SSSP

Springer
Series in
Social
Psychology

Springer Series in Social Psychology

Attention and Self-Regulation: A Control-Theory Approach to Human Behavior
Charles S. Carver/Michael F. Scheier

Gender and Nonverbal Behavior
Clara Mayo/Nancy M. Henley (Editors)

Personality, Roles, and Social Behavior
William Ickes/Eric S. Knowles (Editors)

Toward Transformation in Social Knowledge
Kenneth J. Gergen

The Ethics of Social Research: Surveys and Experiments
Joan E. Sieber (Editor)

The Ethics of Social Research: Fieldwork, Regulation, and Publication
Joan E. Sieber (Editor)

Anger and Aggression: An Essay on Emotion
James R. Averill

The Social Psychology of Creativity
Teresa M. Amabile

Sports Violence
Jeffrey H. Goldstein (Editor)

Nonverbal Behavior: A Functional Perspective
Miles L. Patterson

Basic Group Processes
Paul B. Paulus (Editor)

Attitudinal Judgment
J. Richard Eiser (Editor)

Social Psychology of Aggression: From Individual Behavior to Social Interaction
Amelié Mummendey (Editor)

Directions in Soviet Social Psychology
Lloyd H. Strickland (Editor)

Sociophysiology
William M. Waid (Editor)

Compatible and Incompatible Relationships
William Ickes (Editor)

Facet Theory: Approaches to Social Research
David Canter (Editor)

Action Control: From Cognition to Behavior
Julius Kuhl/Jürgen Beckman (Editors)

SSSP

Sociophysiology

Edited by
William M. Waid

Springer-Verlag
New York Berlin Heidelberg Tokyo

Dr. William M. Waid
Institute of Pennsylvania Hospital
University of Pennsylvania
Philadelphia, Pennsylvania 19104
U.S.A.

New Jersey Psychological Institute
93 West Main Street
Freehold, New Jersey 07728
U.S.A.

QP
360
.S623
1984

With 14 Figures

Library of Congress Cataloging in Publication Data
Main entry under title:
Sociophysiology.
   (Springer series in social psychology)
   Includes indexes.
   1. Psychology, Physiological. 2. Social psychology.
I. Waid, William M.
QP360.S623   1984   152   84-5434

© 1984 by Springer-Verlag New York Inc.
All rights reserved. No part of this book may be translated or reproduced in any form without
written permission from Springer-Verlag, 175 Fifth Avenue, New York, New York 10010,
U.S.A.
The use of general descriptive names, trade names, trademarks, etc., in this publication,
even if the former are not especially identified, is not to be taken as a sign that such names,
as understood by the Trade Marks and Merchandise Marks Act, may accordingly be used
freely by anyone.

Typeset by Publishers Service, Bozeman, Montana.
Printed and bound by R.R. Donnelley & Sons, Harrisonburg, Virginia.
Printed in the United States of America.

9 8 7 6 5 4 3 2 1

ISBN 0-387-90861-7 Springer-Verlag New York Berlin Heidelberg Tokyo
ISBN 3-540-90861-7 Springer-Verlag Berlin Heidelberg New York Tokyo

Preface

Research on the interactions of social psychological and physiological processes has become a major focus of interest among psychologists in the past two decades. The study of these interactions deserves a central role in psychology because biological determinants of complex behavior are often postulated, or even assumed, and, conversely, pathophysiological processes are often vaguely attributed to psychological or social processes, such as stress.

Sociophysiology was designed to bring together in one volume a representative sample of the broad range of work currently being done in the area of social psychophysiology. Some of the chapters provide a review of the literature while others focus more specifically on current programs of research. All provide new insights into basic relationships and several provide broad integrative schemes.

Sociophysiology can serve as a text for both graduate and higher level undergraduate courses in psychophysiology or social psychology. The authors represented provide an extensive overview of the discipline and are in the forefront of stimulating further theoretical and empirical development.

I am grateful to all those who encouraged and supported this project, including colleagues at the Institute of Pennsylvania Hospital and the University of Pennsylvania where it was initiated and at the New Jersey Psychological Institute where it was completed. A special thanks is due the staff of Springer-Verlag for their role in bringing this volume to completion.

Contents

Part I. Biological Background **1**

1. Origins of Sociophysiology **3**
William M. Waid

Psychotherapy as Social and Physiological Interaction 4
Origins of Physiological Response to Social Stimuli 14

2. Methods in Sociophysiology **21**
Robert M. Stern and William J. Ray

Introduction: All Psychophysiology as Sociophysiology 21
Recording Bodily Responses... 22
Concepts Related to the Interpretation of Recordings 35
New Vistas 39

3. An Evolutionary Perspective on Human Social Behavior **47**
Arne Öhman and Ulf Dimberg

Some Basic Evolutionary Biology 49
Implications for Human Social Behavior............................... 66
Concluding Discussion.. 75

4. The Sociophysiology of Infants and Their Caregivers **87**
Ross A. Thompson and Ann M. Frodi

The Meaning of the Cardiac Response.................................. 88
The Cardiac Response and Socioemotional Responsiveness in Infants .. 91
The Cardiac Response and Adult Reactions to Infant Smiles and
Cries.. 99
Conclusion... 108

Part II. Physiology of Social Cognition, Perception, Learning, and Memory **115**

5. Autonomic Self-Perception and Emotion **117**
  Edward S. Katkin, Jim Blascovich, and Marlon R. Koenigsberg

  Introduction and Background 117
  Visceral Perception and Emotion 120
  Visceral Perception: Methods and Procedures.......................... 124
  Conclusions.. 135

6. The Physiological Bases of Nonverbal Communication **139**
  Ross Buck

  Spontaneous versus Symbolic Communication........................... 139
  Primary Motivational/Emotional Systems 142
  Motor Systems of Emotional Expression............................... 146
  Mechanisms of Excitation and Inhibition in Emotional Expression 150
  The Physiological Bases of Nonverbal Communication................ 156
  Summary 157

7. Physiological Mediation of Attitude Maintenance, Formation, and Change **163**
  Mark P. Zanna, Richard A. Detweiler, and James M. Olson

  Attitudes and Psychophysiology 163
  Attitude Formation and Psychophysiology 168
  Attitude Change and Psychophysiology................................ 173

Part III. Physiology and Social Behavior **197**

8. Social Interaction and Psychophysiology **199**
  John B. Gormly

  Introduction... 199
  Psychophysiological Activity and Psychotherapy 199
  Psychophysiological Activity, Coronary-Prone Personality, and Social Interactions 204
  Psychophysiological Activity and Interpersonal Disagreement 205
  The Experimental Approach: Conformity as a Deceptive Act........... 207
  The Correlational Approach: A Study on Psychophysiological Traits and Social Behavior Patterns.. 211

9. Cognition, Arousal, and Aggression **225**
  Brendan Gail Rule and Andrew R. Nesdale

  Constructs of Arousal, Frustration, Cognition, and Aggression 226
  Arousal, Cognition, and Anger 229
  Anger and Aggression 231

Effects of Additional Arousal Sources on Anger and Aggression 235
Aggression Catharsis.. 240
Conclusions... 242

10. Social Processes, Biology, and Disease............................. **249**
Lawrence F. Van Egeren

Introduction.. 249
Levels of Organization.. 254
Explanation of Social-Biological Relations 272
Conclusions... 277

Author Index   **283**

Subject Index   **295**

Contributors

Jim Blascovich, Department of Psychology, State University of New York at Buffalo, Buffalo, New York 14226, U.S.A.

Ross Buck, Department of Communication Sciences, University of Connecticut, Storrs, Connecticut 06268, U.S.A.

Richard A. Detweiler, Department of Psychology, Drew University, Madison, New Jersey 07940, U.S.A.

Ulf Dimberg, Department of Clinical Psychology, University of Uppsala, Uppsala 75142, Sweden.

Ann M. Frodi, Department of Psychology, University of Rochester, Rochester, New York 14627, U.S.A.

John B. Gormly, Department of Psychology, Rutgers State University, New Brunswick, New Jersey 08903, U.S.A.

Edward S. Katkin, Department of Psychology, State University of New York at Buffalo, Buffalo, New York 14226, U.S.A.

Marlon R. Koenigsberg, Department of Psychology, State University of New York at Buffalo, Buffalo, New York 14226, U.S.A.

Andrew R. Nesdale, Department of Psychology, University of Western Australia, Perth, Australia.

Arne Öhman, Department of Clinical Psychology, University of Uppsala, Uppsala 75142, Sweden.

James M. Olson, Department of Psychology, University of Western Ontario, London, Ontario N6A 5C2, Canada.

William J. Ray, Department of Psychology, Pennsylvania State University, University Park, Pennsylvania 16802, U.S.A.

Brendan Gail Rule, Department of Psychology, University of Alberta, Edmonton, Alberta T6G 2E9, Canada.

Robert M. Stern, Professor and Chairman, Department of Psychology, Pennsylvania State University, University Park, Pennsylvania 16802, U.S.A.

Ross A. Thompson, Department of Psychology, University of Nebraska, Lincoln, Nebraska 68588-0308, U.S.A.

Lawrence F. Van Egeren, Department of Psychiatry, Michigan State University, Lansing, Michigan 48824, U.S.A.

William M. Waid, Institute of Pennsylvania Hospital, University of Pennsylvania, Philadelphia, Pennsylvania 19104, U.S.A., and New Jersey Psychological Institute, Freehold, New Jersey 07728, U.S.A.

Mark P. Zanna, Department of Psychology, University of Waterloo, Waterloo, Ontario N2L 3G1, Canada.

Part I
Biological Background

Chapter 1
Introduction: Origins of Sociophysiology

William M. Waid

Since the emergence in the 1950s of studies of the reciprocal effects of social psychological and physiological processes in psychotherapy, psychophysiologists have become increasingly interested in the effects of social variables on human physiology, and social/personality and clinical psychologists have become increasingly interested in the psychophysiological level of social processes. Shapiro and his colleagues reviewed the work in this area some years ago (Shapiro & Crider, 1969; Schwartz & Shapiro, 1973). Initially, studies conceptualized as "sociophysiological" (Boyd & DiMascio, 1954; DiMascio, Boyd, & Greenblatt, 1957) focused on the effects of interpersonal behavior on human physiology typically in the context of psychotherapy. A related line of social psychophysiological (Harris & Katkin, 1975) inquiry focused on the interaction of cognitive, social, and physiological determinants of emotion as the fundamental problem of the area (Schachter & Singer, 1962; Harris & Katkin, 1975; Valins, 1966). While such phenomena continue to be of fundamental interest, a much wider array of investigations has now been completed. This volume examines some of the major current programs of research in sociophysiology. As an introduction, this chapter presents an overview of the origins and rationale of sociophysiological research with special focus on electrodermal activity (EDA).

In organizing this volume, chapters were conceptualized that would reflect the major current programs of research in sociophysiology, but that would also address broadly conceptualized logical components of a comprehensive overview of the sociophysiological domain. Thus, this initial chapter provides an overview and rationale for sociophysiological inquiry. In Chapter 2 a discussion of the prerequisite technical aspects of psychophysiological methodology is provided by Stern and Ray. Ohman and Dimberg then present an evolutionary biological perspective on human social behavior. Ohman and his associates' extensive programmatic research on the differential conditioning of human physiological response to biologically "prepared" versus "unprepared" stimuli is the centerpiece of this discussion.

Thompson and Frodi present an enlightening discussion of the physiological correlates of social interactions involving infants and their parents. Some of the research discussed suggests that at this critical initial level of social interaction individual differences in physiological responsivity, and perhaps conditionability, play a role in the quality of the interaction.

In contrast to the evolutionary and ontogenetic perspective of these chapters, Katkin, Blascovich, and Koenigsberg discuss their most recent studies probing the relationship between emotion and self-perception of autonomic nervous system activity. This work represents some of the most recent attempts to refine our understanding of the interaction of cognitive and physiological processes in the determination of emotional states.

Subsequent chapters discuss the physiological correlates of major aspects of social behavior that have been the focus of social psychology over the past two decades. Buck reviews the physiological correlates of nonverbal communication and presents a model of the physiological basis of this fundamental and intensively studied form of communication. Zanna, Detweiler, and Olson present a thoroughly documented model of the physiological mediation of attitude formation, maintenance, and change. The physiological correlates of adult social interaction is the topic reviewed by Gormly. This discussion reflects Gormly's intensive investigation of the significance of individual differences in physiological reactions that correlate with complex social behavior. Rule and Nesdale discuss the physiological correlates of aggression and present a model of the interaction of cognitive and physiological processes in determining aggressive behavior.

Finally, Van Egeren offers a comprehensive overview of the interaction of social and biological processes in the production of disease. Sociophysiology is an extension of the more basic discipline of psychophysiology, and as Hassett (1978) has observed, the two basic applied fields to emerge from psychophysiology are biofeedback and polygraph testing. In both of these applied fields, interest in social factors affecting what were once conceptualized purely as psychophysiological processes is on the increase. In Van Egeren's review of social processes, biology and disease, an eloquent rationale emerges for the effectiveness of biofeedback and behavioral medicine techniques. A review of the effects of social, personality, and cognitive processes on polygraph testing has been presented elsewhere (Waid & Orne, 1981) and will not be repeated here.

Psychotherapy as Social and Physiological Interaction

Investigations of the processes involved in psychotherapy (Boyd & DiMascio, 1954; Lasswell, 1936) gave the initial impetus to studies of EDA and other psychophysiological reactions during social interaction. In an incisive review of some of these studies, Lacey (1959) concluded that despite, or perhaps because of, the exquisite sensitivity of autonomic responses to the immediate social context, these responses would not be reliable indicators of the patient's progress.

Dittes (1957a), for example, found that across 30 sessions of psychotherapy the patient's initially frequent electrodermal responses (EDRs) to "embarrassing sex statements" declined significantly. (This decline was independent of any overall habituation to interaction.) In a follow-up of 43 sessions with the same patient,

Dittes (1957b) found that the subject gave significantly more EDRs in sessions that were rated as "unpermissive" (therapist was critical and demanding) than in sessions which were rated as permissive. There was a significant tendency for embarrassing sex statements to evoke EDRs in the unpermissive, but not in the permissive sessions. Thus, the patient's reduced electrodermal arousal to troublesome materials was apparently mediated by the permissive climate the therapist offered. When an unpermissive climate reigned the subject was again aroused by troublesome material.

The findings of this extensive study of a single subject have been conceptually replicated by Martin (1964) with a large sample. Subjects who were treated formally by the experimenter gave larger EDRs to sexual stimuli than did subjects who were treated in a "permissive" manner.

In another study discussed by Lacey (1959), Cohen, Silverman, and Burch (1956) had 5 subjects listen to a list of 30 words on 2 different occasions. If a word evoked either high or low EDRs on both occasions, it was selected for use in a third session in which an attempt was made to enhance the EDR to some stimuli and decrease it to others. The experimenter probed the subject as to why a given word might have evoked emotion in him in the previous sessions. Some words were explored in depth with the subject while others the experimenter cut off discussion abruptly, but politely. A third presentation of the word list was then made. Words which had been discussed in depth evoked little EDR on the third presentation, even though they had evoked large ones before, while "cut-off" words evoked large EDRs.

Lacey concluded that

> The results of Dittes, and of Cohen, Silverman, and Burch, imply that the specific situation is a powerful determinant of the magnitude of somatic response to provocative stimuli. They suggest, I think, that the somatic changes occurring in therapy cannot be utilized as a criterion of the effectiveness of therapy in diminishing somatic effects (or "arousal," or "emotional") outside of the therapeutic situation. If the disappearance of GSR upon exploration of sexual content is a function of the disappearance of the cues of threat and punishment derived from the therapist, and if GSR can be made to re-appear by the therapist becoming less gentle, more threatening, then we have no guarantee that the patient will not be as somatically aroused as he ever was when he detects "threats" in his environment and interpersonal interactions.

These conclusions were followed by a temporary decline in interest in the autonomic correlates of psychotherapy (Roessler et al., 1975). A more structured approach to the use of psychophysiology in social interactions, however, has flourished—the detection of deception (e.g., Waid & Orne, 1981).

Behavior therapy with its more overt, though frequently somewhat trivial, target behaviors has made successful use of autonomic processes as both components and indicators of therapeutic progress (Mathews, 1971). The findings of Hoehn-Saric, Frank, and Gurland (1978) and Hoehn-Saric et al. (1972) suggest that the arousal processes indexed by autonomic activity are indeed an important component of insight psychotherapy also, but that they can more fruitfully be systematically manipulated to aid therapeutic change rather than monitored as evaluation measures.

Regardless of their implications for the problems of utilizing autonomic responses as indicators of the course of psychotherapy, these studies testify to the sensitivity of autonomic responses, particularly electrodermal responses, to the immediate social climate in which interaction occurs. They also suggest some specific aspects of social interaction which may affect electrodermal arousal. Criticism, or unpermissiveness, appears to produce electrodermal arousal, whereas acceptance, or permissiveness, reduces it (Dittes, 1957b). Discussion of potentially anxiety-arousing material reduces subsequent ED arousal to the material (Cohen, Silverman, & Burch, 1956). Once such social-electrodermal interrelations are more systematically understood, the use of electrodermal activity in understanding the course of psychotherapies of various sorts may be more promising. Fortunately, there is an increasing body of knowledge about the autonomic, particularly the electrodermal, underpinnings of these behaviors, much of which is discussed in subsequent chapters of this volume.

Furthermore, advances in our understanding of the biological significance of electrodermal activity have been made. The remainder of this chapter discusses how physiological reactions come to affect and be affected by social processes. This entails brief accounts of the biology of the electrodermal response and the relationship of the EDR to cognitive, emotional, and learning processes.

Origins of Arousal

The relationship of physiological systems to social processes can be better appreciated if placed in the context of the physiological substrates of the system and of its relationship to fundamental behavioral and cognitive processes. A detailed account of the most fundamental, proximal determinants of physiological arousal to social stimuli would be beyond the scope of this volume since these determinants must be, ultimately, the same structures and processes which produce physiological arousal to alerting stimuli (Sokolov, 1963) or to strong (Hovland & Riesen, 1940), noxious (Epstein, 1973), or phobic (Mathews, 1971) stimuli. Arousal induced by a social stimulus or by, for example, the appearance of a phobic stimulus, or a noxious stimulus, is most probably produced via one series of final common pathways. Stern and Ray review the physiological substrates in their chapter on psychophysiological methodology. The biological substrates of electrodermal arousal are outlined here as an example of how understanding the substrates of an autonomic response system can enhance the clarity of sociophysiological findings.

The most general neurological account of electrodermal activity is that it reflects the inflow to the skin of discharges of the sympathetic branch of the autonomic nervous system (ANS) (Edelberg, 1972). Stimulation of the sympathetic trunk elicits an electrodermal response and unilateral sympathectomy abolishes responses ipsilaterally (Schwartz, 1934). In the central nervous system, electrical stimulation of at least three independent anatomical areas of the brain produces electrodermal responses: the limbic cortex, via the hypothalamus, the premotor cortex, and certain parts of the reticular formation. The relation to limbic cortex is one reason that electrodermal activity is frequently interpreted as reflecting emotional processes, while the relation to the premotor cortex implies a motor-accessory role. Electrodermal responses can also be elicited from the mesencephalic reticular formation, linking electrodermal activity to the classic notion of arousal (Morruzzi & Magoun, 1949). On the inhibitory side, at least the frontal cortex and the bulbar portions of the reticular formation have suppressive effects on electrodermal activity.

Further insight into the autonomic and central nervous system significance of electrodermal activity is given by pharmacological and biochemical studies. Ax (1953), Clemens (1957), and Hare (1972) found that a subcutaneous injection of epinephrine increased skin conductance level (SCL) and Ax (1953) and Burch and Greiner (1960) found that epinephrine increased the frequency of nonspecific EDRs. Ax also found that norepinephrine increased nonspecific EDRs and SCL. Since the transmitter at the preganglionic and sweat gland sites is acetylcholine (Guyton, 1961), such action must be due to central activation, even though norepinephrine and epinephrine cross the blood-brain barrier only with difficulty (Koella, 1975). The principal area of the brain in which uptake of circulating catecholamines does occur is the posterior hypothalamus (Weil-Malherbe, 1960), which also is a critical site for electrical elicitation of the EDR (Davison & Koss, 1975). Burch and Greiner also found that penothal, acting centrally, reduced the number of nonspecific EDRs. Amphetamine also increases (Lader, 1969), while chlorpromazine decreases, palmar sweating, both acting centrally (Goodman & Gillman, 1975).

Cholinomimetic agents, e.g., pilocarbine and carbamylcholine, produce copious sweating (Guyton, 1961), but this is presumably due to direct effects on the neuroeffector junction, which is cholinergic, rather than to central effects.

Central nervous system stimulants and depressants in everyday use also have excitatory and inhibitory effects, respectively, on electrodermal activity. Amphetamine and caffeine both increase the rate of nonspecific EDRs and retard the usual decline in amplitude of the EDR to repetitions of 100-dB tones (Lader, 1969). Alcohol and the "minor" tranquilizers, in contrast, reduce the amplitude of the EDR to noxious (Greenberg & Carpenter, 1957) as well as emotional verbal stimuli (Lienert & Traxler, 1959).

From an endogenous perspective, Frankenhaeuser, Froberg, Hagdahl, Rissler, Bjorkvall, and Wolff (1967) found that in response to stress, levels of excreted epinephrine as measured in the urine paralleled skin conductance levels closely and that both physiological measures correlated with performance and subjective arousal in similar ways.

Whatever the neurophysical mechanisms, they may be determined genetically. Substantial evidence is accumulating that the origins of individual differences in electrodermal functioning may be in part genetic. Studies using the twin method (Hume, 1973; Lader & Wing, 1966; Zahn, 1977) have reported significant heritability components for skin conductance level, spontaneous EDRs, and magnitude of response to tasks such as mental arithmetic. Such genetic effects on autonomic functioning could be one route by which the genetic factors postulated by sociobiologists (Wilson, 1975) determine social behavior. Such genetic-physiological-behavioral links need to be established empirically, however, rather than assumed.

Electrodermal Arousal and Behavior

Whatever the biological mechanisms may be, understanding the manner in which electrodermal arousal relates to the elements of behavior and cognition is a further prerequisite for the present volume. Berlyne (1967) and Gellhorn (1967) have both presented general theories of the role of physiological arousal in behavior. In both of these accounts, though they differ in detail, physiological arousal is viewed as a manifestation of central nervous system processes which intervene between stimulus and response to energize behavior. In neither is arousal necessarily considered a unitary dimension (e.g., Duffy, 1962; Malmo, 1959). This is in accord with recent conceptualizations (Lacey, 1967) of arousal as multidimensional.

Whether electrodermal arousal is regarded as unitary or as multiply determined, fundamental psychological processes, from attention (Solley & Thetford, 1967), memory (Berlyne, 1967), and intensity of subjective experience (McCurdy, 1950), to locomotion, manipulation, and defense (Edelberg, 1973), appear to be facilitated by appropriate increases in the electrodermal component of arousal. Some of these processes may also be facilitated by white noise stimulation, by electrical stimulation of specific brain centers, and by central nervous system stimulants, each of which also increases electrodermal arousal (Berlyne, 1967).

Regardless of the ultimate conceptualization of electrodermal-behavioral relations, the literature is broadly consistent with the idea of electrodermal arousal reflecting a sensitizing, central neural activity which facilitates perception, encoding, and reacting to stimuli and basically supplements purely informational properties of stimuli.

Why the neural activity manifested in *skin*, the body's most peripheral organ, is related to so many "central" psychological processes has been discussed by Edelberg (1972; 1973). To summarize, whereas sweating on most of the body is thermoregulatory in nature, sweating on the palms of the hands and the soles of the feet is related to tactile, manipulative, protective, and locomotive functions. The pliability of the skin's surface is determined mainly by its water content, which depends in large part on sweat gland activity. Appropriate hydration of the skin has been shown to enhance tactile sensitivity (Edelberg, 1973), grip (Darrow, 1936), and resistance to abrasion (Wilcott, 1966), as in locomotion and grasping. If fine touch is thought of as a prototype of exploratory or investigatory behavior (e.g., Berlyne, 1960) and grasping and locomoting as prototypes of "emergency" behaviors, then the link between the skin's responses and processes we think of as "psychological" fits within an evolutionary context. Touching, grasping, and locomoting can be, and typically are, inhibited in most social settings, of course. The sweat responses which accompany such behavior, in contrast, normally cannot be inhibited even when the overt behaviors are. Emotional sweating may also have functioned, at least in the evolutionary history of the species, as olfactory communication. Comfort (1971) has presented an argument for the likelihood of human pheromones, and Russell (1976) and McBurney, Levine, and Cavanaugh (1977) have presented evidence of human olfactory discrimination between the sweat of different individuals. Russell found a significant tendency for male and female subjects to make olfactory discriminations between the sweat of males and females.

McBurney et al. found highly significant concordance across individuals in their rankings of the pleasantness-unpleasantness of the sweat of several individuals in addition to discrimination between their own and another's sweat. Although the odorous contribution to sweat originates in the apocrine glands, the eccrine sweat glands are responsible for the diffusion of the odorous substance (Montagna, 1975). Further studies in this line of inquiry may have important implications for the evolutionary role of human sweating.

To summarize, palmar sweating influences the effectiveness of a wide range of tactual and perceptual-motor activity, and as such should be considered in the light of its adaptive significance. Similar functional relationships must exist for other psychophysiological systems.

Physiological Arousal and Sociocognitive Processes

The significance of social stimuli and the emission of social behaviors are modulated by complex cognitive processes. The relationship of physiological arousal to such processes has been a fundamental problem in sociophysiology. Most research in this area has evolved from models of the role of physiological arousal in *emotion*, as formulated by Schachter and Singer (1962), Valins (1966), and Mandler (1975), and from Lazarus' (1966; 1968) concept of cognitive appraisal and stress. By defining their interest in arousal vis-à-vis emotion and stress, these theorists necessarily present less general theories than Gellhorn and Berlyne. Nonetheless, these theories have had a greater impact on sociophysiological research. Katkin and his colleagues describe their most recent research on the problem in their chapter in this volume. A précis of previous research is a helpful introduction to that chapter.

The Schachter and Singer Paradigm

The models espoused by Schachter and Singer and later by Valins (1966) have been phrased in terms of the historic debate concerning peripheral versus central mediation of emotions. Schachter and Singer (1962) found that subjects given epinephrine but misinformed of its arousing effects imitated either the euphoric or angry behavior of a confederate, and rated themselves euphoric or angry to a greater extent than subjects given placebo and than subjects given epinephrine but accurately informed of its arousing effects. Schachter and Singer's interpretation of these findings was that any emotional experience or behavior, e.g., anger or euphoria, results from the same generalized physiological arousal in combination with a cognition of the context of that arousal. The arousal alone, independent of context, is insufficient to produce emotion, however, since knowledge of an artificial source of the arousal (in this case, a dose of epinephrine) blocks the emotional behavior. The context of the arousal also was concluded to be insufficient in itself since subjects given placebo imitated the confederates less than the misinformed epinephrine subjects. Although Schachter and Singer's conclusions have been faulted on a number of grounds, several studies are consistent with their findings.

Erdeman and Janke (1978) recently attempted to replicate certain aspects of Schachter and Singer's study. Subjects were given either ephedrine, a sympathomimetic agent, or placebo under disguised circumstances (i.e., neither group had any ostensible reason to attribute subsequent arousal to the substances they had ingested) and then treated in a way designed to evoke either mild annoyance, mild euphoria, or a neutral state. Consistent with Schachter and Singer, Erdeman and Janke found no differences in the subsequent moods of anger or euphoria of neutral subjects who had ingested placebo. Among subjects who had ingested ephedrine, however, subjects in the anger condition showed significantly more dysphoria than subjects in the euphoria condition. Heart rate and systolic pressure were both significantly elevated among ephedrine but not among placebo subjects.

Although neither Schachter and Singer nor Erdeman and Janke measured the electrodermal response, the type of physiological manipulation they investigated has been shown to affect the electrodermal system. Clemens (1957) and Hare (1972) found that a similar dose of epinephrine increased skin conductance levels, and Burch and Greiner (1960) found that it increased the frequency of nonspecific EDRs. Amphetamine, a sympathomimetic agent with effects similar to ephedrine, also increaese EDA.

Marshall and Zimbardo (1979), in contrast, have reported a failure to replicate Schachter and Singer's findings of enhanced euphoria in epinephrine-misinformed subjects exposed to a euphoric model. They conclude that there is no evidence that adrenalin-induced physiological arousal can enhance positive affect, but rather that the sympathetic nervous system arousal thus produced inevitably produces negative affect. Unfortunately, Marshall and Zimbardo did not, in fact, replicate one of the most critical components of Schachter and Singer's procedures. The former's instructions to epinephrine-misinformed subjects included symptoms which are indeed induced by epinephrine. While this discrepancy may explain the failure to replicate, psychophysiological studies of the psychology of *humor* provide more substantial evidence in support of the affective plasticity of sympathetic arousal, at least of moderate degrees, and against the notion of negative affective bias.

Both Godkevitch (1976) and Langevin and Day (1972) have found humorous material to evoke increased electrodermal activity and the latter investigators found that material receiving the highest ratings for funniness tended to evoke the largest electrodermal changes. Schachter and Wheeler (1962) found that subjects who were injected with epinephrine considered a movie more amusing than control subjects who were injected with saline, who, in turn, found the film more amusing than a third group injected with chlorpromazine.

Ironically, the controversy over peripheral (James—Lange) versus central (Cannon—Bard) predominance in the mediation of emotionality, which spurred the research, cannot be resolved on the basis of these studies. While both the Schachter and Singer and the Erdeman and Janke studies confirm the importance of "unexplainable" physiological arousal in emotionality, the importance of the *peripheral* autonomic changes in producing emotionality is inseparable from the arousal of the central brain process which effects the autonomic changes. Although epinephrine crosses the blood-brain barrier with some difficulty, it does appear to have central effects. Ephedrine, used by Erdeman and Janke, crosses the blood-brain barrier readily. Furthermore, the peripheral activation produced by epinephrine, especially its pressor effect, doubtless produces, afferently, central activation. In summary, this complex feedback loop has not been penetrated by the studies under consideration. Nonetheless, the critical point for the present discussion is well established by these studies: sympathomimetic agents which produce autonomic arousal, particularly electrodermal, concommitantly enhance the emotive aspects of behavior and cognition. There seems little reason to suppose, however, that it is the peripheral manifestations of this arousal which are critical, though they may serve a critical scientific function in reflecting the intensity of the central process.

Thus, it would be premature to conceptualize all social behavior which may be considered "emotional" in terms of nonspecific physiological arousal paired with cognition of the social context. While Schachter and Singer have provided a theoretical framework for understanding how autonomic arousal and complex cognition can interact to produce emotional behavior, the extent to which nonspecific physiological arousal is involved in socioemotional behavior needs to be documented for a broader range of social behavior.

While the evidence supports the theory that moderate increases in arousal may enhance either negative or positive affect, this may well be untrue for larger increases in arousal which may produce only negative affect.

Misattribution of Arousal

Valins (1966) subsequently attempted to show that emotional experience could be reduced to cognitive processes independent of actual physiological changes, specifically to the perception (or misperception) of arousal. Harris and Katkin (1975) have reviewed investigations of Valins' hypothesis, so it is unnecessary to do so here. To summarize their conclusions, subsequent research (e.g., Hirschman, 1975) has found that the false physiological feedback used by Valins is itself arousing, electrodermally. Thus, subjects who are given false physiological feedback cannot be said to be affected only by their misperception of arousal since they are indeed more aroused than control subjects.

Perceived Arousal and Emotion

Mandler (1975) nonetheless places great importance on the *perception* of actual arousal as critical to emotion. In an effort to construct a purely psychological model, he uses heart rate alone as an index of arousal because heart rate has been found to be discriminable to many people. He explicitly disavows as such an index electrodermal activity and any other physiological measure which has not been found to be discriminable. A model of emotion based on heart rate alone as the index of arousal may be quite useful heuristically (just as useful as the present effort to describe only the electrodermal correlates and consequences of social behavior), but to base the choice of this measure on its discriminability by the individual is conceptually costly. The only physiological factors allowed to play a part in such a model are ones which are within the conscious perception of the subject. Thus both hormones and neurotransmitters, in addition to most electrophysiological phenomena such as electrodermal activity, are thereby excluded from even eventual consideration. The value of such a model is unclear. Nonetheless, despite the self-imposed restrictions of his model, Mandler's conceptualization of the role of autonomic arousal in emotion is, in the final analysis, little different from that of Berlyne and Gellhorn: "I assume that it is autonomic nervous system activity that turns many . . . response patterns into emotions . . . The ANS arousal system may modify and potentiate any behavior . . ." (p. 116).

Appraisal and Arousal

Although their emphases on cognitive, social, and physiological processes differ, all of these views (Schachter & Singer, 1962; Valins, 1966; Mandler, 1975) concur in the notion that cognitive appraisal is critical to emotionality. Lazarus (1968) has reviewed the efforts of himself and his colleagues to delineate the nature of the cognitive processes which result in stress or emotion. In summary, this research has shown that a stressful stimulus will produce less stress reaction, including electrodermal activity, if the appraisal of the harmful significance of the events is altered in certain ways. In the first such study (Speisman, Lazarus, Mordkoff, & Davison, 1964), subjects watched a film, *Subincision*, portraying a series of crude genital operations on adolescent boys in a Stone Age culture in Australia. Skin conductance levels were raised by a sound track emphasizing the operation's harmful consequences and lowered both by a "denial" sound track and by a sound track conveying the theme of intellectualized detachment. Later studies (e.g., Lazarus & Alfert, 1964) replaced the sound-track approach with orienting statements given before the subjects watched the film and yielded similar results. Similar findings have been obtained using a film depicting horrifying accidents in a woodworking shop (Lazarus, Opton, Nomikos, & Rankin, 1965).

These experimental manipulations of subjects' appraisal of threatening stimuli were particularly effective with subjects who displayed styles of thinking which were compatible with the style of the manipulation (Speisman et al., 1964).

An unfortunate limitation of the laboratory studies in this series is that all involved vicarious stress. While the results are of great importance, it nonetheless must be asked whether similar manipulations of cognitive appraisal would have such effects on direct stress.

Mastery, Control, and Arousal

In contrast, a series of studies of the psychophysiology of sport parachuting (Fenz, 1964; Fenz & Epstein, 1967; Fenz & Jones, 1972) has developed another useful perspective on the processes modulating stress reactions in a dramatic field context involving extreme levels of stress.

Novice parachutists were found to show increased levels of physiological arousal, including skin conductance, from the night preceding up to the moment of their jump. Experienced parachutists, in contrast, showed a quite different temporal pattern of arousal rather than simply a reduced level of arousal. The highest level of physiological arousal occurred at a time considerably before the moment of the jump. It declined thereafter to the moment of the jump and after landing (Fenz & Epstein, 1967).

This finding of little overall difference is in accord with findings of Bloom, Euler, and Frankenhaeuser (1963) that both novice and very experienced military parachutists gave large increases in both urinary adrenalin and noradrenalin in response to a jump and that they did not differ. Comparing these studies also reveals the utility of continuous recordings of a process such as electrodermal activity. Although parachuting appears to be equally stressful for novices and for experienced jumpers in terms of gross neuroendocrine response, there are critical differences between the two groups in the temporal patterns of physiological response as indicated by electrodermal activity.

Fenz and Epstein concluded that fear of a stressful event does not simply dissipate, but rather is inhibited or controlled. The functional role of this pattern of arousal, early anticipatory arousal followed by a period of sustained decline (i.e., mastery of the arousal), was documented in a later study. Fenz and Jones (1972) found that the better parachutists, among both experienced and beginning jumpers, showed a sharp increase in arousal early during the jump sequence, followed by a sharp decline in arousal which extended to the moment when the subject jumped. Poorer performers, in contrast, reached their highest levels of arousal at the moment of the jump.

If good performers are thought of as those who have gained more control over the behavioral components of the jump sequence, then these findings are consistent with those of another line of inquiry. Noxious stimuli over which a person has control evoke smaller EDRs than stimuli matched for noxiousness and duration, but which occur without the person's control (Corah & Boffa, 1970; Pervin, 1963). It has not been possible to completely separate personal control from predictability (Averill, 1973), i.e., if the person controls the stimuli he knows when they will occur. Knowledge of just when a noxious stimulus will occur reduces the EDR (Lykken & Tellegen, 1972; Waid, 1979) and magnitude estimations of the intensity of the stimulus (Waid, 1979). Nonetheless, outside the laboratory, mastery of stress, as in sport parachuting, may involve making stressful events predictable by means of controlling them.

It is likely that these changes in electrodermal activity as a function of predictability or controllability, though transient, reflect processes whose cumulative effect can be that of long-term changes in physiological functioning. A program of research by Weiss (1972) has documented that similar but persistent conditions of unpredictability and/or uncontrollability of noxious stimuli produces severe ulceration in the rat. This animal model of ulceration is certainly consistent with psychophysiological studies, though the direct links between psychophysiological measures and the biochemical level have yet to be forged.

Summary

In summary, it appears that physiological arousal and cognitive registration of an emotional context must occur conjointly to produce emotional behavior or experience (Harris & Katkin, 1975). The precise nature of the cognitive processing or appraisal of the context may vary, however, depending upon personality and cognitive style (Lazarus, 1968), experience (Fenz & Jones, 1972), coping skill (Fenz & Epstein, 1967), temporal information (Lykken & Tellegen, 1974; Waid, 1979), and degree of personal control (Corah & Boffa, 1970; Pervin, 1963), with marked consequences for physiological arousal. Thus, the same context or stimuli may or may not evoke marked physiological arousal depending upon the way in which it is processed cognitively. Such cognitive factors are typically conditioned by the individual's social environment (e.g., Schachter & Singer, 1962).

Origins of Physiological Response to Social Stimuli

Since most psychophysiological research has examined the effects of highly controlled physical stimuli, an informative manner in which to begin consideration of sociophysiological phenomena is by comparing social with physical effects on electrodermal activity.

Any social stimulus would presumably be sufficient to elicit the electrodermal component of the orienting response, just as are simple stimuli such as innocuous tones or lights (Sokolov, 1963). Such responses are probably vestiges of the tactile-motor accessory role played by palmar sweating (Edelberg, 1972; 1973). Orienting responses quickly disappear, however, upon repetition of such stimuli, so a social stimulus which persists in evoking EDRs would presumably be evoking something more than an orienting response. Further, some social stimuli may be innate elicitors of large persistent electrodermal responses analogous to those elicited by a sudden loud or painful stimulus.

Attention and Emotion

Geer and Klein (1969) made an informative comparison of stimuli presumed to elicit orienting with stimuli hypothesized to evoke arousal beyond that of orienting. Subjects viewed 10 color slides of individual men visible from the trunk up, followed by 5 similar slides turned upside down or by 5 slides right side up but each depicting the corpse of a victim of violent death. Expressing the EDR to the last 5 slides as a proportion of the mean EDR to the last 3 of the habituation slides (i.e., the 10 normal pictures), subjects seeing the corpses responded about 9 times as much, electrodermally, as those seeing the "dis-habituating" inverted slides. Geer and Klein concluded that in situations such as seeing the results of violent death a large component of electrodermal arousal is superimposed upon an orienting component and that such responses cannot be considered simply as orienting responses. Such responses are more likely related to the adaptive role of electrodermal activity in locomotion (e.g., flight) and defense (Edelberg, 1972; 1973).

In summary, much of the electrodermal arousal to social stimuli may reflect rather minor demands of attention, as in the responses to the incongruously posed men in Geer and Klein's inverted slides. There are other social stimuli, however, which evoke huge changes in electrodermal activity and appear to be a part of the "emergency" reaction rather than only correlates of attending. There is no need, however, to postulate a discontinuity between such levels of arousal. Attending may be intensified, though also narrowed in focus (Easterbrook, 1959), under emergency conditions. Thus, electrodermal activity under such circumstances reflects processes *in addition to*, rather than in place of, attention.

Social Stimuli as Conditioned Stimuli for Arousal

Whether a reflection of attentional or of emergency processes, electrodermal arousal plays a role in social behavior and this role is amplified by the relative ease with which it comes to be evoked by previously insufficient stimuli. An innate origin for the arousing properties of most social stimuli is unlikely since many are mediated symbolically, and individuals differ considerably in precisely what social stimuli are highly arousing. However, whether by the gradual build-up of connections through the repetitive pairing of the insufficient and sufficient stimuli, or by direct awareness of the stimuli contingencies, innocuous stimuli become capable of eliciting electrodermal arousal which they otherwise would not regularly elicit (Grings & Dawson, 1973).

Staats and Staats (1958) have shown in a number of studies that such a process is capable of producing positive or negative attitudes toward otherwise neutral stimuli. It has been suggested (Page, 1969) that the procedures used to establish attitudes through classical conditioning are subject to the influence of demand characteristics (Orne, 1962). Zanna, Kiesler, and Pilkonis (1970), however, have obtained the conditioning of attitudes even when demand characteristics are eliminated or minimized. Of particular interest from the present perspective is the finding that only subjects who showed concurrent acquisition of conditioned EDRs later showed the attitude effects.

Appraisal of Social Stimuli

Lazarus's (1968) work on cognitive appraisal provides a model of another way in which some social stimuli may acquire such arousal-eliciting properties, a model similar to that of "instructed conditioning." Any stimuli, including purely social ones, which are appraised as threatening will evoke large changes in arousal. Thus, when social stimuli acquire threatening properties for an individual, through learning, experience, or simply instruction, they will subsequently be appraised as threatening and consequently become arousing. Knowing how certain social stimuli come to have such properties is of less importance, of course, than is utilizing this fact to determine which precise social stimuli have such properties for an individual or group of interest.

Further, while it may be of considerable interest to understand whether a given social stimulus has innate or acquired arousal-eliciting properties, this is not necessarily crucial to understanding and making use of the role of such arousal in ongoing social behavior. Speech phobic subjects, for example, show significant electrodermal arousal when merely contemplating speaking before a group (Van Egeren, Feather, & Hein, 1971). Both systematic densitization (Paul, 1966) and biofeedback (Gatchel & Proctor, 1976) have been used successfully in reducing such arousal, resulting in a decline in phobic behavior and an enhancement in public speaking capacity. It is not known, however, whether the maladaptive arousal previously evoked by having to speak in public was acquired through unpleasant experiences or whether it originated in constitutional factors in the subjects. Whether the electrodermal arousal in social stimuli was innate or acquired, however, reducing it played an important role in modifying social behavior.

Ontogeny of Electrodermal Arousal

It is also important to note that electrodermal responses can be elicited within the first day of life (Crowell et al., 1965), and that even in infancy EDRs reflect something about the state of the individual. Stechler, Bradford, and Levy (1966) found that when infants attended to a grid stimulus they gave larger skin potential responses to auditory stimuli than when there was no grid to attend to. Although conditioning of the EDR in infancy has not been demonstrated, nor its absence indicated (Fitzgerald & Brackbill, 1976), other autonomic processes, which have received more attention among infancy investigators, have been found to condition under certain circumstances, e.g., temporal conditioning. It can be concluded from Fitzgerald and Brackbill's (1976) review that some forms of conditioning of autonomic processes occur even in early infancy, but that these may show great stimulus (both conditional and unconditional)-response specificity.

The remaining chapters in this volume treat many of the topics summarized here in more detail, and extend the psychophysiological approach to major areas of social psychological inquiry.

Acknowledgment. The writing of this chapter and the editing of the book were supported in part by a grant from the Institute for Experimental Psychiatry.

References

Averill, J. R. (1973). Personal control over aversive stimuli and its relationship to stress. *Psychological Bulletin, 80,* 286-303.

Ax, A. F. (1953). Physiological differentiation between fear and anger in humans. *Psychosomatic Medicine, 15,* 433.

Berlyne, D. E. (1960). *Conflict, arousal, and curiosity.* New York: McGraw-Hill.

Berlyne, D. E. (1967). Arousal and reinforcement. In D. Levine (Ed.), *Nebraska Symposium on Motivation* (Vol. 15). Lincoln, NE: University of Nebraska Press.

Bloom, G., Euler, U. S. von, & Frankenhaeuser, M. (1963). Catecholamine excretion and personality traits in paratroop trainees. *Acta Physiologica Scandinavica, 58,* 77.

Boyd, R. W., & DiMascio, A. (1954). Social behavior and autonomic physiology: A sociophysiological study. *Journal of Nervous and Mental Disease, 120,* 207-212.

Burch, N. R., & Greiner, T. H. (1960). A bioelectric scale of human alertness: Concurrent recordings of the EEG and GSR. *Psychiatric Research Reports, 12,* 183-193.

Clemens, T. L. (1957). Autonomic nervous system responses related to the Funkenstein test: To epinephrine. *Psychosomatic Medicine, 19,* 267-274.

Cohen, S. I., Silverman, A. J., & Burch, N. R. (1956). A technique for the assessment of affect change. *Journal of Nervous and Mental Disease, 124,* 352-360.

Comfort, A. (1971). Likelihood of human pheromones. *Nature, 230,* 432-433, 479.

Corah, N. L., & Boffa, J. (1970). Perceived control, self-observation, and response to aversive stimulation. *Journal of Personality and Social Psychology, 16,* 1-4.

Crowell, D. H. (1965). Galvanic skin reflex in newborn humans. *Science, 148,* 1108-1111.

Darrow, C. W. (1936). The galvanic skin reflex (sweating) and blood pressure as preparatory and facilitative functions. *Psychological Bulletin, 33,* 73-94.

Davison, M. A., & Koss, M. C. (1975). Brainstem loci for activation of electrodermal response in the cat. *American Journal of Physiology, 229,* 930-934.

DiMascio, A., Boyd, R. W., & Greenblatt, M. (1957). Physiological correlates of tension and antagonism during psychotherapy: A study of 'interpersonal physiology.' *Psychosomatic Medicine, 19,* 99-104.

Dittes, J. E. (1957a). Extinction during psychotherapy of GSR accompanying "embarrassing" statements. *Journal of Abnormal and Social Psychology, 54*, 187-191.

Dittes, J. E. (1957b). Galvanic skin responses as a measure of patient's reaction to therapist's permissiveness. *Journal of Abnormal and Social Psychology, 55*, 295-303.

Duffy, E. (1962). *Activation and behavior*. New York: Wiley.

Easterbrook, J. A. (1959). The effect of emotion on cue utilization and the organization of behavior. *Psychological Review, 66*, 183-201.

Edelberg, R. (1961). The relationship between the galvanic skin response, vasoconstriction, and tactile sensitivity. *Journal of Experimental Psychology, 62*, 187-195.

Edelberg, R. (1972). Electrical activity of the skin: Its measurement and uses in psychophysiology. In N. S. Greenfield & R. A. Sternbach (Eds.), *Handbook of psychophysiology*, New York: Holt, Rinehart, & Winston.

Edelberg, R. (1973). Mechanisms of electrodermal adaptations for locomotion, manipulation, or defense. In E. Stellar & J. M. Sprague (Eds.), *Progress in physiological psychology, 5*.

Epstein, S. (1973). Expectancy and magnitude of reaction to a noxious UCS. *Psychophysiology, 10*, 100-107.

Erdman, G., & Janke, W. (1978). Interaction between physiological and cognitive determinants of emotions: Experimental studies on Schachter's theory of emotions. *Biological Psychology, 6*, 61-74.

Fenz, W. D. (1964). Conflict and stress as related to physiological activation and sensory, perceptual, and cognitive functioning. *Psychological Monographs, 78*.

Fenz, W. D., & Epstein, S. (1967). Gradients of physiological arousal in parachutists as a function of an approaching jump. *Psychosomatic Medicine, 29*, 1.

Fenz, W. D., & Jones, G. B. (1972). Individual differences in physiologic arousal and performance in sport parachutists. *Psychosomatic Medicine, 34*, 1-8.

Fitzgerald, H. E., & Brackbill, Y. (1976). Classical conditioning in infancy: Development and constraints. *Psychological Bulletin, 83*, 353-376.

Frankenhaeuser, M., Froberg, J., Hagdahl, R., Rissler, A., Bjorkvall, C., & Wolff, B. (1967). Physiological, behavioral, and subjective indices of habituation to psychological stress. *Physiology and Behavior, 2*, 229-237.

Gatchel, R. J., & Proctor, J. D. (1976). Effectiveness of voluntary heart rate control in reducing speech anxiety. *Journal of Consulting and Clinical Psychology, 44*, 381-389.

Geer, J. H., & Klein, K. (1969). Effects of two independent stresses upon autonomic responding. *Journal of Abnormal Psychology, 74*, 237-241.

Gellhorn, E. (1967). *Principles of autonomic-somatic integrations: Physiological basis and psychological and clinical implications*. Minneapolis: University of Minnesota Press.

Godkevitch, M. (1976). Physiological and verbal indices of arousal in rated humour. In A. J. Chapman and H. C. Foot (Eds.), *Humor and laughter: Theory, research and applications*. London: Wiley.

Goodman, L. S., & Gillman, A. (Eds.). (1975). *The pharmacological basis of therapeutics*. New York: MacMillan.

Greenberg, L. A., & Carpenter, J. A. (1957). The effect of alcoholic beverages on skin conductance and emotional tension. *Quarterly Journal of Studies of Alcohol, 18*, 190-204.

Grings, W. W., & Dawson, M. E. (1973). Complex variables in conditioning. In W. F. Prokasy & D. C. Raskin (Eds.), *Electrodermal activity in psychological research*. New York: Academic Press.

Guyton, A. C. (1961). *Textbook of medical physiology*. Philadelphia: W. B. Saunders Company.

Hare, R. D. (1972). Psychopathy and physiological responses to adrenalin. *Journal of Abnormal Psychology, 79*, 138-147.

Harris, V. A., & Katkin, E. S. (1975). Primary and secondary emotional behavior: An analysis of the role of autonomic feedback on affect, arousal, and attribution. *Psychological Bulletin, 82*, 904-916.

Hassett, J. (1978). *A primer of psychophysiology*. San Francisco: W. H. Freeman.

Hirschman, R. (1975). Cross-modal effects of anticipatory bogus heart rate feedback in a negative emotional context. *Journal of Personality and Social Psychology, 31*, 13-19.

Hoehn-Saric, R., Liberman, B., Imber, S. D., Stone, A. R., Pande, S. K., & Frank, J. D. (1972). Arousal and attitude change in neurotic patients. *Archives of General Psychiatry, 26*, 51.

Hoehn-Saric, R., Frank, J. D., & Gurland, B. J. (1968). Focused attitude change in neurotic patients., *Journal of Nervous and Mental Disease, 147*, 124.

Hovland, C. I., & Riesen, A. H. (1940). Magnitude of galvanic and vasomotor response as a function of stimulus intensity. *Journal of General Psychology, 23*, 103-121.

Hume, W. I. (1973). Physiological measures in twins. In G. Claridge, S. Canter, and S. I. Hume (Eds.), *Personality differences and biological variations: A study of twins* (pp. 87-114). Oxford: Pergamon Press, Ltd.

Koella, G. B. (1975). Neurohumoral transmission and the autonomic nervous system. In L. S. Goodman & A. Gillman (Eds.), *The pharmacological basis of therapeutics*. New York: MacMillan.

Lacey, J. I. (1959). Psychophysiological approaches to the evaluation of psychotherapeutic process and outcome. In E. A. Rubinstein & M. B. Parloff (Eds.), *Research in psychotherapy* (pp. 160-208). Washington, DC: American Psychological Association.

Lacey, J. I. (1967). Somatic response patterning and stress: Some revisions of activation theory. In M. H. Appley & R. Trumbull (Eds.), *Psychological stress* (pp. 14-42). New York: Appleton.

Lader, M. (1969). Comparison of amphetamine sulphate and caffeine citrate in man. *Psychopharmacologia, 14*, 83-94.

Lader, M. H., & Wing, L. (1966). *Physiological measures, sedative drugs, and morbid anxiety*. London: Oxford University Press.

Langevin, R., & Day, H. I. (1972). Physiological correlates of humor. In J. H. Goldstein and P. E. McGhee (Eds.), *The psychology of humor*. New York: Academic Press.

Lasswell, H. D. (1936). Certain changes during trial (psychoanalytic) interviews. *Psychoanalytic Review, 23*, 241-247.

Latane, B., & Darley, J. M. (1968). Group inhibition of bystander intervention in emergencies. *Journal of Personality and Social Psychology, 10*, 215-221.

Lazarus, R. S. (1966). *Psychological stress and the coping process*. New York: McGraw-Hill.

Lazarus, R. S. (1968). Emotions and adaptation: Conceptual and empirical relations. *Nebraska Symposium on Motivation, 16*, 175-266.

Lazarus, R. S., & Alfert, E. (1964). The short-circuiting of threat. *Journal of Abnormal and Social Psychology, 69*, 195-205.

Lazarus, R. S., Opton, E. M., Jr., Nomikos, M. S., & Rankin, N. O. (1965). The principle of short-circuiting of threat: Further evidence. *Journal of Personality, 33*, 622-635.

Lienert, G. A., & Traxler, W. (1959). The effects of meprobamate and alcohol on galvanic skin response. *The Journal of Psychology, 48*, 329-334.

Lykken, D. T., & Tellegen, A. (1972). On the validity of the preception hypothesis. *Psychophysiology, 9*, 125-132.

Malmo, R. B. (1959). Activation: A neurophysiological dimension. *Psychological Review, 66*, 367-386.

Mandler, G. (1975). *Mind and emotion*. New York: Wiley.

Marshall, G. D., & Zimbardo, P. G. (1979). Affective consequences of inadequately explained physiological arousal. *Journal of Personality and Social Psychology, 37*, 970-988.

Martin, B. (1964). Expression and inhibition of sex motive arousal in college males. *Journal of Abnormal and Social Psychology, 68*, 307-312.

Mathews, A. M. (1971). Psychophysiological approaches to the investigation of densitization and related procedures. *Psychological Bulletin, 76*, 73-91.

McBurney, D. H., Levine, J. M., & Cavanaugh, P. M. (1977). Psychophysical and social ratings of human body odor. *Personality and Social Psychology Bulletin, 3*, 135-138.

McCurdy, H. G. (1950). Consciousness and the galvonometer. *Psychological Review, 157,* 322-327.

Montagna, W. (1975). The skin. In *Biological anthropology: Readings from Scientific American.* San Francisco: W. H. Freeman & Co.

Moruzzi, G., & Magoun, H. W. (1949). Brainstem reticular formation and activation of the EEG. *Electroencephalography and Clinical Neurophysiology, 1,* 455-473.

Orne, M. T. (1962). On the social psychology of the psychological experiment: With particular reference to demand characteristics and their implications. *American Psychologist, 17,* 776-783.

Page, M. (1969). Social psychology of a classical conditioning of attitudes experiment. *Journal of Personality and Social Psychology, 11,* 177-186.

Paul, G. L. (1966). *Insight vs. densitization in psychotherapy.* Stanford, CA: Stanford University Press.

Pervin, L. A. (1963). The need to predict and control under conditions of threat. *Journal of Personality, 31,* 570-587.

Roessler, R., Bruch, H., Thum, L., & Collins, F. (1975). Physiologic correlates of affect during psychotherapy. *American Journal of Psychiatry, 29,* 26-36.

Russell, M. J. (1976). Human olfactory communication. *Nature, 260,* 520-522.

Schachter, S., & Singer, J. E. (1962). Cognitive, social, and physiological determinants of emotional state. *Psychological Review, 69,* 379-399.

Schachter, S., & Wheeler, L. (1962). Epinephrine, chlorpromazine, and amusement. *Journal of Abnormal and Social Psychology, 65,* 121-128.

Schwartz, H. G. (1934). Reflex activity within the sympathetic nervous system. *American Journal of Physiology, 109,* 593-604.

Schwartz, G. E., & Shapiro, D. (1973). Social psychophysiology. In W. F. Prokasy & D. C. Raskin (Eds.), *Electrodermal activity in psychological research.* New York: Academic Press.

Shapiro, D., & Crider, A. (1969). Psychophysiological approaches in social psychology. In G. Lindzey & E. Aronson (Eds.), *The handbook of social psychology* (Vol. 3, 2nd ed., pp. 1-49). Reading, MA: Addison-Wesley.

Sokolov, E. N. (1963). *Perception and the conditioned reflex.* New York: Macmillan.

Solley, C. M., & Thetford, P. E. (1967). Skin potential responses and the span of attention. *Psychophysiology, 3,* 397-402.

Speisman, J. C., Lazarus, R. S., Mordkoff, A. M., & Davidson, L. A. (1964). The experimental reduction of stress based on ego-defense theory. *Journal of Abnormal and Social Psychology, 57,* 37-40.

Staats, A., & Staats, C. (1958). Attitudes established by classical conditioning. *Journal of Abnormal and Social Psychology, 57,* 37-40.

Stechler, G., Bradford, S., & Levy, H. (1966). Attention in the newborn: Effect on motility and skin potential. *Science, 151,* 1246-1248.

Valins, S. (1966). Cognitive effects of false heart-rate feedback. *Journal of Personality and Social Psychology, 4,* 400-408.

Van Egeren, L. F., Feather, B. W., & Hein, P. L. (1971). Densensitization of phobias: Some psychophysiological propositions. *Psychophysiology, 8,* 213-228.

Waid, W. M. (1979). Perceptual perpardness in man: Brief forewarning reduces electrodermal and psychophysical response to noxious stimulation. *Psychophysiology, 16,* 214-221.

Waid, W. M., & Orne, M. T. (1981). Cognitive, social and personality processes in the physiological detection of deception. *Advances in Experimental Social Psychology, 14,* 61-106.

Weil-Malherbe, H. (1960). The passage of catecholamines through the blood-brain barrier. In J. R. Vane, G. E. W. Wolstenholme, & M. O'Connor (Eds.), *Adrenergic mechanisms.* Boston: Little, Brown & Company.

Weiss, J. M. (1972). Psychological factors in stress and disease. *Scientific American, 226,* 104-113.

Wilcott, R. C. (1966). Adaptive value of arousal sweating and the epidermal mechanism related to skin potential and skin resistance. *Psychophysiology, 2,* 249-262.

Wilson, E. O. (1975). *Sociobiology, the new synthesis.* Cambridge, MA: Harvard University Press.

Zahn, T. P. (1977). Autonomic nervous system characteristics possibly related to a genetic predisposition to schizophrenia. *Schizophrenia Bulletin, 3,* 49-60.

Zanna, M. P., Kiesler, C. A., & Pilkonis, P. A. (1970). Positive and negative attitudinal affect established by classical conditioning. *Journal of Personality and Social Psychology, 14,* 321-328.

Chapter 2
Methods in Sociophysiology

Robert M. Stern and William J. Ray

Introduction: All Psychophysiology as Sociophysiology

Just as all psychological experiments involving at least one subject and one experimenter are social psychological studies, all psychophysiological experiments are really sociophysiological studies. To quote from Shapiro and Crider (1969), "a growing understanding of the social psychology of the psychophysiological experiment points up sources of variation in physiological measures and, conversely, the remarkable sensitivity of those measures to social attitudes such as race, sex, and status leads to a fuller appreciation of the impact of social factors on individual behavior" (pp. 37-38).

Three brief examples from our laboratory of the influence of race, sex, and status in sociophysiological investigations follow.

A graduate student was interested in the effects of proximity, or interpersonal distance, on peripheral blood flow. Recording was done using a photocell transducer and telemetry so that the subjects could be freely moving. The subject was instructed to walk slowly toward another individual, a laboratory assistant, who remained stationary. The question asked by the experimenter was "will there be detectable differences in the subjects' peripheral blood flow when they are 20 feet, 10 feet, 5 feet, and 2 feet from the laboratory assistant?" The answer provided by the data was positive. But perhaps even more interesting and relevant to this chapter was the finding that the race of the stationary laboratory assistant affected the peripheral blood flow of the subject along with proximity. White students approaching a black assistant showed greater vasoconstriction than white students who approached a white assistant.

In another experiment we were interested in studying the effect of repeated electric shocks on various autonomic nervous system (ANS) responses in males and females. As is commonly done, we presented to each subject a series of brief shocks each slightly stronger than the previous one and asked the subject to set his or her own maximum limit, the level that would then be presented several times in the actual study. We never did get to compare ANS responding to shocks of the same absolute level in males and females because the males tolerated significantly higher shock levels than the females. Two of the male subjects fainted rather than indicate that the shock level was too high. The experimenter was female.

The final example of the ever-present relationship between social variables and psychophysiology has to do with status. We were examining the ability of college students to control voluntarily their electrodermal activity with and without feedback. Subjects were told that during a rest period they were to think about lying on the beach or some similar image and to let their skin conductance decrease. In addition, subjects were instructed that during a respond period they were to think of something arousing, such as a painful experience (Epstein, 1973), and thereby make their skin conductance increase. In a pilot study, laboratory assistants found that many subjects could control their electrodermal activity when provided with feedback. However, when one of us (RMS) was the experimenter and used current students as subjects, few showed this ability. After considerable frustration, an explanation came in the form of a comment made independently by two subjects to a student assistant. What they said in effect was that during the respond period, they did not permit themselves to have arousing images because they were embarrassed, as they thought their teacher could tell what they were thinking via the electrodes on their hands!

Previous reviews of the area of sociophysiology, or social psychophysiology as it was then called, include the following: Kaplan and Bloom, 1960; Schwartz and Shapiro, 1973; Shapiro and Crider, 1969; and Shapiro and Schwartz, 1970.

It is the purpose of this chapter to introduce the reader to physiological measurement. We will discuss (1) general issues related to the recording of bodily responses, (2) how specific physiological measures are recorded, (3) concepts related to the interpretation of physiological measurements, and (4) new vistas. For a more detailed introduction the interested reader should consult Stern, Ray, and Davis (1980). Technical discussions of specific measures presented in more detailed form are found in Martin and Venables (1980).

Recording Bodily Responses

Organization of the Nervous System

The terminology of the nervous system reflects an anatomical organizing principle. The central nervous system (CNS) is composed of all cells within the bony enclosure of the spinal cord and skull, whereas the peripheral nervous system includes those neurons outside of these structures. The CNS is subdivided into the brain and spinal cord, with each of these structures further divided along anatomical lines. Physiological measures that are mediated by the CNS include electroencephalography (EEG or brain potentials), electromyograms (EMG or muscle potentials), electro-oculograms (EOG, eye movement potentials), and respiration.

The peripheral nervous system is also divided into two main parts: the somatic system and the autonomic nervous system. While the somatic system is concerned with adjustment between the external world and the organism, the ANS deals more with internal regulation of the organism. The ANS is further divided into two parts, depending upon where the neurons originate along the spinal cord. The sympathetic division originates within the thoracic and lumbar sections of the spinal cord, whereas the parasympathetic division originates in the cranial and sacral regions. Table 2-1 summarizes the action of the ANS. In general, the sympathetic division activates the body, while the parasympathetic division conserves the resources of the body and helps return physiological functioning to a state of equilibrium. For example, increases in heart rate, sweating, and vasoconstriction of the peripheral blood vessels are all stimulated by the sympathetic nervous system. The parasympathetic system, on the other hand, decreases heart rate, controls erection of the genitalia, stimulates peristalsis of the gastrointestinal tract, and increases tearing and salivation. The sympathetic system acts more diffusely, whereas the parasympathetic system displays independent action in each of its parts.

A familiarity with the structure and function of the nervous system is essential if one is to select the most appropriate physiological measures to record in a particular study. Decisions must be made with regard to CNS and ANS and within the latter,

Table 2-1 Action of the Autonomic Nervous System

Structure	Function	Parasympathetic Nervous System	Sympathetic Nervous System
Eyes Iris	Constriction	+	−
Eyes Lens	Accomodation	+	−
Lacrymal glands	Tears	+	−(?)
Nasal mucosa	Secretion, dilation	+	−
Salivary glands	Salivation	+	−(?)
Gastrointestinal tract	Peristalsis	+	−
Stomach glands	HCL, pepsin, & mucus	+	0
Pancreas (islet cells)	Insulin	+	0
Heart (rate)	Acceleration	−	+
Lungs (bronchia)	Dilation	−	+
Adrenal medulla	Adrenaline	0	+
Peripheral blood vessels	Vasoconstriction	?	+
Sweat glands	Sweating	0	+
Pilomotor cells	Piloerection	0	+
Internal sphincters Bladder Intestine	Contraction	−	+
Bladder wall Lower bowel	Contraction	+	−
Genitalia	Erection	+	−

Note. (+) indicates a facilitative effect and (−) an inhibitory effect. The upper portion of the table emphasizes facilitative effects of the cranial parasympathetics, the bottom separates the sacral parasympathetic effects, and the central portion emphasizes sympathetic facilitative effects. From R. M. Stern, W. J. Ray and C. M. Davis. *Psychophysiological recording*, New York: Oxford University Press, 1980. Reprinted with permission.

between responses that are mediated by the sympathetic, parasympathetic, or both. For example, if you wish to study sexual arousal in males while they view erotic films, you would not only record electrodermal activity since it is related to sweat gland activity, which is a sympathetic response. Sexual arousal is a parasympathetic response. In some cases, rather than recording nervous system responses, it might be more fruitful to measure hormonal levels, e.g., epinephrine.

Equipment

One could perform physiological assessment without any equipment other than one's own ability to observe and sense changes in another's body. Pulse rate could be measured by counting the pulses at any one of the arteries of the body. Another measure of autonomic activity could be approximated by feeling the palms and estimating the amount of sweating that has taken place before, for example, one gives an important speech. One could likewise notice pupillary changes as another person reacts to varying stimuli. These equipmentless types of measurement have been performed for thousands of years and are still in use today as exemplified by the physician feeling the pulse of a patient or by the salesman watching a customer's reaction as new merchandise is displayed. Although assessments performed in this manner may be useful and even fairly accurate, it is difficult to quantify and compare objectively measurements on different occasions under varying conditions. Investigators have thus sought objective methods that yield permanent records of the various physiological measures. In this section of the chapter we will discuss the equipment necessary for obtaining these recordings.

Electrodes and transducers. When one makes any movement or even thinks about a movement, bioelectrical activity from the relevant muscle(s) can be recorded. This bioelectrical activity results from biochemical changes and may be recorded from the surface of the skin. In order to record this electrical activity, two small metal disks, electrodes, are placed in contact with the surface of the skin. Electrodes are used to record any electrical activity resulting from biochemical changes within the body. This includes not only muscle activity (EMG) but also the activity of the cardiac muscle or heart (EKG), the electrical activity found on the scalp (EEG), electrical activity resulting from changes in the gastrointestinal tract (EGG), and the activity resulting from the movement of the eyes (EOG).

From a technical standpoint, electrodes are much more than simply connections to the skin from which bioelectrical activity can be recorded (Cromwell, Weibell, Pfeiffer, & Usselmann, 1973). Electrodes aid in converting ionic potential generated by muscle and other cells into electrical potentials which can be measured. For technical reasons (Lykken, 1959), the most common electrodes today are made of silver-silver chloride (Ag-AgCl) disks encased in a plastic housing. The electrode itself does not touch the skin because it is recessed slightly in the plastic housing; contact with the skin is made through a paste or jelly-like substance capable of conducting electrical activity. Most commercially available silver-silver chloride electrodes and electrode paste are of high quality and will serve adequately for most sociophysiological research. However, additional considerations regarding proper electrode selection and placement and appropriate electrolytes may be found in introductory (Stern, Ray, & Davis, 1980) and more advanced texts in psychophysiology (Brown, 1967; Martin & Venables, 1980) as well as in biomedical instrumentation references (Cromwell, Arditti, Weibell, Pfeiffer, Steele, & Labok, 1976; Geddes, 1972).

One extremely important concern in making bioelectrical recordings is proper skin preparation. Without proper skin preparation and electrode placement, the bioelectrical signal will not only be reduced in amplitude but will contain unwanted artifacts since the outer layer of skin is composed mainly of dead cells, dirt, and oils. The latter must always be removed by cleaning the skin with alcohol. For some measures (EMG) rubbing the skin with an abrasive pad or with an electrolyte containing a mild abrasive is also necessary. Once the electrodes are attached by using adhesive collars and an electrolyte, the electrical connection should be checked through the use of an impedance meter or ohmmeter. Generally, impedance or resistance levels below 10,000 ohms are considered acceptable.

Signals of relatively large amplitude such as the EKG can be recorded with minimal effort; small signals, however, such as EEG require greater care and a lower impedance for high quality recordings to be made. Once the electrical activity is recorded from the surface of the skin, the next step requires that the signal be amplified and/or conditioned by a polygraph so that it can be viewed and quantified.

Polygraphs. The main component of a physiological recording system is a polygraph. A polygraph is an instrument for conditioning, amplifying, and reproducing physiological signals from various response systems. In the same way that a stereo amplifier is actually made up of two separate amplifiers, one for each stereo channel, a polygraph is composed of anywhere from 2 to 32 separate amplifiers, each capable of reproducing a specific type of physiological signal. Conceptually, a polygraph can be divided into three main components: (1) a signal conditioner or coupler; (2) a preamplifier and amplifier; and (3) a device for displaying the signal.

Couplers. A coupler is designed to condition the signal coming from the subject. Some couplers change the form of the signal in order to meet the requirements of the preamplifier. Other couplers contain specialized circuits for use with transducers which record blood pressure, respiration, skin resistance, and so forth. In addition, some couplers perform selective filtering or compute rate measures, for example, heart rate.

Amplifiers. The signal goes from the coupler to the preamplifier which increases its amplitude to a level that can be accepted by the power amplifier. The power amplifier in turn multiplies the signal until it is of sufficient potential to drive the writer units, interface with a computer, and/or control some type of display. The output of most polygraph amplifiers is approximately 1 volt. This means that a bioelectrical signal such as EEG which is in the microvolt range (one-millionth of a volt) requires amplification of a million times before it can drive the pen or writer unit of a polygraph.

Because of the large amplification factor used in sociophysiological research, it is often necessary to remove unwanted electrical activity or interference by using filters. Filtering often takes place in the amplification section of the polygraph, although some couplers also contain filters. Lowpass filters allow only frequencies *below* a certain frequency to pass, whereas highpass filters allow only frequencies *above* a certain frequency to pass. A lowpass and a highpass filter may also be combined to allow the passing of a certain frequency band or range as is done for the purpose of detecting alpha waves in the EEG (waves in the 8-12-Hz range). Finally, notch filters may be set at certain frequencies such as at 60 Hz for filtering out electrical interference from normal wall current.

Conceptually, psychophysiologists speak of two types of amplifiers: AC and DC amplifiers. AC amplifiers are designed to reproduce rapid *changes* in a bioelectrical signal without remaining absolutely faithful to the slow changes in the bioelectrical potential difference between the electrodes connected to the person. The DC amplifier, on the other hand, does faithfully reproduce slow-changing potentials. Practically, this means that one should use a DC amplifier for such slow-changing measures as temperature, skin potential, and contingent negative variation (a slow-changing potential recorded from the brain) and an AC amplifier for more rapidly changing potentials such as heart activity, EEG, and EMG (muscle potentials). Through the use of a time-constant, the AC amplifier filters out the DC or slow moving component; the shorter the time constant, the less low frequency or slow-moving component will be displayed.

Pen-writers. The most common device for displaying the electrical signal is a pen-writing unit which traces the physiological signal on paper. As useful as visual inspection may be, new forms of data reduction often make paper recorders inadequate today. Many psychophysiological laboratories now connect the polygraph either directly, that is, "on-line," or indirectly, that is, "off-line," to a digital computer.

Computers and tape recorders. On-line means that the computer is being used to analyze the data at the same time that it is being collected. In order to accomplish this, the physiological signal is sent from the power amplifier of the polygraph to the analogue-to-digital (A-to-D) converter section of the computer, where the analogue or continuous physiological signal is changed into a discontinuous or discrete set of numbers. The computer can then perform numerical calculations on these numbers. Off-line refers to collecting the physiological signal on some type of recording device such as an FM tape recorder for later analysis at a time when the subject is not connected to the equipment. Physiological signals must be recorded on a special type of tape recorder, an FM tape recorder, since normal voice recorders, AM tape recorders, cannot faithfully reproduce frequencies below 50-100 Hz. Following this brief introduction to the equipment necessary for sociophysiological recordings, we now turn to the measures themselves.

Recording Specific Response Systems

Brain. Numerous studies have utilized the electroencephalogram (EEG) as a means of inferring cognitive and emotional activity in the brain. Recent interest has been focused on the particular hemisphere involved in the processing of given stimuli with EEG activity used to infer hemispheric utilization (see Donchin, Kutas, & McCarthy, 1977, for a review of this area). However, because of the equipment and technical sophistication required for EEG measurements, only recently have social psychologists started to use this measure.

Electroencephalography is generally divided into two major divisions: spontaneous EEGs, which is generally thought of as brain wave activity, and event-related potentials (ERPs). (The latter will not be discussed in this chapter since it has not been used in sociophysiology.) The EEG is a measure of electrical activity recorded from the surface of the scalp. Although there is an ongoing debate related to the origin of the EEG (Elul, 1972), since the brain is composed of billions of neurons, it is difficult, if not impossible, to know exactly what is being recorded when one examines the EEG.

Electrically, the typical EEG is in the microvolt range and thus requires considerable amplification for good recordings. EEG activity is specified in terms of frequency, with the main frequency bands being designated by Greek letters. Delta (0-4 Hz) is present in deep sleep and coma states. Theta (4-8 Hz) is present as one approaches sleep and in other reverie-like activities.

Most sociophysiological studies use either a measure of alpha activity (8-12 Hz) or beta activity (15-30 Hz). Alpha is considered to be a measure of noncortical processing in contrast with beta, which is often seen as a measure of cognitive activity. Thus it is assumed in many EEG studies that beta represents cognitive activity and alpha represents more of a resting state. Using this formulation Gale and his colleagues (Gale, Kingsley, Brookes, & Smith, 1978) monitored the EEGs of pairs of females when they made eye contact according to the experimenters' instructions (i.e., smile, direct gaze, avert gaze). Since either of the two females could be doing any of the three instructions, there were nine conditions: gaze-gaze, gaze-smile, smile-gaze, smile-avert, and so forth. Using a beta range of 13-19 Hz, Gale et al. reported that EEG responsiveness varies with eye contact and that averted gaze is less arousing than direct gaze. Gale and his associates (Gale, Spratt, Chapman, & Smallbone, 1975) in a previous study looked at EEG activity as a function of distance between two subjects and found higher arousal with closer proximity. As with the later study, direct gaze was associated with higher arousal regardless of the distance between subjects.

Muscles. Muscular activity has been used both as an assessment measure for discussing such constructs as anxiety and relaxation (Jacobson, 1938) and as a treatment modality when fed back to an individual in clinical biofeedback (Ray, Raczynski, Rogers, & Kimball, 1979). The most common technique for recording muscular activity is the surface recorded electromyogram (EMG), which is the result of action potentials spreading over the skeletal muscle cells following neural stimulation. With increased stimulation and the resultant increased activity or tension, numerous motor units begin to fire. However, the EMG is most representative during tension and not as valid during movements themselves (Lippold, 1952).

EMG activity can range from a few microvolts to the millivolt range and thus the amplifier settings depend on the type of activity that one is concerned with. EMG activity generated by a subject completely at rest might be 1-3 μV; a subject imagining that he or she was performing an activity might show a ten-fold increase in EMG activity, and a subject who voluntarily contracts a muscle might show EMG activity in the millivolt range. The frequency of muscle activity likewise may range from a few hertz to over 1000 Hz, although most of the signal power is between 10 and 150 Hz. It should be noted, though, that polygraph pen units rarely function accurately above 75 Hz; if only a general tension level is desired this should pose little problem.

Recording artifact-free EMGs from subjects who are in a resting state is extremely difficult because of the low level of the signal and the frequent presence of 60-Hz interference from the AC power lines. A 60-Hz notch filter should not be used when recording EMG since some of the muscle potential activity occurs at this frequency.

Muscle activity is recorded from the surface of the skin in much the same way as heart rate activity is recorded, but with more care because of the low level of the signal. There are several important considerations that should be noted when making EMG recordings. First, both electrodes should be placed over the same muscle or muscle group. Davis, Brickett, Stern, and Kimball (1978) have noted that most biofeedback researchers report that they record frontalis activity but actually record with one electrode over each of the two frontalis muscles. This produces needless complications in the interpretation of the recording. Second, the electrodes, when possible, should be on a line parallel with the muscle fibers. And third, the distance between the electrodes determines whether they are recording the activity of single motor units (1-2 cm between electrodes) or a general index of muscle tension. Even with careful placements, activity from other nearby muscles may also be picked up. Thus, it is not possible to make the claim that one is recording from only a specific muscle when surface electrodes are used.

A recent sociophysiological study in which EMG was recorded is described by Cacioppo and Petty (1979). Those authors examined the extent to which the magnitude of EMG responses over the perioral region (lips) varies with cognitive response processes in persuasion. They found that EMG from the perioral region generally increased during a period in which subjects were to collect their thoughts in preparation for an impending counter attitudinal advocacy. However, EMG activity from a normal muscle group, trapezius, did not increase. The authors concluded that the magnitude of EMG recorded from the perioral region reflect the extent of covert linguistic processing.

Eyes. Measurements related to the eyes can be both the most simple and most complicated of sociophysiological assessments. They are the most simple since the idea behind these measures stem from the age-old adage that the eye is the mirror of the soul. They are the most complicated since they require some of the most sophisticated equipment, the interpretation of which lies in a complex maze of theoretical speculation. For researchers interested in social process, eye contact has offered a simple measure of social interaction (Rubin, 1973). Likewise, direction of gaze has offered a possible indirect indication of hemispheric brain functioning (Bakan, 1969).

Pupillography. It is well known that the pupil of the eye responds to changes in illumination, but it has also been suggested that the pupil responds to changes in emotionality. Darwin, in the 1870s, reported that emotions such as fear and surprise were accompanied by pupillary changes. Although there were scattered studies of pupil changes since the time of Darwin, it was not until the last 20 years and the work of Hess that there has been systematic growth in the area. Hess reported that when showing a series of pictures to a research assistant he noticed that his assistant's pupils became larger when presented a nude rather than a landscape. Following this initial observation, he began a series of studies to determine the pupillary response to numerous psychological stimuli (see Hess, 1975, for a history of this work). According to Hess, attraction to a stimulus results in pupillary dilation and distasteful or unappealing stimuli produce pupillary constriction.

One example of the use of pupillography in sociophysiology is described in an article by Barlow (1969). Barlow showed slides of Lyndon Johnson, George Wallace, Martin Luther King, and an unknown person to subjects classified as liberal or conservative. The liberal subjects showed pupillary dilation while viewing slides of Johnson and King and constriction to Wallace. Conservative subjects showed just the opposite response.

Janisse (1977) has recently reviewed the work of Hess and others in this area and concluded that there is still much controversy over the relationship of psychological factors and pupillary responses. Upon closer inspection, the pupillary response is seen to be influenced by numerous factors, both psychological and physiological which include age, fatigue, information load, incentive, taste, alcohol, relaxation, habituation, and numerous specific responses to light, color, and focal point (Tryon, 1975).

The measurement of pupil size has involved either photographing the eye with a camera or using a computer-directed electronic scanning device. Pupil size change is then calculated and used for analysis. Both the camera technique which may produce 20,000 to 100,000 separate measurements in one study, and the electronic scanning technique which requires expensive equipment and extensive calibration for each subject pose limitation to the use of pupillography in sociophysiology.

Eye movement. Social psychologists have been interested in eye movement, particularly eye contact as an index of attraction, intimacy, and interpersonal communication (Argyle & Cook, 1976). Other psychologists have examined the effects of intrapersonal variables such as information processing and emotionality (Ehrlichman & Weinberger, 1978). The simplest method of determining direction of gaze is by observation and in interpersonal studies this has been concluded to be a reliable method of measurement. If, on the other hand, one were interested in finer differentiations of movement such as those that occur during reading (Oster & Stern, 1980), electrical recording of eye movements is recommended.

The basis of electrical eye movement recording or the electrooculogram (EOG) is the potential difference between the front and the back of the eye, that is, the cornea is 0.4-1.0 mV positive with respect to the retina. Thus, if electrodes are placed either on each side of the eyes, for horizontal movement, or above and below an eye, for vertical movement, an electrical potential can be recorded which varies as the eye moves. With appropriate calibration, eye position can then be determined from either paper records or with the use of a laboratory computer.

Respiratory system. Respiration refers to the process by which oxygen is supplied to cells and carbon dioxide is removed. The aspects of respiration that sociophysiologists usually measure are breathing rate and amplitude, the latter being an indirect measure of the depth of breathing. The normal rate of respiration in man is about 12 breaths per minute, and the usual depth (tidal volume or total volume of each breath) is 400-600 ml for healthy adults.

Examples of the use of respiration as a dependent variable in sociophysiology are not very common. Frequently, when respiration is recorded, it is used as a check against possible artifacts in other response measures caused by breathing irregularities. A deep breath, intentional or not, will usually bring about a greater change in ANS responses than will manipulation of the independent variable (Stern & Anschel, 1968). The effect of respiration on heart rate has long been of interest to physiologists. Sinus arrythymia refers to the rhythmic increases and decreases in heart rate produced by normal respiration in many subjects.

One subarea of sociophysiology in which respiration has received considerable attention is the detection of deception. Riddle (1925) described the characteristic respiratory pattern of people bluffing during a poker game. In more typical detection of deception situations, both laboratory and field, a variety of measures of respiration have been used: rate, amplitude, variability in both of these measures, and the relative duration of inspiration and expiration.

Respiration is modified by both the CNS and ANS, particularly the parasympathetic branch. Respiratory activity is highly responsive to changes in the concentrations of carbon dioxide and oxygen in the blood. It should be noted, however, that the level of carbon dioxide is much more important for the regulation of breathing than the level of oxygen. For additional information on the physiological basis of respiration, see Comroe (1965).

Four methods of recording respiration rate and amplitude are air-pressure pneumograph, impedance, air temperature, and strain gauge. The relative insensitivity of the air-pressure pneumograph and various shortcomings of the impedance and air temperature methods have stimulated interest in using a wire, crystal, or ceramic strain gauge attached to a rubber or elastic strap which is placed around the subject's chest. A commonly used transducer is a 10-inch open strain gauge made of silastic (a synthetic rubber) tubing filled with mercury. A small current is passed through the mercury as the subject inhales, the mercury column is stretched thinner, thereby increasing the resistance in the circuit. As he exhales, the resistance decreases. The respiratory transducer is usually placed around the chest somewhere between the nipple line and the base of the sternum.

In determining respiration rate, the obvious and most common procedure is simply to count the number of complete respiratory cycles per minute. A more accurate method is to measure the distance between successive cycles and then convert to a measure of intercycle interval in units of seconds. None of the methods commonly used for recording respiration amplitude yields absolute data. Therefore, the data obtained are usually expressed in relative terms. One must decide how much deeper than normal respiration amplitude can be before causing disruptive artifacts in other measures. As a rule of thumb, it is suggested that if the amplitude of a respiratory cycle is twice as large or greater than the previous cycle, other physiological responses that occur for at least the next 20 s should not be considered valid data.

Cardiovascular system. Three major measures of the functioning of the cardiovascular system which are of interest to social scientists are heart rate, blood pressure, and vasomotor activity.

Heart rate. The heart contracts following an impulse from specialized cells within it referred to as pacemaker cells. This initial impulse results in the contraction of the atrium and then the ventricles which produces the distribution of blood first to the lungs and then to the body. The depolarization of the ventricles results in the characteristic spike (QRS complex) of bioelectrical potential that can be seen in the electrocardiogram (EKG). In order to record the depolarization of the atrium and ventricles, one need only place two electrodes on the skin, fairly far apart. The QRS complex of the EKG is approximately 1 mV in amplitude with a frequency of approximately 1 Hz. Thus, the recording equipment used must be able to amplify the signal at least 1000 times; an AC amplifier is generally used which minimizes drift in the electrical signal on paper.

There are two common ways in which the frequency of heart beating are reported: heart rate (HR) and interbeat-interval (IBI). Heart rate is measured in terms of the number of beats per time period, usually minutes. Most polygraphs also have a special coupler referred to as a cardiotachometer to electronically determine and display heart rate. Interbeat-interval, on the other hand, is the amount of time between successive heart beats. While many researchers previously determined this measure from the polygraph records themselves, today more and more investigators use computers in quantifying this measure. Although heart rate and interbeat-interval are highly related, problems can arise when one measure is converted into another for purposes of analysis (Khachaturian, Kerr, Kruger, & Schachter, 1972).

Graham (1978 a,b) has also suggested that the measure and the time units should be considered carefully to produce statistically unbiased means. For example, one has the choice of either recording the first 12 *beats* following a stimulus or the first 12 *seconds* following a stimulus. To complicate matters, each of these choices may be recorded in either beats per minute or in interbeat-intervals, and depending on the study, these four possible combinations may actually produce different results using the same set of subjects. Although complicated, the matter of heart rate or IBI measurement need not be difficult if the researcher considers carefully the type of question being asked and the most appropriate measure to answer it.

Shapiro (1975) reported an interesting example of a sociophysiological study involving heart rate. He compared the heart rate of kibbutz girls and urban girls living in Israel the day before, immediately before, and a week after receiving an injection. He was testing the hypothesis that kibbutz children would be less aroused by stress. The results showed that the heart rate of the kibbutz girls was lower the day before. Shapiro then used "day before" as a covariate for the following days and found that heart rate immediately before the injection and one week later was significantly slower for the kibbutz children.

Blood pressure. The maximal or systolic blood pressure occurs when the ventricle of the heart contracts. The subsequent relaxation of the ventricle is associated with the period when blood pressure is at a minimum, the diastolic blood pressure. Blood pressure is reported as systolic over diastolic with the standard unit of measurement being millimeters of mercury (mmHg). The so-called normal blood pressure is said to be about 120/80 mmHg, although such factors as age, diet, posture, and weight are important to consider (Brobeck, 1973).

Blood pressure changes during coitus, an example of a sociophysiological study, was reported by Fox and Fox (1969). These experiments were conducted with an individual married couple with 11 years of mutual coital experience. They took place in complete privacy and in the familiar surroundings of their own bedroom. Their results showed that systolic blood pressure rose from 120 mmHg to 175 mmHg at the moment of onset of ejaculation in the male, while the female peaked at 200 mmHg during orgasm. Blood pressure was then seen to drop sharply to below resting level during resolution or postorgasmic phase and then return to normal.

The most common method of measuring blood pressure involves a sphygmomanometer and a stethoscope, the equipment used by most physicians. The sphygmomanometer cuff is placed around the person's arm and then inflated to cut off all arterial blood flow. As the pressure in the cuff is reduced, tapping sounds (Korotkoff sounds) are heard in the stethoscope, placed over the brachial artery below the cuff, as blood begins to flow again. The point at which the first sound is heard is referred to as systolic blood pressure. As pressure in the cuff is reduced further, the sounds change through a series of well described stages until no sound is heard. The measurement at this point is considered to be the diastolic blood pressure.

Polygraph couplers have been designed to produce a permanent record by replacing the stethoscope with a microphone whose output is displayed on the polygraph tracing superimposed over the pressure record as the cuff is deflated. Problems emerge in quantifying these data, however, as a visual judgment must be made as to the first and last sounds as they appear on the chart paper, and the inflation and deflation of the cuff itself may be a strong stimulus for the subject. There is also a limit to the number of blood pressure recordings that can be taken during any one session, and repeated measures may actually artificially alter readings through tissue changes. Finally, large variations may be seen in an individual's readings during a session (Tursky, 1974). Hence, using blood pressure as an assessment device should be approached with caution.

Vasomotor activity. Vasomotor changes are often noticed as cold hands or feet as one is about to take an exam or meet someone important. One of the early demonstrations of vasomotor changes was reported by Mittelman and Wolff (1939) in the form of a case history. These investigators recorded the skin temperature of a finger of a young girl while they interviewed her concerning her troubled relationship with her mother. Drops in skin temperature are caused by vasoconstriction. As might be expected, when the girl was first asked a question about her mother, her finger temperature was 34 °C. It dropped to 22 °C within 30 min. The smaller the diameter of the blood vessels in the skin, the smaller the area of warm blood at the surface of the body and consequently the lower the skin temperature.

There are two commonly used measures of vasomotor activity: blood volume and pulse volume. Blood volume reflects slow changes in the amount of blood in the arm, finger, leg, or toe, whereas pulse volume is a more rapid change reflecting both the contraction of the heart as well as peripheral changes. Blood volume measurements are made with a transducer connected to a DC amplifier, while pulse volume measurements are made with an AC amplifier.

The most popular method for recording blood volume and pulse volume is with a photoelectric plethysmograph. A photoelectric plethysmograph consists of a light source in the infrared range and a photodetector. Depending on the particular photoelectric plethysmograph, the light is either measured as it passes through the tissue (more blood equals less light passing through) or as it bounces off the blood (the detector is on the same side as the light source).

While the recording of vascular activity is relatively simple, the interpretation and accurate quantification of this measure is a difficult task. Many factors such as room temperature, variation in skin characteristics, difficulty of exact placement from person to person and on the same person on different occasions, and even variations in the intensity of the light source make absolute vasomotor measurement impossible and relative ones complicated. (See Cook, 1974, for a more detailed discussion of factors that influence vasomotor activity.)

Electrodermal activity. Electrodermal activity (EDA) has been recorded more frequently than any other sociophysiological measure. Why is this such a popular measure? Many who record EDA today share the basic belief expressed by Carl Jung in 1907 and by present-day lie detector operators that verbal responses do not tell all, but that EDA does reveal the secrets of "mental life." Today we think of EDA as a measure of the state of the organism's interaction with his environment. Edelberg (1972) reminds us that the skin has a special significance because it both receives outside information and responds to signals from within.

There are two different methods for measuring electrodermal activity, both dating back to the 1800s. The first method passes a current through the skin from an external source and measures the changes in resistance of the skin to this current. Today, the reciprocal of resistance, skin conductance, is usually recorded for a number of reasons (Venables & Christie, 1973). The second method, referred to as skin potential, does not use an external current but measures the electrical activity at the surface of the skin.

Skin conductance and skin potential may be examined in regard to responses to specific stimuli (phasic activity), general basal level (tonic level), or changes which cannot be attributed to a specific stimulus (spontaneous activity).

Eccrine sweat glands, a special type of sweat gland, are intimately involved in EDA. Eccrine sweat glands are concentrated in the palms of the hands and soles of the feet. What makes them of particular interest to psychologists is that they respond primarily to "psychic" stimulation, whereas other sweat glands respond more to increases in temperature. The eccrine sweat glands are innervated by the sympathetic branch of the ANS, but the chemical transmitter at the postganglionic synapse is acetylcholine, not noradrenaline, as would be expected in the sympathetic nervous system. This is worth noting because many make the mistake of generalizing from EDA recording to all other sociophysiological activity. Generalizing from one channel of data is always risky, but particularly so when the single measure used is an exception to the rule.

The most common EDA measure used in behavioral research is that of skin conductance. Skin conductance is usually recorded from the palmar surface of the hands. If a bipolar placement is to be used, the electrode sites on the hand are cleaned but not abraded; with monopolar recording, the inactive site (usually on the arm) is abraded. Skin conductance responses are recorded using a special coupler that imposes a small constant voltage across the two electrodes.

One example of the use of electrodermal responses (EDRs) in sociophysiology is a study by Stern and Lewis (1968) which examined the relationship between the ability of actors to control their EDRs and express emotions on the stage. During one 10-min period subjects were instructed to make as many EDRs as possible and during another 10-min period they were to inhibit their EDRs. All subjects received continuous visual feedback of their responses. No relationship was found between ability to control EDRs and emotional expression as measured by the ratings of directors. However, method actors, those individuals who express emotions through the use of personal emotional memory, were able to control their EDRs at a significantly higher level than nonmethod actors.

A second example of the use of EDA in sociophysiology was recently reported by Waid and Orne (1981). These investigators studied the effect of the ethnic background of a polygraph examiner and subjects during a test of detection of deception. The examiner was of Irish heritage; the subjects were native-born U.S. college students of the following ethnic backgrounds: English, German, Irish, Italian, Jewish, and Scottish. In response to biographical interview questions, the students of Irish heritage gave significantly smaller EDRs than did the other ethnic groups. And during a deception test, the Irish subjects had the smallest number of detections of any of the groups.

While this measure, EDA, like vascular activity, is relatively easy to record, the quantification of skin conductance is a complex matter and may involve quantification of response amplitudes and frequency of spontaneous responses, as well as other aspects of the responses themselves. In addition, Venables and Christie (1973) have reported a number of factors that may influence skin conductance responses, including such subject factors as age, sex, race, and stage of the menstrual cycle and such environmental factors as temperature, humidity, time of day, day of week, and season of the year.

Concepts Related to the Interpretation of Recordings

Concepts discussed in this section are generalizations that workers in this field have arrived at based on thousands of experiments. A familiarity with these concepts will not only provide the reader with information about certain relationships between social and physiological variables but will also alert the reader to factors—other than the independent variables—which might influence the data in sociophysiological studies. With an understanding of these generalizations, the reader should be better equipped to design new studies and to understand earlier publications.

Arousal and Habituation

Arousal. The concept of arousal or activation has its roots in Cannon's (1915) notion of the unified body preparing for fight or flight. Duffy (1957) extended this concept to include the intensity aspect of all behavior. She (Duffy, 1962) hypothesized an inverted U-shaped curve relating level of activation or arousal and performance. Other researchers such as Malmo (1959) and Lindsley (1951) sought to determine the relationship between physiological changes and behavior. Much of this work viewed arousal as forming a continuum going from very low arousal (e.g., sleep) to hyperarousal. Arousal was often related to the Yerkes-Dodson law reported in 1908 which suggested that better performance is found with medium arousal than with either low or high arousal. Since much of the theoretical work was based on animal studies, there was a general blending of the terms arousal and emotionality, with both being seen as moving on a continuum from low to high. This is in contrast to Darwin's (1872) suggestion that emotionality serves a communicative function and thus is organized around certain core expressions such as joy, surprise, sadness, and so forth. An excellent review of the question of emotionality directed at social psychologists has been published by Leventhal (1980).

In 1962 Schachter and Singer published an article in *Psychological Review* which relates generalized arousal to emotions. They suggested that *both* arousal and cognition are necessary for emotion. They based this conclusion on a study in which one group of subjects was given injections of epinephrine in the guise of a study on the effects of vitamins on vision. These subjects were then placed with either a euphoric or angry confederate. From a combination of behavioral measures, self-report measures, and physiological measures taken at the end of the session, these authors concluded that once one is aroused, labeling plays an important role in determining the nature of one's emotionality if the arousal could not be explained by the subject. Schachter and Singer (1962) state ". . . precisely the same state of physiological arousal could be labeled 'joy' or 'fury' or any of a great diversity of emotional labels, depending upon the cognitive aspects of the situation" (p. 381).

The work of Schachter and Singer has stimulated interest in the concept of arousal: what is arousal, is it perceived arousal or actual physiological arousal that is important, and what happens when one receives false feedback of physiological responses (cf. Stern, Botto, & Herrick, 1972). The answers to such questions are not simple. For example, Lacey (1967) has pointed out the low intercorrelation between different physiological measures and thus presents one with the difficulty of choosing any one particular physiological measure (e.g., heart rate) as an index of arousal. In addition Lacey suggests that in order to understand the concept of arousal one must differentiate among cortical arousal, autonomic arousal, or behavioral arousal. This is supported by research on anxiety (Borkovec, 1976) in which cognitive and somatic responses differ. The main conclusion to be drawn is that the concept of a simple arousal continuum with all physiological variables responding similarly is not supported.

Not only has the Schachter and Singer work led to a number of studies in sociophysiology, it has also generated a great deal of controversy. Maslach (1979 a,b) has criticized the Schachter and Singer work on a number of methodological and conceptual grounds. (See also the response of Schachter and Singer, 1979.) This is a most enlightening and instructive debate which not only points to many important questions in sociophysiology but also many areas in which our conceptualizations remain unclear.

Habituation. The concept of habituation is just as basic to sociophysiology as the concept of arousal. They are in a sense complementary. Whereas arousal suggests responding to a stimulus, habituation describes the cessation or diminution of responding that occurs with repeated presentation of the same stimulus.

Habituation always occurs with repeated presentation of the same stimulus, except in cases of unusually intense stimulation. (See the discussion of defensive responses below.) Habituation will be slower the greater the intensity of stimulation, the more unique the stimulus, and the more complex the stimulus. Habituation will also be affected by the rate of presentation of the stimuli and the duration of each presentation. If the subject is required to make a behavioral response—for example, to rate the subjective intensity of the stimuli—habituation will be somewhat inhibited. For more information about habituation of autonomic responses, see Graham (1973).

Orienting and Defensive Responses

Orienting responses. Having discussed habituation, it is fitting to move on to the description of and distinction between orienting responses and defensive responses. An important first distinction is that orienting responses habituate rapidly, whereas defensive responses habituate very slowly.

The orienting response is the group of reactions which usually occur to novel stimuli; it is the "what is it" response (Pavlov, 1927).

Lynn (1966) has summarized the components of the orienting response as follows:

1. There is an increase in the sensitivity of sense organs.
2. The organism turns its head, and in some cases its ears, toward the stimulus.
3. There is a decrease in irrelevant motor activity and an increase in general muscle tone.

4. EEG shows faster and lower-voltage activity.
5. Vasoconstriction occurs in the periphery (limbs) and vasodilation in the head.
6. Skin conduction increases.
7. Respiration shows a delay followed by an increase in amplitude and a decrease in frequency.

Defensive responses. The defensive response habituates very slowly. This response protects us from the possible dangers of very intense stimulation. Its function apparently is to limit the effect on the body of intense stimuli. Those components of the defensive response which are different from the orienting response are listed below.

1. There is a decrease in the sensitivity of sense organs.
2. The organism tends to move away from the stimulus.
3. Vasoconstriction occurs in the periphery and in the head.
4. Heart rate increases.

Homeostasis and Autonomic Balance

Homeostasis. The word homeostasis has been used to describe both a state of the organism and a process which takes place within the organism. When we refer to the homeostatic state, we are identifying equilibrium, stability, constancy, and the like. What we are really describing is a steady-state internal environment providing the right temperature, nourishment, oxygen, and fluids for optimal functioning of all cells. The mechanism that underlies the homeostatic process is negative feedback. An example of a negative feedback system outside of our bodies is the thermostat which controls the temperature of a room. The thermostat senses the temperature; the warmer the room, the less heat it allows in.

The general concept of homeostasis as first stated by Claude Bernard—"Le fixité du milieu interieur est la condition de la vie libre,"[1] and later supported by Cannon (1939) in his book *The Wisdom of the Body*—captured the imagination of physiologists and psychologists alike. The maintenance of equilibrium was accepted by some as the unifying principle of motivation and, indeed, as a model for many other aspects of behavior. In our opinion, it is no more meaningful to specify the homeostatic state of the whole organism than it is to specify the stability of an entire university. In both cases, some parts (physiological systems or departments) may be very stable, while others are not.

Autonomic balance. Most internal organs, such as the heart, are innervated by both branches of the autonomic nervous system: the sympathetic nervous system (SNS) and the parasympathetic nervous system (PNS). The rate at which the heart beats is determined by the relative excitation from the SNS and PNS, or the autonomic balance. Autonomic balance may, therefore, be considered one specific part of homeostasis.

Eppinger and Hess (1915) were the first to classify people as vagotonics or sympathicotonics. Vagotonics (from vagus nerve, the primary parasympathetic nerve)

---

[1] "Stability of the internal environment is the necessary condition for a healthy life."

are individuals who show unusually large responses to drugs which stimulate the PNS. Sympathicotonics are persons who show unusually large responses to drugs which stimulate the SNS. The interested reader is referred to early work on autonomic balance by Gellhorn, Cortell, and Feldman (1941) and Darrow (1943). The person who has done the most research in the area of autonomic balance is Wenger (1972), who developed a technique for comparing an individual's resting scores on a group of ANA measures with the scores of other individuals and, in so doing, came up with an estimate of autonomic balance for each subject.

Law of Initial Values

Wilder (1967) was the first to call attention to the relationship of the size of a response to the prestimulus level and to name it the law of initial values (LIV). He reported that the greater the prestimulus level, the smaller the response to stimulation. It is a principle that is often supported, but it does not hold at all prestimulus levels, for all subjects, or for all ANS measures.

If we examine the evidence for the LIV from empirical studies, we find the following. For heart rate, most investigators have found that their results support the LIV. Skin resistance has also been found by most investigators to follow the LIV, but skin conductance usually does not. A few additional studies have found support for the LIV with blood pressure and respiration.

How would one know if his data supported the LIV? An investigator could either calculate the correlation between the prestimulus levels and the magnitude of the responses to stimulation, or could construct a scattergram. If a significant correlation does exist, how might it be removed? Two methods are available for statistically neutralizing the LIV: Lacey's (1956) Autonomic Lability Score, and covariance (Benjamin, 1967). If possible, the experimenter tries to ensure that LIV does *not* affect his data by administering stimulation at similar initial levels.

Stimulus-Response Specificity and Individual Response Stereotypy

Stimulus-response specificity. By definition, stimulus-response specificity exists if a stimulus brings about a similar pattern of physiological responding from most subjects. Some investigators sought evidence of stimulus-response specificity to support James' (1884) theory that the perception of bodily changes is what constitutes emotion. Ax (1953) created a laboratory situation in which one group of subjects was made angry and another fearful. He recorded a large number of bodily responses and found that about half of them differentiated between fear and anger situations. Davis (1957) sought response patterns to some very simple stimuli with no notion of uncovering the physiological correlates of fear, repulsion, and the like. The various bodily responses recorded showed significant differentiation among the four stimulus situations: paced key pressing, listening to noises, looking at pictures, and receiving cutaneous stimulation.

Individual response stereotypy. Individual response stereotypy refers to idiosyncratic responding. Will psychiatric patients, who frequently complain of head and neck pain, show a different pattern of bodily responses in a stress situation than patients who frequently complain of heart palpitations? That was the basic question asked by Malmo and Shagass (1949) in the first of a series of studies on what they came to call symptom specificity. They recorded heart rate changes, muscle potentials from the neck, and other physiological measures from both groups of patients. The exciting finding was that even when stress consisted of only moderate thermal stimulation, and the subjects were not reporting that they were in pain, the head and neck complainers showed a significant increase in muscle potential from the neck, while the group that normally complained of palpitations showed a significant change in their heart rate.

Lacey and his co-workers conducted several studies during the 1950s (e.g., Lacey and Lacey, 1958) to see if the principle of symptom specificity would hold for non-psychiatric patients. Using various groups of subjects and several different stressors, they found that individuals tend to respond by showing the greatest degree of activity in the same physiological system, no matter what the stress. For many subjects their pattern of physiological responding was repeated from stressor to stressor. This is what is meant by individual response stereotypy.

Stimulus-response specificity and individual response stereotypy probably exist to some degree in all sociophysiological studies. The practical question is how serious is this problem, and what can and should be done about it? We cannot make a blanket statement concerning the proportion of the total variance in all future studies which will be attributable to stimulus-response specificity and individual response stereotypy, as it will no doubt vary considerably. However, the problem does not appear serious if careful consideration is given to the selection of physiological responses to be measured and the number of subjects. Stimulus-response specificity tells us that we should record not just one but several physiological measures and examine the pattern of responses to our various stimulus situations. Individual response stereotypy, on the other hand, alerts us to the problem of a few subjects making idiosyncratic responses in a situation where quite a different pattern of responses might be expected.

New Vistas

During the past 20 years there has been an increasing number of studies in which investigators have recorded physiological variables as a means of understanding social processes. In this concluding section, we want to discuss briefly the following four areas of potentially productive sociophysiological research: (a) individual responding (e.g., arousal) as a mechanism for understanding processes such as helping behavior or reaction to persuasion; (b) interpersonal patterns of responding as a means of delineating such constructs as empathy and communication; (c) the manner in which one's physiology communicates information to another person; and (d) the manner in which false physiological feedback has an impact on one's attitudes and beliefs. The first two areas use sociophysiological variables as a means of understanding a particular process, such as helping behavior or empathy, whereas the last two areas view the sociophysiological measures as containing information which is perceived and processed in the context of individual and social interaction.

Individual Responding

Research in the first area asks such questions as, how might sociophysiological factors help us to better understand social processes? One recent example of this is the work of Piliavin, Dovidio, Gaertner, and Clark (1981). These researchers have been interested in what factors influence the degree to which one person will help another in an emergency situation. In their chapter, Piliavin et al. indicate that initially they proposed a simple arousal model which suggested that as arousal increased, the probability of helping would also increase. This type of thinking is supported by independent research such as that of Shotland and Stebbins (1980) in which they reported higher levels of arousal from self-report and observational measures for subjects who intervened in an emergency situation. (The model of arousal for much of this work is similar to that articulated by Duffy or suggested in the Schachter and Singer work, that of a simple continuum of arousal.) However, Piliavin et al. further along in their chapter draw from the work of Sokolov (1965) and that of Lacey (1967) to suggest that there are two arousal systems which correspond to orientation (OR), or the input of information, and defensive reaction (DR), or the gating out of information. As could be gathered from the discussion of the OR and DR in the previous section of this chapter an important part of this model would be the intensity of the stimulus as it relates to the type of helping behavior seen.

Another example of research from the first area would be that of attitude change. For example, Cacioppo, Petty, and Quintanar (1982) have examined the relationship between EEG activity and cognitive responses to persuasion. This type of research may be expanded to ask broad questions of how we process information. As we gain more understanding in what we can learn from using sociophysiological measures it may be possible to identify subject variables which will help to explain some of the inconsistencies found in certain social psychological areas. For example understanding how a particular person processes violence seen on television may be useful in pointing out what types of violence have the potential to be arousing and for whom.

Interpersonal Interactions

A second area of potential importance for sociophysiological research is that of interpersonal interactions. This area of research has not been adequately explored although there are analogue studies in the clinical literature. For example, Coleman, Greenblatt, and Solomon (1956) followed a series of 44 psychotherapy sessions in which heart rate of both therapist and client were recorded. One intriguing finding of this work was that the heart rate of the therapist responded in a similar way to that of the client, and thus might in some way be related to such constructs as empathy. Another interesting finding was that physiological processes were related to psychological relationship factors such that physiological measures changed as a function of whether the therapist was interested in his own internal processes or paying attention to the client. Other researchers from this period reported similar findings; many of these studies are reviewed by Lacey (1959). A reading of this review should offer a number of interesting ideas which could be translated into the realm of sociophysiological research.

Physiological Communication

The previous applications described instances in which social factors effected bodily change, the usual case in sociophysiology. At this point we want to mention the possiblity of studying the other direction, namely, bodily changes which affect social variables.

Let us assume a couple is out on a date for the first time. If at the end of the evening the male notices that his companion's pupils are small and her hands cold, he will probably rightly conclude that she really isn't very interested in him. On the other hand, if her pupils are large and her hands warm, this might be interpreted by the male to mean that she was interested in intensifying their interaction.

This is just one of many possible examples of nonverbal communication that takes place not via body position but rather via visible bodily changes which are brought about by autonomic nervous system responses to social situations. In addition to hand temperature and pupil size, two other bodily changes that commonly respond to social factors and are easily observable are vascularity of the skin (blushing) and sweating. In extreme cases, these responses can be not only embarrassing but an impediment to carrying out one's job. We were recently consulted by a physician who was trying to help a young lawyer who perspired from the forehead to such an extent in court when he was having difficulty with a certain aspect of a case that the opposing lawyer could make good use of this information.

False Feedback of Physiological Information and Attitudes

In 1966, Valins reported the first of a series of experiments involving the cognitive effects of false heart rate feedback. Extending Schachter's theory of emotion (Schachter & Singer, 1962), Valins stated that the *belief* that one's heart beat is increasing or decreasing, with the actual physiological change occurring, is sufficient to affect behavior. There have been several criticisms of Valins' interpretation of the mechanisms involved in the false feedback studies (e.g., Stern, Botto, & Herrick, 1972), but the procedure used might lend itself to a series of studies on the effect of false feedback from a confederate on the attitudes of subjects. For example, while college-age males are viewing slides of nude females, we might play for them an electronically generated audio tape which they are told is the taped heart rate of another individual, recorded while the other person watched the same slides. The immediate question is what will be the effect on the subject's own heart rate and attitude concerning the attractiveness of a particular slide when he hears what he thinks is another person's heart rate increase or decrease? And what will be the effect of manipulating the status of the "other person?" Would conformity of actual heart rate and/or attitude differ if the other person was a star athlete, president of a fraternity, or a homosexual? Obviously, this same type of study could be done with alternative stimulus material such as statements concerning social issues rather than slides of nude women.

Understanding the inexact manner in which physiological and cognitive measures relate to each other offers a challenge to the sociophysiological researcher. As we develop new techniques for analysis and descriptions of both psychological and physiological variables, it will clearly be an exciting time as social psychologists and psychophysiologists bring together their individual understanding for a more complete picture of human functioning.

References

Argyle, M., & Cook, M. (1976). *Gaze and mutual gaze*. New York: Cambridge University Press.
Ax, A. F. (1953). The physiological differentiation between fear and anger in humans. *Psychosomatic Medicine, 15*, 433-442.
Bakan, P. (1969). Hypnotizability, laterality of eye movement, and functional brain asymmetry. *Perceptual and Motor Skills, 28*, 587-590.
Barlow, J. D. (1969). Pupillary size as an index of preference in political candidates. *Perceptual and Motor Skills, 28*, 587-590.
Benjamin, L. S. (1967). Facts and artifacts in using analysis of covariance to "undo" the law of initial values. *Psychophysiology, 4*, 187-206.
Borkovec, T. D. (1976). Psychophysiology and cognitive processes in the regulation of anxiety. In G. E. Schwartz & D. Shapiro (Eds.), *Consciousness and self regulation* (Vol. 1). New York: Plenum.
Brobeck, J. R. (Ed.). (1973). *Best and Taylor's physiological basis of medical practice*. Baltimore: Williams & Wilkins.
Brown, C. C. (Ed.). (1967). *Methods in pyschophysiology*. Baltimore: Williams & Wilkins.
Cacioppo, J. T., & Petty, R. E. (1979). Attitudes and cognitive response: An electrophysiological approach. *Journal of Personality and Social Psychology, 37*, 2181-2199.
Cacioppo, J. T., Petty, R. E., & Quintanar, L. R. (1982). Individual differences in relative hemispheric alpha abundance and cognitive responses to persuasive communication. *Journal of Personality and Social Psychology, 43*, 623-636.
Cannon, W. B. (1915). *Bodily changes in pain, hunger, fear and rage*. New York: Appleton-Century-Crofts.
Cannon, W. B. (1939). *The wisdom of the body* (2nd ed.). New York: Norton.
Comroe, J. H., Jr. (1965). *Physiology of respiration*. Chicago: Yearbook Medical Publishers.
Coleman, R., Greenblatt, M., & Solomon, H. C. (1956). Physiological evidence of rapport during psychotherapeutic interviews. *Diseases of the Nervous System, 17*, 2-8.
Cook, M. R. (1974). Psychophysiology of peripheral vascular change. In P. Obrist, A. H. Black, J. Brener, & L. DiCara (Eds.), *Cardiovascular psychophysiology*. Chicago: Aldine.
Cromwell, L., Weibell, F. J., Pfeiffer, E. A., & Usselmann, L. B. (1973). *Biomedical instrumentation and measurements*. Englewood Cliffs, NJ: Prentice-Hall.
Cromwell, L., Arditti, M., Weibell, F. J., Pfeiffer, E. A., Steele, B., & Labok, J. (1976). *Medical instrumentation for health care*. Englewood Cliffs, NJ: Prentice-Hall.
Darrow, C. W. (1943). Physiological and clinical tests of autonomic function and autonomic balance. *Physiological Review, 23*, 1-36.
Darwin, C. (1872). *Expression of the emotions in man and animals*. London: Murray.
Davis, C. M., Brickett, P., Stern, R. M., & Kimball, W. H. (1978). Tension in the two frontales: Electrode placement and artifact in the recording of forehead EMG. *Psychophysiology, 15*, 591-593.
Davis, R. C. (1957). Response patterns. *Transactions of the New York Academy of Science, 19*, 731-739.
Donchin, E., Kutas, M., & McCarthy, G. (1977). Electrocortical indices of hemispheric utilization. In S. Harhad, R. W. Doty, L. Goldstein, J. Jaynes, & G. Krauthamer (Eds.), *Lateralization in the nervous system*. New York: Academic Press.
Duffy, E. (1957). The psychological significance of the concept of "arousal" or "activation." *Psychological Review, 64*, 265-275.
Duffy, E. (1962). *Activation and behavior*. New York: Wiley.
Edelberg, R. (1972). Electrical activity of the skin. In N. S. Greenfield & R. A. Sternbach (Eds.), *Handbook of psychophysiology*. New York: Holt, Rinehart & Winston.

Ehrlichman, H., & Weinberger, A. (1978). Lateral eye movements and hemispheric asymmetry: A critical view. *Psychological Bulletin, 85,* 1080-1101.

Elul, M. R. (1972). The genesis of the EEG. *International Review of Neurobiology, 15,* 227-272.

Eppinger, H., & Hess, L. (1915). *Vegatonia, mental and nervous disease* (monograph No. 20). New York: Nervous and Mental Disease Publishing (translated from the 1910 German original).

Epstein, S. (1973). Expectancy and magnitude of reaction to a noxious UCS. *Psychophysiology, 10,* 100-107.

Fox, C. A., & Fox, B. (1969). Blood pressure and respiratory patterns during human coitus. *Journal of Reproductional Fertility, 19,* 405-415.

Gale, A., Kingsley, E., Brookes, S., & Smith, D. (1978). Cortical arousal and social intimacy in the human female under different conditions of eye contact. *Behavioural Processes, 3,* 271-275.

Gale, A., Spratt, G., Chapman, A. J., & Smallbone, A. (1975). EGG correlates of eye contact and interpersonal distance. *Biological Psychology, 3,* 237-245.

Geddes, L. A. (1972). *Electrodes and the measurement of bioelectric events.* New York: Wiley-Interscience.

Gellhorn, E., Cortell, L., & Feldman, J. (1941). The effect of emotion, sham rage, and hypothalamic stimulation on the vago-insulin system. *American Journal of Physiology, 133,* 532-541.

Graham, F. K. (1978a). Normality of distributions and homogeneity of variance of heart rate and heart period samples. *Psychophysiology, 15,* 487-491.

Graham, F. K. (1978b). Constraints on measuring heart rate and period sequentially through real and cardiac time. *Psychophysiology, 15,* 492-495.

Graham, F. K. (1973). Habituation and distribution of responses innervated by the autonomic nervous system. In H. V. S. Peeke & M. J. Herz (Eds.), *Habituation: Vol. 1, Behavioral studies.* New York: Academic Press.

Hess, E. H. (1975). *The tell-tale eye.* New York: Van Nostrand Reinhold.

Jacobson, E. (1938). *Progressive relaxation.* Chicago: University of Chicago Press.

James, W. (1884). What is emotion? *Mind, 9,* 188-204.

Janisse, M. P. (1977). *Pupillometry.* Washington, DC: Hemisphere Publishing.

Jung, C. G. (1907). On psychophysical relations of the associative experiment. *Journal of Abnormal Psychology, 7,* 247-255.

Kaplan, H. B., & Bloom, S. W. (1960). The use of sociological and social-psychological concepts in physiological research: A review of selected experimental studies. *Journal of Nervous and Mental Disorders, 131,* 128-134.

Khachaturian, Z. S., Kerr, J., Kruger, R., & Schachter, J. (1972). A methodological note: Comparison between period and rate data in studies of cardiac function. *Psychophysiology, 9,* 539-545.

Lacey, J. I. (1956). The evaluation of autonomic responses: Towards a general solution. *Annals of the New York Academy of Science, 67,* 123-163.

Lacey, J. I. (1959). Psychophysiological approaches to the evaluation of psychotherapeutic process and outcome. In E. A. Rubenstein and M. B. Parloff (Eds.), *Research in psychotherapy* (Vol. 1). Washington D.C.: American Psychological Association.

Lacey, J. I. (1967). Somatic response patterning and stress: Some revisions of activation theory. In M. H. Appley & R. Trumbull (Eds.), *Psychological stress.* New York: Appleton-Century-Crofts.

Lacey, J. I., & Lacey, B. C. (1958). Verification and extension of the principle of autonomic response-stereotypy. *American Journal of Psychology, 71,* 50-73.

Leiderman, P. H., & Shapiro, D. (Eds.). (1964). *Psychobiological approaches to social behavior.* Stanford, CA: Stanford University Press.

Leventhal, H. (1980). Toward a comprehensive theory of emotion. In L. Berkowitz (Ed.), *Advances in experimental social psychology.* New York: Academic Press.

Lindsley, D. B. (1951). Emotion. In S. S. Stevens (Ed.), *Handbook of experimental psychology.* New York: Wiley.

Lippold, O. C. J. (1952). The relations between integrated action potentials in a human muscle and its isometric tension. *Journal of Physiology, 117,* 492-499.

Lykken, D. T. (1959). Properties of electrodes used in electrodermal measurement. *Journal of Comparative and Physiological Psychology, 52,* 629-634.

Lynn, R. (1966). *Attention, arousal and the orientation reaction.* Oxford: Pergamon Press.

Malmo, R. B. (1959). Activation: A neurophysiological dimension. *Psychological Review, 66,* 367-386.

Malmo, R. B., & Shagass, C. (1949). Physiological study of symptom neurosis in psychiatric patients under stress. *Psychosomatic Medicine, 11,* 25-29.

Maslach, C. (1979a). Negative emotional biasing of unexplained arousal. *Journal of Personality and Social Psychology, 37,* 953-969.

Maslach, C. (1979b). Emotional consequences of arousal without reason. In C. E. Izard (Ed.), *Emotions in personality and psychopathology.* New York: Plenum.

Martin, I., & Venables, P. H. (Eds.). (1980). *Techniques in psychophysiology.* New York: Wiley.

Mittelmann, B., & Wolff, H. G. (1939). Affective states and skin temperature: Experimental study of subjects with "cold hands" and Raynaud's syndrome. *Psychosomatic Medicine, 1,* 271-292.

Oster, P. J., & Stern, J. A. (1980). Measurement of eye movement. In I. Martin & P. H. Venables (Eds.), *Techniques in psychophysiology.* New York: Wiley.

Pavlov, I. P. (1927). *Conditional reflexes: An investigation of the physiological activity of the cerebral cortex.* London: Oxford University Press.

Piliavin, J. A., Dovidio, J. F., Gaertner, S. L., & Clark, R. D. (1981). *Emergency intervention.* New York: Academic Press.

Ray, W. J., Raczynski, J. M., Rogers, T., & Kimball, W. H. (1979). *Evaluation of clinical biofeedback.* New York: Plenum.

Riddle, E. M. (1925). Aggressive behavior in a small social group. *Archives of Psychology,* No. 78.

Rubin, Z. (1973). *Liking and loving: An invitation to social psychology.* New York: Holt, Rinehart & Winston.

Schachter, S., & Singer, J. E. (1962). Cognitive, social and physiological determinants of emotional state. *Psychological Review, 69,* 379-399.

Schachter, S., & Singer, J. E. (1979). Comment on Maslach and Marshall-Zimbardo experiments. *Journal of Personality and Social Psychology, 37,* 989-995.

Schwartz, G. E., & Shapiro, D. (1973). Social psychophysiology. In W. F. Prokasy & D. C. Raskin (Eds.), *Electrodermal activity in psychological research.* New York: Academic Press.

Shapiro, A. H. (1975). Behavior of kibbutz and urban children receiving an injection. *Psychophysiology, 12,* 79-82.

Shapiro, D., & Crider, A. (1969). Psychophysiological approaches in social psychology. In G. Lindzey & E. Aronson (Eds.), *Handbook of social psychology* (Vol. 3). Reading, MA: Addison-Wesley.

Shapiro, D., & Schwartz, G. E. (1970). Psychophysiological contributions to social psychology. *Annual Review of Psychology, 21,* 87-112.

Shotland, R. L., & Stebbins, C. (1980). Bystander response to rape: Can a victim attract help? *Journal of Applied Social Psychology, 10,* 510-527.

Sokolov, E. N. (1965). The orienting reflex, its structure and mechanisms. In L. G. Veronin, A. N. Leontrev, A. R. Luria, E. N. Sokolov, and O. S. Vinogradova (Eds.), *Orienting reflex and exploratory behaviour.* Washington, DC: American Institute of Biological Sciences.

Stern, R. M., & Anschel, C. (1968). Deep inspirations as stimuli for responses for the autonomic nervous system. *Psychophysiology, 5,* 132-141.

Stern, R. M., Botto, R. W., & Herrick, C. D. (1972). Behavioral and physiological effects of false heart-rate feedback: A replication and extension. *Psychophysiology, 9,* 21-29.

Stern, R. M., & Lewis, N. L. (1968). Ability of actors to control their GSRs and express emotions. *Psychophysiology, 4,* 294-299.

Stern, R. M., Ray, W. J., & Davis, C. M. (1980). *Psychophysiological recording*. New York: Oxford University Press.

Tryon, W. W. (1975). Pupillometry: A survey of sources of variation. *Psychophysiology, 12,* 90-93.

Tursky, B. (1974). The indirect recording of human blood pressure. In P. Obrist, A. H. Black, J. Brener, & L. DiCara (Eds.), *Cardiovascular psychophysiology*. Chicago: Aldine.

Valins, S. (1966). Cognitive effects of false heart-rate feedback. *Journal of Personality and Social Psychology, 4,* 400-408.

Venables, P. H., & Christie, M. J. (1973). Mechanisms, instrumentation, recording techniques and quantification of responses. In W. F. Prokasy & D. C. Raskin (Eds.), *Electrodermal activity in psychological research*. New York: Academic Press.

Waid, W. M., & Orne, M. T. (1981). Cognitive, social and personality processes in the physiological detection of deception. In L. Berkowitz (Ed.), *Advances in experimental social psychology* (Vol. 14). New York: Academic Press.

Wenger, M. A. (1972). Autonomic balance. In N. S. Greenfield & R. A. Sternbach (Eds.), *Handbook of psychophysiology*. New York: Holt, Rinehart & Winston.

Wilder, J. (1967). *Stimulus and response: The law of initial value*. Bristol, England: Wright.

Yerkes, R. M., & Dodson, J. D. (1980). The relation of strength of stimulus to rapidity of habit-formation. *Journal of Comparative Neurological Psychology, 18,* 459-482.

Chapter 3
An Evolutionary Perspective on Human Social Behavior

Arne Öhman and Ulf Dimberg

Like so many of the individuals whose behavior it purports to explain, psychology has an ambivalent, if not neurotic, relationship to its parents. This is particularly true for its most legitimate mother discipline, biology, where the ambivalence can take advantage of a tendency toward a split personality in the discipline itself. Just at about the time Wilhelm Wundt set the stage for psychology by marrying philosophy and physiology, the seed to the split was planted in Charles Darwin's theory of the evolution of species.

Physiology is very much in line with traditional natural science. Its ideal is to analyze entities in terms of their parts. Isolating the parts relies on anatomy, and the specification of mechanisms relies on biochemistry. A primary aim is to establish general laws. Thus, physiology adheres to reductive explanations in terms of physical systems disclosed through experimental analysis on isolated subsystems. Good examples of the fruitfulness of this approach are easily found, for example, in our knowledge of the cardiovascular system (e.g., Rushmer, 1976).

Evolutionary biology, on the other hand, is of a different kind. It deals with undivided, complete organisms in dynamic interaction with specific environments. It feeds on diversity and individual differences in seeking to understand the unique fit between the individual organisms building up a species and their ecological niche. Thus, it shows little concern with reductive explanations and even with general physical laws. Although "the processes of organic evolution are consistent with the laws of the physical sciences, . . . , it makes no sense to say that biological evolution has been 'reduced' to physical laws." Its explanation "is meaningful only at the level of complexity of" the involved processes and systems themselves (Mayr, 1978, p. 45). Indeed, some biologists even conclude that organic evolution is not a deterministic process at all because of the chance factors taking part in genetic mutations and recombinations, on the one hand, and the enormous complexities of the interactions between a great number of ecological factors in natural selection, on the other (Plotkin & Odling-Smee, 1981a). This built-in indeterminacy of the evolutionary process, then, makes predictions about future evolutionary events virtually impossible, which sharply sets biology apart from physics where prediction is one of the hallmarks.

Physiology had the edge during the first decades of psychology's independent development and so could profit from early affective bonding. Thus, few psychologists have really questioned the legitimacy of physiological mechanisms for their science. Of course, the attitude may differ depending upon whether one is interested in, say, sensory processes or social psychology, but as the title of this book implies, there is an audience broad enough to be captured by the juxtaposition of social psychology and psychophysiology for a publisher to bet on it. The most influential systems in psychology (e.g., Hull, 1943) were explicitly modeled on physical science, and so had a natural place for physiology, which adhered to the same scientific ideals. It is not surprising, therefore, that "physiological psychology" is an acknowledged subdiscipline of our field and a celebrated one at that.

For the other aspect of the split image biology offers behavioral sciences, evolutionary biology, the story is quite different. Although some influential psychologists have operated with causal mechanisms similar to those of the evolution (e.g., Skinner, 1969), biological ideas have failed to make a strong impact on psychology. Rather than having given rise to subdisciplines within psychology, they have, without much concern, been given away to other sciences, such as ethology. In fact, it has been argued that some profound implications for psychology of Darwin's work still, after more than 100 years, have not even started to permeate our science (Ghiselin, 1973).

While few psychologists would be willing to seriously challenge the assertion that the *ultimate* causes of human behavior must be sought in the evolution of our species, most would be very uncomfortable to admit that the evolution has useful specific insights to offer the understanding of *proximal* behavioral causes. The greatest feat of the evolution, it is held, is that it has freed humans from immediate biological determinism (usually understood as "instinctual") in favor of individual adaptations developed through learning. In this way, a basis has been provided for psychology to start fresh and to concentrate on environmental and experiential rather than on biological factors as determinants of behavior.

We think that the pivotal concept for psychology's ambivalence to biology is "genetics." The theory of evolution is predicated on heritability of the evolving traits. That is to say, their variability must, at least partially, be under genetic control. Without a systematic correlation between the overt phenotype and an underlying genotype, natural selection could operate but would not result in evolution (e.g., Barash, 1977). During this century, psychology has been dominated by Americans, and American psychology, "no matter what it tries, . . . will always be behaviorist at heart" (Wispé & Thompson, 1976, p. 346). Although it could be argued that behaviorism's legacy eventually may be eroding, the erosion process appears not to have touched one of its central tenets, environmentalism, most clearly spelled out in a famous quote from Watson (1930, p. 104). This tenet has been backed by deeply felt convictions in American ideology, without which the idealism attached to "a whole host of American folk heroes—Lincoln in politics, Edison and Ford in industry, Thorpe in sports'—would not exist (Wispé & Thompson, 1976, p. 346). To question environmentalism, in some respects, is to question the American Dream. Since an evolutionary perspective by necessity involves endorsement of genetic determinism, it implies a challenge to environmentalism. No wonder, therefore, that few

Americans have tried such a perspective, and that those who have dared to try typically have had a limited impact. Thus, the relevance of biological ideas for behavior was left to European ethnologists to explore (e.g., Eibl-Eibesfeldt, 1975), particularly during the period when behaviorism was at its peak influence.

More recently, a serious new biologically inspired assault has been framed towards the behavioral terrain under the banner of sociobiology (e.g., Barash, 1977; Wilson, 1975; 1978). Parallel to that, biological ideas have eventually begun to find their way into the traditional heartlands of psychology (e.g., see Seligman & Hager, 1972; Johnston, 1981). Time may be ripe, therefore, for psychology to begin a therapeutic process aimed at resolving its neurotic relationship to biology. "Sociophysiology" in our view, therefore, should not limit itself, like psychophysiology often does, to the elucidation of physiological correlates of behavioral processes. Rather we think it is important to keep in mind that the "physiology" occurs inside a social being which has been shaped into an integrated whole by evolution. The extent to which measuring physiological correlates turns out rewarding for the psychologist is because evolution has provided the necessary physiological and metabolic foundation for whatever behavior tendencies it has selected. Thus, the physiological responses measured by psychophysiologists are parts and parcels of the organism's integrated reaction, as shaped by evolution to meet environmental demands. It is a basic tenet of this chapter that the odds of eliciting such integrated reactions are better if investigators attend to evolutionary considerations in their choice of stimulus situations. By doing this, we argue, not only would we elicit more meaningful responses, but the likelihood for the social psychologist to find empirical relationships that transcend the limitations of the laboratory would also be vastly improved.

The first part of this chapter contains a discussion of some themes from evolutionary biology which we feel are of central interest to psychologists. More specifically, we shall first discuss an issue briefly touched on above, namely, the role of genetic diversity in evolution with special attention to its implication for psychology. Second, we shall develop a conceptual framework which provides an evolutionary perspective on psychology, with special emphasis on the interrelationship between genetics, learning, and culture in the shaping of behavior, and particularly human social behavior. Third, some of the implications of this perspective will be illustrated by a brief description of research on emotional responding to human facial expression, which we have been engaged in for the last few years. Finally, in the concluding section of the chapter, the implications of our evolutionary framework for sociophysiology will be discussed and critically evaluated.

Some Basic Evolutionary Biology

Human Evolution and Genetic Diversity

If we date the birth of our species from the moment in time some five million years ago when our hominoid ancestors lifted their knuckles from Africa's savannahs to become the biped *Australopithecus*, modern man, or *Homo sapiens* as we know him, has been around for only about 1 percent of the total time of our evolution (e.g.,

Dobzhansky, Ayala, Stebbins, & Valentine, 1977; Washburn, 1978b; Wilson, 1978). Moreover, only for a quarter of that time period, or 10,000 years, has man defected from the hunter-gatherer life of his predecessors to develop agriculture and urban civilizations. And it is only during the last tenth of this last period that we have created a technology which essentially changes the conditions for all life on our planet. This enormous acceleration in the pace of our evolution is the paradoxical results of a brain which, as pointed out by Washburn (1978b), was "developed under conditions that have long ceased to exist" (p. 146). At least quantitatively, the human brain has not changed appreciably during the last 200,000 years, in spite of the enormous change in our living conditions during this period (Dobzhansky et al., 1977). Perhaps it is no wonder, then, that contemporary students of our species feel that its evolutionary history is only of passing interest to their topic, particularly if they are interested in behavior.

This recent spurt in our evolution can be almost completely attributed to the brain's capacity to generate and control behavior. It is through behavior we interact with our environment to produce changes that create new conditions for our development. However, the key role for behavior in evolution need not be restricted to our species. In the words of a famous biologist,

> behavior often—perhaps invariably—serves as a pacemaker in evolution. A change in behavior, such as the selection of a new habitat or food source, sets up new selective pressures and may lead to important adaptive shifts. There is little doubt that some of the most important events in the history of life, such as the conquest of land or of the air, were initiated by shifts in behavior. (Mayr, 1978, p. 47)

A similar idea has been voiced by an influential psychologist: "Behavior arising from ontogenic contingencies may make phylogenic contingencies more or less effective. Ontogenic behavior may permit a species to maintain itself in a given environment for a long time and thus make it possible for phylogenic contingencies to operate" (Skinner, 1969, p. 203). Note, however, that whereas Mayr talks about behavior in general, ontogenetic behavior for Skinner refers to behavior *learned* under ontogenetic reinforcement contingencies. What he suggests, then, is that learning through behavior can act back on the biological evolution to influence the course it takes.

If behavior is a pacemaker for evolution, and more so for our own than for other species, and if our behavior is controlled by a brain developed under circumstances very different from those prevalent today, a reasonable conclusion would be that evolutionary considerations are of little consequence for the understanding of present-day man. What matters for this task is to understand behavior, and behavior is mediated by a brain which essentially has freed itself from the conditions of its creation. Moreover, this brain generates learned behavior which can act back on the biological evolution itself. Therefore, the latter process is not necessarily primary to the first.

To bolster the assertion that evolutionary biology is of little concern for the understanding of modern man, one could invoke arguments from that discipline itself. Biological evolution feeds on diversity. As natural selection picks out the adaptive traits, genetic variability is lost, and more so the more important and adaptive the particular trait is (e.g., Dobzhansky, 1972). As bipedal gait is a hallmark in human evolution (Washburn, 1978b), it is shown by every human being developed under normal circumstances. Thus, it is highly *inherited*, yet its variability would show essentially zero *heritability* because differences between individuals (0, 1, or 2 legs) would be completely determined by environmental factors, in this case most likely accidents. According to this view, humans would be a product of evolution showing important inherited traits, such as bipedal walk, extreme manual skills, and capacities for language and culture. However, virtually all differences between individuals would be attributable not to heritability, that is, genetic differences, but to environmental effects and cumulated experience. The only present and recent evolution of interest, according to this view, would be the one taking place at the level of culture, and as revealed by the work of anthropologists and historians. In sum, human psychology would best be understood in terms of basic capacities shared by all members of the species, and the interaction between these capacities and social and cultural factors. We surmise that this is the perspective taken by most contemporary psychologists, and by some biologists as well (e.g., Washburn, 1978a). As summarized by a celebrated member of the latter group, Dobzhansky says, "In a sense, human genes have surrendered their primacy in human evolution to an entirely new, nonbiological or superorganic agent, culture. However, it should not be forgotten that this agent is entirely dependent on the human genotype" (Wilson, 1978, p. 22).

The reservation voiced in the last sentence of this quote is an important one, however. Even if heritability could be of negligible importance for the understanding of human behavior, the fact that many important capacities are inherited could imply a role for evolutionary biology in psychology. It would suggest that humans are not blank slates for experience to write on, but that constraints operate to shape behavior into predetermined directions. Language is a case in point because for this, the perhaps most human of all capacities, it is quite clear that biological factors are of central importance (e.g., Lenneberg, 1967). Another possibility is to argue that humans are *generalists*, who have been selected for general educability, and which have thus, once and for all, transcended the boundaries of biology.

These views both essentially entail that the biological evolution of humans has been brought to a stop, and that evolution continues entirely at the cultural level. However, just as it would be foolish to disregard the role of culture for human behavior, it may not be justified to completely deny the possibility of a continuing biological evolution. To continue quoting Dobzhansky (1972):

> Cultural evolution is superimposed on the biological . . . . Culture did not suddenly fall from heavens, complete and unalterable. Its genetic basis was compounded gradually by natural selection from genetic building blocks that existed in man's precultural ancestors. The formation of this genetic basis was due to positive feedback between biological and cultural evolutions. Neither culture nor its genetic basis is now fixed and stationary. For good as for ill, they continue evolving. (Dobzhansky, 1972, p. 528; see also Dobzhansky et al., 1977, pp. 457-459)

As pointed out in the introduction to this chapter, for biological evolution to continue, the variance of the involved traits must have at least partly a genetic basis. In other words, not only must humans have inherited capacities to behave, but behavior differences must also be heritable. Indeed, from a biological perspective anything else would be quite alarming. The genetic diversity of a species is too precious a biological capital for lighthearted expenditure. Even though central functions must be genetically and physiologically buffered to guarantee a nonvariable outcome (Dobzhansky, 1972), mechanisms have also evolved to maintain diversity in the gene pool of a species (e.g., Ayala, 1978; Dobzhansky et al., 1977). Lacking such genetic diversity, a species would have rid itself of one of its most important resources to meet new environmental challenges. This basic theoretical argument can be supplemented by empirical ones.

By help of techniques from modern molecular biology, it has been established that the genetic diversity in populations are much larger than was formerly thought (e.g., Ayala, 1978; Plomin, DeFries, & McClearn, 1980). This diversity provides the basis for the success typically achieved in breeding attempts through artificial selection (e.g., see Barash, 1977). As we all know, such attempts have been spectacularly successful with various domestic animals, both at the morphological and behavioral level. As mammals, such animals have a genetic diversity (measured as heterozygosity) similar to that of man (Ayala, 1978). By implication, then, if such animals are sufficiently diverse in their genetic makeup to be susceptible to biological evolution, humans must also be. There is also direct evidence available, where behavior geneticists, by help of twin and adoption studies, have generated data indicating a genetic component in the variance of many human behavioral traits, such as, intelligence or some types of psychopathology (e.g., see Plomin et al., 1980).

In conclusion, then, compelling arguments can be advanced for the theses that both inheritance and heritability have roles to play in the analysis of human behavior. However, the specific nature of these roles remains, in most instances, completely obscure. To be able to discuss in a more articulate manner the ways biology takes part in the shaping of behavior, we devote the next section to an outline of some basic concepts of evolutionary biology and of their interaction in the determination of behavior.

A Framework from Evolutionary Biology

The outline given here draws heavily on the distinction between closed and open genetic programs proposed by Mayr (1974) and on the multiple-level model of evolution of Plotkin and Odling-Smee (1981a). The outline is schematically illustrated in Figure 3-1.

Information referents. Adaptation is a central, albeit often problematic (Lewontin, 1978), concept in evolution, which we shall return to. Suffice it to say here that the fit between organism and environment which we call adaptation together with individual diversity provides the starting point for evolutionary theory. Because an effective adaptation requires a congruence between itself and some feature in the environment, one could argue that it requires knowledge, or the storing of information, about the environment (Plotkin & Odling-Smee, 1981a). A pivotal problem for evolutionary biology then becomes to what extent the postulation of only one information storage device, e.g., in the gene pool, would be sufficient to account for the evolution. Plotkin and Odling-Smee (1981a) answer this question in the negative,

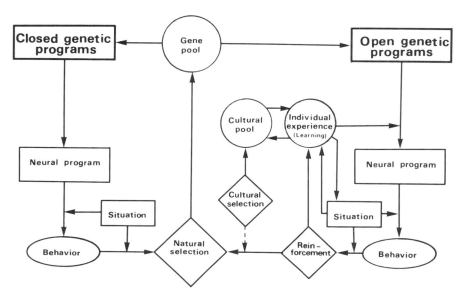

Figure 3-1. A multiple-level evolutionary perspective on the control of behavior. Two basic loops are involved, one with closed and the other with open genetic programs. Nested within the latter are loops for learning and for culture. Circles denote information referents, and diamonds denote evaluative processes. The gene pools contain closed genetic programs, which can be transformed to neural programs without additional specific input. Given an appropriate stimulus situation, the neural program generates behavior, which is directly evaluated by natural selection. The outcome of this selection process is fed back as changes in the relative frequencies of alleles in the gene pool. Open genetic programs also reside in the gene pool. Their transformation to neural programs requires input from the individual experience of the organism, i.e., they are modified by learning. Learning occurs about and within a stimulus situation, and results in the generation of learned behavior which is evaluated by reinforcement processes, so that successful behavior is retained. The reinforcement process is calibrated by natural selection. Groups of animals that are able to learn by observing each other or through communication can develop a transindividual cultural pool. This pool is the result of learning, and it helps to structure the learning experiences of the individual taking part in the culture. The content of the cultural pool is determined by a process of cultural selection, which, as indicated by the dashed line, is imperfectly controlled by natural selection.

and claim that several storage devices or evolutionary levels are necessary. Because of the central role they give to information for adaptation, they suggest that evolutionary levels are best defined in terms of sites of information storage. Disregarding one of their levels (cf. Campbell, 1981), we can operate with three levels, the gene pool, individual experiences or learned "engrams" stored in the central nervous systems of individuals, and a cultural pool of information built up by the totality of shared experience in a group of individuals. These three information sites or *referents* are illustrated as circles in Figure 3-1.

The gene pool. The gene pool is basic to evolution. It represents all the possible genes, or gene variants, alleles, that reside in the complete population building up a species. An individual has a sample from this gene pool in his genotype, a subset of which is expressed in his phenotype. Thus, much genetic variance remains hidden in the gene pool in each generation and can only be revealed by special techniques such as, e.g., inbreeding.

Genetic and neural programs. The genotype of an individual can be described as a set of genetic programs. The DNA segment constituting a gene does not intervene directly to control behavior. It works through manufacturing proteins that may function as enzymes, structural components, or in other biological roles. These proteins, then, work through many intermediaries of different kinds to ultimately result in manifest morphological structures or behavior. Genes can be understood in informational terms as sets of instructions for the elaboration of biological entities. According to Mayr (1974), we can distinguish between *closed* and *open* genetic programs. A genetic program does not control behavior directly. First it has to be translated into a neural program (Figure 3-1). If this translation occurs without additional specific input to that from the genetic program, we are dealing with a closed program. For such programs, then, there is no specific role presupposed for the environment. For open genetic programs, on the other hand, specific environmental input is necessary in the translation process resulting in the neural program (Figure 3-1).

Note that the neural program gives rise to behavior only given an "appropriate" situation (see Figure 3-1). In fact, one could say that it is the nature of this situation, which, in an evolutionary sense, determines whether an open program is necessary. If the situation is highly stable over generations, then a closed program is appropriate. However, if the situation varies, particularly within a generation, then an open program has the adaptive edge because it allows the individual to tailor his behavior after his particular environment.

From this perspective, then, behavior is always jointly determined by a neural program and a particular stimulus situation (which includes events occurring both outside and inside the organism). Depending on the nature of the situation and the evolutionary history of the species, the neural programs may be more or less completely determined by the genetic program alone. In other words, the two types of genetic programs are located on a continuum. Thus, one can reasonably talk about relatively closed or relatively open programs. For example, it is clear that environmental effects are discernible even in behaviors often presumed to be controlled by tightly closed programs (e.g., Hailman, 1969), and environmental effects may occur prenatally (Gottlieb, 1976). Completely closed programs may be rare when the topic concerns mammalian behavior. Nevertheless, it is important to realize that even cases of very modifiable behaviors are predicated on genetic programs, which have been actively shaped by evolution. Thus, even the most flexible behaviors owe their versatility to an evolutionary history distilled in genes. It is not appropriate, then, to think about some rigid and primitive behaviors as controlled by genes and other more advanced and complex behaviors as controlled by experience. All behaviors depend on genetic programs, and that environment has a role to play and the extent of this role is to the credit of these programs.

However, at the present state of knowledge, it must be frankly admitted that this statement is an *in principle* one. It does not imply that the route from behavior over neural to genetic programs is an easy one to travel. In fact, it is a major weakness with most applications of evolutionary constructs in psychology that the relationship between the genetic program and behavior most often proves elusive. This relationship is probed from "the ultimate end" by evolutionary biologists and ethologists and from "the proximate end" by psychologists, with neuroscientists trying to map the middle ground. Most likely, there is still a long time before these forces can be joined and the road open for leisurely travel. In our view, however, the likelihood of the forces to find each other would be much improved by the emergence of a unifying framework encompassing the disparate aspects of the task. It is our contention that the starting point for such a framework is best sought in evolutionary biology because the theory of evolution serves well as a unifying framework for biology in general, and in some important respects psychology is a biological discipline.

Natural selection. The behaviors controlled by closed genetic programs are directly evaluated by natural selection, and the result is preserved as changes in the relative frequency of alleles in the gene pool (Figure 3-1). The currency for this evaluation is *inclusive fitness* (e.g., Barash, 1977), that is, the relative representation of the individual's genes in the gene pool of the next generation. Thus, it includes both the traditional Darwinian fitness defined in relative numbers of surviving offspring, and the relative number of kins' offspring, which share genes with the individual. Inclusive fitness can be gained, then, through one's own, or through the promotion of kins', breeding success. This extension of the fitness concept can be used to address an otherwise intractable problem for evolutionary theory. By engaging in altruistic acts, many animals appear to defy the necessarily selfish Darwinian credo. For example, alarm calls when a predator is discovered are ubiquious among social animals. Yet the promotion of escape for companions occurs at the potential risk of bringing the caller to the immediate attention of the predator. However, by taking inclusive fitness into account, it can be shown that the probability of the altruistic act should vary with genetic overlap between the giver and receiver on the one hand, and the mutual cost-benefit ratios on the other (Hamilton, 1964; see also Alexander, 1975; Barash, 1977; Hoffman, 1981; and Maynard Smith, 1978).

Ordinarily, when we talk about natural selection, we think in terms of "survival of the fittest," that is, *directional selection* (e.g., Barash, 1977; Dobzhansky et al., 1977). By picking out individuals adaptively deviating from the norm, directional selection permits a population to adjust its gene pool according to slow changes in the ecology, or to take advantage of favorable mutant genes entering the pool. To remove deleterious mutations and to homogenize the gene pool, extremes in either direction can be removed by *stabilizing (or normalizing) selection. Disruptive (or diversifying) selection*, finally, occurs when either extreme in a distribution is suited to exploit different subhabitats, with the intermediate cases less suited for either (e.g., see Dobzhansky et al., 1977).

It is important to realize that natural selection operates on individuals, which implies compromises between many adaptive features. "Because an organism is a bundle of selective compromises, no single one of its attributes is likely to be maximized or optimized" (Alexander, 1975, p. 83). Thus, the unit of selection is never a piece of behavior, but the individual to whose fitness it contributes. This limitation in the action of natural selection prompted Plotkin and Odling-Smee (1981a) to postuate new levels of selection, where selection could operate within an individual. In considering these possibilities, we move from the closed to the open programs.

Learning. The great adaptive advantage with open genetic programs is that they leave spaces to be filled in by individual experience. In this way, they allow the individual organism to adjust its behavior according to the specific subarea of the ecological niche he occupies. Whereas closed genetic programs presuppose a common environment for the species which changes only very slowly over generations, the learning entailed in open programs can accommodate a much more variable and more rapidly changing environment. Thus, through learning, organisms can cope with environmental changes occurring within the time span of a generation, and they can exploit a much broader habitat by adjusting their behaviors to a greater range of environments than would be possible on the basis of information stored only in the gene pool.

Information about the environment acquired through learning resides in the central nervous system of the individual organism as changes in the neural program. Thus, it is tied to a concrete individual to benefit his behavior, with no necessary effects on others. This sets this information referent apart from the gene pool (see Plotkin & Odling-Smee, 1981a), which does not reside in individuals but in breeding populations. Genetic information, then, differs from learned in that it is automatically shared among many individuals. Another important difference between these two information referents concerns the unit of selection. For the gene pool, this unit is, as we have seen, the individual. For learning, however, selection affects individual behaviors. In short, in the former case selection occurs *between* individuals and in the latter it occurs *within* individuals. This is the basic reason for the detailed individual fit between an organism's behavior and the environment which can be achieved through learning. However, such a fit must conform to the requirements of natural selection. As shown in Figure 3-1, the within-organism selection which results in learning is evaluated by natural selection between organisms, so that only genes that prepare for biologically advantageous learning are retained in the gene pool.

Many authors have commented on the similarities between the mechanism of natural selection and learning through trial-and-error, reinforcement, or operant conditioning (e.g., Campbell, 1975; Plotkin & Odling-Smee, 1981b; Skinner, 1969; 1971; Staddon, 1975). In both cases, we are dealing with a formula which can be described as variation-selection-retention (Campbell, 1975) or generate-test-regenerate (Plotkin & Odling-Smee, 1981b). That is to say, we start with the generation of a more or less "blind" variation among which successful units can be selected. This selection procedure is then retained as changes in the relative frequencies of the units of the original variation.

The basic difference between selection at the level of the gene pool and at the level of learned behaviors, however, is that effects of the former are transindividual in the sense that they are left in the gene pool for future generations, whereas the effects of the latter die with the brain of the individual. Selection of learned behaviors, therefore, cannot affect the biological evolution directly (see Figure 3-1). It can affect the gene pool only indirectly by contributing to the breeding success of the individual. And what may be transferred between generations in this way is not the learning itself, but a capacity for it. The selection level of learning, therefore, is subsidiary to, or nested under, the primary level of natural selection (Plotkin & Odling-Smee, 1981a).

The cultural pool. The most important limitation of the learning level is that it remains specific for the individual. Adaptations achieved at this level, then, cannot directly benefit other individuals whether they are genetically related or not. If learning would remain the most advanced selection level, it would imply that every individual had to go through the painstaking steps of interaction with his environment to acquire the necessary information. However, if two conditions are met, a new level, transcending the individual, can develop (Plotkin & Odling-Smee, 1981a). First, a group of individuals must exist. Second, these individuals must be capable of *communicating* with each other (through other channels than the genes). That is to say, the individuals must be able to adjust their behavior according to what they learn from other individuals, either through observation or through specialized communication systems. Given the validity of these two requirements, experience acquired by one individual can be transferred to other members of the group, thereby shortcutting the lengthy interaction between organism and environment which often is necessary for individual learning. In short, the stage has been set for *culture*. Basically, a *culture* is a set of shared experiences which are based on the spread of information within the group. Unlike individual, personal experience, cultural experience transcends the generations. The information building up a culture can be said to reside in a *cultural pool*. This word usage highlights some important similarities with the concept of a gene pool. Both concepts refer to totalities, the former to the total set of items available in the cultural pool, and the latter to the total set of genes carried by all living individuals in a population. Thus, both are abstractions in the sense that they reside in collections of individuals rather than in any single physical entity (Plotkin & Odling-Smee, 1981a).

However, like the results of learning, the information in the cultural pool must be represented in the individual brains of the group members, and like learning it must have access to their behavioral repertoires in order to operate on the environment. It is clear, therefore, that learning and culture represent two levels that are tightly interwoven, yet partly independent. In several respects, learning is primary to culture. First, information for the cultural pool is gained through learning both by the sender and the receiver. That is, both the origin and the spread of information rely on this mechanism. Second, the learning level can exist on its own without a cultural level, whereas the reverse is not possible. It is clear, then, that culture is nested under learning, which, as we have seen, is nested under the gene pool (see Figure 3-1) (Plotkin & Odling-Smee, 1981a).

A distinguishing feature of the cultural level is its dependence on communication between members of the group. The epitome of such a communication system, of course, is the human language. However, the system does not need to approach this level of complexity in order to form the basis for a culture. The critical requirement goes back to the fact that culture is nested under learning and implies that what is communicated is the result of learning. Thus, even quite complex communication signs that do not depend on learning, e.g., the quite elaborated courtship displays of many species, cannot provide the basis for culture. It is the communication system that provides the counterpart to genetic inheritance in the cultural pool because it provides the means for cultural items to propagate themselves and thus remain in the cultural pool. Because this method of propagation is independent of the generation lag, cultural evolution is vastly faster than the biological evolution (Dobzhansky et al., 1977). Thus, once a cultural evolution is under way, the odds are that the divergence between the biological and cultural evolution will accelerate over time, which may explain the recent enormous spurt in the evolution of our species briefly referred to earlier.

Cultural evolution occurs because cultural items or features, like genes, can be viewed as replicators with an ability to propagate themselves (Williams, 1981). This provides the basis for describing the cultural evolution in terms of the same variation-selection-retention formula as previously discussed for learning and natural selection (e.g., Campbell, 1975). However, several problems are more difficult to deal with at this level than at the other two. First, as pointed out by Williams (1981), "for a cultural feature to prevail, it is necessary and sufficient for it to be effective at replicating itself in the environment provided by society" (p. 257). Thus, it is not necessary that it directly affects the fitness of the individual. Yet, because culture is presumed to be nested under the gene pool (via learning), the capacity for culture must have evolved precisely because of its adaptive benefits to the individual. This implies that culture is built on a biological basis (e.g., Dobzhansky et al., 1977), but that the specific contents of cultural pools are not directly determined by fitness considerations. Of course, fitness requirements still provide limitations in determining biological boundaries which cultural evolution cannot cross without severe consequences for the populations involved, the predicament of our species in the age of nuclear armament being a case in point. But while extreme cases like this example can be dealt with, the problem of specifying even the *basis* for cultural selection in more ordinary cases remains quite bothersome. Not only is the basis for selection troublesome, but also the units for selection remain problematic. In some cases, cultural development most likely affects the individuals quite directly, such as with tool and weapon manufacture, but in other cases the selection must occur at the social system level (see Campbell, 1975, for a discussion of this problem). Such selection at the social system level implies "a selective retention of organizational principles and ideologies, independent of the fate of individuals, if these organizational forms and belief systems contributed to the social system functionality, as expressed in the conquest and conversion of other peoples" (Campbell, 1975, p. 1106). Campbell (1975) goes on to invoke independent but converging evolutions of "complex division-of-labor, urban, apartment house, stored-food" societies several times in ancient Mexico and Peru, China, and Europe as support for the thesis of cultural evolution through adaptive selection.

This short discussion should suffice to point out both the appeal and the risk with analogizing between biological and cultural evolution. Even if some of the similarities are striking, there are also important differences. First, in contrast to Darwinian biological evolution, the cultural evolution is Lamarckian in the sense that acquired characteristics can be transferred to new generations (e.g., Plotkin & Odling-Smee, 1981a; Wispé & Thompson, 1976). Second, as already alluded to, because of its Lamarckian character and because of the efficiency of language in transmission of information, cultural evolution can occur much faster than biological evolution (e.g., Dobzhansky et al., 1977; Wispé & Thompson, 1976). Third, "although neither biological nor social evolution is teleological, maybe social evolution is a little more so" (Wispé & Thompson, 1976, p. 342); that is to say, "the conscious planning and foresight that can guide cultural evolution into new channels has no counterpart in organic evolution" (Dobzhansky et al., 1977, p. 471). Finally, conspicuous as it may seem, particularly in our own species, cultural evolution is secondary to the biological in the sense that it cannot ultimately evade being evaluated by natural selection (Plotkin & Odling-Smee, 1981a). We can only hope that, for our own species, this evaluation shall not take place in the holocaust of a nuclear war.

Relationships Between Levels of Selection

In the previous sections, we have introduced three information referents upon which selection processes operate to generate adaptive behavior. The selection levels clearly interact with each other. Following Plotkin and Odling-Smee (1981a), we have argued that culture is nested under learning, and that learning is nested under the gene pool (see Figure 3-1). In some respects, this gives a primary or basic role to biological evolution because it affects the other levels in a "bottom-up" type of relationship. This relationship can be described in terms of *biological constraints* acting on learning (Hinde & Stevenson-Hinde, 1973; Seligman & Hager, 1972) and culture (e.g., Eibl-Eibesfeldt, 1979; Wilson, 1978). However, the opposite type of relationship between levels, that is, "top-down," is also possible and often involves claiming the *priority of culture* for human behavior. These two relationships will be discussed in this section, which will end with a discussion about the mutual dependence between the bottom-up and top-down relationships in the evolution of human behavior.

Biological constraints on learning. As indicated in Figure 3-1, learning results from the evaluation of behaviors in particular situations. Successful behaviors and confirmed expectancies about relationships in the environment are likely to be retained, whereas unsuccessful behaviors and disconfirmed expectancies are lost. As is obvious in the figure, however, this evaluation process must be calibrated by natural selection. This implies that the within-organism evaluation resulting in learning is, in turn, assessed by the between-organism evaluation of natural selection, and the result is fed back to the gene pool. Thus, individuals with a successful capacity for learning are likely to leave more offspring than individuals with less successful learning capacities. It is the capacity for learning, then, which becomes represented in the gene pool. The diversity and generality of this capacity is a basic and controversial issue in the psychology of learning.

Some of the founders of the scientific study of learning were interested not in learning per se, but in intelligence. Intelligence was thought to be manifested in learning ability. This ability was typically viewed as a unitary general capacity, understood as multiplexity in potential stimulus-response connections. Thus, this general process view of learning allowed the ordering of creatures from protozoas to hominoids on a divine ladder of nature, "the Scala Naturæ" (Hodos & Campbell, 1969). This conception provided a theoretical underpinning for the use of animals in learning experiments as a mere methodological convenience. In spite of the frequency of animal experiments among students of learning, then, the interest was primarily on human rather than on animal behavior (Schwartz, 1981). The insights the experiments offered could be generalized up and down the ladder of nature simply by assuming differences in the number of stimulus-response connections different species could learn. Biology could enter this scheme only through the primary reinforcers, that is, the stimuli the organisms needed to encounter in their environment in order to survive. Such reinforcers served to "stamp in" stimulus-response connections or to increase the probability for recurrence of the behavior sequence resulting in reinforcement. In other words, students of learning accepted only the minimum requirement implied in the relationship between reinforcement and natural selection in Figure 3-1, that organisms must know what is good for them.

Some of these basic assumptions (albeit not as crudely formulated as here) have permeated psychologists' attempts to understand learning, and it is only recently that they have come under fire within the field itself (e.g., Garcia, McGowan, & Green, 1972; Johnston, 1981; Lockhard, 1971; Seligman & Hager, 1972), and attempts have been made to articulate the role of biology in learning (e.g., Johnston & Turvey, 1980; Rozin & Kalat, 1971; Seligman, 1970).

From a biological perspective such as that implied in Figure 3-1, it could be argued that learning is best viewed as adaptive specializations (Rozin & Kalat, 1971) which have evolved to assist the individuals of a specific species to solve the typical problems that their ecology poses (Johnston, 1981; Johnston & Turvey, 1980). Knowledge about such processes, it is held, cannot be gained from observations on arbitrarily chosen species in artificial situations characterized by arbitrary contingencies between stimuli and responses (e.g., Seligman, 1970). Such a strategy would only pay off given the validity of the general process view, where it could be argued that the very arbitrariness of the observations would guarantee that the generality of the data would not be confounded by species-specific idiosyncrasies. However, from the other perspective, such situations would only generate arbitrary data, completely lacking relevance for the species studied in its natural ecology. Instead, the biological perspective argues that one has to start with intensive study of a specific species in its natural habitat to delineate *what* it is that it learns. Only after that stage is it possible to proceed to the laboratory to design ecologically relevant experiments that could find out *how* it learns (Johnston, 1981). To the extent that this view talks about generalized intelligence, it would argue that its evolution involves making adaptive specializations originating in specific situations accessible for use by other behavior systems in new situations (Rozin, 1976). In some respects, then, such a strategy is similar to cognitive subcomponent theories of human intelligence (e.g., Sternberg, 1980).

In the present terminology, biologically highly constrained learning would be controlled partly by relatively closed genetic programs, whereas the general-process type of learning would be exclusively controlled by quite open programs. This implied continuity between closed and open programs helps to point out the improductivity of arguing about *whether* learning is biologically constrained or not. Clearly, there are instances of quite constrained learning, such as imprinting (e.g., Hinde, 1974; Rajecki, 1973) or the acquisition of taste aversions (e.g., Garcia et al., 1972; Revusky, 1977; Rozin & Kalat, 1971), and clearly there are other types of learning, particularly in humans, where it is difficult to give a major role to biological constraints. A more sensible strategy would be to discuss whether it is possible to suggest types of behaviors or situations which tend to covary with the continuum between closed and open genetic programs.

Mayr (1974) suggested that one way of classifying behavior which would address this issue is in terms of the response it elicits from the environment. This implies that the classification primarily concerns what Skinner (1969) denotes operant behavior since it deals with behaviors that operate, or have effects, on the environment. When the behavior is directed to physical aspects of the environment, the environment is passive. This is what Mayr calls noncommunicative behavior. Behavior which prompts an active response, at least potentially, from its recipient, on the other hand, is broadly designated as communicative behavior. This category can, in turn, be subdivided according to whether the responding individual is a member of the same or a different species. In the former case, Mayr talks about intraspecific behavior, which then denotes all social behaviors, and in the latter case he talks about interspecific behavior, where the relationship between predator and prey is a case in point.

From the general principle that "selection should favor the evolution of a closed program when there is a reliable relationship between a stimulus and only one correct response" (Mayr, 1974, p. 657), Mayr goes on to argue that noncommunicative behavior should be much more dependent on open genetic programs than communicative behavior. "Noncommunicative behavior leading to an exploitation of natural resources should be flexible, permitting an opportunistic adjustment to rapid changes in the environment and also permitting an enlargement of the niche as well as a shift into a new niche" (Mayr, 1974, p. 657).

Noncommunicative behavior, then, concerns interaction between the organism and the physical environment. Use of the term "physical environment" to encompass the ecologies of all species highlights what these ecologies have in common, namely, adherence to the physical laws of nature. Thus, for example, all mobile species encounter events that are spatially and temporally structured, they find out that events have causes which tend to be temporally and spatially proximate to their effects, and they find out that their behavior affects their environment. These generalities are likely to prompt independent but convergent evolutions of psychological apparatuses which allows the analysis of the environment, including its causal structure. Knowledge of such structures, of course, would be highly conducive to survival for the individual. It would involve short-term adaptive mechanisms such as perception and action and very long-term mechanisms dealt with by biological evolution.

In between these extremes, however, there is a need for mechanisms extending over medium time ranges (Johnston & Turvey, 1980), which could take advantage of regularities in the environment to achieve behavior changes optimalizing the fit between the individual and his immediate surroundings. Such mechanisms would allow the organism to decide, on the basis of its individual experience, which events lead to what consequences, and which behaviors have what effects on the environment. To sort out these types of relationships, animals have evolved quite sophisticated associative apparatuses (e.g., Rescorla, 1972, 1980; Rescorla & Holland, 1982), which are useful in epistemic analyses of all aspects of the physical environment. According to Revusky (1977) this type of analysis explains why the acquisition of taste aversions, which has been taken as the prototype of biological constrained learning (e.g., Rozin & Kalat, 1971; Seligman, 1970), still shows the typical characteristics of Pavlovian conditioning in spite of its highly divergent parameter values (Logue, 1979). Because they have evolved to match higher order invariants in the physical characteristics of our planet, these types of mechanisms would be quite general across species, and they would not be seriously constrained by having evolved in particular environments. In other words, they provide a rationale for the general process view, but restrict it to a particular category of behavior, interacting with the physical surroundings. It is precisely in this respect that humans in practice have demonstrated their independence of particular ecologies in spreading their habitats all over the planet, and in transforming the environments profoundly to adapt it to their needs. Moving around in a crowded city indeed is different from foraging over pleistocene savannahs, yet the information that is a prerequisite for successful use of the genetic programs controlling such behaviors may be independent of these specific contexts. As pointed out by Schwartz (1974), it is precisely the evolutionary irrelevance of present-day man's ecology which allows insights about the processes controlling his behavior to be gained from experiments on arbitrary species in artificial situations. In other words, Schwartz (1974) claims that such experiments may be more helpful in teaching us something about humans, rather than about animals.

While biological constraints may be relatively unimportant for learned behaviors interacting with the physical environment, they may be much more important for communicative behavior, or for respondent rather than for operant behavior. Emotions provide an important instance of respondent behavior (Skinner, 1969). To take just one example, a quite compelling argument can be raised for the thesis that one class of intense aversive emotions, phobias, reflects biologically prepared learning (Seligman, 1971; see also Wilson, 1978). Phobias typically are seen to objects or situations providing some danger or threat to pretechnological man, such as snakes, heights, large open spaces, etc., rather than to objects providing a threat to modern man, such as hand weapons or broken electrical equipment. Furthermore, their ease of acquisition, extreme resistance to extinction, and refractoriness to rational arguments about the lack of real danger, set them apart from the normal learned fears studied in the laboratory (Seligman, 1971; Öhman, 1979).

These theoretical ideas have been corroborated empirically by Öhman and co-workers (Öhman, 1979; Öhman, Fredrikson, & Hugdahl, 1978). For example, autonomic responses conditioned to potentially phobic stimuli such as snakes and spiders are more persistent than similar responses conditioned to electrical outlets (Hugdahl & Kärker, 1981) or hand weapons (Öhman, 1979). In terms of Mayr's (1974) classificatory scheme, these phenomenon could be construed as belonging to interspecific behavior. Thus, at least for some phobias one could argue that they are remnants from a period when the early mammals were the preys of reptiles (cf. Sagan, 1977).

The third category proposed by Mayr (1974) is intraspecific behavior. Such behavior is directed towards members of the same species, and thus encompasses all social behavior. According to Mayr (1974), it is the category which is most influenced by closed genetic programs. However, because social behavior is the main target of this chapter, a detailed discussion of this topic has to await its own heading.

The priority of culture. As we have seen in the previous section, an active debate has been flourishing recently about the role of biological factors in learning. In comparison, little can be said about the role of biological constraints on culture. However, there is no lack of proposals: "far from being irrelevant to human behavior, biology is the matrix in which culture is embedded and which bounds it in extremely complex and flexible, but by no means trivial ways" (van der Berghe, 1978, p. 33). Thus, one could argue not only that humans have a biological propensity for culture, but also that the specific manifestations of culture are biologically constrained (e.g., Wilson, 1978). That is to say, only a finite set of cultural features are possible, and the boundaries of this set are determined by the gene pool. On the basis of cultural universals (e.g., Eibl-Eibesfeldt, 1979; Murdock, 1945), it could be claimed that just as linguistic universals are taken as indicating innate "deep structures" or a universal grammar (e.g., Chomsky, 1968), the cultural universals may reflect biologically given "cultural grammars" which constrain the surface expressions of culture. This analogy helps to point out that cultures in spite of their seemingly enormous heterogeneity at the observational level still at a deeper level could reflect a limited set of potentially identifiable rules of biological origin, in the same way as all languages, in spite of their diversity, reflect the constraints of a common universal grammar. However, this issue should not detract us from a more conspicuous one, that culture appears to take precedence over biological evolution so that in the case of modern man it allows direct manipulations even with the basic information packages of the gene pool.

Culture is one result of the preponderance of open genetic programs in the control of human behavior. According to our conceptual scheme (Figure 3-1), however, culture is dependent on learning. In a sense these higher levels which both are predicated on open programs can be thought of as evolving through needs arising from shortcomings of the lower levels (Plotkin & Odling-Smee, 1981b). For example, the crudeness of the between-organism selection affecting the gene pool is considerably refined by the within-organism selection of specific behaviors occasioned through learning; culture, in turn, alleviates the failure of learning to affect other individuals than the one in which it takes place. From this type of consideration, the step is not large to claim that the new levels, and particularly the cultural one, take precedence over lower levels (e.g., Lewontin, 1981; Plotkin & Odling-Smee, 1981b; Skinner, 1969). From biological considerations alone, man is a biped tied to the ground, with morphological features which would make any direct attempt to realize Icarian wishes suicidal. However, through his general intelligence and technological skills distilled in culture, man has developed into the most successful flyer of all, and the only one which can leave the atmosphere he shares with other flying creatures. Thus, "far from being constrained by lower-level limitations, culture transcends them and feeds back to lower levels to relieve constraints. Social organization, and human culture in particular, are best understood as negating constraints rather than being limited by them" (Lewontin, 1981, p. 245).

The priority of culture for humans is further enhanced by the fact that few organisms adapt passively to their environment (Lewontin, 1981). Rather they recreate and restructure this environment through their activity. For most species, these changes in the environment are either controlled by quite closed genetic programs, such as nest-building, or are unintended side effects of other behaviors. It is only for humans that such environmental restructuring takes on an intentional component which is deeply embedded in culture. Culture provides the ideology motivating, and the technological means allowing, environmental interventions. The effects of these interventions are then fed back to modify the culture, so that culture and culturally reshaped environment become inextricably tied to each other. To a considerable extent, the manmade environment *is* his culture. Because information in the cultural pool transcends the generations, environmental restructuring cumulates over generations. Thus, the net effect is a tremendous change from the habitat of our hunter-gatherer ancestors to the urban civilization of modern man. Because behavior evolved to closely match environmental demands, our radically different environment makes our behavior so different from our ancestors' that it is difficult to see the connection. Yet the connection is right there in the gene pool, which contains the open genetic programs that made these profound changes possible.

Mutual dependence of open and closed genetic programs. By focusing on the consequences of our open genetic programs in changing our environment, it is easy to lose sight of their evolutionary origin and of their interaction with, and dependence on, relatively closed genetic programs. In one sense this interaction is antithetical, because to meet the demands of the open program strategy, evolution had to take a direction which reduced the possibilities to utilize changes in the gene pool as a means of meeting ecological challenges. The open program strategy, as we shall see shortly, requires a long period of parental dependence, which implies that the selection for learning ability and general intelligence also resulted in selection for longevity and long generation time. Furthermore, as we also shall see, it required high parental investment in the offspring, and a K-selection instead of an r-selection strategy (few offspring with low death rate as opposed to many offspring and a high death rate; e.g., see Barash, 1977). All these factors tend to reduce the scope and speed of natural selection, with the associated changes in allelic frequencies, as a means for adaptive adjustments to changing environment (van der Berghe, 1981).

These losses at the basic selection level, then, had to be offset by greater efficiency at other levels, and particularly at the cultural level, whose Lamarckian character and speed of penetrance made it ideally suited for this task. In a very real sense, then, one could argue that humans have given up potentials at the genetic level to be able to rely more heavily on culture for their continuing adaptation.

However, in other cases, the open program strategy owes its evolution not to the negating of the importance of closed programs, but on their utilization as a necessary requirement for the evolution of open programs. For evolution to bet as one-sidedly on open programs as it has done for humans, it needs some guarantees from relatively closed programs. To realize the adaptive potential of open genetic programs, a time of apprenticeship is needed. The more the species rely on open programs, the longer this time must be. As we know, this development has reached its extreme in the higher primates, and particularly in man. However, in order for apprenticeships to bear fruit in increased capacity, a responsible master is needed for protection, modeling, and supervision in the acquisition of relevant skills. Few creatures are as vulnerable as human infants, and no other animal takes as long to reach maturity. In fact, the very vulnerability of the human neonate may be the prize paid for a brain capable to meet the informational demands of the dominating open genetic programs. The brain size of the human neonate is likely to reflect an evolutionary compromise between forces acting to enlarge the female pelvis for easier (and safer) childbirths and forces keeping it at an optimal size for biped locomotion (Dobzhansky et al., 1977). One way to circumvent this constraint on brain size may have been to leave a substantial part of the brain's maturation to occur postpartum (Dobzhansky et al., 1977). Thus, for humans, the two conditions for a strategy stressing open genetic programs, large brain size and prolonged parental care (Mayr, 1974), simply demand a caregiver to provide nutrition, shelter, and protection in infancy, and to give guidance in learning the relevant behaviors throughout childhood. Without the offspring staying close to a caregiver ready to accept these responsibilities, an open program strategy could not have evolved, and, as a consequence, we would see no humans. This parent-offspring relationship, therefore, is far too critical to be in itself left in the uncertain hands of open genetic programs. This is precluded by the capriciousness of most ecologies, which could seriously jeopardize the relationship if it were highly dependent on the inscription from the environment in the formation of its neural program. Thus, the odds are persuasive that the emergence of the open program strategy in humans was predicated on the availability of sets of relatively closed genetic programs subserving a stable parent-offspring relationship. This type of analysis, then, provides a theoretical backing for evolutionary-ethological theories of infantile attachment such as that of Bowlby (1969) (for reviews and evaluative analyses of such theories, see Mineka & Soumi, 1978; Rajecki, Lamb, & Obmascher, 1978). This type of theory presumes that parents have a biologically determined readiness to recognize and immediately develop affectional bonds to their infants, who, in turn, are similarly biologically prepared to reciprocate this affection by showing filial behavior resulting in their staying close to the parent. Note that we are talking about "readiness" and "preparedness" in this context, which implies that the programs are only relatively closed. Thus, there is a role for learning even here, e.g., in achieving mutual recognition (e.g., see Hinde, 1974). Furthermore, it is perhaps worth stressing that the relationship need not be an exclusive parent-child one. To some extent, some aspects of the relationships can be taken over by other individuals such as siblings (e.g., Harlow & Harlow, 1970; Mineka & Soumi, 1978).

The importance that we give to parent-offspring attachment as a prerequisite for the phylogenetic emergence of an open program strategy has an ontogenetic counterpart in the interaction between attachment and exploratory behavior systems postulated by Bowlby (1969). Once the infant has formed an attachment to the parent, the latter can be used as a "secure base" for exploratory escapades in the surroundings. "The presence of an attachment figure, particularly one who is believed to be accessible and responsive, leaves the baby open to stimulation that may activate exploration" (Ainsworth, 1979, p. 935). Such exploratory behavior enriches the experience taking part in the transformation of open genetic programs to neural programs controlling behavior and in modifications and elaborations of already established neural programs.

This discussion serves to illustrate the important point that an evolutionary perspective may endorse the priority of culture for human behavior yet argue that the very basis for this priority must be based on biological constraints in other respects. *Just because* human behavior is controlled by learning and culture to such a dominating extent, one must assume the existence of some much more rigidly biologically controlled behaviors to have the evolutionary equation make sense. If we accept the evolutionary perspective, it means that we give up the old nature-nuture discussion and instead start analyzing the interplay between relatively open and relatively closed genetic programs in the control of various types of human behavior.

Implications for Human Social Behavior

In the preceding section we argued that emotional attachment between parent and child is likely to have an evolutionary base in relatively closed genetic programs. In this respect, attachment behavior can serve as a prototype for what Mayr (1974) termed intraspecific behavior, that is, behavior directed towards conspecifics or, more generally, social behavior.

Biological Constraints on Social Behavior

According to Mayr (1974), at least at the animal level, intraspecific behavior is the category most governed by closed genetic programs. This is because some of these behaviors, like mutual parent-child attachment, are extremely important from an evolutionary perspective. Courtship behavior is another case in point. Not only is such behavior the *modus operandi* for the propagation of genes, but courtship display also serves another critical evolutionary role as an isolation mechanism between species. Recognition of the species-specific display, and appropriate response to it, is the most economical means of preventing the wasting of gametes in evolutionary unproductive sexual behavior (e.g., Ayala, 1978). Sexual activity in general, therefore, is likely to be quite tightly controlled by closed genetic programs. For socially living species, the variety of social behaviors is enlarged, and therefore successful functioning for the individual requires recognition and appropriate responding to many social signals. "Since much of the behavior directed toward other conspecific individuals consists of formal signals, and since there is a high selective premium for these signals to be unmistakable, the essential components of the phenotype of such signals must show low variability and must be largely controlled genetically" (Mayr, 1974, p. 657).

This dominance of closed genetic programs in the control of social behavior is diluted in cultural species such as humans. Indeed, we required that the critical communicative system for culture was based on learning, explicitly excluding genetically programmed signal systems. With human language, social exchange can utilize an extremely efficient and flexible system, which, although biologically constrained, still is controlled by rather open genetic programs. Nevertheless, face-to-face communication seldom is restricted to the linguistic level, but also involves a level of nonverbal communication which interacts with and modifies the meaning of the verbal responses (e.g., see Harper, Wiens, & Matarazzo, 1978). Such nonverbal communication may involve many elements reminiscent of the more rigid and primitive communication systems of animals (e.g., Eibl-Eibesfeldt, 1980). Indeed, plausible arguments can be raised for suggesting an evolutionary basis for aspects of nonverbal communication. For example, some gestures like the "eyebrow flash," appear to be quite universal across widely different cultures (Eibl-Eibesfeldt, 1979). Furthermore, this type of social interaction occurs in an ecology which has not changed appreciably during the evolution of the human species (e.g., Bowlby, 1969). Parents today define a large segment of the infant's visual, auditory, and tactile world in the same way as parents of similar appearance determined the external world of their infants hundreds of thousands of years ago. Similarly, infants were as ubiquitous in the worlds of their parents at that time as they are for contemporary parents. A similar logic applies to face-to-face contacts between adults. Thus, nonverbal communication gestures, whose functionality prompted their incorporation in the gene pool a very long time ago, may retain some of that functionality today because the ecology of close social encounters has not changed appreciably. Thus, in the same vein as the drastic change in our physical surroundings between hunter-gatherer and modern life argues for the openness of programs controlling interactions with this aspect of the environment, the constancy of the small group ecology argues for a larger role for closed genetic programs in face-to-face interactions with fellow humans.

These relatively closed genetic programs which control some nonverbal communication systems interact intimately with the open programs controlling social learning. Appropriate identification of nonverbal signals, indeed, is a requirement for observational learning. To learn from observation, an individual has to be able to recognize what a conspecific is doing, and, no less important, his emotional reactions to doing it. Finding out that someone else inserts something in his mouth that appears to be good-tasting and pleasure-inducing is much more conducive to imitation than observing a reaction of disgust to a potential food item. A capacity for observational learning is an enormous evolutionary asset for socially living species because it abbreviates the acquisition process of often complex behaviors, and it saves individuals from repeating costly, and even fatal, mistakes made by conspecifics (Bandura, 1977). Moreover, as we have seen, observational learning fulfills the necessary requirements as a means for developing culture. Once again we see how closed and open genetic programs are likely to interact even in behaviors which serve to bring about the most advanced level of human adaptation, that of culture. Like the more important communication channel for humans, language, social learning is a product of biological evolution which, although assisting in transcending this organic process, is intricately embedded in an evolutionary web of open and closed genetic programs.

Emotional Facial Expressions

In the previous sections, we have argued that social signaling is likely to be controlled to a substantial degree by closed genetic programs. For humans, as for other primates, the face provides one of the most important sources for nonverbal social communication. The heavy genetic loading of this behavior category was recognized in the pioneering work of Darwin (1872) in his "The Expression of Emotion in Man and Animals." Because they are putatively controlled by closed programs, facial expressions are likely to be easily identified and to induce meaningful physiological responses. Furthermore, they can be easily represented for experimental purposes without severe losses in ecological validity, and they can be scaled by quite elaborated procedures (e.g., Ekman, Friesen, & Ellsworth, 1972). Therefore, facial expressions provide an important category of stimuli of great potential interest for the sociophysiologist. In this section, we shall review some background data pointing to the basis of facial expressions in closed genetic programs and then go on to describe a project of our own where facial expressions have been studied in a sociophysiological context.

Production of facial expressions. If facial expressions are based primarily on closed genetic programs, one would expect them to be universal among humans. Second, they should appear early in the human behavior repertoire, and their emergence should be relatively independent of environmental influences. Finally, homologous expressions should be expected among other primates. All these propositions have extensive support in existing data.

First, cross-cultural studies (Eibl-Eibesfeldt, 1980; Ekman, 1972; 1973) have demonstrated quite convincingly that some distinct emotional facial expressions are virtually universally found. Second, developmental studies have shown that infants display distinct facial expressions such as smiles within the first week of life (for reviews, see Vine, 1973; Sroufe & Waters, 1976; Oster & Ekman, 1978). Furthermore, emergence of emotional expressions in the face appears to be relatively little affected by the environment because both congenitally blind and blind-and-deaf born children display emotional facial expressions (Eibl-Eibesfeldt, 1973). Finally, facial expressions are ubiquitous in the social life of other primates as a means of controlling social interaction (Chevalier-Skolnikoff, 1973; Goodall, 1968; Hinde, 1974), and comparative studies suggest that facial displays have a common evolutionary origin and are homologous to human facial expressions (Andrew, 1963;

1965; van Hooff, 1972). Presumably, relatively fixed sets of genetically controlled facial expressions have evolved because of their usefulness in the organization of social interaction. In face-to-face interaction, they provide immediate information about the state of the sender and thus also about the interaction which is likely to follow. For example, smiles are important ingredients in the strategy of friendly encounters (Eibl-Eibesfeldt, 1980). It is interesting to note, therefore, that the human smile and laughter can be viewed as the concatenation of two primate displays, one indicating submissiveness, and the other playfulness (van Hooff, 1972). This massive evidence clearly supports an evolutionary basis for the production of facial emotional expressions.

Recognition of facial expressions. If production of facial expressions has an evolutionary basis, then the same must be true for recognition of such displays. An animal who forces an intruder to withdraw because of an impressive threat display profits because he does not have to share resources, but the intruder also profits because he does not risk being hurt in fighting the self-confident occupant of the resource. Thus, if human facial expressions are determined by biologically given facial affect programs (Ekman, 1972), it follows that humans must also be predisposed to decode and react adaptively to facial stimuli. Again, the data are overwhelmingly in favor of this suggestion. Facial expressions of emotions are recognized across widely different cultures (Ekman, 1972) and under degraded stimulus conditions, such as long distances (Hager & Ekman, 1979). Similarly, direction of gaze is accurately perceived (Gibson & Pick, 1963). Furthermore, studies on human infants demonstrate that different emotional expressions can be distinguished by infants in the 3-6 month age (LaBarbera, Izard, Vietze, & Parisi, 1976; Young-Browne, Rosenfeld, & Horowitz, 1977). Finally Sackett (1966) reported that infant rhesus monkeys reacted emotionally to facial displays from adults even when reared in isolation. It is clear, therefore, that both the production and the recognition and reaction to human facial expressions are likely to be controlled by quite closed genetic programs. Indeed, a more extravagant claim may be warranted. "The universal facial expressions of emotions are perhaps the only satisfactorily documented phylogenetic adaptions in human beings" (Izard, 1979, p. 39).

Conditioning to facial stimuli. Emotional facial expressions have evolved in different contexts depending on which particular emotion they are associated with. Aversive emotions like pain, fear, and anger (but not anxiety) are primarily associated with the agonistic behavior system, which typically is activated during conflicts between conspecifics (e.g., Scott, 1980). Anger may signal impending attack, and fear may signal readiness to yield in cases of hostile approaches. Because of the adaptive assets of keeping this type of conflict at the signaling level, without having to test each challenge and risk injury, it is not surprising that these emotions are clearly distinguishable in the face. Other types of emotions, such as surprise or happiness, are associated with other behavior systems such as explorative behavior, play, or infantile attachment, which in important respects are antagonistic to agonistic behavior. This differential origin of emotions in potentially antagonistic behavior systems could be expected to result in biological constraints on the associa-

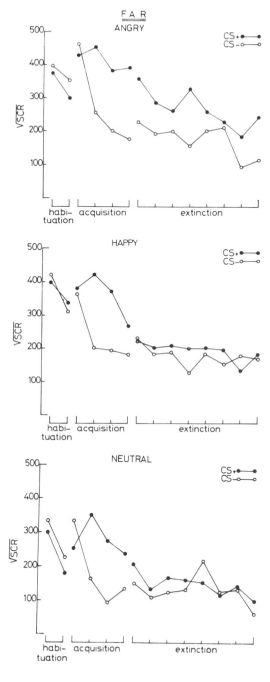

BLOCKS OF TWO TRIALS

bility of emotions with particular facial expressions. Thus, from an evolutionary perspective, one would expect the facial expressions of agonistic emotions such as fear and anger to be more easily associated with pain and aversion than would, say, happiness. In Seligman's (1970) terminology, anger and fear would be biologically prepared to enter into associations with aversion, whereas happiness would be contraprepared to do so. This proposition is extensively supported by human experimental data.

Öhman and Dimberg (1978) presented pictures of angry, neutral, or happy faces as signals for aversive stimuli (mild electric shocks to the fingers) in a Pavlovian conditioning paradigm with skin conductance as the dependent measure for three different groups of students. The subjects were required to discriminate between two stimulus persons by having one of them followed by the electric shock. As can be seen in the left part of Figure 3-2, responses to the three types of facial expressions did not differ appreciably before conditioning. In the middle panels, it is obvious that introduction of the unconditioned stimulus (US) after one of the conditioned stimuli (CSs) resulted in reliable differential responding in all three groups, with no between-groups difference. However, for the neutral and happy expressions, this effect was quite fragile because as soon as the US was omitted during extinction (right panels) differential responding was lost in these groups. This contrasts markedly with the anger group where differential responding persisted throughout the extinction phase. These findings were essentially replaced by Orr and Lanzetta (1980) in a study using fearful rather than angry expressions. Lanzetta and Orr (1980; 1981) extended the data base significantly by presenting fearful, neutral, or happy faces in compound with a neutral stimulus (a tone) as signals for an aversive US. By testing the component CSs separately during extinction, they were able to draw conclusions about the relative effectiveness of the facial stimuli in becoming associated with the aversive US. They found that fearful expressions overshadowed to tone, whereas the tone overshadowed the happy expression (Lanzetta & Orr, 1980; 1981). A neutral expression, finally, did not differ from the tone (Lanzetta & Orr, 1981). This series of studies then supports the notion that different CSs are differentially effective in entering into associations with particular USs (cf. Seligman, 1970).

From an evolutionary point of view, one would expect the direction of the facial display to be critical, especially for anger displays. Even if the mere presence of a threat display increases the level of activation in groups of primates (e.g., Goodall, 1968), the display is by far most significant for the individual who is the target of

---

Figure 3-2. Skin conductance responses conditioning to facial stimuli. Three separate groups of individual were conditioned to pictures of angry, happy, and neutral facial expressions (top, middle, and bottom panel, respectively). Each subject saw repeated, random presentations of pictures of two different persons expressing the same emotion. One of these conditioned stimuli (the CS+) was followed by the shock unconditioned stimulus during the acquisition phase, whereas the other (the CS−) was never followed by shock. No difference between groups or pictures was observed during initial, nonreinforced presentations (the habituation phase). During the acquisition phase, the reinforced cue (the CS+) evoked reliably larger responses than the nonreinforced cue (the CS−), which showed pronounced habituation over trials. When the shock was omitted (extinction), differential responding to the CS+ and the CS− remained almost unaltered in the subjects conditioned to angry faces, but disappeared immediately in the two other groups.

attention. If all individuals would react, group cohesiveness would suffer. However, if an anger display suddenly would be changed in its direction, a pronounced response would be expected in the individual who now becomes the target. Data of relevance for these hypotheses were presented by Dimberg and Öhman (1983). They demonstrated that angry faces were effective CSs only when directed toward the subject. Angry faces directed away were as ineffective as happy faces in inducing resistance to extinction. Furthermore, in a second experiment, where the direction of the stimulus person's facial display was shifted between acquisition and extinction, they showed that what was critical was what direction the display had during extinction. Thus, subjects conditioned to a person directing his angry face away showed persistent responding when the direction was changed so that they now were the target for the display. However, subjects conditioned with the face directed toward them stopped responding immediately when the face was directed away during extinction.

These latter findings suggest an evolutionary meaningful hypothesis. It appeared that the subjects learned something about the stimulus person irrespective of the direction of his anger display when the face was paired with the aversive US. However, this learning was evident in performance only when the display was directed at the subject during extinction. Evolutionarily speaking, facial displays are always asssociated with specific individuals. Thus, an individual who has pain associated with the anger display of a conspecific not only learns something about anger displays, but, more importantly, he learns something about the individual showing the display. This type of learning is conducive to the development of stable dominance relationships and dominance ranks among animals (e.g., Bernstein, 1981; Hinde, 1974), one function of which is to decrease both the incidence and intensity of agonistic encounters within the group.

The hypothesis that the effect of angry facial expression is mediated by the person was directly tested by Dimberg (1984). He shifted the person but kept the expression constant between acquisition and extinction. Thus, one group of subjects saw angry faces expressed by different persons during acquisition and extinction, and another group saw different persons expressing happiness. Both groups immediately lost differential responding with the change in stimulus person, which indicates that the effect indeed was mediated by the person.

In the first shift experiment (Dimberg & Öhman, 1983, Experiment 2), subjects showing the effect of angry faces only when it was directed to them still were conditioned to an angry face, even if it was directed away. To see whether an angry face is necessary during acquisition, Dimberg (1984) shifted expressions from anger to happiness, and vice versa, keeping the stimulus person constant. Again, it was demonstrated that persistent differential responding during extinction occurred only for the group having an angry face during this phase in spite of the fact that they were conditioned to a happy expression. However, in an additional experiment, he was able to document that anger, although not necessary during acquisition, still contributed to enhanced resistance to extinction by its presence during acquisition.

In his final experiment, Dimberg (1984) supplemented these findings suggesting an excitatory role for anger and fear expressions in aversive conditioning with data indicating an inhibitory role for the happy expression. One group of subjects was

conditioned to a happy face directed away and another group to a happy face directed toward the observer. The logic behind this manipulation was that the potential inhibitory effect of a happy face would be removed by having it directed away, analogous to the effect of direction on angry displays (Dimberg & Öhman, 1983, Experiment 1). During extinction, both groups were exposed to the same stimulus persons,
but now showing an angry expression directed at the observer. The results are shown
in Figure 3-3. The group which had the happy expression directed at the observer
during acquisition did indeed show less resistance to extinction than the group conditioned to a happy face directed away. These data, then, support the proposition that
happy expressions have an inhibitory effect when used as CSs in aversive conditioning. Thus, in agreement with the data of Lanzetta and Orr (1981), our finding demonstrates that angry facial expressions are prepared for excitatory aversive conditioning, whereas happy expressions are inhibitory (or contraprepared) for this type
of learning. Furthermore, our data are consistent with expectations from an evolutionary perspective with regard to the effect of direction of the display, as well as
with regard to the critical role played by the stimulus person in mediating the effect.

Facial responses to facial stimuli. The previous series of studies demonstrated that
physiological responses to facial stimuli are modified by Pavlovian conditioning
depending on whether the emotional expression is congruent with the aversive US
or not. However, because autonomic responses do not allow conclusions about the
specific quality of emotional response, all we can say from the autonomic data is
that the subjects were emotionally activated. One way of gaining access to the
qualities of emotion is to use the face as an output system in addition to its use as an
input system. The facial expressions that give observers information about what
type of emotion a person is experiencing are produced by changes in the facial
muscles which can be picked up by electronic transducers. Indeed, Schwartz and co-
workers (Schwartz, Fair, Salt, Mandel, & Klerman, 1976a,b; Schwartz, Fair, Mandel, Salt, Mieske, & Klerman, 1978; Schwartz, Ahern, & Brown, 1979; Schwartz,
Brown, & Ahern, 1980) have demonstrated differential patterns of electromyographic (EMG) activation during imagery-induced emotions. Pleasant emotions
such as happiness resulted in elevated EMG activity in the zygomatic muscle,
whereas unpleasant emotions such as sadness or anger enhanced activity in the corrugator muscle. The zygomatic muscle extends from the cheekbone to the corner of
the mouth, and mediates the lifting of the latter in a smile, whereas the corrugator
hides behind the eyebrow to mediate the frowning of an angry facial display
(Hjortsjö, 1970). In other words, happy thoughts induced aspects of a smile, and
angry thoughts produced aspects of an angry expression. However, whether one
should talk about specific emotions in this way or merely about a differentiation between positive and aversive emotional states is too early to decide.

  If facial displays are powerful stimuli with an evolutionary backing, one would
expect them to more or less reflexively elicit responses in the observer. Whereas the
conditioning data indicate that responses to facial stimuli are more or less likely to
be channeled in different directions as a result of a pavlovian contingency, the facial
EMG technique enables a more detailed assessment of the emotional qualities
elicited by facial stimuli even before conditioning. Dimberg (1982) measured EMG

Arne Öhman and Ulf Dimberg

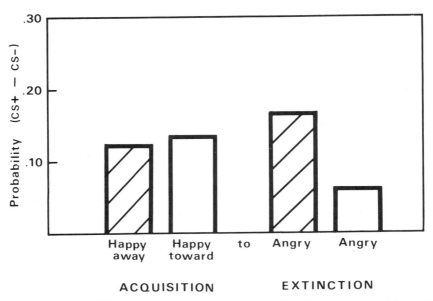

Figure 3-3. Mean differential skin conductance responding to reinforced (CS+) and nonreinforced (CS−) pictures of happy facial expressions. One group of subjects was conditioned with the stimulus person looking away (Happy away) and another group with the stimulus person directing his expression at the observer (Happy toward). During acquisition, when the CS+ was reinforced by an electric shock unconditioned stimulus, the groups did not differ. During extinction, however, when both groups were exposed to the same stimulus person as during acquisition but now directing his *angry* expression toward the observer, the Happy away group showed reliably more resistance to extinction than the Happy toward group. This result implies that an inhibitory effect of happy expression on aversive conditioning was offset by having the display directed away during acquisition.

from the zygomatic and the corrugator during exposures to pictures showing angry or happy facial expressions. These pictures elicited reliable heart rate decelerations, and skin conductance responses, which, however, did not differentiate the two stimulus conditions. In contrast, such differentiation was clearly available in the EMG data. As can be seen in Figure 3-4, the happy face clearly enhanced activity in the zygomatic, and showed a tendency to inhibit activity in the corrugator, whereas the angry expression had the opposite effect, that is, corrugator enhancement and no effect on the zygomatic. Vaughan and Lanzetta (1980) extended these data by reporting EMG results from subjects exposed to a videotaped model displaying a facial pain response to ostensible electric shock punishment in a memory task. Their results indicated increased activity in the muscle narrowing the eye, the orbicularis oculi, and in the muscle clenching the jaw, the masseter, but no change in a pain-irrelevant facial muscle, the medial frontalis. These EMG changes, then, provide a pattern consistent with the facial response to pain (Hjortsjö, 1970). Vaughan and Lanzetta (1980) argued from the details of their findings that the observer's facial response in fact mimicked the response of the stimulus person, rather than

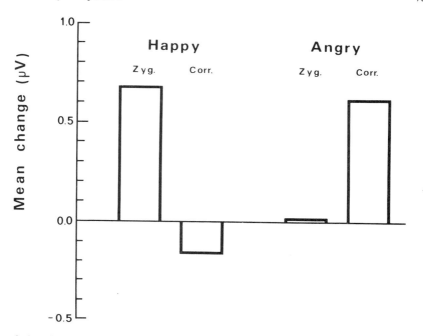

Figure 3-4. Electromyographic changes from prestimulus baseline in the zygomatic (Zyg.) and corrugator (Corr.) muscles in subjects exposed to pictures of happy and angry facial expressions. The zygomatic pulls the corner of the mouth and the corrugator frowns the eyebrow. These data, then, suggest that a happy face evokes enhanced activity in a muscle mediating a smile, and that the angry face evoked enhanced activity in a muscle controlling one of the facial gestures of anger.

merely categorized the stimuli as pleasant or unpleasant. These findings suggest that facial expressions evoke systematic and specific patterned responses in the observer's face, which tend to mimic the specific expression displayed by the stimulus person. The specificity of this response, of course, is compatible with what one would expect from behavior which, as shown earlier, is highly likely to be governed by closed genetic programs. In fact, given the minimal stimulus situations, pictures in Dimberg's (1982) case, and a videotaped sequence in the case of Vaughan and Lanzetta (1980), the reliability of the findings is quite surprising and prompts questions about how powerful responses one would be able to observe in more naturalistic settings.

Concluding Discussion

The purpose of this chapter has been to spell out an evolutionary perspective on human behavior which we regard as useful for the sociophysiologist. Indeed, in the last section we attempted to illustrate this usefulness by reviewing experimental data that originated from such a perspective. In this concluding discussion we, first, discuss limitations and dangers inherent in this perspective, and second, we outline what we regard as some of its most important implications for sociophysiology.

Problems with an Evolutionary Perspective

Evolutionary theory serves as a unifying biological perspective on psychological phenomena. In stressing its role as a perspective rather than as a specific theory, we have in mind something akin to Kuhn's (1962) distinction between paradigm and normal science, or between metatheory and scientific theory (Johnston & Turvey, 1980). That is to say, evolutionary theory provides a framework for posing a number of questions about psychological phenomena, suggests a general direction in which answers are to be sought, and provides methodological recommendations for how one is to go about seeking the answers. Failure to appreciate this distinction is apt to give rise to problems. For example, while the difficulties in submitting many of the propositions in this chapter to direct empirical tests would be embarrassing if our aim was theoretical rather than metatheoretical, it is to miss the point to apply this type of criticism, because as metatheory it is evaluated primarily in terms of its fruitfulness in prompting new theoretical developments and research. Furthermore, by treating it as theory about behavior rather than as a perspective on behavior, severe mistakes are likely to be committed in the explanation of specific psychological phenomena. The theory of evolution, indeed, is a seductive intellectual tool, which easily leads the proponent astray. While there are different theories of evolution that quibble about various aspects of the process (e.g., see the comments on the paper by Plotkin & Odling-Smee, 1981a), the general theory of organic evolution is, as claimed by Barash (1977), "probably as close to truth as we can get in the natural science" (p. 9). This combination of intellectual appeal and scientific status sometimes provides a danger in leading people to go beyond their facts. However,

> no matter how powerful the theory of evolution, there is no way to go directly from the theory to the interpretation of human behaviors. The theory guides research. It does not provide conclusions ... an accepted theory (such as the theory of evolution based on natural selection) may be terrible liability if misapplied. All the prestige of the theory then supports the mistakes. (Washburn, 1978a, pp. 412-413)

In short, evolutionary speculations can never replace empirical knowledge about human psychology. However, the way we go about gaining such knowledge may be very much affected by whether we subscribe to an evolutionary perspective or not, as we shall see shortly.

Applying the theory of evolution directly to interpret human behavior involves a series of hazards which often are more or less completely neglected when enthusiastic biologists try to extend the area of application of their science. As a unifying theory, evolutionary theory implies a continuity between species, which is taken to legitimate the interpretation and elucidation of human behavior in terms of animal data. As pointed out by many authors, this approach can explain anything by utilizing the enormous degree of freedom there is in choosing among all available species as a basis for comparisons. Washburn (1978a) argues that any interspecies comparison must take knowledge about the human level as a point of departure; otherwise, uniquely human adaptations are likely to be missed, and the comparison becomes misleading both for the human and the animal side. The sociocultural level of humans provides a unique context which is not shared by other species, but which determines the very meaning of the concepts we use when talking about human behavior. For example, as pointed out by Washburn (1978a), human sexual behavior occurs inside (or outside) culturally determined marriage customs, which is apt to make any attempt to elucidate it from animal mating systems misleading. Without this cultural context, a very incomplete and inaccurate picture of human sexuality is likely to emerge.

Any evolutionary interpretation of human behavior requires at least three steps. The behavior in question must be described in meaningful units, its heritability must be demonstrated, and its adaptive significance must be ascertained. In a critique of sociobiology, Lewontin (1979) shows that all these steps are fraught with difficulties. First, descriptory units are problematic even with regard to more tangible morphological components. For example, is the hand a suitable evolutionary unit in terms of genetics and ecological pressures, or should, say, the thumb be considered a unit of its own? Such problems, of course, are magnified when behavior is at issue. While psychologists put great effort into carefully defining and measuring behavior characteristics under interest, to assess its stability across time and different situations, to enumerate its empirical correlates, and then perhaps eventually attempt to assess its potential genetic basis, for example, by twin studies, the primary present-day evolutionary advocates, the sociobiologists, appear happy to merely postulate a genetic basis for "a very odd assortment of behaviors—altruism, cheating, spite, deception, creativity, and reciprocity, to mention only a few" (Washburn, 1978a, p. 406). Such behavior categories often reflect reifications of loose constructs, conflations of meaning-context, e.g., the use of animal aggression to elucidate human warfare, and the confusion of levels in treating social and political systems as nothing but the collective activity by individuals (Lewontin, 1979). With regard to heritability, we have already concluded that it has a role to play in human behavior, but that its details most often remain obscure. Furthermore, arguments about evolutionary origins of traits require knowledge about genetic variance, which inevitably is lost because of evolution itself (Lewontin, 1979). Finally, evolutionary arguments require ascertaining the adaptive significance of behavioral traits which may prove exceedingly difficult.

According to Lewontin (1978), the task of the evolutionary biologist is often understood as the working out of an adaptionist program, "to construct a plausible argument about how each part functions as an adaptive device" (p. 161). This task is difficult, indeed. First, the concept of adaptation is, in itself, refractory to analysis (see Lewontin, 1978). Second, although adaptations need experimental verifications, such verifications are most often very difficult to achieve, particularly when human behavior is at issue. Lacking empirical possibilities, what remains is often "imaginative reconstructions" (Lewontin, 1979) which entirely relies on plausibility. Third, the assumption in the adaptionist program that all morphological parts and behaviors must be adaptive is not valid (Lewontin, 1979). For example, natural selection picks the individuals with the higher fecundity, which are not necessarily always the best adapted ones (Lewontin, 1978; 1979).

In concert, all these difficulties make evolutionary theory as applied by the sociobiologists an unsuitable theory about human behavior. Specific theoretical propositions have to be sought elsewhere. If we want to increment our knowledge about humans, there is no alternative but to study humans. In doing so, however, knowledge about evolution may be helpful in shaping our thinking and methodological approaches. In the next section, these implications will be examined for a specific context, social knowing.

Evolutionary Implications for Social Knowing

In previous sections, we argued from a general evolutionary basis that social cues largely controlled by closed genetic programs play an important role in human social behavior. Our argument implies that evolutionary pressures have shaped both the sender and the receiver end of social communication. Thus, evolutionary pressures must have been exerted to equip man with very efficient apparatuses for directly perceiving even complex aspects of other persons' behavior. Man has evolved in a social setting to be a social creature, and to be biologically successful in this role he must have been able to discern important characteristics of surrounding group members. To efficiently fulfill his role, he had to recognize features such as gender, dominance, friendly or hostile intentions and even such complex attributes as trustworthiness on the basis of minimally informative cues. In other words, evolution would have tuned our perceptual systems to pick up whatever invariants there are in, e.g., gait, movement patterns, or facial expressions, which correlate with such characteristics.

Common assumptions in contemporary social psychology do not agree with this evolutionary premise. Typically, it is assumed that what is out there contains little specific information so that a heavy load is put on complex cognitive mechanisms to sort out what is going on. Thus, one stresses the indirect, inferential, and deliberate character of social perception, where what is ultimately identified is heavily influenced by the individual's rather than by the environment's contribution. Rather than being concerned with the pickup of useful information, perceptual processes are viewed as enriched from the inside by cognitive systems in inferring from poor external cues what is happening in the outside world.

Recently, Gibson's (1966; 1979) ecologically inspired challenge of the indirect approach to perception has been extended to the domain of social perception by Baron (1981) and Runeson and Frykholm (1984). Baron (1981) proposes a "social knowing continuum" which extends from direct or perception-based to indirect or cognition-based knowing. At the former extreme, information from the surrounding world is directly picked up by mechanisms shaped through evolution to make use of whatever information there is in the stimulus array to support identification of biologically relevant objects or events. In our terminology, this end of the continuum would be controlled by closed genetic programs. At the other end, however, knowing occurs through indirect means like conscious reasoning, which is highly dependent on the cognitive structures available to the individual. Here, open genetic programs must be assumed to play a dominating role. In line with the general environmentalist bias of psychology commented on earlier, social psychologists have tended to stress the cognitive end of this dimension much more than the perceptual end. Baron (1981) argues that this bias should be reversed, so that indirect cognitive mechanisms are invoked only if a Gibsonian analysis of the stimulus field fails to reveal the necessary invariants for direct perceptual pickup.

The direct and indirect ends of the social knowing continuum were pitted against each other in a vicarious instigation experiment on empathy by Hygge (1976). His subjects viewed identical staged sequences of interaction between the experimenter and an alleged fellow subject who was actually a confederate. Both the subject and the confederate ostensibly heard tones over earphones, and the confederate complained vigorously over the unbearable high intensity of one of the tones she was receiving. From Stotland's (1969) theorizing about empathy, it was hypothesized that the explanation given for the confederate's discomfort would influence the subject's emotional responding to it. According to Stotland, empathic responding occurs because of a process of identification where the observer, by help of cognitive mechanisms, vicariously puts himself in the position of the sufferer. Facilitating this role-taking process, then, would enhance empathy. This type of explanation is clearly placed at the indirect end of the social knowing continuum. From the direct end, one would simply argue that what matters is to recognize directly that someone else is suffering, with no necessary role for complex cognitive transformations for emotional empathy to occur. Hygge (1976) manipulated ease of identification by telling half his subjects simply that the strong intensity was due to wrong intensity setting for the tone received by the confederate, whereas for the other half, the confederate allegedly suffered from an ideosyncratic hearing disorder making some pitches highly aversive. For both groups, the experimenter talked the confederate into continuing in the experiment with unchanged stimulus parameters because "changing them now would ruin the data." Skin conductance responses to the tones were ostensibly measured from both "subjects" before and after the interaction sequence. Both the instruction groups enhanced their responses to the tones during the trials following as compared to those preceding the scene, but the groups did not differ from each other. Hygge (1976) interpreted these data to suggest that seeing the suffering other was sufficient for empathic emotional responding, with no additional effects from manipulation of the identification process.

The ecological approach to social perception has been significantly extended by Runeson and Frykholm (1984). Following Baron's (1981) lead that a primary task is to determine whether there is specific information available in the stimulus array, they demonstrated by help of principles from mechanics, biomechanics, and motor control theory that the anatomy of the human body in action provides specific visual information which quite directly gives the observer access not only to what the actor does, but also to his complex attributes such as gender, expectations, intentions, and even attempts to deceive. Their theoretical analysis, then, suggests that quite specific information is available about even very complex attributes of the actor. From this premise, there is but a short step to argue that evolution has tuned our perceptual apparatus to respond exactly to this information because of its biological usefulness. Runeson and Frykholm (1984) went on to demonstrate empirically that subjects are in fact able to use this potential information in a series of experiments where the actors' movements were visible only through light patches attached to their joints (cf. Johansson, 1973). For example, the actor's expectations were readily seen in the lead-in movements for lifting a box because observers were able to judge the expected weight quite accurately from this information alone. The intended length of a throw was similarly discernible from seeing only the throwing movement of the actor. Gender in both children and adults could be quite accurately perceived from complex movement patterns alone. Finally, and perhaps most significantly, attempts to deceive the observer about one's sex, or the weight one was lifting, were quite unsuccessful. Indeed, both the actual and the intended sex, as well as the actual and deceptively intended weight of a box, were independently perceived. The ease with which deception was identified is interesting from an evolutionary perspective because without such a capacity, evolution of reciprocal altruism would be difficult (Trivers, 1971). Altruism, of course, is the *raison d'être* of sociobiology (e.g., Barash, 1977), but to extend it into the human domain (e.g., see Hoffman, 1981), it is highly desirable to be able to supplement the more restricted kin selection theory with one allowing reciprocal altruism (e.g., Alexander, 1975), if evolutionary oriented theories even shall come close to accounting for the data (cf. Campbell, 1975).

Implications for Sociophysiology

Research of the kind considered in the previous section demonstrates that perhaps the most significant contribution of evolutionary biology to social psychology is philosophical and methodological. Evolutionary considerations suggest that humans have evolved to be responsive to very specific aspects of the informational inflow, that is, those aspects that carry the biologically useful information. By utilizing "smart mechanisms" (Runeson, 1977), perceptual systems are able to directly extract the information they need, without pressures to invoke higher cognitive processes or extensive, complex computations. In short, the organisms and its ecological niche are mutually tuned to each other, so that they must be regarded as co-implicative rather than as independently definable (Johnston & Turvey, 1980; Lewontin, 1978).

A methodological implication of this premise is that simplification of the stimulus situation in artificial laboratory settings always involves a risk of losing the significant environmental support for naturally integrated behavior, so that the subject has no option but to cognitively control his behavior in whatever way he deems appropriate. In the natural environment, the conspicuous cues apparently controlling behavior are embedded in a fabric of interwoven background events which in more or less subtle ways may modify responding to the primary cues. The redundancies and probabilistic relationships between cues may have been used by evolution to shape responding to the total pattern, including the background, so that its removal in the laboratory may involve a significant change in the conditions (Petrinovich, 1979). Following Brunswik (1956), it could be argued that systematic experimental designs need to be supplemented with representatively designed experiments to make sure that the evolutionary and ecologically relevant dimensions are represented in the experiment. In Brunswik's (1956) words, systematic experiments allow statements about what is possible, but not about what is probable in the natural environment. From an evolutionary perspective, then, an analysis of the ecology is a necessary preliminary for any psychological inquiry (e.g., Johnston & Turvey, 1980; Johnston, 1981; Petrinovich, 1979).

If the sociophysiologist is interested in the full, integrated response to complex social situations, including its physiological correlates, the validity of his potential findings are at the mercy of the ecological validity of the stimulus situation. It is much easier to posit that the complete pattern of physiological response is evoked from a situation engendering direct perceptual mechanisms controlled by relatively closed genetic programs than from a situation eliciting no specific response but a series of cognitively integrated hunches. Merely having subjects watch movies supposed to elicit various emotions is not conducive to result in differential physiological activation patterns (Frankenhaeuser, 1975), whereas carefully staged sequences involving ecologically relevant fear and anger stimuli (Ax, 1953), or the use of carefully selected and trained good imaginers (Weerts & Roberts, 1976) can provide quite unequivocal data on physiological differentiation of emotions.

In our view, then, evolutionary considerations are highly pertinent for the emergent discipline of sociophysiology, particular as they endorse an ecological approach to psychology (see Johnston & Turvey, 1980; Turvey, Shaw, Reed, & Mace, 1981). An important tenet of this chapter is that evolutionary theory serves as a perspective which helps shape the specific research activities in psychology. By stressing its role at this level, it is possible to endorse the relevance of evolutionary theory for psychology, yet remain skeptical about some of the excesses often associated with its applications in the direct interpretation of psychological phenomena. As stated by an evolutionary biologist and physical anthropologist with a good sense for the requirements of behavioral sciences, "fortunately, it is possible to accept the theory of evolution and the importance of genetics without ignoring the known historical record, social science, or the psychology of the individual" (Washburn, 1978a, p. 416).

Acknowledgment. Preparation of this chapter was facilitated by grants from the Swedish Council for Research in the Humanities and Social Sciences.

References

Ainsworth, M. D. S. (1979). Infant-mother attachment. *American Psychologist, 34,* 932-937.

Alexander, R. D. (1975). The search for a general theory of behavior. *Behavioral Science, 20,* 77-100.

Andrew, R. J. (1963). Evolution of facial expression. *Science, 142,* 1034-1041.

Andrew, R. J. (1965). The origins of facial expression. *Scientific American, 213* (4), 88-94.

Ax, A. F. (1953). The physiological differentiation of fear and anger in humans. *Psychosomatic Medicine, 15,* 433-442.

Ayala, F. J. (1978). The mechanism of evolution. *Scientific American, 239* (3), 48-61.

Bandura, A. (1977). *Social learning theory.* Englewood Cliffs, NJ: Prentice-Hall.

Barash, D. P. (1977). *Sociobiology and behavior.* New York: Elsevier.

Baron, R. M. (1981). Social knowing from an ecological event perspective: A consideration of the relative domains of power for cognitive and perceptual modes of knowing. In J. Harvey (Ed.), *Cognition, social behavior, and the environment*. Hillsdale, NJ: Erlbaum.

Bernstein, I. S. (1981). Dominance: The baby and the bathwater. *Behavioral and Brain Sciences, 4*, 419-457.

Bowlby, J. (1969). *Attachment and loss*. Vol. 1. *Attachment*. London: Hogarth Press.

Brunswik, E. (1956). *Perception and the representative design of psychological experiments*. Berkeley: University of California Press.

Campbell, D. T. (1975). On the conflicts between biological and social evolution and between psychology and moral tradition. *American Psychologist, 30*, 1103-1126.

Campbell, D. T. (1981). Levels of organization, selection, and information storage in biological and social evolution. *Behavioral and Brain Sciences, 4*, 236-237.

Chevalier-Skolnikoff, S. (1973). Facial expression of emotion in nonhuman primates. In P. Ekman (Ed.), *Darwin and facial expression*. New York: Academic Press.

Chomsky, N. (1968). *Language and mind*. New York: Harcourt, Brace & World.

Darwin, C. (1872). *The expression of emotion in man and animals*. London: Murray.

Dimberg, U. (1982). Facial reactions to facial expressions. *Psychophysiology, 19*, 643-647.

Dimberg, U. (1984). Facial expressions as excitatory and inhibitory stimuli for conditioned autonomic responses. Manuscript submitted for publication.

Dimberg, U., & Öhman, A. (1983). The effects of directional facial cues on electrodermal conditioning to facial stimuli. *Psychophysiology, 20*, 160-167.

Dobzhansky, T. (1972). Genetics and the diversity of behavior. *American Psychologist, 27*, 523-530.

Dobzhansky, T., Ayala, F. J., Stebbins, G. L., & Valentine, J. W. (1977). *Evolution*. San Francisco: Freeman.

Eibl-Eibesfeldt, I. (1973). The expressive behavior of the deaf and blind born. In M. von Cranach & I. Vine (Eds.), *Social communication and movement*. London: Academic Press.

Eibl-Eibesfeldt, I. (1975). *Ethology: The biology of behavior*. New York: Holt, Rinehart & Winston.

Eibl-Eibesfeldt, I. (1979). Human ethology: Concepts and implications for the sciences of man. *Behavioral and Brain Sciences, 2*, 1-26.

Eibl-Eibesfeldt, I. (1980). Strategies of social interaction. In R. Plutchik & H. Kellerman (Eds.), *Emotion: Theory, research, and experience* (Vol. 1). New York: Academic Press.

Ekman, P. (1972). Universals and cultural differences in facial expressions of emotion. In J. K. Cole (Ed.) *Nebraska Symposium on Motivation* (Vol. 19). Lincoln, NE: University of Nebraska Press.

Ekman, P. (1973). Cross-cultural studies of facial expression. In P. Ekman (Ed.), *Darwin and facial expression*. New York: Academic Press.

Ekman, P., Friesen, W. V., & Ellsworth, P. (1972). *Emotion in the human face: Guidelines for research and an integration of findings*. New York: Pergamon Press.

Frankenhaeuser, M. (1975). Experimental approaches to the study of catecholamines and emotion. In L. Levi (Ed.), *Emotions: Their parameters and measurement*. New York: Raven Press.

Garcia, J., McGowan, B. K., & Green, K. F. (1972). Biological constraints on conditioning. In A. H. Black & W. F. Prokasy (Eds.), *Classical conditioning II: Current research and theory*. New York: Appleton-Century-Crofts.

Ghiselin, M. T. (1973). Darwin and evolutionary psychology. *Science, 179*, 964-968.

Gibson, J. J. (1966). *The senses considered as perceptual systems*. Boston: Houghton-Mifflin.

Gibson, J. J. (1979). *The ecological approach to visual perception*. Boston: Houghton-Mifflin.

Gibson, J. J., & Pick, A. D. (1963). Perception of another person's looking behavior. *American Journal of Psychology, 76*, 386-394.

Goodall, J. (1968). The behavior of free-living chimpanzees in the Gombe Stream Reserve. *Animal Behavior Monographs, 1*, 161-311.

Gottlieb, G. (1976). Conceptions of prenatal development: Behavioral embryology. *Psychological Review, 83*, 215-234.

Hager, J. C., & Ekman, P. (1979). Long-distance transmission of facial affect signals. *Ethology and Sociobiology, 1*, 77-82.

Hailman, J. P. (1969). How an instinct is learned. *Scientific American, 221* (6), 98-106.

Hamilton, W. D. (1964). The genetical theory of social behaviour: I and II. *Journal of Theoretical Biology, 7*, 1-52.

Harlow, H. F., & Harlow, M. K. (1970). Developmental aspects of emotional behaviour. In P. Black (Ed.), *Physiological correlates of emotion*. London: Academic Press.

Harper, R. G., Wiens, A. N., & Matarazzo, J. D. (1978). *Nonverbal communication: The state of the art*. New York: Wiley.

Hinde, R. A. (1974). *Biological bases of human social behaviour*. New York: McGraw-Hill.

Hinde, R. A., & Stevenson-Hinde, J. (1973). *Constraints on learning*. London: Academic Press.

Hjortsjö, C. H. (1970). *Man's face and mimic language*. Malmö, Sweden: Nordens Boktryckeri.

Hodos, W., & Campbell, C. B. G. (1969). Scala naturae: Why there is no theory in comparative psychology. *Psychological Review, 76*, 337-350.

Hoffman, M. L. (1981). Is altruism part of human nature? *Journal of Personality and Social Psychology, 40*, 121-137.

Hugdahl, K., & Kärker, A. C. (1981). Biological vs. experiential factors in phobic conditioning. *Behavioural Research and Therapy, 19*, 109-115.

Hull, C. L. (1943). *Principles of behavior*. New York: Appleton-Century-Crofts.

Hygge, S. (1976). Information about the model's unconditioned stimulus and response in vicarious classical conditioning. *Journal of Personality and Social Psychology, 33*, 764-771.

Izard, C. E. (1979). Comment on "Human ethology: Concepts and implications for the sciences of man" by I. Eibl-Eibesfeldt. *Behavioral and Brain Sciences, 2*, 39.

Johansson, G. (1973). Visual perception of biological motion and a model for its analysis. *Perception and Psychophysics, 14*, 201-211.

Johnston, T. D. (1981). Contrasting approaches to a theory of learning. *Behavioral and Brain Sciences, 4*, 125-139.

Johnston, T. D., & Turvey, M. T. (1980). A sketch of an ecological metatheory for theories of learning. In G. H. Bower (Ed.), *The psychology of learning and motivation* (Vol. 14). New York: Academic Press.

Kuhn, T. S. (1962). *The structure of scientific revolutions*. Chicago: The University of Chicago Press.

LaBarbera, J. D., Izard, C. E., Vietze, P., & Parisi, S. A. (1976). Four- and six-month-old infants' visual responses to joy, anger, and neutral expressions. *Child Development, 47*, 535-538.

Lanzetta, J. T., & Orr, S. P. (1980). The influence of facial expressions on the classical conditioning of fear. *Journal of Personality and Social Psychology, 39*, 1081-1087.

Lanzetta, J. T., & Orr, S. P. (1981). Stimulus properties of facial expressions and their influence on the classical conditioning of fear. *Motivation and Emotion, 5*, 225-234.

Lenneberg, E. (1967). *The biological foundations of language*. New York: Wiley.

Lewontin, R. C. (1978). Adaptation. *Scientific American, 239* (3), 157-169.

Lewontin, R. C. (1979). Sociobiology as an adaptionist program. *Behavioral Science, 24*, 5-14.

Lewontin, R. C. (1981). On constraints and adaptation. *Behavioral and Brain Sciences, 4*, 244-245.

Lockhard, R. B. (1971). Reflections on the fall of comparative psychology: Is there a message for us all? *American Psychologist, 25*, 168-179.

Logue, A. W. (1979). Taste aversion and the generality of the laws of learning. *Psychological Bulletin, 86*, 276-296.

Maynard Smith, J. (1978). The evolution of behavior. *Scientific American, 239* (3), 136-145.

Mayr, E. (1974). Behavior programs and evolutionary strategies. *American Scientist, 62,* 650-659.

Mayr, E. (1978). Evolution. *Scientific American, 239* (3), 39-47.

Mineka, S., & Soumi, S. J. (1978). Social separation in monkeys. *Psychological Bulletin, 85,* 1276-1400.

Murdock, G. P. (1945). The common denominator of culture. In R. Linton (Ed.), *The science of man in the world crisis.* New York: Columbia University Press.

Öhman, A. (1979). Fear relevance, autonomic conditioning, and phobias: A laboratory model. In P. O. Sjödén, S. Bates, & W. S. Dockens III (Eds.), *Trends in behavior therapy.* New York: Academic Press.

Öhman, A., & Dimberg, U. (1978). Facial expressions as conditioning stimuli for electroder-mal responses: A case of preparedness? *Journal of Personality and Social Psychology, 36,* 1251-1258.

Öhman, A., Fredrikson, M., & Hugdahl, K. (1978). Towards an experimental model for sim-ple phobic reactions. *Behaviour Analysis and Modification, 2,* 97-114.

Orr, S. P., & Lanzetta, J. T. (1980). Facial expressions of emotion as conditioned stimuli for human autonomic responses. *Journal of Personality and Social Psychology, 38,* 278-282.

Oster, H., & Ekman, P. (1978). Facial behavior in child development. In W. A. Collins (Ed.), *Minnesota symposia on child psychology* (Vol. 14). Hillsdale, NJ: Erlbaum.

Petrinovich, L. (1979). Probabilistic functionalism: A conception of research method. *American Psychologist, 34,* 373-390.

Plomin, R., DeFries, J. C., & McClearn, G. E. (1980). *Behavioral genetics: A primer.* San Francisco: Freeman.

Plotkin, H. C., & Odling-Smee, F. J. (1981a). A multiple-level model of evolution and its implications for sociobiology. *Behavioral and Brain Sciences, 4,* 225-235.

Plotkin, H. C., & Odling-Smee, F. J. (1981b). Possible mechanisms for a multiple-level model of evolution. *Behavioral and Brain Sciences, 4,* 257-268.

Rajecki, D. W. (1973). Imprinting in precocial birds: Interpretation, evidence, and evalua-tion. *Psychological Bulletin, 79,* 48-58.

Rajecki, D. W., Lamb, M. E., & Obmascher, P. (1978). Toward a general theory of infantile attachment: A comparative review of aspects of the social bond. *Behavioral and Brain Sciences, 3,* 417-464.

Rescorla, R. A. (1972). Informational variables in Pavlovian conditioning. In G. H. Bower (Ed.), *The psychology of learning and motivation* (Vol. 6). New York: Academic Press.

Rescorla, R. A. (1980). *Pavlovian second-order conditioning. Studies in associative learning.* Hillsdale, NJ: Erlbaum.

Rescorla, R. A., & Holland, P. C. (1982). Behavioral studies of associative learning in animals. *Annual Review of Psychology, 33,* 265-308.

Revusky, S. (1977). Learning as a general process with an emphasis on data from feeding experiments. In N. W. Milgram, L. Krames, & T. M. Alloway (Eds.), *Food aversion learn-ing.* New York: Plenum.

Rozin, P. (1976). The evolution of intelligence and access to the cognitive unconscious. In J. M. Sprague & A. N. Epstein (Eds.), *Progress in psychobiology and physiological psychol-ogy.* New York: Academic Press.

Rozin, P., & Kalat, J. W. (1971). Specific hungers and poison avoidance as adaptive speciali-zation of learning. *Psychological Review, 78,* 459-486.

Runeson, S. (1977). On the possibility of "smart" perceptual mechanisms. *Scandinavian Journal of Psychology, 18,* 172-179.

Runeson, S., & Frykholm, G. (1984). Kinematic specification of dynamics as an informa-tional basis for person and action perception: Expectation, gender recognition, and deceptive intention. *Journal of Experimental Psychology: General, 112,*585-615.

Rushmer, R. F. (1976). *Structure and function of the cardiovascular system.* Philadelphia: Saunders.

Sackett, G. P. (1966). Monkeys reared in isolation with pictures as visual input: Evidence for an innate releasing mechanism. *Science, 154,* 1468-1473.

Sagan, C. (1977). *The dragons of Eden: Speculations on the evolution of human intelligence.* London: Hodder & Stoughton.

Schwartz, B. (1974). On going back to Nature: A review of Seligman and Hager's Biological boundaries of learning. *Journal of the Experimental Analysis of Behavior, 21,* 183-198.

Schwartz, B. (1981). The ecology of learning: The right answer to the wrong question. *Behavior and Brain Sciences, 4,* 159-160.

Schwartz, G. E., Ahern, G. L., & Brown, S.-L. (1979). Lateralized facial muscle responses to positive and negative emotional stimuli. *Psychophysiology, 16,* 561-571.

Schwartz, G. E., Brown, S.-L., & Ahern, G. L. (1980). Facial muscle patterning and subjective experience during affective imagery: Sex differences. *Psychophysiology, 17,* 75-82.

Schwartz, G. E., Fair, P. L., Mandel, M. R., Salt, P., Mieske, M., & Klerman, G. L. (1978). Facial electromyography in the assessment of improvement in depression. *Psychosomatic Medicine, 40,* 355-360.

Schwartz, G. E., Fair, P. L., Salt, P., Mandel, M. R., & Klerman, G. L. (1976a). Facial muscle patterning to affective imagery in depressed and nondepressed subjects. *Science, 192,* 489-491.

Schwartz, G. E., Fair, P. L., Salt, P., Mandel, M. R., & Klerman, G. L. (1976b). Facial expression and imagery in depression: An electromyographic study. *Psychosomatic Medicine, 38,* 337-347.

Scott, J. P. (1980). The function of emotions in behavioral systems: A systems theory analysis. In R. Plutchik & H. Kellerman (Eds.), *Emotion: Theory, Research, and Experience* (Vol. 1). New York: Academic Press.

Seligman, M. E. P. (1970). On the generality of the laws of learning. *Psychological Review, 77,* 406-418.

Seligman, M. E. P. (1971). Phobias and preparedness. *Behavior Theory, 2,* 307-321.

Seligman, M. E. P., & Hager, J. E. (Eds.) (1972). *Biological boundaries of learning.* New York: Appleton-Century-Crofts.

Skinner, B. F. (1969). *Contingencies of reinforcement: A theoretical analysis.* New York: Appleton-Century-Crofts.

Skinner, B. F. (1971). *Beyond freedom and dignity.* New York: Knopf.

Sroufe, L. A., & Waters, E. (1976). The ontogenesis of smiling and laughter: A perspective on the organization of development in infancy. *Psychological Review, 83,* 173-189.

Staddon, J. E. R. (1975). Learning as adaptation. In W. K. Estes (Ed.), *Handbook of learning and cognitive processes* Vol. 2: *Conditioning and behavior theory.* Hillsdale, NJ: Erlbaum.

Sternberg, R. J. (1980). Sketch of a componential subtheory of human intelligence. *Behavioral and Brain Sciences, 3,* 573-614.

Stotland, E. (1969). Exploratory investigations of empathy. In L. Berkowitz (Ed.), *Advances in experimental social psychology* (Vol. 4). New York: Academic Press.

Trivers, R. L. (1971). The evolution of reciprocal altruism. *Quarterly Review of Biology, 46,* 35-57.

Turvey, M. T., Shaw, R. E., Reed, E. S., & Mace, W. M. (1981). Ecological laws of perceiving and acting: In reply to Fodor and Pylyshyn (1981). *Cognition, 9,* 237-304.

van der Berghe, P. L. (1978). *Man in society.* New York: Elsevier.

van der Berghe, P. L. (1981). Multiple-level evolution: A disagreement to disagree. *Behavioural and Brain Sciences, 4,* 253-254.

van Hooff, J. A. R. A. M. (1972). A comparative approach to the phylogeny of laughter and smiling. In R. A. Hinde (Ed.), *Nonverbal communication.* Cambridge, England: Cambridge University Press.

Vaughan, K. B., & Lanzetta, J. T. (1980). Vicarious instigation and conditioning of facial expressive and autonomic responses to a model's expressive display of pain. *Journal of Personality and Social Psychology, 38,* 909-923.

Vine, I. (1973). The role of facial-visual signalling in early social development. In M. von Cranach & I. Vine (Eds.), *Social communication and movement.* London: Academic Press.

Washburn, S. L. (1978a). Human behavior and the behavior of other animals. *American Psychologist, 33,* 405-418.

Washburn, S. L. (1978b). The evolution of man. *Scientific American, 239* (3), 146-154.

Watson, J. B. (1930). *Behaviorism.* New York: Norton.

Weerts, T. C., & Roberts, R. (1976). The physiological effects of imagining anger-provoking and fear-provoking scenes. *Psychophyiology, 13,* 174 (Abstract).

Williams, G. C. (1981). A defense of monolithic sociobiology and genetic mysticism. *Behavioral and Brain Sciences, 4,* 257.

Wilson, E. O. (1975). *Sociobiology: The new synthesis.* Cambridge, MA: Harvard University Press.

Wilson, E. O. (1978). *On human nature.* Cambridge, MA: Harvard University Press.

Wispé, L. G., & Thompson, J. N., Jr. (1976). The war between the words. Biological versus social evolution and some related issues. *American Psychologist, 31,* 341-347.

Young-Browne, G., Rosenfeld, H. M., & Horowitz, F. D. (1977). Infant discrimination of facial expression. *Child Development, 48,* 555-562.

Chapter 4

The Sociophysiology of Infants and Their Caregivers

Ross A. Thompson and Ann M. Frodi

Psychophysiological measures are attractive to behavioral scientists for many reasons. They can be precisely recorded and provide a broader range of measurement than most other kinds of assessment tools. They are extremely sensitive to changes in arousal and behavioral state and can be used with subjects of various ages since response parameters are broadly comparable throughout most of the life span. Furthermore, the attractiveness of these measures is heightened by theoretical formulations which relate physiological activation to various psychological processes in a relatively straightforward fashion. Thus, psychophysiological measures offer precise, sensitive assessments of phenomena which are otherwise frustratingly difficult to appraise.

In this chapter, we consider the uses and limitations of psychophysiological measures in research concerning the socioemotional responses of infants and their caregivers. Recent years have witnessed a burgeoning interest in the development of infant-parent relationships, and in the effects of individual differences in the harmony of the interactions between a baby and adult (e.g., Ainsworth, Blehar, Waters, & Wall, 1978; Brazelton, Tronick, Adamson, Als, & Wise, 1975; Field, 1979a, 1981; Frodi & Lamb, 1978, 1980; Stern, 1977; Thompson & Lamb, 1983). In much of this research, psychophysiological measures—particularly the cardiac response—have provided direct, sensitive assessments of underlying arousal which have been particularly useful in interpreting more subtle kinds of behavioral or subjective responses. Used in convergent fashion, they have yielded important information concerning dimensions of infant and parent responsiveness.

Among the variety of physiological response measures available to the behavioral scientist, heart rate has been used most often in studies of infants and their caregivers. This is due primarily to interpretational formulations which link changes in the direction of cardiac activity (acceleration or deceleration) to important aspects of the organism's transactions with the environment. We open our discussion with a review and evaluation of this work and indicate several important considerations for the researcher who uses physiological measures to study psychological processes in human subjects. Although we focus upon cardiac measures in this review, we think these considerations are relevant to research applications of other physiological measures as well.

Our subsequent review of research employing psychophysiological measures consists of two parts. In the first, we discuss studies employing heart rate measures to appraise the socioemotional responses of infants. Because of the baby's limited behavioral repertoire and the subtlety of many infant behaviors, cardiac measures have been valuable convergent indices of the baby's socioemotional reactions to stimulus events. In addition to discussing existing studies, we suggest several additional areas of research in which cardiac data can provide useful information.

We then turn to the other half of the infant-parent dyad and discuss how physiological measures have been employed in studies concerning the caregiver's responsiveness to infant smiles and cries. This research literature provides a multifaceted picture of the motivational processes underlying a parent's caregiving behaviors and how these are influenced by characteristics of the infant and of the parent. Together with subjective mood assessments, psychophysiological measures have yielded important information about normal and maladaptive infant-parent interactions.

Throughout, this review reflects our optimism concerning the advantages offered by psychophysiological measures—particularly cardiac activity—to students of infant and parent responsiveness. While inferring psychological processes on the basis of physiological assessments must always be done cautiously, the research we discuss demonstrates some of the useful applications of psychophysiological assessments in research efforts to better understand the socioemotional dimensions of the infant-parent relationship.

The Meaning of the Cardiac Response

Interest within the behavioral sciences in the applications of heart rate data has been stimulated primarily by the formulations of John and Beatrice Lacey (Lacey, 1959; Lacey & Lacey, 1970, 1974), who have related cardiac acceleration to a person's "rejection of the environment," while "environmental intake" or receptiveness has been associated with cardiac deceleration. The importance of this formulation can best be appreciated when viewed in the context of contemporary thinking. Two decades ago, autonomic (especially sympathetic) nervous system activity was viewed as a general and unidimensional indicator of "arousal," "activation," or "psychological tension" in the organism (e.g., Duffy, 1962; Lindsley, 1951; Malmo, 1959). There were two important implications of this approach. One was that the variety of autonomic indicators, such as heart rate, respiration, electrodermal activity, vasconstriction, and other indicators, should intercorrelate highly in response to stimulus events, or at least exhibit directional consistency. The second was that ANS activity was viewed as a derivative of the cortical processes which elicit arousal in an organism (i.e., an effector system) rather than as independently influencing central processing of stimulus events.

In reviewing the research relevant to this perspective, Lacey (1959) found sufficient evidence to question both the usefulness of a unidimensional arousal construct, and the validity of viewing autonomic responses solely as effector systems.

He found, for example, that autonomic measures do not intercorrelate well under certain stimulus conditions, both because individuals often exhibit a stronger response on one autonomic index than on another (a phenomenon Lacey called "individual response stereotypy") and because of underlying directional variation as well. Thus, patterns of autonomic arousal appear to be multiply determined and are not simple, direct derivatives of organismic activation. In addition, Lacey proposed that some autonomic systems—most notably, the cardiac response—have their own independent contributions to cortical processing. Reviewing the neurophysiological literature, Lacey and Lacey (1958, 1970) marshalled evidence to indicate that increases in cardiovascular activity exert an inhibitory effect upon cortical activity through their influence upon pressure receptors located in the aortic arch and carotid sinus. The functioning of cardiovascular-CNS mechanisms, they concluded, constitutes a negative feedback system in which increased heart rate activity results in decreased sensory and motor acuity, while cardiac deceleration results in improved cortical functioning. This was, of course, the opposite of the formulation proposed by the activation theorists. The results of derivative research, particularly in reaction-time studies, have been generally supportive of this approach (e.g., Lacey & Lacey, 1970; Lacey, Kagan, Lacey, & Moss, 1963).

Importantly, the Laceys also proposed that the direction of cardiac activity may be related to the organism's *intended* transaction with the environment.

> Far from being the "end of the chain," then, these *autonomic responses become stimuli* to internal receptors, whose activation may well lead reflexively to changes in the relationship of the organism to the environment, in terms both of the organism's accessibility to environmental inputs and the organism's motor outputs. . . . In a sense, then, the acceleration or deceleration of the heart could be considered to be something like an instrumental act of the organism, leading either to increased ease of "environmental intake," or to a form of "rejection of the environment." (Lacey, 1959, p. 199; see also Lacey & Lacey, 1970) (Reprinted by permission of the author and of the American Psychological Association.)

Rather than operating merely as an effector system, then, cardiac activity itself was viewed as either facilitating or inhibiting cortical processing as part of the organism's total response "package."

The Lacey formulation has been subject to a number of critiques (e.g., Elliot, 1972; Hahn, 1973) as well as empirical challenges (e.g., Lazarus, Speisman, & Mordkoff, 1963). Foremost among these have been objections to the breadth with which the bipolar "environmental intake"–"rejection of the environment" dimension has been defined, especially in research contexts. Like many global indices of psychological functioning, this dimension has been conceptually elusive, particularly in attempts to operationalize these terms in ways which are relevant to specific stimulus conditions. Furthermore, its meaning has become blurred over time as a greater variety of research findings have been interpreted within this theory. For example, serial time-estimation tasks entail the kind of concentration—and "rejection" of competing stimuli—which would be associated with cardiac acceleration in the Laceys' formulation. Instead, heart rate slowing is typically the accompanying response, which is explained in terms of "response intention" (Lacey & Lacey, 1970). In short, definitional ambiguity contributes to the breadth of psychological processes to which the theory can be applied, but does not foster its efficient testing in research contexts.

Part of this problem, of course, is that a variety of influences can affect cardiac activity independently of an organism's intended transaction with the environment. These include verbalization instructions (Campos & Johnson, 1966), respiration (Sroufe & Morris, 1973), muscle activity (Obrist, Webb, Sutterer, & Howard, 1970a; 1970b), and behavioral state (Campos & Brackbill, 1973; Graham & Jackson, 1970). Indeed, Obrist and his colleagues (Obrist, 1976; Obrist, Howard, Lawler, Galosy, Meyers, & Gaeblein, 1974; Obrist, Webb, & Sutterer, 1969; Obrist, Webb, Sutterer, & Howard, 1970a; 1970b) have proposed that changes in cardiac activity are primarily a derivative of the metabolic demands of the body musculature attendant to the initiation or inhibition of motor activity. It is certainly true that muscular exertion—involved not only in gross motor activity but also in laughing, crying, and other behaviors—fosters an increase in heart rate, and its cessation a decline in cardiac activity. It is unclear, however, whether this is an entirely adequate explanation for observed changes in cardiac rate in various stimulus contexts (see Elliot, 1972; Hahn, 1973; Sroufe & Waters, 1977).

In short, the cardiac response is a multidetermined event, and inferences concerning the psychological meaning of heart rate must take these alternative influences into consideration. Although psychological processes and behaviorial activity frequently covary in a consistent manner (e.g., orienting to a stimulus is usually accompanied by behavioral stilling), there is clearly no simple, straightforward relationship between complex psychological states in humans and the direction of cardiac activity. This means that the investigator must control for other potential sources of influence before making psychological interpretations of cardiac changes. This can be done through a variety of controls on motor behavior, the use of direct and indirect convergent measures of psychological responding, and, in some instances, through the use of statistical procedures (see Campos, 1976; Graham & Jackson, 1970; Lewis, 1974; Sroufe & Waters, 1977).

Despite these objections (and, in some ways, because of them), the Laceys' formulation has generated a great deal of interest among behavioral scientists who have found this interpretive framework useful for studying aspects of cognitive and affective processes. Some of this research has been devoted to understanding the complex motivational processes underlying a parent's caregiving behaviors, and, in particular, a caregiver's responsiveness to the smiles and cries of infants. Using the hypothesized intake-rejection dimension, researchers have assessed the physiological and phenomenological responses of adults to these socioemotional signals of infants and have studied how adult responses are affected by characteristics of the infant as well as of the adult. We review this research in a subsequent section of this chapter.

In the developmental study of cardiac functioning, Frances Graham and her colleagues (Graham, 1979; Graham & Clifton, 1966; Graham & Jackson, 1970) have offered a reformulation of the Laceys' approach which has proven useful to understanding cardiac behavior in young infants. Linking the Laceys' neurophysiological formulations with Sokolov's (1963) theory of orienting and defensive arousal systems, Graham views heart rate activity as part of the organism's generalized, reflexive response to environmental events. Cardiac deceleration is regarded as a component of the orienting reflex (OR), a response system which enhances sensory receptivity and strengthens cortical associative processes. According to Graham, the OR is typically elicited by any change in ongoing stimulation. Acceleration of heart rate, on the other hand, is viewed as part of the defensive reflex (DR), which functions to limit the effects of high-intensity, unpleasant stimulation. More recently, Graham (1979) has also described the DR as an "output-enhancing" system which facilitates motor readiness for a response and has suggested that this response system may serve as a more generalized "activation" system for the organism since it frequently occurs in response to stimuli at moderate intensity levels as well as high-intensity stimulus events.

Much of the research deriving from Graham's formulation has focused upon the conditions evoking attentional orienting (and cardiac slowing) in young infants. Several researchers have found, for example, that onset of the OR varies according to the complexity of stimulus events from a very young age (e.g., Kagan & Lewis, 1965; Lewis, Kagan, Campbell, & Kalafat, 1966; McCall & Kagan, 1967). Other research has concerned whether cardiac decleration can be observed in newborns, which would support the early, adaptive functions of the orienting response (see Berg & Berg, 1979, for a review). In contrast, much less developmental research has examined the development of the DR or "activation" response, even though this response system is most relevant to early socioemotional development. In the next section, we review research in which cardiac responding has been used as an indicator of the development of fearful reactions to depth perception and, more pertinently, unfamiliar adults. We also suggest potentially fruitful applications of cardiac data for future researchers.

Taken together, whether viewed from the standpoint of the organism's intended transaction with the environment or the functioning of reflexive response systems, the bidirectional quality of heart rate responding seems to provide the behavioral researcher with meaningful information about the relationship between the human organism and the environment. To be sure, the interpretation of cardiac data is always contingent upon the evaluation of alternative explanations for observed changes in the direction of response (including motor activity, vocalization, etc.), and this compels the researcher to use heart rate measures in the context of other convergent indices of psychological functioning. Employed in this context, however, cardiac measures can provide a significant increase in measurement sensitivity.

The Cardiac Response and Socioemotional Responsiveness in Infants

The sensitivity of cardiac activity offers several advantages when appraising the socioemotional reactions of infants. Because infants are nonverbal and have a limited behavioral repertoire, the range of meaningful responses which can be reliably measured is necessarily limited, especially at young ages. Moreover, apart from a set of readily identified behaviors (such as smiling, laughing, and crying), infant facial and vocal expressions of affect are often subtle and difficult to assess.

For example, an infant who greets the approach of an unfamiliar adult with behavior stilling, raised eyebrows, clear and focused eyes, and a partially opened mouth may be indicating attentional interest on one hand, or the escalation of wariness on the other. In instances like these, when behavioral responses are poor discriminators, the bidirectional heart rate response can provide a valuable convergent index of the baby's emotional reaction.

Unfortunately, however, relatively little research has employed cardiac measures as a convergent index of socioemotional responding in social contexts. For this reason, our discussion in this section is heuristic as well as substantive: in addition to discussing a number of existing research applications, we also indicate important areas for future work in which heart rate measures are likely to be informative. Our discussion begins with research concerning the development of fear responses in infants to cues of depth perception on the "visual cliff" apparatus, to provide a paradigmatic example of the value of cardiac data in interpreting the subtle behavioral reactions of young infants. Then we turn to studies concerning infant reactions to unfamiliar adults to show how heart rate measures have been used to appraise the early development of sociability.

Fear on the Visual Cliff

The visual cliff was designed by Gibson and Walk (1960; Walk & Gibson, 1961) to assess depth perception in the young of different species. The apparatus consists of a large glass-covered table which is divided into two sections. One section, called the "shallow" side, consists of a checkered surface resting immediately beneath the glass. The other section, called the "deep" side, has the checkered surface about 40 inches below the glass. These sections are divided by a small board which straddles the two halves of the apparatus.

The typical procedure for testing depth perception consists of placing the infant on the center board, and then having the mother beckon or call to the baby from either the deep or shallow side of the apparatus. If the infant crosses the shallow side to get to mother but refuses to cross the deep side, depth perception (and fear of depth) may be inferred. Depth perception has been demonstrated in this way in locomotor human infants, as well as in the young of other species (e.g., Gibson & Walk, 1960; Walk & Gibson, 1961).

The major disadvantage of this procedure, of course, is its reliance upon locomotor responses, making it impossible to assess depth perception in human infants much before the second half of the first year of life. An alternative procedure, however, remedies this difficulty. By directly placing infants on either the shallow or deep side of the cliff, researchers can observe whether the deep side differentially elicits indications of fear or distress in prelocomotor infants. In this situation, cardiac activity can provide useful information concerning infant reactions to these perceptual cues. Thus, we might expect to note heart rate acceleration in prelocomotor infants who could perceive depth—and feared it—when placed directly onto the deep side of the cliff (i.e., the DR), but showed no such response to the shallow side. In contrast, there should be no difference in cardiac activity between deep- and shallow-side placements in the absence of depth perception.

In a developmental study, Schwartz, Campos, and Baisel (1973) assessed the cardiac and behavioral responses of 5-month-old (prelocomotor) and 9-month-old (locomotor) infants to the visual cliff. Each infant was given two placements on each side of the cliff in the mother's absence. Both behavioral and cardiac measures were obtained; the latter were converted into change scores in relation to a prestimulus baseline. All response measures were time-locked in order to obtain precise temporal comparisons across the different measures.

Their results were striking. Both the 5-month-old and the 9-month-old infants showed differential responding to the deep side of the cliff, but in markedly different ways. As expected, the older babies displayed cardiac acceleration on the deep side of the cliff, with little change in heart rate on the shallow side. The younger infants, on the other hand, exhibited strong *deceleratory* responses to the deep side coupled with no change to the shallow side. In short, cues of perceptual depth were discriminated by infants at both ages, but the responses of the younger infants reflected orienting and interest (i.e., the OR), in contrast to the more fearful reactions of the older babies (i.e., the DR).

Analyses of the behavioral data provided support for this conclusion while indicating the greater sensitivity of the cardiac data. Measures of positive and negative vocalizations and limb movements yielded no age differences, whereas the measure of visual attention did show age changes. However, intercorrelations among the cardiac and behavioral variables showed that heart rate responses correlated negatively with positive vocalizations, positively with negative vocalizations, and negatively with ratings of visual attention. In short, heart rate slowing was associated with indices of focused attention and positive affect, and cardiac acceleration co-occurred with distress vocalizations.

In this study, then, the interpretation of the developmental shift in cardiac responses to the deep side of the cliff was corroborated by the behavioral measures. In addition, the absence of any consistent correlations between heart rate and gross-motor activity (i.e., limb movement) disconfirmed an alternative interpretation of changes in cardiac activity as an epiphenomenon of changes in somatic movement (e.g., Obrist et al., 1970a, 1970b). Moreover, it was clear that cardiac activity was more sensitive to developmental changes than were most of the behavioral measures. Taken together, these data suggest a developmental change in the nature of infants' reactions to cues of perceptual depth which parallels the development of locomotor ability. In locomotor infants, depth cues elicit indications of fear and distress, while prelocomotor infants evidently perceive depth without responding fearfully (see Campos, 1976; Campos, Hiatt, Ramsay, Henderson, & Svejda, 1978).

Stranger Reactions

A developmental phenomenon which undergoes a similar shift at about the same time concerns infants' reactions to strangers. For quite some time, developmental investigators have noted that negative reactions to unfamiliar adults begin sometime during the second half of the first year of life (e.g., Bronson, 1972; Schaffer, 1966). So widely accepted was the development of stranger fearfulness during this time that one investigator called it the "8-month anxiety" (Spitz, 1965). More recently, however, the generality of this phenomenon was called into question by Rheingold and Eckerman (1973), who reported that few of the infants they observed showed frank fear of strangers during this period, and many responded in a sociable, affiliative manner. For this reason, they doubted that stranger anxiety was a significant developmental milestone in the first year.

Since the Rheingold and Eckerman critique, researchers have sought to refine the construct of "stranger anxiety" as well as to identify the factors which influence how infants react to unfamiliar adults. Some investigators, for example, have studied the influence of contextual factors, such as the mother's presence (Campos, Emde, Gaensbauer, & Henderson, 1975; Morgan & Ricciuti, 1969; Skarin, 1977), the manner of the stranger's approach (Bretherton, 1978), where the assessment occurs (Sroufe, Waters & Matas, 1974), and similar variables. In addition, methods of assessing stranger reactions have also been improved, reflecting an awareness that most infants respond to an unfamiliar adult with a mixture of mild negative reactions ("wariness") and sociable responses.

Clearly, cardiac measures can provide useful convergent data in studies of stranger responsiveness by helping researchers to interpret the more subtle behavioral responses of infants. Prolonged staring at the stranger coupled with cardiac acceleration, for example, may indicate an increase in wariness, whereas accompanying heart rate slowing may reflect greater interest and attention in the absence of wariness.

In one such application, Campos, Emde, Gaensbauer, and Henderson (1975) assessed the convergence of heart rate and behavioral responses of infants to a strange adult. In their developmental study, 5- and 9-month-old infants seated in high-chairs were filmed as they were slowly approached by an unfamiliar adult. Simultaneously, heart rate was recorded by a polygraph which was synchronized with the film record. The mode of approach consisted of four 15-s phases: an *entry* phase (with the stranger speaking conversationally to the child from a distance of about 13 ft), an *approach*, an *intrusion* (stranger reaches out to child), and an *exit* phase. An additional feature of this study was the assessment of infants in mother's presence and in her absence. Cardiac activity was converted into change scores as described earlier; behavioral responses consisted of ratings of the infant's facial expression, gaze direction, motor activity, and a summary judgment of overall distress.

The findings from the cardiac and behavioral measures were highly consistent. First, a developmental shift was observed for heart rate as well as for measures of facial expression and gaze direction. The younger infants showed cardiac deceleration to the stranger's presence coupled with a generally interested, positive facial expression and gazing directed to the stranger's face. The older infants, in contrast, showed marked heart rate acceleration combined with a more sober, negative facial expression and more frequent gaze-avoidance of the stranger. Overall, the 5-month-olds were rated as showing less distress than the 9-month-olds. Interestingly, of the behavioral measures, the global index of motor activity was least sensitive to these developmental differences.

Second, this cardiac-behavioral convergence was reflected in other ways. All measures, for example, were sensitive to the different stages of the stranger's approach: there were more indications of fear or wariness (and concomitant heart rate increases) as the stranger moved closer. In addition, Campos and his colleagues selected a subset of infants at each age who were rated as showing a progressively increasing amount of distress reflected in their facial expressions. For these babies, regardless of age, cardiac activity simultaneously accelerated in a highly consistent fashion.

There was also evidence, however, for the greater sensitivity of cardiac activity. For example, the heart rate measure varied significantly according to mother's presence or absence, with higher acceleration when the infant was alone with the stranger. This difference was also reflected in the global distress rating, but not on the other behavioral measures. Thus, cardiac activity was more sensitive to certain dimensions of stress than were the behavioral indicators, and this has been found by other investigators as well. For example, Sroufe, Waters, and Matas (1974) found that infants' cardiac responses to an approaching stranger were more acceleratory in an unfamiliar laboratory setting compared to the familiar home environment. Their behavioral measures were less sensitive to this contextual influence.

Other investigators have also found a concordance between cardiac and behavioral measures of stranger responsiveness in infants. Waters, Matas, and Sroufe (1975) compared the cardiac responses of infants rated "wary" and "non-wary" during the intrusion phase of a stranger approach (babies showing clear-cut distress were excluded from this analysis). Peak heart rate accelerations were significantly higher for wary infants at 6, 7, and 8 months of age. Similarly, Provost and Décarie (1974) coded the behaviors of 9- and 12-month-olds as "accepting" or "rejecting" during a prolonged stranger approach. The former group showed uniphasic cardiac decelerations throughout the stranger approach, while the latter exhibited large acceleratory responses. In both groups, however, heart rate increased as the stranger became more proximal.

Taken together, these findings reflect the important contributions of cardiac assessments to understanding developmental changes in stranger responsiveness during the first year. Consistently, cardiac decelerations have been associated with behavioral indications of attention and interest, while heart rate increases have been linked to subtle cues of wariness and aversion in infants. Throughout this research, cardiac responses have proven to be the more sensitive measures, while their interpretation has been securely based in the convergent behavioral data.

From the standpoint of developmental theory, these patterns of findings are meaningful ones. The findings of Campos' research group indicate, in particular, that important changes in the appraisal of certain stimulus events seem to occur during the second half-year of life. On both the visual cliff and during the approach of an unfamiliar adult, earlier indications of interest and orienting change into aversive reactions in the older infant. Whether this is due to cognitive maturity, the development of fearfulness as a response system, specific kinds of developmental experiences, or other factors is currently the focus of further research inquiry.

The Interpretation of Cardiac Responses

With this broad array of evidence for the interpretability of the bidirectional cardiac response, why not use cardiac activity as a single, reliable index of socioemotional responsiveness in infants? Why is its interpretation dependent upon convergent behavioral measures which are, on the whole, less sensitive?

The primary reason we cannot make simple, straightforward inferences concerning the psychological meaning of cardiac activity is that heart rate is subject to influences which do not fit easily into an environmental intake-rejection dimension. One example of this is smiling. In a reanalysis of their earlier study, Emde, Campos, Reich, and Gaensbauer (1978) looked at the cardiac accompaniments to the *positive* reactions of infants to the approaching stranger. They found that for the 9-month-olds, instances of smiling were accompanied by heart rate increases during the stranger's entry phase. For the 5-month-olds, in turn, cardiac declerations were of smaller magnitude when the infant smiled. Smiling was also accompanied by heart rate increases at other points in the stranger approach at both ages. Other analyses indicated that the relationship between smiling and heart rate acceleration was not directly mediated by an accompanying increase in motor activity, although there were some associations between smiling and activity level.

Another example of interpretational complexity is noted by Campos (1976; Campos et al., 1975), who has observed that certain kinds of high-intensity crying are associated with marked cardiac slowing. For example, when an infant cries hard and then continues to exhale without producing sound, it is accompanied by a high-magnitude deceleration which persists briefly before heart rate increases again. Campos has interpreted this bradycardia as a physiological reflex intruding upon a primarily acceleratory cardiac pattern.

Both phenomena create difficulty for straightforward interpretations of heart rate activity in terms of environmental receptiveness and rejection. In the first case, cardiac acceleration seems to be a derivative of a more generalized state of arousal experienced by the child and certainly does not reflect a defensive reaction. In the latter case, there is a competing physiological response confounding a dominant acceleratory trend which cannot be interpreted as environmental intake. Thus, the sensitivity of heart rate responding is a mixed blessing; it provides more acute assessments of the organism's environmental transactions, but is a complexly determined response system as well. Identification of the factors underlying a change in cardiac activity thus requires the use of convergent behavioral indices.

These interpretational complexities are well illustrated in Lewis, Brooks, and Haviland's (1978) study of cardiac-behavioral convergence in infants. Selecting individual cases from a larger sample, they presented several examples of how the heart rate and facial expressions of infants failed to converge in the theoretically expected manner during a graduated stranger approach. In some instances, for example, smiling at the stranger was accompanied by cardiac acceleration; in others, subtle facial indications of wariness were not accompanied by increased heart rate. While there are interpretational problems inherent in the use of ideographic data such as these, they demonstrate some of the difficulties in relying upon cardiac data alone to draw inferences concerning a baby's psychological appraisal of events. Heart rate cues alone, when interpreted within the intake-rejection formulation, sometimes led to interpretations which were contradicted by the behavioral evidence. In addition, these stranger-approach sequences were conducted in the mother's presence, and thus the infant's reactions to the stranger were probably milder than they would have been in mother's absence (see Campos et al., 1975 and discussion above; also Skarin, 1977). The greater subtlety of these reactions could also have contributed to the cardiac-behavioral dyssynchrony noted by Lewis and his colleagues.

In short, because heart rate responses are multidetermined and competing influences are especially apparent in more subtle stimulus conditions, cardiac measures alone do not yield informative inferences concerning underlying psychological processes. These interpretations must always depend upon convergent behavioral measures.

Other Applications

The added sensitivity of cardiac activity in research contexts must, of course, be balanced against added equipment costs, inconvenience to subjects and researchers, and other difficulties in gathering heart rate data. We feel, however, that the potential advantages of cardiac data have not yet been exploited by students of early socioemotional development and merit further consideration. In this section, we describe some of these areas of application.

Cardiac activity and the temporal patterning of emotional responses. Current models of socioemotional development emphasize the importance of the infant's cognitive processing or "appraisal" of stimulus events prior to the onset of an emotional response (e.g., Rothbart, 1973, 1976; Sroufe, 1979). Such a linkage between cognitive and socioemotional processes is an important conceptual tool in the developmental study of affect. But how do we examine the nature of this appraisal process—its duration, for example, or its temporal course? Cardiac measures may be useful by providing a highly sensitive assessment of cognitive processing of stimuli *prior to* the onset of a specific emotional reaction.

To be sure, the extent to which cardiac reactions consistently precede emotional ones is not entirely clear. Campos and his colleagues (1975), for example, indicated that there was no consistent precedence of cardiac activation over emotional reaction in the infants they observed. However, analyzing beat-by-beat scores during a stranger approach, Waters and his colleagues (1975) reported one case in which gaze-aversion occurred in an infant as heart rate was accelerating but just prior to its peak. After gaze-aversion, heart rate decelerated again. Because of this, Waters (Waters et al., 1975; Sroufe & Waters, 1977) has suggested that gaze-aversion serves a "cut-off" function in infants to limit the escalation of distress in threatening circumstances, such as a stranger approach. Its purpose is to enable the infant to disengage from threatening stimuli before distress climaxes and to permit the infant a period of settling before reengaging the stranger. Unfortunately, no other data were reported beyond this single case; Field (1981), however, has noted similar observations during arousing bouts of mother-infant interaction.

Another perspective on the temporal patterning of cardiac-affective reactions is provided by Vaughn and Sroufe (1979), who analyzed the temporal relationship between cardiac acceleration and infant crying during an incongruity game with the mother. Employing a microanalytic approach, they reported that heart rate at 10 beats prior to the onset of crying was significantly faster than during a prestimulus baseline, and that heart rate continued to accelerate in linear fashion until the beginning of a cryface (typically three beats prior to cry) and finally the cry itself. Although there was no assessment of motor activity, they reported that typically the infant was stilled and attentionally fixed upon the mother during this build-up period (approximately 4-5 s long). They interpreted this acceleratory trend to reflect the baby's cognitive appraisal or evaluation of mother's activity prior to a distress response. Because of the gradual buildup, they concluded, cardiac acceleration was clearly not simply a derivative of increased motor activity which accompanies crying itself.

Such an information-processing view of emotional arousal is, of course, consistent with the frequently reported observation of an initial, brief, phasic cardiac slowing at the first appearance of a stranger, followed by the tonic acceleration noted in older infants (Campos et al., 1975; Sroufe et al., 1974; Sroufe & Waters, 1977; Vaughn & Sroufe, 1979). This momentary, affectively neutral period of appraisal could show important development changes as well as meaningful variability in different stimulus conditions. The sensitivity of cardiac responding could thus be useful to understanding these influences upon emotional arousal.

Cardiac activity and mother-infant interaction. Recent interest in the development of the mother-infant relationship has focused on early interactions and their mutual regulation by the mother and baby (e.g., Brazelton, Tronick, Adamson, Als, & Wise, 1975; Stern, 1974a, 1974b, 1977). Mothers, of course, have a range of behaviors with which to modulate social exchanges with their infants. The baby's repertoire, by contrast, is more limited and during the early months relies heavily upon directed gazing and gaze-aversion (Stern, 1974a, 1977). The appraisal of cardiac activity over the course of brief mother-infant interactions may help to explain the functions of these behaviors for the baby.

Field (1981; see also Field, 1979a; 1979b) has used cardiac measures in this manner to study infants' attentional responses to maternal social activities. In her research, 3- and 4-month-old babies were observed in several different interactional situations with the mother: one in which the mother was highly intrusive and overactive, another in which she was naturally interactive, and a third in which she was subdued and inexpressive. Behavioral and cardiac data were gathered for each 3-min interactive session. Field reported that both the duration of attention to mother and cardiac activity varied with mother's interactive animation. When the mother was naturally interactive, the infant gazed at her longer and exhibited small increases in heart rate. In contrast, when mothers were either overactive or subdued, infants showed marked gaze-avoidance and significantly elevated heart rate.

Field has interpreted these differences in terms of the baby's information-processing capabilities. Interaction with the mother is likely to be a stimulating experience to young infants, with the degree of stimulation linked to the quality of the mother's interactive behaviors. When mothers are gradual and well-modulated in their interactive bids (which normally occurs during their face-to-face exchanges), infants can respond with sustained attention, and they continue to orient to her. However, when mothers are overactive, they present greater information-processing demands, requiring "time-out" (gaze-aversion) for the baby's processing and eliciting cardiac acceleration (DR) due to "stimulus overload" (Field, 1979a). Field thus argues that gaze-aversion modulates escalating arousal in highly stimulating circumstances, in a manner similar to that proposed by Waters. In the situations in which the mother was subdued, on the other hand, Field suggests that gaze-aversion may have resulted from the mother's violation of the baby's interactive expectations for her. Although the possible role of motor activity (e.g., limb movement, crying) as a variable mediating the relationship between gaze-aversion and heart rate increases was not completely assessed, Field (1981) presented some data indicating that cardiac accelerations were not due to observable motor movements in infants in certain conditions.

Research of this kind illustrates some of the potentially useful applications of cardiac data to the study of mother-infant interaction and its effects upon the baby. Further research could fruitfully be devoted to exploring the effects of more subtle variations of maternal activity upon infant arousal (e.g., changes in the quality or intensity of her facial expressions, vocalizations, etc.), as well as variations in behavior due to the caregiver's gender (fathers compared to mothers) and caregiving experience.

Summary

As we have indicated, cardiac data provides such useful information in studies of early socioemotional development because it helps researchers interpret the subtle behavioral reactions of infants. This has clearly been the case in studies of depth perception and stranger reactions, and, we suggest, heart rate measures can be equally valuable in other areas of research. While the psychological inferences drawn from cardiac responses depend upon convergent behavioral measures, the sensitivity of heart rate makes it a valuable assessment tool.

Focusing on infant responsiveness is, of course, only part of the picture provided by infant-parent interaction: cardiac measures can also provide useful information about adult's reactions to a baby's smiles and cries. We now turn to this area of research inquiry.

The Cardiac Response and Adult Reactions to Infant Smiles and Cries

Psychophysiological measures have also been used to study adult responses to infants. In this research, psychophysiological indices have been employed in convergence with pencil-and-paper mood assessments to study the effects of a baby's socioemotional signals upon the adult. The purpose of these studies has been to understand some of the complex motivational processes underlying adult responsiveness to a baby, and how this varies according to infant and adult characteristics.

More than in infancy research, studies of this kind have employed a variety of psychophysiological measures, including skin conductance, skin potential, and diastolic and systolic blood pressure responses in addition to heart rate. Cardiac measures, however, have figured most prominently in these studies and are therefore the focus of our review.

In this section, we discuss both the rationale for using cardiac measures in studies of adult responsiveness and then review the results of research in this area. Following this, we describe several specific studies which have sought to identify variations in adult responsiveness as a function of characteristics of the infant (e.g., temperament, prematurity, etc.) and characteristics of the adult (e.g., caregiving experience, gender, etc.).

Adult Responsiveness to Infant Signals

What are the motivational characteristics underlying an adult's responsiveness to a baby's smiles and cries? According to ethologically oriented theorists like Bowlby (1969) and Lamb (1978), the infant's socioemotional signals figure prominently in the maintenance of proximity to an adult, which is the goal of these and other "attachment behaviors." On one hand, infant smiling entices adults into remaining nearby by eliciting positive affect. On the other hand, the aversive quality of infant crying promotes caregiver proximity to relieve the baby's distress. In the latter case, of course, feelings of sympathy or empathy for the baby must also be aroused so that the adult approaches rather than avoids the baby (Murray, 1979). Importantly, with both smiling and crying, infant signaling and adult responsiveness create important early contexts for caregiver-infant interaction, such as in face-to-face play encounters, or the relief of the infant's distress (Thompson & Lamb, 1983). Thus, an appreciation of the effects of the infant's socioemotional signals upon the adult can contribute to a better understanding of the development of infant-parent relationships and how they are influenced by salient characteristics of each partner.

The bidirectional cardiac response can be a useful measure of adult responses by providing an index of physiological arousal to accompany more subjective assessments of mood state. Furthermore, when interpreted within the context of the Laceys' bipolar continuum, the direction of change in cardiac responding provides valuable information about the quality of an adult's responsiveness. That is, heart rate acceleration may be taken as an indication of activation or negative arousal, while cardiac slowing may reflect an attentional, orienting response. In research of this kind, when combined with other physiological indices of arousal (i.e., skin conductance increases) or aversion (i.e., diastolic blood pressure increases; see Frodi, 1978), cardiac responses can contribute importantly to a multidimensional portrayal of physiological activation to infants' smiles and cries.

This strategy was used in an initial set of studies conducted by Frodi and her colleagues concerning the physiological and phenomenological responses of adolescents and adult parents to infant smiles and cries (Frodi & Lamb, 1978; Frodi, Lamb, Leavitt, & Donovan, 1978). In these investigations, male and female subjects viewed a 6-min videotaped episode of a 5-month-old infant who was viewed first as alert and quiescent (2 min), then as either smiling or crying (2 min), and finally as quiescent again (2 min). During these presentations, heart rate, skin conductance, and systolic and diastolic blood pressure responses were recorded. These data were later analyzed as change scores in relation to a prestimulus baseline value. Following the presentations, subjects were then asked to fill out a mood adjective checklist to describe their subjective reactions to each of the three videotape segments.

Frodi and her colleagues reported that infant smiling and crying elicited different responses on both physiological and phenomenological measures. Diastolic blood pressure and skin conductance measures were significantly higher during the crying segments for both the parents and adolescents. The smiling segments, in contrast, elicited no changes on these measures. For the adolescents, infant crying segments also evoked cardiac acceleration, while heart rate slowing was the typical response to the smiling segments. Heart rate data were not recoverable for adults in this early work, although in a later study (Frodi & Lamb, 1980), similar cardiac responses were noted in an adult control group. Finally, the mood adjective checklist responses revealed that both groups reported feeling happier when viewing the smiling infant, but significantly more distressed and irritated when the baby was crying. Interestingly, the adolescents also reported feeling more "sorry for" the crying baby, a finding which was not replicated with the adult sample who had infants of their own!

Taken together, these findings indicate that smiling and crying in infants yield distinctly different socioemotional responses in both adult caregivers and adolescents. In short, smiling results in attentiveness and positive affect, while crying is clearly an aversive stimulus, indexed both physiologically and phenomenologically.

Other studies have replicated this pattern of findings. For example, Doerr, Disbrow, and Caulfield (1977) monitored the physiological responses of parents to a sequence of 12 videotaped scenes of parent-infant interaction. The scenes were either pleasant (e.g., the child was happily engaged in play), unpleasant (e.g., the child was shown fussy and irritable), or neutral (pastel-colored light only). They reported that unpleasant scenes elicited increases in heart rate and skin conductance, whereas the pleasant scenes did not.

There is some evidence that the aversive quality of the infant cry may consist primarily of its auditory component—the abrasive, high-pitched scream—rather than just the sight of the screwed-up cryface on a distressed baby. Both Donovan, Leavitt, and Balling (1978) and Wiesenfeld and Klorman (1978) have reported that *silent* pictures or videotapes of infant crying produced cardiac slowing in mothers, although the mood ratings reported by Wiesenfeld and Klorman indicated significantly greater feelings of aversion to the distressed baby. Donovan and her colleagues also found that the order of presentation influenced cardiac responsiveness. When the crying images were preceded by pictures of a smiling baby, the deceleratory response was larger than when the crying pictures were shown first.

Thus, the sound of an infant crying may contribute more to its perceived aversiveness to adult caregivers than the visual image of a distressed baby presented alone. Such a conclusion accords well with the proximity-eliciting functions of infant crying—that is, its adaptive value of summoning the attention of caregivers from a distance (Bowlby, 1969). When the visual image of a distressed infant is presented alone, on the other hand, the adult must devote greater effort to "read" or interpret infant facial cues in the absence of a compelling, clear-cut auditory signal. This is reflected in cardiac slowing (OR) when viewing a silent picture of an upset baby.

Variations in Responsiveness Due to Infant Characteristics

Infant familiarity. In the research reported thus far, adolescents and adults were responding to the socioemotional cues of unfamiliar infants. In a series of investigations, Wiesenfeld and his colleagues have sought to determine whether a caregiver's responses differ according to whether the cues were produced by their own child or not. In an initial study, Wiesenfeld and Klorman (1978) reported that brief (10-15 s duration), silent videotaped segments of infant crying and smiling elicited significant cardiac accelerations when mothers were viewing their own infants. In contrast, tapes of unfamiliar infants produced primarily deceleratory responses. In a second study, Wiesenfeld, Malatesta and DeLoach (1981) presented brief audiotapes of infant crying to mothers while monitoring their heart rate and skin conductance responses. They reported that when mothers heard their own infants crying, they responded with a marked increase in skin conductance and a cardiac response characterized by an initial deceleration followed by an acceleratory change. In contrast, the cardiac response to the cries of an unfamiliar child was uniformly deceleratory and was accompanied by a much smaller change in skin conductance. Mothers also rated their own baby's cries as significantly more unpleasant than those of an unfamiliar baby.

Wiesenfeld and Malatesta (1982) suggest that these patterns of responsiveness reflect a caregiver's differential attachment to a specific infant—that is, one's own baby. When seeing or hearing the cues of an unfamiliar child, a mother's response is one of orienting and attention, but not of arousal per se. In contrast, the sight or sound of her own baby elicits cardiac acceleration and other indications of excitement and arousal in a mother. In the case of infant smiling, the acceleratory response seems to reflect positive affect and enjoyment (as it may with infants; see Emde et al., 1978, and discussion above). In the case of infant crying, on the other hand, Wiesenfeld and Malatesta suggest that heart rate increases reflect the caregiver's "empathetic distress" for the baby's upset.

While the finding of differential responsiveness to familiar smiles and cries is not unexpected, it is less clear why the cries of an unfamiliar infant elicited cardiac slowing in these studies, while cardiac acceleration was more characteristic of the adults studied by Frodi and her colleagues, as described above. Methodological differences between these laboratory groups may help explain the discrepancy. Videotaped vignettes were significantly longer in duration in Frodi's research (2 min) compared to Wiesenfeld's studies (15 s), and both visual and auditory cues were combined in Frodi's work. Thus, the impact of infant crying may have been significantly greater in the research conducted by Frodi and her colleagues. In addition, differences in task orientation may have influenced the different patterns of adult responsiveness. While in Frodi's research adults were simply asked to pay attention to the videotaped vignettes, Wiesenfeld and colleagues (1981) asked each parent to identify whether the cry belonged to her own infant or not after each stimulus segment. It is thus possible that cardiac slowing reflected the mother's sustained monitoring of the unfamiliar infant's cries in order to decide whether they were produced by her own infant or not. Wiesenfeld and his colleagues found, in fact, that the mothers in their study identified their own infants' cries with near-perfect accuracy, and that most of their errors were ones of false positives—that is, incorrectly believing that an unfamiliar cry was actually produced by their own child. Thus, there may have been greater uncertainty when listening to an unfamiliar cry ("*Could* this be my baby?"), reflected in physiological indices of sustained attention and orienting.

Temperament and birth status. Acoustic and spectrographic analyses indicate that the quality of crying exhibited by premature infants, babies rated as temperamentally "difficult," and infants with perinatal complications differ importantly from the cries of normal infants (e.g., Boukydis, 1980; Zeskind & Lester, 1978; see review by Boukydis, 1981). The former groups tend to have more abrasive and higher-pitched cries which are arrythmic and unpredictable in their temporal course. These differences have an important influence on parental perceptions of the cry and their responsiveness to it. For example, Boukydis (1980) examined the skin potential responses of 24 parent couples and 12 nonparent couples who listened to 24-s audio recordings of different infant cries. The infants producing these cries varied in temperament, according to parent ratings on the Infant Characteristics Questionnaire (Bates, Freeland, & Lounsbury, 1979): four were rated as difficult, four as easy, and four as average babies. Boukydis found that the cries of the difficult infants elicited the highest skin potential responses in adults. In contrast, the easy infants elicited the lowest skin potential responses, with the average infants' cries falling in between.

In another study (Frodi, Lamb, Leavitt, Donovan, Neff, & Sherry, 1978), 64 mothers and fathers were shown videotapes of either premature or full-term crying infants; these tapes consisted of quiescent-cry-quiescent segments as previously described. Consistent with earlier research by this group, the crying episodes elicited marked increases in parental diastolic blood pressure, skin conductance, and heart rate responses. However, the cry of the premature infant elicited significantly greater autonomic arousal across all physiological measures than did the cry of the full-term infant. This was accompanied by mood ratings indicating greater irritation, annoyance, and disturbance while hearing the premature infant's cry. In addition, this study was designed to independently assess the effects of the cry characteristics (i.e., the auditory stimulus) and the facial appearance of the infant (i.e., the visual stimulus) in counterbalanced fashion. Sound tracks were dubbed so that half of the normal and half of the premature infants were paired with the cry of a normal baby, while the other half emitted the cry of a premature infant. Frodi and her colleagues found that, in general, the premature cry itself was a more potent stimulus than the facial appearance of the premature baby, but the strongest activation occurred when the cry *and* face of the premature infant appeared together.

Interestingly, similar differential effects can occur simply due to how a baby is labeled. Frodi, Lamb, Leavitt, and Donovan (1978) manipulated parental frame of reference by describing the infant in a videotaped presentation as either normal, temperamentally difficult, or premature. Adult caregivers showed greater activation when the baby was labeled premature than to the other labeling conditions, especially on the skin conductance measure. Thus, a parent's interpretational set also has a strong influence upon the quality of responsiveness to infant crying, independent of the aversive characteristics of the cry itself. Since parents tend to infer more complex psychological motives in the cries of difficult babies—describing them as "frustrated" or "wanting attention" rather than just being hungry or cold (Boukydis, 1980)—it is easy to see how a parent's interpretational set, together with the aversive acoustic properties of the cry itself, could contribute to impaired infant-parent interactions in cases of prematurity, prenatal or perinatal problems, or temperamental difficulty.

Variations in Responsiveness Due to Adult Characteristics

Gender. The research evidence is mixed concerning gender differences in adult responsiveness to infant smiles and cries. On physiological assessments, Boukydis (1980) and Frodi and her colleagues (Frodi et al., 1978a, 1978b; Frodi & Lamb, 1978) both reported no significant differences between male and female subjects, and differences on mood assessments were likewise small and inconsistent. Frodi and Lamb (1978) have contended that these findings argue against the existence of innate sex differences in caregiving capacities. On the other hand, Wiesenfeld and his colleagues (1981) reported that mothers, but not fathers, showed evidence of differential physiological responsiveness to the sound of their own infant crying. In contrast to mothers, fathers exhibited cardiac deceleration to *both* familiar and unfamiliar crying segments. Since the fathers in this study were also strikingly less accurate than the mothers in correctly identifying the source of the cry, consistent heart rate slowing may have derived from the fathers' continued efforts to determine whether the cry came from their own child or not. Additional research may help in reconciling these divergent findings by exploring further the effects of these variations in response set.

Prior caregiving experiences. In view of the importance of a parent's interpretational set, it seems likely that the nature of prior caregiving experiences would have an influence upon an adult's responsiveness to infant smiles and cries. On the question of the *amount* of caregiving experiences, however, the evidence is inconsistent. Wiesenfeld and Malatesta (1982) reported that multiparous mothers responded with cardiac acceleration of greater magnitude to the sound of their own infants' crying compared to primiparous mothers. There were no differences reported on the other measures. On the other hand, Boukydis (1980) reported that primiparas displayed greater activation (i.e., skin potential responses) to cry audiotapes than did multiparas. Finally, as indicated earlier, Frodi and her colleagues have found comparable patterns of physiological responsiveness to infant smiling and crying in adolescent and adult samples.

Another perspective on the effects of caregiving experience concerns variations in the *quality* of prior experiences. For example, characteristics of a mother's own baby may influence how she responds to infant smiles and cries. In a study by Frodi, Lamb, and Willie (1981), the birth status of the mother's own child was found to influence her perceptions of infant crying. Sixteen mothers of premature babies and 16 mothers of full-term infants viewed and heard videotapes of crying premature and full-term infants. As expected, in both groups of mothers, the onset of crying by either infant evoked increases in diastolic blood pressure, skin conductance, and cardiac activity. However, the mothers who had premature infants of their own responded with heightened arousal to the cries of both kinds of infants. Frodi and her colleagues suggested that the mothers of premature infants might have become sensitized to the atypical features of their own babies and thus exhibited a heightened generalized sensitivity to the stimulus babies presented in this study.

Adult responsiveness may also be influenced by how they perceive the temperament of their own baby. Parents who regularly have to contend with a crying, fussy baby may interpret an infant's socioemotional cues much differently than parents who perceive their baby to be more placid. In order to assess the importance of this variable, Donovan, Leavitt, and Balling (1978) assessed mothers' perceptions of their own infants and measured the cardiac and skin conductance responses of these mothers as they watched silent pictures of a crying and smiling 3-month-old. Half the mothers saw the smiling picture prior to the crying picture, with the order reversed for the others. Mothers who perceived their own infants as temperamentally difficult were physiologically less responsive to the picture presented second, whether of smiling or crying, than were the mothers of temperamentally "easy" babies. They concluded that the former group seemed less sensitive to the *change* in infant affective expressions, perhaps as a result of their prior caregiving experiences.

In an intriguing investigation, Donovan (1981) has suggested that one of the factors mediating variations in caregiver responsiveness may be the mother's history of success or failure in soothing her infant's crying. Drawing upon current theories of learned helplessness (Seligman, 1975; 1978), Donovan has proposed that recurrent experiences of unsuccessful caregiving ministrations would render a mother less sensitive and competent in future instances of infant distress. Such an hypothesis would help to explain the differences in caregiver responsiveness in the study described above.

To test this idea, Donovan subjected 48 mothers to one of the three pretreatment conditions varying their ability to control infant crying and then observed their responses to a series of test trials entailing instrumental responses to terminate crying audiotapes. There were three pretreatment conditions: one in which mothers could successfully terminate the cry audiotape by pushing a button ("escape"), a second in which button-pressing was unsuccessful in terminating the cry ("inescape"), and a third, control condition, in which mothers listened to the cry tapes without having any instrumental response at all. After 35 pretreatment trials, the mothers were then observed in a second situation in which a different instrumental response was effective in terminating the cry for mothers in all 3 pretreatment conditions. In these test trials, the onset of the cry was preceded by a 10-s anticipatory period during which the impending cry was signaled by means of a light. Throughout these test trials, both cardiac and behavioral responses were monitored.

Donovan found that mothers in the inescape pretreatment group responded with impaired performance on the test trials compared to mothers in the other two groups. They failed to terminate the cry more frequently and were generally slower to use the termination response compared to other mothers. On the cardiac measures, Donovan reported that only mothers who had earlier been successful in terminating the cry (i.e., those in the "escape" condition) displayed heart rate slowing during the anticipatory phase. Mothers in the other groups exhibited either no change in cardiac activity, or heart rate acceleration.

Donovan's findings thus indicate one of the ways in which prior experiences may either hinder or facilitate a caregiver's responsiveness to infant cues. Mothers with successful prior experience in soothing an infant's crying may be more attentive to the cry on future occasions, and more successful in caregiving ministrations. In contrast, earlier failures at soothing infant distress may render a caregiver less attentive and generally less competent at soothing behaviors on future occasions. These laboratory results provide a basis for further investigation of variations in caregiver responsiveness and its correlates in more naturalistic circumstances.

Dimensions of personality. Differences in the personality characteristics of caregivers have, of course, figured prominently in theoretical and empirical considerations of caregiving competence (see review by Lamb & Easterbrooks, 1981). Only one study, however, has been designed to appraise these differences using psychophysiological measures. Wiesenfeld, Whitman, and Malatesta (1981) differentiated "high-empathy" and "low-empathy" female undergraduates on the basis of their responses to a pencil-and-paper measure of emotional empathy (Mehrabian & Epstein, 1972). Heart rate measures were recorded while the women observed a series of silent videotapes of smiling, crying, and quiescent infants. These episodes were then viewed a second time, during which a series of subjective mood assessments were completed.

Wiesenfeld and his colleagues reported that high-empathy and low-empathy groups differed in their overall cardiac responses to the videotaped episodes: high-empathy women showed a significant acceleratory trend to the infant stimuli, while low-empathy women exhibited no appreciable heart rate change. Women in the high-empathy group also responded with higher-magnitude skin conductance responses. Convergent ratings of the facial expressions of these undergraduates while they viewed the videotaped episodes yielded no significant differences, however. The mood assessments, in turn, indicated that high-empathy subjects felt significantly greater happiness when the smiling infant was viewed, and greater sadness in watching the sad baby, than did the low-empathy subjects. (These findings are not convergent data, strictly speaking, since the mood assessments were obtained during a second viewing of the videotaped episodes.) In short, the high-empathy women displayed more intense reactions to the infant stimuli, indexed both physiologically and phenomenologically.

Interestingly, this study is one of the few in which adults who are not parents have been assessed. It would therefore be useful to know whether similar differences could be observed in adult women (and men) who have infants of their own. If so, it would provide a valuable perspective on the construct of "maternal sensitivity" which has been so strongly implicated in the development of individual differences in infant-parent relationships (e.g., Ainsworth, 1973; Ainsworth, Bell, & Stayton, 1974).

The child-abusing parent. The confluence of experiential and personality-based influences on adult caregiving is well illustrated in the case of child abuse (see Parke, 1977; Parke & Collmer, 1975, for recent reviews). Two recent studies have found significant differences between abusing and nonabusing parents in their psychophysiological responses to stimuli involving children. Frodi and Lamb (1980) compared the heart rate, blood pressure, and skin conductance responses of 14 abusive and 14 nonabusive mothers who were shown videotapes of a smiling and a crying baby in the fashion earlier described (i.e., quiescent/smile or cry/quiescent segments). Each parent saw both videotapes in counterbalanced order. Frodi and

Lamb reported that both abusers and nonabusers responded to the crying infant with cardiac acceleration and increases in diastolic blood pressure and skin conductance, although these increases were generally greater among the abusers. On the mood ratings, abusive parents also reported greater annoyance and less sympathy than did the nonabusive parents.

When viewing the smiling baby, however, the responses of abusers and nonabusers were strikingly different. Like other parents tested by Frodi and her colleagues, the nonabusive parents responded to infant smiles with negligible changes or declines in cardiac activity and other indices of physiological arousal. The abusers, on the other hand, responded with increased physiological activation on all three measures, and their mood ratings indicated greater indifference and less happiness when seeing the smiling baby compared with nonabusers. In short, it was difficult to distinguish between abusers' reactions to smiling and crying infants, especially on the cardiac measures. They reacted as if both kinds of socioemotional signals were aversive to them.

A somewhat similar study was conducted by Doerr, Disbrow, and Caulfield (1977). In this research, abusive parents, neglectful parents, and a normal parent control group viewed videotaped sequences of pleasant and unpleasant parent-infant interactions. On the basis of both cardiac and skin conductance data, abusive and neglectful parents failed to differentiate between pleasant and unpleasant episodes, whereas the control parents did so significantly and in the expected manner. In general, the neglectors exhibited lower levels of physiological activation to the stimulus materials, and the abusers somewhat higher levels, compared to the matched control group.

Both Frodi and Lamb (1980) and Doerr and his colleagues (1977) accounted for their findings by arguing that abusive and neglectful parents responded insensitively to child-related stimuli, whether positive or negative in affective tone. These differences may arise from factors in the premorbid personality of these parents or as a result of a history of unsuccessful interactions with their children—interactions which were unsuccessful either because the children were difficult to manage or because the adults were lacking parenting skills, or both. More extensive longitudinal study is required to address these questions of etiology.

Interestingly, in the research we have reviewed, high-magnitude cardiac activation to infant cues has been found to be characteristic of both abusive parents (Frodi & Lamb, 1980) and high-empathy undergraduate women (Wiesenfeld, Whitman, & Malatesta, 1981). Of course, similar patterns of physiological arousal do not necessarily reflect similar motive states: the mood measures in these studies indicated much greater sympathy and interest on the part of the undergraduates. Moreover, methodological differences between these studies render problematic a direct comparison of their findings (e.g., silent videotapes vs. videotapes with audio; caregiving vs. noncaregiving adult subjects; different modes of analysis of cardiac data, etc.). Nevertheless, these results suggest important areas of future investigation concerning individual differences in caregiving competence and their developmental origins. We suggest that the convergent use of psychophysiological measures and subjective mood assessments will continue to yield informative findings in this area of inquiry.

Summary

Taken together, these studies exemplify the preemptory impact of a baby's socioemotional signals upon adults. A baby's smiling and cooing not only produce feelings of interest and happiness, but cardiac signs of orienting and attention. Even more compelling, however, is the infant cry, which elicits multiple signs of physiological activation and subjective feelings ranging from irritability and annoyance to sympathy and concern. These influences upon the adult also vary according to infant and adult characteristics, suggesting that any thoroughgoing analysis of the impact of infant socioemotional cues upon adult responsiveness must take into consideration the familiarity of the baby and the adult's prior caregiving experiences, as well as intrinsic characteristics of each partner.

In this research, psychophysiological measures—particularly the cardiac response —have provided a highly sensitive appraisal of adult responsiveness and its correlates. In convergence with mood assessments, they have provided data concerning not only the overall hedonic tone of responsiveness, but also the magnitude of arousal accompanying that response. Their meaning, in turn, has largely been corroborated by the mood measures, although this has, at times, contributed to a broadening of the hypothesized environmental receptiveness-rejection continuum (i.e., Lacey, 1959), particularly with respect to the interpretation of increases in heart rate activity. Nevertheless, when firmly grounded in convergent assessments, the sensitivity of the cardiac response has proven to be a highly valuable measurement tool in these research studies.

Conclusion

Our discussion of the sociophysiology of infants and their caregivers has been wide-ranging: we have considered topics from stranger fear in infants to parental responses to familiar and unfamiliar infant crying. This reflects, in many ways, the broad applications of psychophysiological measures to the study of socioemotional responsiveness of infants and parents. These applications have been highly informative to researchers. Owing to the increased sensitivity of cardiac activity, for example, we now have evidence for a developmental shift in infants' fearful reactions to unfamiliar persons during the first year. We also understand better the effects of infant crying upon adult caregivers, and how these effects vary according to characteristics of the baby (e.g., birth status, temperament) and parent (e.g., caregiving experience, personality). And we can appreciate better the variant interpretations of infant socioemotional cues which may be characteristic of parents who abuse or neglect their young children.

Although cardiac activity has proven to be the more sensitive assessment mode, heart rate and behavioral measures have usually covaried in these research studies. This is to be expected, of course, since both approaches assess different aspects of an organism's response "package" to a stimulus event. This cardiac-behavioral convergence is also important to the interpretation of changes in heart rate since, as we have emphasized, cardiac activity alone is unlikely to yield meaningful inferences of psychological activity apart from convergent behavioral assessments. In all, the value of cardiac measures is their heightened sensitivity to phenomena which are often difficult to appraise with behavioral measures alone.

The convergent value of psychophysiological measures as assessment tools derives, of course, from the interaction of social and physiological processes in the human organism. In studying infants and their caregivers, both response dimensions viewed together will lead to informative conclusions about early socioemotional development.

References

Ainsworth, M. D. S. (1973). The development of infant-mother attachment. In B. Caldwell & H. Ricciuti (Eds.), *Review of child development research* (Vol. 3). Chicago: University of Chicago Press.

Ainsworth, M. D. S., Bell, S. M., & Stayton, D. J. (1974). Infant-mother attachment and social development: Socialisation as a product of reciprocal responsiveness to signals. In M. P. M. Richards (Ed.), *The integration of the child into a social world*. Cambridge, England: Cambridge University Press.

Ainsworth, M. D. S., Blehar, M. C., Waters, E., & Wall, S. (1978). *Patterns of attachment*. Hillsdale, NJ: Erlbaum.

Bates, J. E., Freeland, C. A. B., & Lounsbury, M. L. (1979). Measurement of infant difficultness. *Child Development, 50*, 794-803.

Berg, W. K., & Berg, K. M. (1979). Psychophysiological development in infancy: State, sensory function, and attention. In J. D. Osofsky (Ed.), *Handbook of infant development*. New York: Wiley.

Boukydis, C. F. Z. (1980). An analog study of adult physiological and self report responding to infant cries. *Cry Research Newsletter, 2*, 2-6.

Boukydis, C. F. Z. (1981, April). *Adult perception of infant cry as a social signal*. Paper presented to the biennial meeting of the Society for Research in Child Development, Boston.

Bowlby, J. (1969). *Attachment and loss*, Vol. 1. *Attachment*. New York: Basic Books.

Brazelton, T. B., Tronick, E., Adamson, L., Als, H., & Wise, S. (1975). Early mother-infant reciprocity. In *Parent-infant interaction* (Ciba Foundation Symposium 33). Amsterdam: Elsevier.

Bretherton, I. (1978). Making friends with one-year-olds: An experimental study of infant-stranger interaction. *Merrill-Palmer Quarterly, 24*, 29-51.

Bronson, G. W. (1972). Infants' reactions to unfamiliar persons and novel objects. *Monographs of the Society for Research in Child Development, 37* (Serial No. 148).

Campos, J. J. (1976). Heart rate: A sensitive tool for the study of emotional development in the infant. In L. P. Lipsitt (Ed.), *Developmental psychobiology: The significance of infancy*. Hillsdale, NJ: Erlbaum.

Campos, J. J., & Brackbill, Y. (1973). Infant state: Relationship to heart rate, behavioral response, and response decrement. *Developmental Psychobiology, 6*, 9-19.

Campos, J. J., Emde, R. N., Gaensbauer, T. J., & Henderson, C. (1975). Cardiac and behavioral interrelationships in the reactions of infants to strangers. *Developmental Psychology, 11*, 589-601.

Campos, J. J., Hiatt, S., Ramsay, D., Henderson, C., & Svejda, M. (1978). The emergence of fear on the visual cliff. In M. Lewis & L. Rosenblum (Eds.), *The development of affect*. New York: Plenum.

Campos, J. J., & Johnson, H. J. (1966). The effects of verbalization instructions and visual attention on heart rate and skin conductance. *Psychophysiology, 2*, 305-310.

Doerr, H. O., Disbrow, M. A., & Caulfield, C. (1977, October). *Psychophysiological response patterns in child abusers*. Paper presented to the annual meeting of the Society for Psychophysiological Research, Philadelphia.

Donovan, W. J. (1981). Maternal learned helplessness and physiologic response to infant crying. *Journal of Personality and Social Psychology, 40,* 919-926.

Donovan, W. J., Leavitt, L. A., & Balling, J. D. (1978). Maternal physiological response to infant signals. *Psychophysiology, 15,* 68-74.

Duffy, E. (1962). *Activation and behavior.* New York: Wiley.

Elliott, R. (1972). The significance of heart rate for behavior: A critique of Lacey's hypothesis. *Journal of Personality and Social Psychology, 22,* 398-409.

Emde, R. N., Campos, J., Reich, J., & Gaensbauer, T. J. (1978). Infant smiling at five and nine months: Analysis of heartrate and movement. *Infant Behavior and Development, 1,* 26-35.

Field, T. M. (1979a). Interaction patterns of preterm and term infants. In T. M. Field, A. M. Sostek, S. Goldberg, & H. H. Shuman (Eds.), *Infants born at risk.* New York: Spectrum.

Field, T. M. (1979b). Visual and cardiac responses to animate and inanimate faces by young term and preterm infants. *Child Development, 50,* 188-194.

Field, T. M. (1981). Infant gaze aversion and heart rate during face-to-face interactions. *Infant Behavior and Development, 4,* 307-315.

Frodi, A. M. (1978). Experiential and physiological responses associated with anger and aggression in women and men. *Journal of Research in Personality, 12,* 335-349.

Frodi, A. M., & Lamb, M. E. (1978). Sex differences in responsiveness to infants: A developmental study of psychophysiological and behavioral responses. *Child Development, 49,* 1182-1188.

Frodi, A. M., & Lamb, M. E. (1980). Child abusers' responses to infant smiles and cries. *Child Development, 51,* 238-241.

Frodi, A. M., Lamb, M. E., Leavitt, L. A., & Donovan, W. L. (1978). Fathers' and mothers' responses to infant smiles and cries. *Infant Behavior and Development, 1,* 187-198.

Frodi, A. M., Lamb, M. E., Leavitt, L. A., Donovan, W. L., Neff, C., & Sherry, D. (1978). Fathers' and mothers' responses to the faces and cries of normal and premature infants. *Developmental Psychology, 14,* 490-498.

Frodi, A. M., Lamb, M. E., & Willie, D. (1981). Mothers' responses to the cries of normal and premature infants as a function of the birth status of their own child. *Journal of Research in Personality, 15,* 122-133.

Gibson, E. J., & Walk, R. D. (1960). The "visual cliff." *Scientific American, 22,* 64-71.

Graham, F. K. (1979). Distinguishing among orienting, defense, and startle reflexes. In H. D. Kimmel, E. H. van Olst, & J. F. Orlebeke (Eds.), *The orienting reflex in humans.* Hillsdale, NJ: Erlbaum.

Graham, F. K., & Clifton, R. K. (1966). Heart-rate change as a component of the orienting response. *Psychological Bulletin, 65,* 305-320.

Graham, F. K., & Jackson, J. C. (1970). Arousal systems and heart rate responses. In H. W. Reese & L. P. Lipsitt (Eds.), *Advances in child development and behavior* (Vol. 5). New York: Academic.

Hahn, W. W. (1973). Attention and heart rate: A critical appraisal of the hypothesis of Lacey and Lacey. *Psychological Bulletin, 79,* 59-70.

Kagan, J., & Lewis, M. (1965). Studies of attention in the human infant. *Merrill-Palmer Quarterly, 11,* 95-127.

Lacey, J. I. (1959). Psychophysiological approaches to the evaluation of psychotherapeutic process and outcome. In E. A. Rubinstein & M. B. Parloff (Eds.), *Research in psychotherapy* (Vol. 1). Washington, DC: American Psychological Association.

Lacey, J. I., Kagan, J., Lacey, B. C., & Moss, H. A. (1963). The visceral level: Situational determinants and behavioral correlates of autonomic response patterns. In P. H. Knapp (Ed.), *Expression of the emotions in man.* New York: International Universities Press.

Lacey, J. I., & Lacey, B. C. (1958). The relationship of resting autonomic activity to motor impulsivity. *Research Publications Association for Research in Nervous and Mental Disease, 36,* 144-209.

Lacey, J. I., & Lacey, B. C. (1970). Some autonomic-central nervous system interrelationships. In P. Black (Ed.), *Physiological correlates of emotion.* New York: Academic Press.

Lacey, J. I., & Lacey, B. C. (1974). On heart rate responses and behavior: A reply to Elliott. *Journal of Personality and Social Psychology, 30,* 1-18.

Lamb, M. E. (1978). Influence of the child on marital quality and family interaction during the prenatal, perinatal, and infancy periods. In R. M. Lerner & G. B. Spanier (Eds.), *Child influences on marital and family interaction: A life-span perspective.* New York: Academic.

Lamb, M. E., & Easterbrooks, M. A. (1981). Individual differences in parental sensitivity: Origins, components, and consequences. In M. E. Lamb & L. R. Sherrod (Eds.), *Infant social cognition.* Hillsdale, NJ: Erlbaum.

Lazarus, P. S., Speisman, J. C., & Mordkoff, A. M. (1963). The relation between autonomic indicators of psychological stress: Heart rate and skin conductance. *Psychosomatic Medicine, 25,* 19-30.

Lewis, M. (1974). The cardiac response during infancy. In R. F. Thompson & M. M. Patterson (Eds.), *Methods in Physiological Psychology. I. Bioelectric recording techniques, Part C. Receptor and Effector Processes.* New York: Academic.

Lewis, M., Kagan, J., Campbell, H., & Kalafat, J. (1966). The cardiac response as a correlate of attention in infants. *Child Development, 37,* 63-71.

Lewis, M., Brooks, J., & Haviland, J. (1978). Hearts and faces: A study in the measurement of emotion. In M. Lewis & L. Rosenblum (Eds.), *The development of affect.* New York: Plenum.

Lindsley, D. B. (1951). Emotion. In S. S. Stevens (Ed.), *Handbook of experimental psychology.* New York: Wiley.

Main, M. B. (1977). Analysis of a peculiar form of reunion behavior seen in some day-care children: Its history and sequelae in children who are home-reared. In R. A. Webb (Ed.), *Social development in childhood: Day-care programs and research.* Baltimore: Johns Hopkins University Press.

Malmo, R. B. (1959). Activation: A neurophysiological dimension. *Psychological Review, 66,* 367-386.

McCall, R. B., & Kagan, J. (1967). Stimulus-schema discrepancy and attention in the infant. *Journal of Experimental Child Psychology, 5,* 381-390.

Mehrabian, A., & Epstein, N. (1972). A measure of emotional empathy. *Journal of Personality, 40,* 525-543.

Morgan, G. A., & Ricciuti, H. N. (1969). Infants' responses to strangers during the first year. In B. M. Foss (Ed.), *Determinants of infant behavior IV.* London: Methuen.

Murray, A. D. (1979). Infant crying as an elicitor of parental behavior: An examination of two models. *Psychological Bulletin, 86,* 191-215.

Obrist, P. A. (1976). The cardiovascular-behavioral interaction—As it appears today. *Psychophysiology, 13,* 95-107.

Obrist, P. A., Howard, J. L., Lawler, J. E., Galosy, R. A., Meyers, K. A., & Gaeblein, C. J. (1974). The cardiac-somatic interaction. In P. Obrist, A. Black, J. Brener, & L. DiCara (Eds.), *Cardiovascular Psychophysiology.* Chicago: Aldine.

Obrist, P. A., Webb, R. A., & Sutterer, J. R. (1969). Heart rate and somatic changes during aversive conditioning and a simple reaction time task. *Psychophysiology, 5,* 696-723.

Obrist, P. A., Webb, R. A., Sutterer, J. R., & Howard, J. L. (1970a). Cardiac deceleration and reaction time: An evaluation of two hypotheses. *Psychophysiology, 6,* 695-706.

Obrist, P. A., Webb, R. A., Sutterer, J. R., & Howard, J. L. (1970b). The cardiac-somatic relationship: Some reformulations. *Psychophysiology, 6,* 569-587.

Parke, R. D. (1977). Socialization into child abuse: A social interactional perspective. In J. L. Tapp & F. J. Levine (Eds.), *Justice and the individual in society: Psychological and legal issues.* New York: Holt, Rinehart & Winston.

Parke, R. D., & Collmer, C. (1975). Child abuse: An interdisciplinary analysis. In E. M. Hetherington (Ed.), *Review of child development research* (Vol. 5). Chicago: University of Chicago Press.

Provost, M., & Décarie, T. G. (1974). Modifications du rythme cardiaque chex des enfants de 9-12 mois au cours de la rencontre avec la personne étrangère. *Canadian Journal of Behavioral Science, 6,* 154-168.

Rheingold, H. L., & Eckerman, C. O. (1973). Fear of the stranger: A critical examination. In H. W. Reese (Ed.), *Advances in child development and behavior* (Vol. 8). New York: Academic.

Rothbart, M. K. (1973). Laughter in young children. *Psychological Bulletin, 80*, 247-256.

Rothbart, M. K. (1976). Incongruity, problem-solving, and laughter. In A. J. Chapman & H. C. Foot (Eds.), *Humour and laughter: Theory, research, and applications*. New York: Wiley.

Scarr-Salapatek, S. (1976). Comments on "Heart rate: A sensitive tool for the study of emotional development in the infant." In L. P. Lipsitt (Ed.), *Developmental psychobiology: The significance of infancy*. Hillsdale, NJ: Erlbaum.

Schaffer, H. R. (1966). The onset of fear of strangers and the incongruity hypothesis. *Journal of Child Psychology and Psychiatry, 7*, 95-106.

Schwartz, A. N., Campos, J. J., & Baisel, E. J. (1973). The visual cliff: Cardiac and behavioral responses on the deep and shallow sides at five and nine months of age. *Journal of Experimental Child Psychology, 15*, 86-99.

Seligman, M. E. P. (1975). *Helplessness: On depression, development, and death*. San Francisco: Freeman.

Seligman, M. E. P. (1978). Comment and integration. *Journal of Abnormal Psychology, 87*, 165-179.

Skarin, K. (1977). Cognitive and contextual determinants of stranger fear in six- and eleven-month-old infants. *Child Development, 48*, 537-544.

Sokolov, E. (1963). *Perception and the conditioned reflex*. New York: Macmillan.

Spitz, R. A. (1965). *The first year of life*. New York: International Universities Press.

Sroufe, L. A. (1979). Socioemotional development. In J. D. Osofsky (Ed.), *Handbook of infant development*. New York: Wiley.

Sroufe, L. A., & Morris, D. L. (1973). Respiratory-cardiac relationships in children. *Psychophysiology, 10*, 377-382.

Sroufe, L. A., & Waters, E. (1977). Heart rate as a convergent measure in clinical and developmental research. *Merrill-Palmer Quarterly, 23*, 3-27.

Sroufe, L. A., Waters, E., & Matas, L. (1974). Contextual determinants of infant affective response. In M. Lewis & L. Rosenblum (Eds.), *The origins of fear*. New York: Wiley.

Stern, D. N. (1974a). Mother and infant at play: The dyadic interaction involving facial, vocal, and gaze behaviors. In M. Lewis & L. Rosenblum (Ed.), *The effects of the infant on its caregiver*. New York: Wiley.

Stern, D. N. (1974b). The goal and structure of mother-infant play. *Journal of the American Academy of Child Psychiatry, 13*, 402-421.

Stern, D. N. (1977). *The first relationship*. Cambridge, MA: Harvard University Press.

Thompson, R. A., & Lamb, M. E. (1983). Individual differences in dimensions of socioemotional development in infancy. In R. Plutchik & H. Kellerman (Eds.), *Emotion: Theory, research and experience*. Vol. 2. *Emotions in early development*. New York: Academic.

Vaughn, B., & Sroufe, L. A. (1979). The temporal relationship between infant heart rate acceleration and crying in an aversive situation. *Child Development, 50*, 565-567.

Walk, R. D., & Gibson, E. J. (1961). A comparative and analytical study of visual depth perception. *Psychological Monographs, 75* (Whole No. 519).

Waters, E., Matas, L., & Sroufe, L. A. (1975). Infants' reactions to an approaching stranger: Description, validation, and functional significance of wariness. *Child Development, 46*, 348-356.

Wiesenfeld, A. R., & Klorman, R. (1978). The mother's psychophysiological reactions to contrasting affective expressions by her own and an unfamiliar infant. *Developmental Psychology, 14*, 294-304.

Wiesenfeld, A. R., & Malatesta, C. Z. (1982). Infant distress: Variables affecting responses of caregivers and others. In L. W. Hoffman, R. Gandelman, & H. Schiffman (Eds.), *Parenting: Its causes and consequences*. Hillsdale, NJ: Erlbaum.

Wiesenfeld, A. R., Malatesta, C. Z., & DeLoach, L. L. (1981). Differential parental response to familiar and unfamiliar infant distress signals. *Infant Behavior and Development, 4*, 281-295.

Wiesenfeld, A. R., Whitman, P. B., & Malatesta, C. Z. (1981). Individual differences in responsivity to infants: Evidence in support of an empathy concept. Unpublished manuscript, Rutgers University. (Earlier version presented at the annual meeting of the Eastern Psychological Association, New York, April, 1981.)

Zeskind, P. S., & Lester, B. M. (1978). Acoustic features and auditory perceptions of the cries of newborns with prenatal and perinatal complications. *Child Development, 49,* 580-589.

Part II
Physiology of Social Cognition, Perception, Learning, and Memory

Chapter 5
Autonomic Self-Perception and Emotion

Edward S. Katkin, Jim Blascovich, and Marlon R. Koenigsberg

Introduction and Background

The purpose of this chapter is to analyze the role of autonomic activity and its perception in the experience and expression of emotion. Although there are many cogent theoretical approaches to the study of emotion, ranging from the purely neurophysiological to the purely cognitive, the focus of this chapter will be on work that has emerged from social psychological explanations of emotional behavior.

Arousal-Based Theories of Emotion

Current theory and research on the relationship between arousal and emotion can be traced to 1884, when William James suggested that emotional experience results from the perception of specific bodily responses. James's theory placed substantial emphasis on the importance of the internal milieu as a determinant of emotional experience, and, although it was influential for a few decades, it lost many of its adherents after it was criticized sharply by Cannon (1927).

Cannon demonstrated that cats could exhibit signs of "emotional behavior" even after they were sympathectomized. According to Cannon, the sympathectomy (i.e., separating the cat's cortex from its autonomically innervated organs) rendered the cat insensate with respect to its viscera. Yet, his cats remained able to express what Cannon called "sham emotion," a pattern of behavior (piloerection, arched back, claw extension) which appeared similar to the "emotional behavior" that would be expected from normal cats in response to threat.

Although it is fruitless to argue about the degree of "emotion" that may be attributed to a cat's behavior, the fact that sympathectomized cats could show any behavior that could be labeled "emotional" convinced Cannon and others that James's peripheral theory of emotion was untenable. In addition, Cannon argued that emotional behavior, as evidenced by motor action and facial expression, had a shorter latency than the autonomic responses it was presumed to follow. Finally, Cannon argued that there was no support for James's implication that there must be a discretely different pattern of arousal for each different pattern of emotional experience.

Thirty years later Schachter and Singer (1962) revived and revised Jamesian theory by dealing directly with the last of the criticisms described above. They agreed with Cannon that there are no unique patterns of autonomic responsivity associated with the experience of distinct emotions. Rather, they postulated that when individuals perceive general arousal, they explain it by labeling their experience as an emotion that is cognitively consistent with available cues from the environmental context. In their classic paper Schachter and Singer reported that subjects whose autonomic arousal was augmented by injections of epinephrine and who were not given specific expectations concerning the effects of those injections tended to respond with a greater degree of emotionality in an experimentally arranged context than a similar group of subjects who were not injected with epinephrine or who, although having been so injected, were given specific expectations about their bodily reactions to them. On the basis of these and other similar data, Schachter and Singer concluded that the experience of emotion required increments in autonomic arousal, the *perception* of such increments, and an available social context to which subjects can attribute the perception of their arousal.

According to Schachter and Singer, the perception of unexplained visceral arousal leads to a relatively neutral, objective search for explanation. Critics of their view, however, have suggested that when an individual experiences unexplained arousal, there is a negative bias, presumably based upon prior experiences of adrenergic arousal, causing the subject to seek out a negative explanation of the unexplained arousal (Marshall & Zimbardo, 1979; Maslach, 1979). Even though these critics have engaged Schachter and Singer (1979) in intense debate concerning the essence of the individual's cognitive response to unexplained arousal, neither they nor Schachter and Singer have questioned the primary assumption that cognitive labeling and, ultimately, the experience of emotion are secondary to the perception of visceral arousal.

Although cognitive-physiological approaches to emotion have reconciled the discrepancy between the variety of emotional experiences and the lack of variety of autonomic response patterns, they have not dealt well with Cannon's other criticisms of Jamesian theory. Harris and Katkin (1975) addressed these criticisms by postulating the existence of "primary" and "secondary" emotions. According to Harris and Katkin,

> Primary emotion is that emotional state that includes ANS arousal and subjective perception of that arousal; secondary emotion is that emotional state that does not necessarily include ANS arousal, but that may include a subject's nonveridical perception of such arousal. (1975, p. 913)

This distinction between primary and secondary emotion is quite similar to Mandler's (1962) distinction between autonomically based and nonautonomically based emotional expressions. According to Mandler, ANS activity is essential for the acquisition of emotions, but it may be unnecessary for their subsequent expression.

Harris and Katkin postulated that after a period of emotional learning, which requires ANS arousal (and perception of that arousal), it is likely that subjects can express secondary emotion, defined as those components of emotional behavior (e.g., motor and verbal behavior) without autonomic arousal. Thus, they hypothesized that Cannon's observation of "sham" emotion in sympathectomized cats was most likely an observation of the "secondary" fear that the cats expressed in the absence of peripheral autonomic feedback. In the presence of an intact ANS, Cannon's cats could have recognized visceral feedback a few seconds after the initiation of their secondary emotional responses, and the perception of this feedback would have been associated with a somewhat different expressiveness, which Cannon might have characterized as "real" and not "sham" emotion. Harris and Katkin's hypotheses concerning primary and secondary emotion remain to be validated empirically. Nevertheless, their view on the issues is not substantially different from other contemporary cognitive views of arousal-based emotion (Marshall & Zimbardo, 1979; Schachter & Singer, 1979) which assume that the *perception* of arousal is the essential stimulus for cognitive labeling behavior.

Arousal-Based Theories of Social and Interpersonal Behavior

In addition to its central role in contemporary theories of emotion, arousal is also an important construct in many theories covering a wide range of other social behaviors. For many of these arousal-based theories of social behavior, some level of awareness or perception of visceral arousal is assumed or at least implied. Included in this group are attitude theories, as well as theories of antisocial and prosocial behavior, and theories of interpersonal behavior.

Attitudes. Perhaps no concepts have received more attention in social psychology than the concepts of attitude and attitude change. Arousal has been regarded implicitly or explicitly as an integral component of attitude and attitude change by a number of theorists. Consistency theories have been the most frequently and popularly emphasized of these explanations. The essential and distinguishing feature of consistency theories is a state of "inconsistency" (or "balance," "incongruity," or "dissonance"). An individual is driven to strengthen or change attitudes in order to eliminate or reduce the inconsistency. Not surprisingly, the nature of most kinds of inconsistency has been explained in terms of arousal. Dissonance theory (Festinger, 1957) provides a good illustration. Festinger originally provided little description of the nature of "dissonance," although he did suggest that it was a kind of "tension." Later, Brehm and Cohen (1962) characterized dissonance as an arousal state. Although a few researchers (Buck, 1970; Gerard, 1967; Gleason & Katkin, 1979; McMillen & Geiselman, 1974) subsequently investigated the physiological arousal properties of the state of dissonance, only recently have the physiological arousal properties of dissonance been theoretically integrated in a comprehensive way (Fazio & Cooper, 1982).

Antisocial and prosocial behavior. Arousal is a critical feature in most theories of aggressive behavior, including both biological and social psychological theories. Research has repeatedly demonstrated a relationship between physiological arousal and aggressive behavior (Baron & Bell, 1977; Donnerstein & Barrett, 1978; Mueller & Donnerstein, 1977; Tannenbaum & Zillmann, 1975; Zillmann, 1971, 1978).

In addition to its important role in antisocial behavior, arousal has been implicated as a component of such prosocial behaviors as "helping." For instance, Piliavin, Piliavin, and Rodin (1975) have postulated that:

> Observation of an emergency arouses the bystander . . . physiological components may include . . . rapid and heavy heartbeat, shortness of breath, "butterflies" in the stomach, and a variety of other reactions associated with startle and shock . . . the bystander will choose the response to an emergency that most rapidly and most completely reduces his arousal, incurring as few net costs . . . as possible in the process. (p. 430)

Interpersonal behavior. Arousal has been postulated to be involved in such processes as social facilitation and interpersonal attraction. For instance, in Zajonc's (1965; 1968) theory of social facilitation, it is hypothesized that the presence of others leads to increased general arousal which in turn facilitates "dominant" responses in an individual's behavior. Similar theories have been proposed by Cottrell (1968; 1972) and by Sanders (1981). Although the work of Zajonc, Cottrell, and Sanders may be differentiated on a number of specific details, all of their theories include the construct of arousal and imply that it is a crucial determinant of subsequent facilitative behavior.

Arousal has also been implicated in theories of interpersonal attraction. Schachter (1959), for instance, demonstrated that fear arousal increases an individual's desire to affiliate with others. Arousal also plays a role in social psychological explanations of liking and loving. Stephan, Berscheid, and Walster (1971), Berscheid and Walster (1974), and Carducci, Cozby, and Ward (1978), for example, have demonstrated that arousal often forms the basis for attributions or misattributions of attraction.

Implications

It seems clear from this very brief review that arousal is an important construct for many theories covering a wide variety of social behaviors. What may not be so clear is the degree to which *awareness* or *perception* of such arousal is important. For most arousal-based theories of social behavior, some level of awareness or perception of visceral arousal is assumed or implied. Many theories are based on an assumption that individuals are accurate perceivers of arousal (Maslach, 1979; Piliavin, Piliavin, & Rodin, 1975; Schachter & Singer, 1962). Of the varieties of theories in which such assumptions have been made, the clearest articulation may be seen in arousal-based theories of emotion. The primary focus of our discussion, therefore, will be on the theoretical role of visceral perception in social psychophysiological theories of emotion, with special emphasis upon attendant methodological and conceptual problems.

Visceral Perception and Emotion

This section will address the potential implications of individual differences in accurate visceral self-detection for four contemporary social-psychophysiological theories of emotion including Schachter and Singer's (1962; 1979) cognitive-physiological theory, Valin's (1966; 1967) nonphysiological, cognitive attribution view, Zill-mann's (1971) excitation-transfer theory, and Harris and Katkin's (1975) notions about the distinction between primary and secondary emotions.

Two-Factor Cognitive-Physiological Theory

One of the crucial assumptions of Schachter and Singer's theory is that "the individual is acutely aware of nontrivial elevations in the level of diffuse physiological arousal he experiences, mainly through interoceptive cues" (Zillmann, 1978, p. 336). The assumption of "nontrivial elevations in arousal" may be critical because there is a substantial amount of data to indicate that in nonaroused states subjects are relatively insensitive to their interoceptive cues. For instance, Penne-baker (1981) has found that nonaroused subjects are relatively insensitive to their own heartbeats and that they are more likely to estimate their cardiac rates on the basis of external task demands than upon awareness of their actual heart rates. Data from our laboratory (Katkin, Blascovich, & Goldband, 1981) also indicate that under normal resting conditions most subjects are relatively unable to detect their heartbeats. These data suggest that cognitive labeling of an emotional state can take place only if a subject accurately detects signs of substantially elevated arousal.

A number of hypotheses about this cognitive-physiological theory of emotional labeling can be tested. First, one can test the notion that accuracy of self-detection increases in the presence of nontrivial elevations in arousal. Second, on the assumption that under conditions of arousal there are individual differences in accuracy of detection, one could test the hypothesis that cognitive searching and labeling will take place to a greater extent among subjects who are more accurate detectors of their excitation than among those who are less accurate detectors. Finally, it may be hypothesized that the phenomenon described by Schachter and Singer should be easier to demonstrate among subjects who have had prior training in visceral self-perception than among subjects who have not had such training. In summary, the cognitive-physiological view of emotions places great emphasis upon the importance of self-perception of arousal as the determining factor in the causal chain that leads to the cognitive labeling of experience; later in the chapter we will present evidence that it now seems possible to test that aspect of the theory directly.

Cognitive Attribution Theory

Valins (1966) did not agree that the accurate self-perception of arousal was required for emotional labeling. He suggested that a subject need not perceive actual autonomic arousal in order to experience an emotion but need only *believe* that he perceived it:

> If . . . it is the cognitive effect of internal events that influences emotional behavior, then the same influence should be observed when subjects think that they have reacted to a given stimulus, regardless of whether or not they have indeed reacted. (Valins, 1966, p. 401)

Valin's position became quite controversial since he suggested that the physiological component of the cognitive-physiological theory is excess baggage. Valins provided data that bogus feedback of a change in cardiac rate caused male subjects to attribute attractiveness to slides of female nudes. This suggests that a subject's emotional response to an external stimulus was affected by his beliefs about the state of his internal milieu, irrespective of the actual state. Subsequent research by a number of investigators (Goldstein, Fink, & Mettee, 1972; Hirschman, 1975; Stern, Botto, & Herrick, 1972) suggested that the bogus feedback employed by Valins may have had the undesired effect of increasing a subject's level of arousal. In that case, it was argued that the cognitive attribution was related to the induced arousal and that the subjects were responding more to the arousal than to the bogus feedback.

If, as Valins suggested, subjects can be misled by bogus feedback and attribute affect based on their *beliefs* about their visceral arousal, then it may be inferred that they are relatively insensitive to their actual arousal; otherwise, they would recognize the discrepancy between the bogus feedback and their own arousal level. This line of reasoning leads to the hypothesis that subjects who are accurate perceivers of their visceral arousal are least likely to respond to the bogus arousal feedback. As has already been discussed, subjects are more likely to be accurate perceivers if they are either in a high state of arousal or if they have been trained in accurate self-perception. Hence, it may be hypothesized that subjects who either are in high arousal states or who have been trained to a high level of accuracy in heartbeat detection should be relatively immune to the bogus feedback effect, whereas untrained subjects, or those in a relatively neutral state of arousal, should be subject to maximum bogus feedback effects. A correlated hypothesis is that under conditions of low arousal the purely cognitive explanation offered by Valins may be adequate to explain emotional labeling, but that under conditions of higher excitation, emotional labeling may be more dependent upon actual arousal and its perception.

Excitation-Transfer Theory

Zillmann (1971) has proposed a modification of cognitive-physiological theory that postulates three rather than two factors. In this three-factor theory, Zillmann posits a dispositional factor along with the excitatory and experiential factors presumed by Schachter and Singer. This dispositional factor is postulated to be a response-guiding mechanism, and Zillmann invokes it to explain motor behavior that may be independent of slower visceral responding. In this view, a stimulus that evokes both a motor response and an excitatory reaction (i.e., arousal) will produce emotional behavior. However, a motor response that is evoked without arousal will be perceived by the individual as nonemotional. Finally, according to Zillmann, a stimulus that evokes an excitatory reaction with no specific motor response will produce a state of cognitive ambiguity, and presumably generate a search for explanation. This latter situation is essentially the situation described by Schachter and Singer.

Excitation-transfer theory is derived from this three-factor theory. The basic theme of excitation-transfer is that the excitatory or arousal reaction decays slowly and that the individual may carry the residue of a past response into a new stimulus situation. In that case, the new stimulus may lead to an excitatory reaction whose total magnitude is the sum of the residue of the previous response plus the new excitatory reaction. Zillman's model is based on the following notions:

The individual can determine the intensity of his excitatory reaction through interoception. However, only comparatively gross changes in the level of excitation will draw the individual's attention and produce an awareness of his state of excitation.

... The individual relates an excitatory reaction of which he becomes aware to the apparent inducing condition and may recall this connection at later times.

... The individual does not identify all factors that contribute to an experienced state of excitation; nor does he apportion his excitation to the various contributing factors. Instead, he tends to ascribe his entire excitatory reaction to one particular, inducing condition.

... Intense excitatory reactions do not terminate abruptly. Because of slow, humoral processes involved in the control of sympathetic excitation, excitation decays comparatively slowly. Residues of this slowly decaying excitation then, may enter into subsequent, potentially independent experiential states. (Zillmann, 1978, p. 359-360)

An essential component of Zillmann's theoretical structure hinges on the assumption that "the individual can determine the intensity of his excitatory reaction through interoception." While Zillmann and his colleagues have supported the general validity of their notion in a number of studies (e.g., Cantor, Bryant, & Zillmann, 1974; Zillmann & Bryant, 1974), they have generally ignored an empirical evaluation of the extent to which their subjects can actually determine the intensity of their excitatory reactions through interoception. Thus, individual differences in visceral perception should be related to the extent to which excitation-transfer occurs. Subjects who are more accurate perceivers of visceral excitation, and who also carry a residue of arousal from one situation to another, should respond with no more, or possibly less, emotion to the second situation than subjects who are less accurate self-perceivers because, being more accurate, they are more likely to recognize that they have transferred a residue of arousal from the prior situation and thus less likely to attribute their total arousal to the second situation. Thus, objective evaluation of visceral self-perception may lead to more refined predictions about emotional experience and behavior than was previously possible from Zillmann's three-factor theory.

Primary and Secondary Emotion

Whereas Zillmann postulated a dispositional factor to deal with the obvious phenomenon that emotional behavior often is manifested too quickly to be explained by visceral responses, Harris and Katkin (1975) postulated the acquisition of "secondary" emotions, which, like conditional responses, are reinforced by subsequent visceral arousal. They speculated that if "Cannon's cats had been sympathectomized at birth and therefore incapable of having *primary* emotions, they would not have been able to acquire secondary emotions and would have been incapable of showing 'sham emotion' " (1975, p. 914).

A subsidiary hypothesis that may be derived from Harris and Katkin is that in the sympathectomized cat there should be more rapid extinction of "sham emotion" after repeated presentations of the emotion-inducing stimulus than in the intact preparation. If, as Harris and Katkin speculate, the secondary emotional response is reinforced by the perception of subsequent excitation, then the sympathectomized preparation should be incapable of having the secondary response reinforced and should show rapid extinction of the behavior. A corollary hypothesis for intact human subjects would be that those subjects who show the poorest accuracy of visceral self-perception are analogous to the sympathectomized preparation and should show fewer instances of emotional expressiveness and greater speed of extinction of secondary emotional responses than those subjects who show the best accuracy.

Harris and Katkin placed great emphasis on the importance of visceral perception in the development of emotion, even while trying to account for the wide variety of emotional expressions manifested in its absence. Empirical assessment of individual differences in visceral self-detection, therefore, is an essential ingredient of hypothesis testing from their model.

Summary

Modern social-psychophysiological approaches to emotion have generated considerable research and discussion concerning the processes by which the cognitive labeling of emotion takes place, but very little research on the processes by which an individual perceives his or her own arousal. While these theories of emotion have generated numerous experimental studies, there has been no experimental approach addressed directly to the fundamental question of the perception of autonomically controlled visceral arousal. Psychological theories concerning the autonomic basis of emotion place heavy emphasis on the role of visceral self-perception, but corresponding empirical research has lagged far behind. It seems clear that the development of objective and quantitative methods for assessing the accuracy of autonomic perception would facilitate empirical study of the relationships among individual differences in the accuracy of visceral perception, visceral arousal, and the experience and expression of emotion.

Visceral Perception: Methods and Procedures

Background

The history of research on visceral self-perception and emotion has been marked by a dependence on subjective rather than objective methods. The few attempts at objective assessment that have emerged have come from theoretical contexts far removed from theories and models of emotion. Although there are a number of theoretical issues that are central to the choice of a technique for assessing visceral perception, the emphasis of this section will be on methodological problems. Specifically, the development of an empirical strategy for evaluating accuracy of visceral self-perception will be discussed.

There will be one clear limitation to this discussion. We will focus only on one index of autonomic arousal—heartbeats. Cardiac self-perception has been most frequently studied, although other visceral activities, such as sweat gland activation (Lacroix & Gowen, 1980) and gastric motility (Whitehead, 1980) also have been investigated. Our emphasis on cardiac activity results primarily from the ease with which heartbeat detection can be assessed, although such assessment is not without flaws. The perception of heartbeats is selected as a prototype because it has both face validity for subjects and because it is a simple, digital signal which lends itself readily to quantitative evaluation. It was our assumption from the outset that if the phenomenon of visceral self-perception could be demonstrated with quantitatively sound, objective techniques, it could be done most readily through the analysis of heartbeat detection. Positive results with this measure would encourage the extension of the research paradigm to other indexes of internal visceral activity. On the other hand, failure to demonstrate the phenomenon with the analysis of heartbeat detection would suggest that we were still not ready to subject the issue of visceral perception to easy experimental analysis.

Although there has been little or no empirical research on the relationship between visceral perception and emotion, there has been considerable development in other areas. Brener (1977), for instance, suggested that the voluntary control of an autonomic response is possible only if an individual can discriminate differential activity of that response. Furthermore, Brener has stipulated that the specificity with which an individual complies with instructions to control an autonomic response voluntarily is determined by the extent to which he or she can discriminate instances of that response independently of other ongoing activities.

According to Brener (1977) and Miller (1978), external feedback (i.e., biofeedback) is useful because it affords a means whereby response discrimination, and thus response control, is possible. In simple terms, both Brener and Miller have suggested that persons who are trained to discriminate a particular response should display improvement in their ability to control that response as well as improvement in their ability to identify specific occurrences of it. For these reasons there has been considerable interest among biofeedback researchers on the development of adequate means for assessing individual differences in accuracy of visceral self-perception.

The majority of recent studies on visceral self-perception have focused on cardiac activity, and the research has usually been concerned with the relationship between self-perception and self-control of heartbeats (or heart rate). Cardiac perception has been assessed with paper and pencil tests, heart rate discrimination tasks, heartbeat tracking tasks, and heartbeat discrimination tasks, and there has been significant variation among procedures within each of these categories (Carroll, 1977; Williamson & Blanchard, 1979a, 1979b).

One of the first systematic attempts to measure visceral perception was the Autonomic Perception Questionnaire (APQ), developed by Mandler, Mandler, and Uviller (1958). The APQ is a subjective, self-report inventory which assesses the frequency and intensity of perceptions of autonomic activity. Mandler et al. (1958) found that scores on the APQ correlated significantly with scores on trait anxiety scales that contained items requiring the subjective report of physiological events. In addition, Mandler et al. reported that persons scoring high on the APQ showed significantly greater autonomic activity than persons who scored low on the APQ.

Subsequent research with the APQ has been disappointing. Although APQ scores are higher among subjects who show high levels of general arousal, there is little or no evidence to support the idea that the APQ score reflects enhanced ability to perceive specific aspects of visceral responsivity. Studies that have compared APQ scores with performance on objectively defined tasks of specific visceral perception (McFarland, 1975; Whitehead, Drescher, & Blackwell, 1976; Whitehead, Drescher, Heiman, & Blackwell, 1977) have obtained negative results. In addition, a number of investigators have tried specifically to test Brener's postulation of a relationship between visceral perception and visceral control, using subjects who score high and low on the APQ and training them in visceral self-control (Bergman & Johnson, 1971; Blanchard, Young, & McLeod, 1972; Blankstein, 1975; Whitehead et al., 1976). Generally, the results have been disappointing; none of these studies has supported the prediction that subjects with higher scores on the APQ would demonstrate better visceral control.

Obviously, the failure to find relationships between APQ scores and visceral control can be explained in many ways. However, most investigators who were engaged in this work generally chose to conclude that the problem resided in the subjective nature of the APQ. Therefore, many of them set out to develop more objective techniques for the assessment of visceral self-perception, with a primary focus on the relationships between perception and self-control, and with little attention to other theoretical ramifications of the ability to measure ANS self-perception objectively and accurately.

McFarland (1975) developed a technique in which subjects were asked to press a button in rhythm with their heartbeats for a specified time period. After completing the detection task, subjects were required to increase and decrease their heart rates in a biofeedback paradigm. McFarland found no relationship between heartbeat perception and heart rate decreases. Unfortunately, McFarland's design did not include a method for determining whether good perceivers performed better than chance. Furthermore, good perceivers simply may have been better at estimating their average heart rate, without actually perceiving their own heartbeats accurately. This technique measures the extent to which a subject can estimate his or her mean heart rate over time and is not particularly sensitive to phasic changes in the heart rate that might occur during the test interval. In order to develop a measure that would more accurately reflect the perceptual sensitivity to phasic changes in heart rate activity, Brener and Jones (1974) developed their "cardiac activity discrimination" test.

The cardiac activity discrimination test assesses the degree to which subjects can discriminate exteroceptive stimuli that are contingent on cardiac activity from exteroceptive stimuli that are independent of cardiac activity. For each trial, a subject receives either contingent stimulation (i.e., stimuli that are triggered by their own heartbeats) or noncontingent stimulation (e.g., stimuli triggered by a pulse generator set to produce a frequency equal to the subject's mean heart rate). Subjects indicate whether the exteroceptive stimuli are contingent or noncontingent on their heartbeats. Using this technique, Brener and Jones (1974) were able to assess the number of correct detections their subjects made and to infer that the number of correct detections was an effective index of cardiac rate discrimination.

There are problems with the Brener and Jones (1974) discrimination measure, however. As Whitehead et al. (1977) have pointed out, in this paradigm it is possible for subjects to discriminate between the two trains of stimuli by manipulating their heart rate (e.g., with a respiratory maneuver) during the train. If the exteroceptive stimuli are affected by such a manipulation, then they are seen by the subjects to be contingent on the heartbeat; if they are not affected, then they are seen to be noncontingent. Although it is not clear how many subjects actually use such a strategy, the fact remains that subjects can do well at the task without ever perceiving their heart rate, simply by manipulating the stimuli indirectly.

Because of this drawback, Whitehead and his collaborators developed a technique in which both contingent and noncontingent signals are generated continuously by a subject's own heartbeats. In addition, Whitehead et al. (1977) analyzed subjects' responses using the theory of signal detection (TSD; see McNicol, 1972). An important feature of TSD is that it allows the investigator to isolate perceptual sensitivity from response bias components of the subject's response pattern. There is a large body of literature on the application of TSD to vigilance and perceptual sensitivity for a variety of perceptual tasks. Whitehead's application of this technique as well as more recent applications by Ashton, White, and Hodgson (1979), extend the methodological elegance of TSD to the analysis of the perception of internal, viscerally generated signals.

In Whitehead's paradigm, subjects are presented with a train of stimuli that are generated by their own heartbeats, after either a 100-ms or a 400-ms delay from each heartbeat. The subject's task is to discriminate between the signals that are delayed for a "short" period and those that are delayed for a "long" period. Obviously, if a subject tries respiratory or muscular manipulations, both sets of stimuli will be affected equally. Also, if the subjects have no actual perceptual sensitivity for their own heartbeats, the two sets of stimuli will be totally indistinguishable. The only way in which subjects can accurately detect the difference between a short and a long delay train of stimuli is by referring to their own actual heartbeats. Thus, perceptual sensitivity scores greater than chance can be obtained only if the subjects are capable of detecting their own heartbeats. Using this paradigm, Whitehead and his collaborators discovered that only a few subjects could make this discrimination. Their findings were subsequently confirmed in our laboratory.

The poor performance of most of Whitehead's subjects, as well as ours, led us to conclude that the discrimination task was too difficult. Consequently, we set out to devise a task that would preserve the valuable features of Whitehead's paradigm, but would be easier for the subjects to discriminate, assuming that they did indeed have accurate perception of their heartbeats. Katkin, Blascovich, and Goldband (1981) and Katkin, Morell, Goldband, Bernstein, and Wise (1982) modified the technique of Whitehead et al. in an attempt to make the discrimination easier, thus improving the sensitivity of the measure. The basic details of this methodological technique are described in Katkin et al. (1981, 1982). In short, the technique preserves the essential features of the Whitehead et al. task, in that one set of signals (S+) has a fixed, invariant relationship to heartbeats and another set of signals (S−) has a variable relationship to the heartbeats. The subject's task is to correctly discriminate S+ from S−.

In order to establish the legitimacy of this new task it was imperative to demonstrate that subjects could not discriminate the S+ from the S− independently of heartbeat discrimination. Therefore, a study was carried out in which subjects were presented with S+ and S− tones generated by tape recordings of their EKGs rather than their on-line EKGs (Katkin et al., 1981). In this experiment all subjects were run in two sessions separated by one week. In the first session all subjects received 120 training trials in which they were asked to discriminate their heartbeats and given veridical feedback about the correctness of their discrimination on every trial. During the second session, the experimental subjects repeated the same procedure, but subjects in the control group were given exteroceptive feedback triggered by tape recordings of their earlier EKGs from the first session. Obviously, for subjects in the control group the relationship between heartbeats and exteroceptive feedback was random. The feedback concerning the correctness of their discrimination was similarly random; therefore, for subjects in the control group, it was expected that there would be only chance level performance on the discrimination task.

The data depicted in Figure 5-1 show the mean signal detection scores for subjects in the two conditions during the first and second sessions. The dependent measure is expressed as 2 arcsin $\sqrt{p(A)}$, a nonparametric approximation of d', the standard measure of perceptual sensitivity (McNicol, 1972). Figure 5-1 shows that subjects in the first session learned to discriminate their heartbeats at a level substantially better than chance (chance performance = 1.57), but that during the second session only the experimental subjects could maintain such performance. Subjects in the control condition, who were responding to nonveridical feedback, showed chance level performance, as expected. Thus, the results of this study demonstrated that subjects could not discriminate the S+ from S− stimuli merely by listening to the tones. Consequently, the task can be used as a valid index of individual differences in heartbeat discrimination ability.

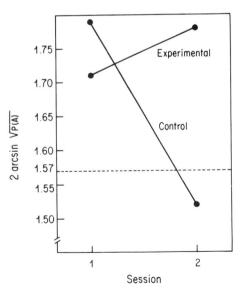

Figure 5-1. Mean accuracy scores (2 arcsin $\sqrt{p(A)}$) for experimental and control subjects in the initial (no manipulation) session and the second (experimental) session. From Katkin et al. (1981) Copyright (1981) by the American Psychological Association. Reprinted by permission of the publisher and author.

Visceral Perception: Empirical Results

Four studies have been completed in our laboratory using the signal detection paradigm described above. Each of these studies was aimed at a specific question concerning individual differences in heartbeat discrimination ability. The overall purpose of this series of studies, however, was to establish the validity of our paradigm for assessing visceral perception, so that future studies on autonomic awareness and emotion would have an adequate methodological base from which to operate.

Heartbeat discrimination and electrodermal lability. The first experiment (Katkin et al., 1982) was conducted to test the validity of the detection paradigm described above. In this study the experimental subjects were presented with a randomly determined mixture of 25 S+ and S− stimulus trains without any performance feedback, followed by 25 additional presentations with performance feedback. The control subjects received 50 consecutive trials without performance feedback. In addition, subjects were subdivided into groups based on their electrodermal lability during a preexperimental rest period. Electrodermal lability is determined by counting the number of skin conductance fluctuations that occur spontaneously during a specified time period, unrelated to any specific stimulation (see Katkin, 1975). The rationale for the division of subjects into electrodermal labiles and stabiles was derived from previous findings that labile subjects are superior to stabile subjects on a variety of tasks that require perceptual discrimination and vigilance (Crider & Augenbraun, 1975; Hastrup, 1979; Sostek, 1978). On the assumption that the discrimination of heartbeats is similar to other perceptual discrimination tasks, we hypothesized that labile subjects would be better at heartbeat discrimination than stabile subjects.

The data from this study are summarized in Figure 5-2, in which it may be noted that only the labile subjects appeared to benefit from training in heartbeat detection, and that neither the labile nor the stabile subjects were adept at the task before training. Statistical analyses confirmed that the two groups did not differ from each other in the pretraining period, but that they showed significant differences from each other after training ($p < .01$). These data suggest that most of the subjects were poor at detecting their own heartbeats without training, but that the labile subjects were more able than the stabile subjects to learn to make the discrimination after receiving performance feedback. This experiment employed 8 male and 33 female subjects. Close inspection of the results indicated that the successful acquisition of discrimination for the labile subjects could be attributed primarily to the few male subjects contained in that group; the female labile subjects showed generally poorer acquisition than their male counterparts. For that reason, a second study was carried out with the specific aim of evaluating the observed sex differences.

Sex differences in heartbeat discrimination. Katkin et al. (1981) replicated and extended the first study, using equal numbers of male and female subjects, and employing a greater number of baseline (no feedback) and training trials. In this study, the subjects received 40 baseline trials followed by 120 feedback trials. The data from this experiment are summarized in Figure 5-3, in which it may be noted

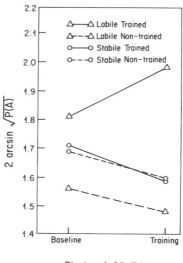

Blocks of 25 Trials

Figure 5-2. Mean accuracy scores (2 arcsin $\sqrt{p(A)}$) for electrodermally labile and stabile subjects before and during discrimination training. Reprinted with permission of the publisher from Katkin et al. (1982).

that there was a significant Groups × Trial Blocks interaction ($p < .01$). Both groups of subjects performed at about chance level during the baseline period, but only the male subjects showed any evidence of acquisition of heartbeat discrimination during the feedback trials. These data confirmed definitively the earlier anecdotal observations; male and female subjects demonstrated clearly different responses to heartbeat discrimination training. Subsequent studies were designed to address different potential contributors to this phenomenon.

Cerebral lateralization and heartbeat discrimination. Hantas, Katkin, and Reed (in press) addressed the potential effects of cerebral lateralization on individual differences in heartbeat discrimination. The decision to examine this variable was based on two assumptions: (1) that heartbeat discrimination is more similar to functions ascribed to the right hemisphere (e.g., spatial, holistic, somesthetic perceptual) than it is to functions ascribed to the left hemisphere (e.g., analytic, verbal); and (2) that females are not as discretely lateralized as males. Hantas et al. speculated that heartbeat discrimination is related to right hemisphere preference and that the apparent ability of male subjects to learn this discrimination better than female subjects might result from more discrete lateralization among males. The idea that there may be clear differences between the sexes in brain lateralization, and that such differences may be related to tasks such as visceral discrimination are supported in the literature.

Recent investigations suggest that the asymmetry patterns of male and female brains differ. It is now widely known that the left cerebral hemisphere in the large majority of right-handers is specialized for language and related functions and that the right cerebral hemisphere is specialized for a variety of nonverbal processes.

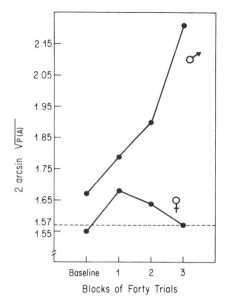

Figure 5-3. Mean accuracy scores (2 arcsin $\sqrt{p(A)}$) for male and female subjects during a baseline period and three subsequent discrimination training periods. From Katkin et al. (1981). Copyright (1981) by the American Psychological Association. Reprinted by permission of the publisher and author.

These include three dimensional visualization, mental rotation, face recognition, and understanding the meaning of facial expression. In male neurological patients, there is a strong association between the nature of psychological deficits observed and the side of the brain that has been injured: Verbal functions are disordered with left-hemisphere lesions and nonverbal functions are disordered with right-hemisphere lesions. In female neurological patients, this association is much weaker, suggesting that the female brain is less functionally asymmetric than the male brain.

Research with normal people has generally confirmed this observation (Levy, 1981, pp. 22-23).

Hantas et al. employed 31 male right-handed subjects who had no first degree left-handed relatives. Before the experiment began, each subject was interviewed individually and asked a series of verbal and spatial questions, as suggested by Gur and Gur (1977). The interviewer recorded each subject's first shift of gaze to the right or left immediately after each question. Directly behind the interviewer, on the other side of a one-way mirror a second observer also recorded the gaze shifts. Interrater reliability (Pearson r) between the interviewer and the second observer was .94. On the basis of these observations 10 subjects were classified as left movers (i.e., right hemisphere preferent), and 10 subjects were classified as right movers (i.e., left hemisphere preferent). Eleven subjects were classified as bidirectional.

All subjects were then run for 40 baseline trials and 120 training trials. The results of this study, which are presented in Figure 5-4, indicated that during the baseline period, left movers performed significantly better than chance, while right movers

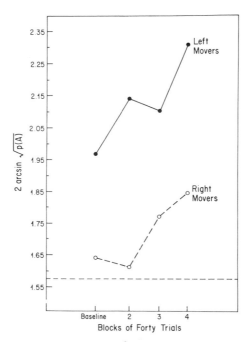

Figure 5-4. Mean accuracy scores (2 arcsin $\sqrt{p(A)}$) for subjects classified on the basis of conjugate lateral eye movements as right movers or left movers during a baseline period and three subsequent discrimination training periods. Reprinted with permission of the publisher from Hantas et al. (in press).

performed only at the chance level. With performance feedback, both groups showed increased discrimination ability. These data are noteworthy for a number of reasons. First, the data demonstrate once again that male subjects show substantial improvement in heartbeat discrimination with performance feedback training. Second, these data show that with the modified paradigm many subjects could discriminate their heartbeats *without* performance feedback training. This finding has substantial importance for establishing the viability of an objective index of visceral self-perception. Finally, these data indicate that heartbeat discrimination ability may be subserved by relative activation of the right hemisphere, which in turn has often been described as subserving emotional rather than verbal, rational functions (Sackeim, Gur, & Saucy, 1978; Schwartz, Davidson, & Maer, 1975; Suberi & McKeever, 1977).

Although these data raise many interesting questions concerning the relationship among laterality, emotion, and autonomic self-perception, they do not clarify the original issue to which they were addressed—sex differences in visceral perception. Not only did the right and left movers in this study show parallel acquisition curves for heartbeat discrimination, but the bidirectional subjects (not shown in Fig. 5-4) also showed an almost identical curve of acquisition, performing at a level midway between the right and left movers throughout the course of the baseline and training periods. It was originally hypothesized that the poor acquisition of discrimination among female subjects might be attributed to less clearly differentiated right hemisphere function. This notion did not receive support from the present data. Therefore, Koenigsberg, Katkin, & Blascovich (1981) conducted a separate study to examine the possibility that a modified instructional set might eliminate the observed sex differences.

Instructions and sex differences in heartbeat discrimination. Koenigsberg et al. (1981) addressed two issues: the effect of instructions on the acquisition of heartbeat discrimination, and the posttraining retention of the acquired discrimination. It was hypothesized that one possible factor contributing to the sex differences obtained in the prior studies may have been motivational or social learning differences between male and female subjects.

In order to test this possibility, Koenigsberg et al. developed a set of extensive instructions which included tape-recorded presentations to the subjects of the sounds of heartbeats followed by S + tones and heartbeats followed by S − tones. In addition, subjects were given extensive preexperimental practice with S + and S − tones in order to put them at ease and clarify thoroughly any misconception they may have had about the task demands. In this experiment "experimental" subjects were given detailed instructions and practice, and "control" subjects were run in an essential replication of the original Katkin et al. (1981) study. Thus, there were two groups of male subjects and two groups of female subjects. In addition to 40 baseline and 120 training trials, an additional 40 trials without performance feedback were added on after training. These trials were included to test for retention of acquired heartbeat discrimination after training.

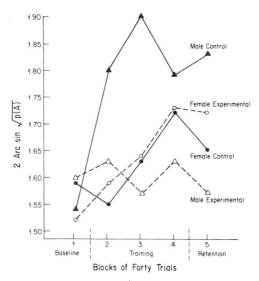

Figure 5-5. Mean accuracy scores (2 arcsin $\sqrt{p(A)}$) for male and female subjects in the standard (control) and the enhanced instruction (experimental) conditions during a baseline period, three subsequent discrimination training periods, and a retention period. From Koenigsberg et al. (1981).

The data from this experiment are depicted in Figure 5-5, in which the following patterns may be observed: (1) all four groups performed at about chance level during the initial baseline period; (2) for the control groups, the earlier pattern of greater acquisition for male than female subjects was replicated; (3) for the experimental groups, the females showed no difference from the female controls, but the males showed a substantial decrement as compared to the male controls, and performed more poorly than either group of females; and (4) during the retention period none of the four groups showed a significant change from the level attained during acquisition.

The results of this study seem to confirm that male and female subjects employ different strategies for solving the heartbeat discrimination task and suggest that the extended instructions employed tended to disrupt or otherwise interfere with the male strategy, but had no apparent effect on the females. In addition, these data provide evidence that after subjects have learned the discrimination they are able to continue to make it, at least for a short time, after the cessation of performance feedback. This latter finding has considerable significance for applications to the study of the relationship between visceral self-perception and other behavior, for it should enable experimenters to evaluate relevant behavior among subjects before and after learned visceral discrimination.

Summary

The results of this series of studies have clarified certain methodological issues, but they have also raised many new questions for future research. First, it is clear that the methods developed are sensitive enough to allow objective and quantitative assessments of heartbeat discrimination; yet, it is likely that either the task demands of this method are sufficiently difficult or the strength of the heartbeat sensation is so weak that few subjects are able to perform well without substantial training. The data also indicate that there are substantial individual differences in the ability to learn to discriminate heartbeats. Primary among these individual differences is gender—males appear to learn the discrimination much more readily than females. Furthermore, it appears that the strategy that male subjects employ to effect the discrimination is disrupted by instructions to focus on listening for heartbeats. It is likely that something akin to somesthetic perceptual processing underlies the heartbeat discrimination. Such a hypothesis is consistent with the finding that right hemisphere preferent subjects show better discrimination without training than left hemisphere preferent subjects.

Differences in electrodermal lability also appeared to be predictive of individual differences in heartbeat discrimination learning. However, this finding may well be affected by sex differences. In the first study, most of the labile subjects were male; in the second study there was an insufficient number of male labile subjects to warrant analysis, but examination of the data suggests that the lability effect may not have replicated and the effect in the first experiment may be attributed to the behavior of the male subjects.

Finally, there is evidence that among males only, using a somewhat easier discrimination task, right hemisphere preference is associated with enhanced heartbeat discrimination ability. On the assumption that the methods at hand are adequate and that there are clear individual differences in visceral discrimination ability on a number of dimensions, each of which has some place in the context of research and theory on emotion, there is reason to believe that empirical testing of the relationship between visceral perception and emotion is feasible and desirable.

Conclusions

This chapter has reviewed the current status of empirical research in one area of visceral self-perception—the discrimination of heartbeats. The potential relevance of this approach for the analysis of the role of peripheral somatic activity in the experience and expression of emotion remains to be tested. The data obtained so far indicate only that it now seems feasible to apply sound, objective methods to the analysis of visceral self-detection; however, a serious analysis of visceral detection in emotions will require extensions of this empirical enterprise to other internal responses such as those of the gastrointestinal tract, as well as to the action of fine muscles. Whitehead (1980) has already provided evidence that subjects are capable of learning to discriminate gastric activity and subsequently to acquire greater voluntary control of otherwise involuntary gastric responses.

There are a host of other issues that remain to be resolved. Using the current methods of analysis, we are able to find only a few subjects who are able to demonstrate better than chance performance on the heartbeat discrimination task. It is unclear whether this represents a true estimate of the population of accurate heartbeat perceivers or whether we are dealing with a task which is so difficult that it masks evidence for more accurate performance. The data obtained by Hantas et al. (in press) using a slightly modified paradigm suggest that more parametric manipulations are in order.

Among the parameters that appear to be promising is arousal level. Jones and Hollandsworth (1981) have demonstrated that exercise-induced cardiac arousal improves accuracy of cardiac self-detection. Current research in our laboratory is addressed to the evaluation of the extent to which psychologically induced arousal may also lead to similar enhancement of cardiac awareness. Further, we will be evaluating the degree to which enhanced accuracy may lead to the attribution of affect as a function of the distinction between exercise induction and psychological induction.

There is clear evidence that male subjects, on average, learn to discriminate their heartbeats with training, whereas female subjects, on average, do not. These differences in acquisition are apparently independent of any differences in pretraining performance, which is poor for both sexes. The data obtained so far indicate that males and females apparently employ different cognitive strategies to learn the discrimination and that extended instructions oriented toward an auditory discrimination strategy seriously impede the otherwise strong acquisition among male subjects.

The data on male subjects suggest the possibility that heartbeat discrimination may be subserved by functions of the right cerebral hemisphere. These data, while preliminary, are consistent with the apparent sex differences in heartbeat discrimination since it is believed that males and females differ with respect to the discreteness of cerebral lateralization. Until further tests of the laterality hypothesis are carried out, however, it is premature to come to any firm conclusions about this matter.

In summary, research on heartbeat discrimination has opened up new possibilities for the empirical evaluation of the one element of peripheral theories of emotion that has usually been reserved for phenomenology—the self-perception of bodily reactions. As is so often the case with new methodological developments, there are more questions than answers to be found in the experimental results.

References

Ashton, R., White, K. D., & Hodgson, G. (1979). Sensitivity to heart rate: A psychophysical study. *Psychophysiology, 16*, 463-466.

Baron, R. A., & Bell, P. A. (1977). Sexual arousal and aggression by males: Effects of type of erotic stimuli and prior provocation. *Journal of Personality and Social Psychology, 35*, 79-87.

Bergman, J. S., & Johnson, H. J. (1971). The effects of instructional set and autonomic perception on cardiac control. *Psychophysiology, 8*, 180-190.

Berscheid, E., & Walster, E. (1974). Physical attractiveness. In L. Berkowitz (Ed.), *Advances in experimental social psychology* (Vol. 7, pp. 158-216). New York: Academic Press.

Blanchard, E. B., Young, L. D., & McLeod, P. (1972). Awareness of heart activity and self-control of heart rate. *Psychophysiology, 9*, 63-68.

Blankstein, K. R. (1975). Note on relation of autonomic perception to voluntary control of heart rate. *Perceptual and Motor Skills, 40*, 533-534.

Brehm, J. W., & Cohen, A. R. (1962). *Explorations in cognitive dissonance.* New York: Wiley.

Brener, J. (1977). Sensory and perceptual determinants of voluntary visceral control. In G. E. Schwartz & J. Beatty (Eds.), *Biofeedback: Theory and research.* New York: Academic Press.

Brener, J., & Jones, J. M. (1974). Interoceptive discrimination in intact humans: Detection of cardiac activity. *Physiology and Behavior, 13*, 763-767.

Buck, R. W., Jr. (1970). *Relationships between dissonance-reducing behavior and tension measures following aggression.* Doctoral dissertation, University of Pittsburgh. Ann Arbor, MI: University Microfilms.

Cannon, W. B. (1927). The James-Lange theory of emotions: A critical examination and alternative theory. *American Journal of Psychology, 39*, 106-124.

Cantor, J. R., Bryant, J., & Zillmann, D. (1974). Enhancement of humor appreciation by transferred excitation. *Journal of Personality and Social Psychology, 30*, 812-821.

Carducci, B. J., Cozby, P. C., & Ward, C. D. (1978). Sexual arousal and interpersonal evaluations. *Journal of Experimental Social Psychology, 14*, 449-457.

Carroll, D. (1977). Cardiac perception and cardiac control: A review. *Biofeedback and Self-Regulation, 2*, 349-369.

Cottrell, N. B. (1968). Performance in the presence of other human beings: Mere presence, audience, and affiliation effects. In E. C. Simmel, R. A. Hoppe, & G. A. Milton (Eds.), *Social facilitation and imitative behavior.* Boston: Allyn & Bacon.

Cottrell, N. B. (1972). Social facilitation. In C. G. McClintock (Ed.), *Experimental social psychology*, pp. 185-236. New York: Holt, Rinehart, and Winston.

Crider, A., & Augenbraun, C. B. (1975). Auditory vigilance correlates of electrodermal response habituation speed. *Psychophysiology, 12*, 36-40.

Donnerstein, E., & Barrett, G. (1978). Effects of erotic stimuli on male aggression toward females. *Journal of Personality and Social Psychology, 36*, 180-189.

Fazio, R. H., & Cooper, J. (1982). Arousal in the dissonance process. In J. T. Cacioppo & R. E. Petty (Eds.), *Social psychophysiology.* New York: Guilford Press.

Festinger, L. (1957). *A theory of cognitive dissonance*. Stanford, CA: Stanford Univ. Press.

Gerard, H. B. (1967). Choice difficulty, dissonance, and the decision sequence. *Journal of Personality, 35*, 91-108.

Gleason, J. M., & Katkin, E. S. (1979). The effects of cognitive dissonance on heart rate and electrodermal response. *Psychophysiology, 16*, 180-181 (Abstract).

Goldstein, D., Fink, D., & Mettee, D. R. (1972). Cognition of arousal and actual arousal as determinants of emotion. *Journal of Personality and Social Psychology, 21*, 41-51.

Gur, R. C., & Gur, R. E. (1977). Correlation of conjugate lateral eye movements in man. In S. Harnad (Ed.), *Lateralization in the nervous system*. New York: Academic Press.

Hantas, M., Katkin, E. S., & Reed, S. D. (in press). Cerebral lateralization and heartbeat discrimination in males. *Psychophysiology*.

Harris, V. A., & Katkin, E. S. (1975). Primary and secondary emotional behavior: An analysis of the role of autonomic feedback on affect, arousal, and attribution. *Psychological Bulletin, 82*, 904-916.

Hastrup, J. L. (1979). Effects of electrodermal lability and introversion on vigilance decrement. *Psychophysiology, 16*, 302-310.

Hirschman, R. D. (1975). Cross modal effects of anticipatory bogus heart rate feedback in a negative emotional context. *Journal of Personality and Social Psychology, 31*, 13-19.

James, W. (1884). What is an emotion? *Mind, 9*, 188-205.

Jones, G. E., & Hollandsworth, J. G. (1981). Heart rate discrimination before and after exercise-induced augmented cardiac activity. *Psychophysiology, 18*, 252-257.

Katkin, E. S. (1975). Electrodermal lability: A psychophysiological analysis of individual differences in response to stress. In I. G. Sarason & C. D. Spielberger (Eds.), *Stress and Anxiety*, pp. 141-176. Washington, DC: Hemisphere Publishing Co.

Katkin, E. S., Blascovich, J., & Goldband, S. (1981). Empirical assessment of visceral self-perception: Individual and sex differences in the acquisition of heartbeat discrimination. *Journal of Personality and Social Psychology, 40*, 1095-1101.

Katkin, E. S., Morell, M. A., Goldband, S., Bernstein, G. L., & Wise, J. A. (1982). Individual differences in heartbeat discrimination. *Psychophysiology, 19*, 160-166.

Koenigsberg, M. R., Katkin, E. S., & Blascovich, J. (1981). The effects of pretraining instructional set on the acquisition and maintenance of heartbeat detection in males and females. *Psychophysiology, 18*, 196-197 (Abstract).

LaCroix, J. M., & Gowen, A. H. (1980). The acquisition of autonomic control through biofeedback: The case against an afferent process—and a possible alternative. *Psychophysiology, 17*, 316 (Abstract).

Levy, J. (1981). Sex and the brain. *The Sciences, 21*, 20-23, 28.

Mandler, G. (1962). Emotion. In R. Brown, E. Galanter, E. Hess, & G. Mandler (Eds.), *New directions in psychology*. New York: Holt, Rinehart, & Winston.

Mandler, G., Mandler, J. M., & Uviller, E. T. (1958). Autonomic feedback: The perception of autonomic activity. *Journal of Abnormal and Social Psychology, 56*, 367-373.

Marshall, G. D., & Zimbardo, P. G. (1979). Affective consequences of inadequately explained physiological arousal. *Journal of Personality and Social Psychology, 37*, 970-988.

Maslach, C. (1979). Negative emotional biasing of unexplained arousal. *Journal of Personality and Social Psychology, 37*, 953-969.

McFarland, R. A. (1975). Heart rate perception and heart rate control. *Psychophysiology, 12*, 402-405.

McMillan, D. L., & Geiselman, J. H. (1974). Effect of cognitive dissonance on alpha frequency activity: The search for dissonance. *Personality and Social Psychology Bulletin, 1*, 150-151.

McNicol, D. (1972). *A primer of signal detection theory*. London: George Allen & Unwin.

Miller, N. E. (1978). Biofeedback and visceral learning. In M. R. Rosenzweig & L. W. Porter (Eds.), *Annual Review of Psychology, 29*, 373-404.

Mueller, C., & Donnerstein, E. (1977). The effects of humor-induced arousal upon aggressive behavior. *Journal of Research in Personality, 11*, 73-82.

Pennebaker, J. W. (1981). Stimulus characteristics influencing estimation of heart rate. *Psychophysiology, 18,* 540-548.

Piliavin, I., Piliavin, J. A., & Rodin, J. (1975). Costs, diffusion, and the stigmatized victim. *Journal of Personality and Social Psychology, 32,* 429-438.

Sackeim, H. E., Gur, R. C., & Saucy, M. C. (1978). Emotions are expressed more intensely on the left side of the face. *Science, 202,* 434-436.

Sanders, G. S. (1981). Driven by distraction: An integrative review of social facilitation research and theory. *Journal of Experimental Social Psychology, 17,* 227-251.

Schachter, S. (1959). *The psychology of affiliation.* Stanford, CA: Stanford Univ. Press.

Schachter, S., & Singer, J. E. (1962). Cognitive, social, and physiological determinants of emotional state. *Psychological Review, 69,* 379-399.

Schachter, S., & Singer, J. E. (1979). Comments on the Maslach and Marshall-Zimbardo experiments. *Journal of Personality and Social Psychology, 37,* 989-995.

Schwartz, G. E., Davidson, R. J., & Maer, F. (1975). Right hemispheric lateralization for emotion in the human brain: Interactions with cognition. *Science,190,* 286-288.

Sostek, A. J. (1978). Effect of electrodermal lability and payoff instructions on vigilance performance. *Psychophysiology, 15,* 561-568.

Stephan, W., Berscheid, E., & Walster, E. (1971). Sexual arousal and heterosexual perception. *Journal of Personality and Social Psychology, 20,* 93-101.

Stern, R. M., Botto, R. W., & Herrick, C. D. (1972). Behavioral and physiological effects of false heart rate feedback: A replication and extension. *Psychophysiology, 9,* 21-29.

Suberi, M., & McKeever, W. F. (1977). Differential right hemispheric memory storage of emotional and nonemotional faces. *Neuropsychologia, 15,* 757-768.

Tannenbaum, P. H., & Zillmann, D. (1975). Emotional arousal in the facilitation of aggression. In L. Berkowitz (Ed.), *Advances in experimental social psychology* (Vol. 8). New York: Academic Press.

Valins, S. (1966). Cognitive effects of false heart-rate feedback. *Journal of Personality and Social Psychology, 4,* 400-408.

Valins, S. (1967). Emotionality and information concerning internal reactions. *Journal of Personality and Social Psychology, 6,* 458-463.

Whitehead, W. E. (1980). Interoception: Relationship of visceral perception to the voluntary control of visceral responses. *Psychophysiology, 17,* 321-322 (Abstract).

Whitehead, W. E., Drescher, V. M., & Blackwell, B. (1976). Lack of relationship between Autonomic Perception Questionnaire scores and actual sensitivity for perceiving one's heartbeat. *Psychophysiology, 13,* 176 (Abstract).

Whitehead, W. E., Drescher, V. M., Heiman, P., & Blackwell, B. (1977). Relation of heart rate control to heartbeat perception. *Biofeedback and Self-Regulation, 2,* 371-392.

Williamson, D. A., & Blanchard, E. B. (1979a). Heart rate and blood pressure biofeedback: I. A review of the recent literature. *Biofeedback and Self-Regulation, 4,* 1-34.

Williamson, D. A., & Blanchard, E. B. (1979b). Heart rate and blood pressure biofeedback: II. A review and integration of recent theoretical models. *Biofeedback and Self-Regulation, 4,* 35-50.

Zajonc, R. (1965). Social facilitation. *Science, 149,* 269-274.

Zajonc, R. (1968). Attitudinal effects of mere exposure. *Journal of Personality and Social Psychology, 9,* 1-27.

Zillmann, D. (1971). The role of excitation transfer in communication-mediated aggressive behavior. *Journal of Experimental Social Psychology, 7,* 419-434.

Zillmann, D. (1978). Attribution and misattribution of excitatory reactions. In J. H. Harvey, W. Ickes, & R. F. Kidd (Eds.), *New directions in attribution research* (Vol. 2, pp. 335-368). Hillsdale, N.J.: Erlbaum.

Zillmann, D., & Bryant, J. (1974). The effect of residual excitation on the emotional response to provocation and delayed aggressive behavior. *Journal of Personality and Social Psychology, 39,* 782-791.

Zimbardo, P. G. (1969). *The cognitive control of motivation.* Glenview, IL: Scott, Foresman.

Chapter 6
The Physiological Bases of
Nonverbal Communication

Ross Buck

Many of the theoretical and empirical issues in the field of nonverbal communication can be clarified by reference to the neural systems underlying emotion and communication. This chapter suggests that specific neural systems underly two sorts of communication processes: *spontaneous* communication which involves the outward expression of motivational/emotional states and *symbolic* communication which involves the intentional expression of propositional messages. This chapter will briefly outline these systems and explore their implications to the study of nonverbal communication.

This chapter begins with definitions of spontaneous and symbolic communication and evidence relating them to right and left hemisphere processing, respectively, is outlined. The nature of the motivational/emotional systems underlying spontaneous communication is then discussed and research on the brain mechanisms underlying facial expression and vocalization is examined. A model of the neural systems underlying the spontaneous expression of motivational/emotional states and two types of voluntary expression, based upon research in primate vocalization, is presented. A number of theories about the inhibition of emotional expression and the neural mechanisms which might underlie this phenomenon are reviewed. Finally, the relationships between these areas of research and their implications for the understanding of the physiological bases of nonverbal communication are discussed.

Spontaneous versus Symbolic Communication

Definitions

Spontaneous communication. Spontaneous communication involves innate tendencies to express motivational/emotional states. These states are based upon neural systems in the subcortical and paleocortical regions of the brain. Spontaneous communication occurs via a biologically shared signal system in that it involves *displays* that have evolved in the service of social coordination (Andrew 1963, 1965; Darwin 1872) and innate tendencies or *preattunements* to respond to such displays in others

(Gibson, 1966, 1977). Such biologically based communication systems may be found in the simplest of creatures and are required for any organized social behavior (cf. Buck, 1981a, 1982; 1984). The expression of such displays is not intentional, but instead involves the automatic expression of an internal motivational/emotional state.

The elements making up displays are *signs*, which are externally accessible aspects of the referents. Dark clouds are a "sign" of rain in that the darkness is an aspect of the referent—the rain—which is externally accessible—the water in the clouds blocks the sunlight. In the same way, the spontaneous expression of a motivational/emotional state is an externally perceivable aspect of that state in that evolution has dictated that an internal state of, say, anger is related to a specific facial expression and/or vocalization. Thus, the content of the spontaneous communication is a motivational/emotional state.

Symbolic communication. Symbolic communication, in contrast, is based upon a socially shared system, the elements of which are *symbols* which bear arbitrary and learned relationships with their referents. Symbolic communication is voluntary in that the sender intends to send a specific message or proposition, and thus the content of symbolic communication is propositional.

Nonverbal Communication in Brain-Damaged Patients

Pantomime recognition and expression. The importance of the distinction between spontaneous and symbolic communication is illustrated by the findings of studies of nonverbal communication in brain-damaged patients (Buck & Duffy, 1980; Buck, 1982). Left hemisphere brain damage in humans which results in aphasic disorders also results in deficits of intentional nonverbal behavior. For example, deaf persons who suffer left hemisphere damage have been found to lose their abilities at signing and finger spelling (Critchley, 1975; Kimura, 1979). Also, a number of studies have demonstrated deficits of gesture and pantomime recognition and/or expression in aphasic patients (Duffy, Duffy, & Pearson, 1975; Duffy & Duffy, 1981; Gainotti & Lemmo, 1976; Goodglass & Kaplan, 1963; Pickett, 1974; Varney, 1978). The degree of gestural/pantomimic impairment has been very closely related to the degree of verbal impairment in these patients, with r's ranging from .48 to .89.

The strength of the relationships between verbal abilities and gestural/pantomimic abilities is difficult to reconcile with the observations of a number of investigators who have commented that nonverbal communication seems to be relatively intact in aphasic patients. For example, Jenkens, Jimenez-Pabon, Shaw, and Sefer (1975) observe that aphasic patients show a "nearly normal competence" for communication via facial expression and gesture. One potential resolution for the apparent contradiction between this statement and the results of the studies above is that the investigators are speaking of different kinds of "nonverbal communication." Specifically, it can be argued that gestural/pantomimic abilities are forms of symbolic communication, as defined above, and that Jenkens and others are speaking of spontaneous communication.

Spontaneous communication. There has long been a distinction in the literature on aphasia between "propositionizing," the use of words for the deliberate communication of a message, and "emotional utterance," which involves the use of words (such as expletives) for the expression of a *presently existing* emotional state. An aphasic patient may swear when frustrated or say "hello" when greeting a friend, but be utterly unable to repeat those words a few moments later when the relevant emotional state has passed. It is possible that these phrases are so overlearned that they are virtually conditioned responses to an internal emotional state. Critchley (1975) has suggested that propositionizing is analogous to pantomime and the intentional posing of expressions, while emotional utterance is analogous to the spontaneous facial/gestural expression of emotion.

Support for this position has been found by Buck and Duffy (1977, 1980; Duffy & Buck, 1979) using a slide-viewing procedure for measuring the spontaneous facial/gestural expression of emotion. In this procedure, subjects are shown a series of emotionally loaded color slides while, unknown to them, their facial/gestural reactions are videotaped. Raters viewing the videotape (without audio) attempt to guess the type of slide shown. The resulting accuracy scores indicate the "sending accuracy" of the subject, defined as the ability of the observers to guess the types of slides viewed (cf. Buck, 1978). This technique evolved from Miller's Cooperative Conditioning Paradigm used to measure the communication of affect in rhesus monkeys (Miller, 1974).

In the application to brain-damaged patients, patients were shown slides of familiar people (nurses and other well-known hospital personnel), unfamiliar people, unpleasant scenes, and unusual scenes. A panel of college students viewed the expression and guessed the slide categories. Results indicated that observers could determine the category of slides viewed by the left-hemisphere-damaged aphasic patients as well as they could from the facial expressions of non-brain-damaged controls. Moreover, right-hemisphere-damaged patients showed significantly lower sending accuracy relative to left-hemisphere-damaged patients and controls, and in fact right-hemisphere-damaged patients did not differ significantly in sending accuracy from a sample of patients with Parkinson's disease, a disorder that has long been associated with a "mask-like" dearth of facial expression. In other words, left-hemisphere-damaged patients who show deficits in verbal communication also show deficits in voluntary nonverbal expression but no deficits in spontaneous nonverbal expression, while right-hemisphere-damaged patients who show no deficits in either verbal or voluntary nonverbal behavior do show lessened spontaneous expressiveness. This led to the suggestion that the distinction between spontaneous and symbolic communication behavior is more basic than the distinction between verbal and nonverbal communication (Buck & Duffy, 1980; Buck, 1981, 1982).

The examination of the relationships between spontaneous expression and verbal and pantomimic abilities is consistent with this analysis (Duffy & Buck, 1979). Pantomime recognition and expression measures were strongly correlated with a measure of verbal ability ($r = .90$ and $.99$, respectively, $p < .001$), and with each other ($r = .91$, $p < .001$), while the measure of spontaneous expressiveness was independent of both the measure of verbal ability ($r=.00$) and the measures of pantomime recognition and expression ($r=.09$ and $.00$, respectively).

The major results of the Buck and Duffy study have been replicated (Borod & Koff, 1982). From these results, Buck and Duffy suggested that the left hemisphere exerts an inhibitory influence over spontaneous nonverbal expression which is mediated by the right hemisphere. We shall return to this explanation below, after examining other evidence relating to the neural systems underlying spontaneous and voluntary expression.

Primary Motivational/Emotional Systems

Spontaneous Expression as Readout

Spontaneous expression is, in effect, a "readout" of the state of primary motivational/emotional systems in externally accessible expressive behavior. Motivation and emotion are considered here to be two sides of the same coin, or different aspects of the same underlying process. Emotion is considered to be the mechanism by which motivational effects are expressed, or "read out," in adaptive/homeostatic responses, spontaneous expressive behavior, and subjective experience (cf. Buck, 1981, 1983). This chapter is most concerned with the readout of emotion in expressive behavior.

Darwin (1872) argued that certain kinds of emotional expression are adaptive to a given species, allowing a coordination of behavior between individuals which is necessary to survival. The precise nature and extent of the external readout depends upon the ecological requirements of the species. The coordination of behavior for sexual reproduction occurs in the simplest of creatures, the threatening/submissive displays of many species allow the establishment of dominance without harmful fights, hunger-related "gaping displays" of nestling birds encourage feeding, etc. In essence, if the expression of a primary motivational/emotional state is important to survival and social coordination, a readout of that state in spontaneous expressive behavior will evolve. This section considers the nature of such states and the neural systems on which they are based.

Definition

In each species, behavior patterns evolve which are adaptive to that species, where adaptive responses are those which "bring the animal into contact with stimuli which are relevant to its survival (approach), and those which remove it from stimuli which are threatening to its survival (withdrawal)" (Glickman & Schiff, 1967, p. 68). The systems underlying these behavior patterns exist at various levels, from simple reflex patterns, through fixed action patterns which may become quite complex, to general patterns of affective response with no fixed action sequence. We shall collectively term these systems *primary motivational/emotional systems*, which may be abbreviated as "primes." They involve active internal processes which are based upon innate mechanisms, but which usually require external stimuli to reach expression. The concept includes phenomena traditionally labeled "motivational" (i.e., the process by which behavior is activated and directed: Young, 1961) and phenomena labeled "emotional," including subjective feelings or affects. It encompasses mechanisms at a number of levels of organization, from the simple reflexes and instincts or fixed action patterns analyzed by ethological theories of innate behavior, through the primary drives emphasized by traditional learning theorists, to primary affect systems analyzed by theorists of emotion.

Because of general similarities in species requirements within the ecosystem of the earth and relationships between species during the course of evolution, some primary motivational/emotional systems are relatively universal, such as the needs for food, water, and oxygen among animals. Others are specific to a given species, reflecting its particular requirements. Examples include the systems of homing in certain pigeons, the systems underlying migratory patterns in many species, patterns of gnawing, burrowing, and hoarding in small rodents, and the particularly long period of attachment to the young in primates.

Reflexes and instincts. The ethological theory of innate behavior patterns is detailed and technical, considering such patterns to involve a complex of levels of organization and stages of functioning. All of these levels and stages involve "primary motivational/emotional systems" in our sense of the term. The simplest forms of motivational/emotional systems are *reflexes*, which are innate response mechanisms in which the response is an automatic, involuntary, and relatively simple function of a stimulus.

Instincts involve innate behavior patterns at a higher level of complexity. The ethologists define instincts as inherited, specific, stereotyped patterns of behavior which have their own energy and are *released*, rather than guided, by environmental stimuli (Cofer & Appley, 1964). In all instinctive behavior "there is a hard core of absolutely fixed, more or less complex automaticism—an inborn movement form" (Thorpe, 1948,p. 3, quoted in Cofer & Appley, 1964, p. 60). This inborn central core has also been termed the *fixed action pattern* (Hess, 1962). Instinctive behavior involves a sequence of events, beginning with an arousing and ordering of behavior, a sustaining of behavior in a given direction, and a terminal phase in which energy is "released" in an appropriate environment. The general pattern of the behavior is predetermined: "hard-wired" into the structure of the organism.

Primary drives. Primary drives differ most markedly from instincts in that the form of the behavior is not predetermined and released by environmental stimuli, but instead the behavior must be *learned* under the *guidance* of environmental stimuli, e.g., via reinforcement. However, like instincts, primary drives are based solidly upon bodily conditions: tissue needs and the operation of deprivation. The concept of drive has often been advanced in opposition to the concept of instinct; indeed it was historically introduced during the 1920s as a replacement for early notions of instinct. However, the concepts of drive and instinct are not necessarily opposed to one another, but instead can both be considered to be different kinds of motivational/emotional systems at different levels of organization.

Primary drives involve behaviors such as eating, drinking, breathing, sleeping, and mating, which are present in virtually all vertebrates and are essential to individual and species survival. They are closely associated with tissue needs and the experimental operation of deprivation. Deprivation makes animals restless and active, and in an environment in which relevant behaviors are reinforced by the lessening of a primary drive, learning occurs.

The drive concept has been successful in dealing with conditions associated with tissue deficits, such as hunger and thirst. However, the use of primary drive theory in the analysis of maternal, migratory, and courting behaviors on one hand, and complex human motives and emotions on the other hand, has not been successful. It appears that the concept of primary drives is useful only within a restricted range of phenomena, and that other concepts, such as those of instincts and primary affects, must be used to analyze other levels of behavior.

Primary affects. The term "primary affects" was introduced in Tomkins' (1962, 1963) theory of emotion and has persisted in the work of Ekman (Ekman, Friesen, & Ellsworth, 1971; Ekman & Friesen, 1975) and Izard (1971; 1977). It covers a variety of types of motivational/emotional states, such as happiness, sadness, fear, anger, and surprise, which Tomkins felt are based upon specific neural substrates and which are each associated with a specific facial display.

Other theorists have adopted dimensional views of emotion in contrast to the typological view of Tomkins, Ekman, and Izard. These approaches assume that emotions vary quantitatively along bipolar dimensions, such as pleasant-unpleasant, strong-weak, and dominant-submissive (Schlosberg, 1952; Russell, 1979; Russell & Mehrabian, 1977).

All of these views of emotion have in common the notion that affective systems exist which (a) are based upon neural substrates, (b) may be associated with tendencies toward external expression, and (c) are associated with subjective experience. Unlike instincts, there are no innate behavior tendencies associated with these systems apart from their innate tendencies toward external display. Unlike drives, these systems are not based upon tissue needs or similar bodily conditions, but rather are reactions to environmental events.

Cognitive motivation. Primary motivational/emotional systems, as we have defined them, are all based upon subcortical and paleocortical systems of great phylogenetic age. There are other kinds of motivational states which do not seem to be based upon these systems. Cognitive motives such as effectance motivation, the need for understanding, the motivation behind the learning of language, and the need for cognitive consistency are motives which seem associated with the development and "housekeeping" of the cognitive system (cf. Buck, 1976, Chapters 8 and 9), and they are not primary motivational/emotional systems in our sense of that term. Such cognitive motives are particularly important in interaction with the primary motivational/emotional systems in the determination of complex processes of coping, conflict resolution, etc. (cf. Buck, 1976, Chapter 10).

Neural Bases

Anatomical structure. We have assumed that each of the primary motivational/emotional systems is associated with a specific neural substrate. These may be anatomically distinct or intertwined with one another. In general, the different system levels noted above correspond to different levels within the central nervous system, with simple reflexes based in the spinal cord and brain stem, species-specific fixed action patterns based in the brain stem and hypothalamus, the primary drives based in or near the hypothalamus, and the primary affects being based upon limbic system as well as brain stem and hypothalamic mechanisms.

The general anatomical structure of the more complex of the primary motivational/emotional systems is presented in Figure 6-1. A great deal is known about the functioning of these neurochemical systems, and due to recent technical advances in the study of the nervous system, this understanding will increase greatly in the near future (cf. Buck, 1976, 1983, 1984). For example, it is well known that the brain stem reticular formation is associated with arousal mechanisms which can affect both the rest of the brain and the body (cf. Lindsley, 1951, 1957) and that the hypothalamus is associated both with mechanisms involving specific drives, such as hunger, thirst, and sex (Grossman, 1979), and with "reward-punishment" systems which course through it on their way between the brain stem and higher centers (Olds & Fobes, 1981). Also, MacLean's (1968, 1969, 1970) notion that the limbic system contains neurochemical systems involving self-preservation, aggression, and fear (particularly involving the amygdala), and systems involving species preserva-

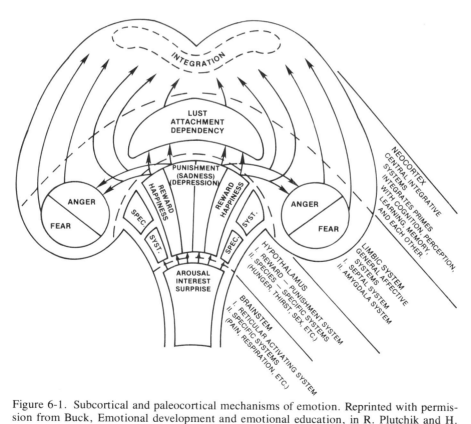

Figure 6-1. Subcortical and paleocortical mechanisms of emotion. Reprinted with permission from Buck, Emotional development and emotional education, in R. Plutchik and H. Kellerman (Eds.), *Emotion in Early Development*. New York: Academic Press, 1983.

tion, sociability, and sex (particularly involving the septal area) is widely accepted. Details of the evidence relating to all of these systems is summarized in Buck (1976).

Theories of motivation and emotion. Different physiologically based theories of emotion and motivation have grown up around different types and levels of primary motivational/emotional systems. Ethological theories of motivation emphasize the analysis of instinctive behavior patterns; arousal theories have been proposed based upon the functioning of the reticular formation (Hebb, 1955; Lindsley, 1957); drive theories have been proposed based upon drive-specific excitatory and inhibitory centers in the hypothalamus (Stellar, 1954); reward-punishment theories have been based upon fiber tracts coursing through the hypothalamus which mediate self-stimulation (Olds & Milner, 1954); and theories encompassing subjective experience have been proposed based upon limbic system mechanisms (MacLean, 1968, 1970). Each of these theories has proved useful, and each has gained its share of empirical support, so that it appears that each is correct as far as it goes but that each is incomplete. It is only when they are taken together that they provide a comprehensive view of the neural bases of motivation and emotion (cf. Buck, 1976, 1983, 1984).

The different theories of the primary affects considered above—the typological versus the dimensional views—can also be seen as relevant to different sorts of identifiable neural systems. The reticular activating system varies along an arousal or intensity dimension, and reward-punishment systems can be thought to vary along an evaluation dimension (pleasant-unpleasant; approach-avoidance, etc.). At the same time, there are also centers in the limbic system associated with relatively distinct motivational/emotional states, such as sex, fear, and anger. Thus, it is not surprising that emotional behavior seems to reflect both kinds of structure.

Motor Systems of Emotional Expression

We have seen that there is evidence that spontaneous and symbolic expression are based upon different neural mechanisms, with spontaneous expression involving a readout of the state of primary motivational/emotional systems. There is also evidence that different motor systems underly spontaneous and symbolic expression (cf. Courville, 1966; Schwartz, Ahern, & Brown, 1979; Steklis & Raleigh, 1979). It has long been recognized by neurologists that voluntary facial movements are controlled via the pyramidal motor system, which originates in the facial area of the motor strip in the precentral gyrus and descends directly via corticobulbar pathways to the facial nuclei in the brain stem. Lesions of this system may impair voluntary facial movements but leave spontaneous expressions intact. Spontaneous facial expressions, in contrast, are controlled via extrapyramidal pathways which are complex and poorly defined. Certain disorders affecting the extrapyramidal system, such as Parkinson's disease, produce the characteristic "mask-like" lack of facial expression and absence of automatic rhythmic movements such as swinging the arms while walking, resulting in a rigid posture and expression "like a statue" (Best & Taylor, 1966, p. 152), all without abolishing voluntary facial movements.

   Another dimension upon which the neural mechanisms underlying emotional expression vary involves whether they deal with the expression only or with the motivational/emotional system that elicits the expression. Electrical stimulation of certain brain regions has been shown to produce facial expressions and vocalizations in both humans and animals, some of which seem "incomplete" and fragmentary, some of which closely resemble spontaneous expression but which nevertheless do not seem to be associated with a motivational/emotional state, and others of which seem clearly to be associated with such states. These studies have shown that the motor control of facial expression is organized and integrated in the brain stem, and that some of these mechanisms involve "hard-wired" systems of coordinated facial, bodily, and autonomic response.

Facial Expression

Instructive illustrations of the role of brain stem mechanisms in facial expression may be found in both the animal and human clinical literatures. In an early study on cats, Weinstein and Bender (1943) found some areas where stimulation produced facial movements which were simple reflex acts—one-sided, tetanoid, and isolated—while other areas produced bilateral, smooth, "life-like" expressions. The latter often occurred in conjunction with autonomic changes which seemed to have functions associated with coughing, swallowing, nursing, defecation, etc. A study of the results of reticular stimulation in 12 human pain patients produced some facial expressions of fear and depression which were nonemotional "fragments of emotions," and other more integrated expressions associated with pain and "a desire to cry" (Wilson & Nachold, 1972). The symptom complex of "pseudobulbar palsy" in humans, associated with bilateral interruption of corticobulbar pathways within the brain stem, can result in uncontrollable outbursts of laughing and crying without emotion (Truex, 1959). Bear (1980) has suggested that the latter is a "pure disorder of emotional expression," involving the disinhibition or excitation of "hard-wired" brain stem mechanisms of expression.

Expressive Vocalization

While relatively few studies have been directed to the study of the neural mechanisms underlying facial expression per se, there have been many systematic studies of the neural bases of spontaneous vocalizations expressive of emotion (cf. MacLean, 1978; Ploog, 1966, 1981). It is reasonable to assume that the results of these studies may be relevant to the analysis of the mechanisms underlying facial expression. First, the facial and vocal expression of emotion serve similar evolutionary functions—emotional expression—via similar peripheral mechanisms; both typically involve the facial musculature. Second, although the literature on facial expression is not as extensive as the literature on vocal expression, much of it is consistent with this assumption. Thus, voluntary and spontaneous systems underlying facial expression can be distinguished; some facial expressions seem to be "hard-wired" into brain stem mechanisms, facial expressions can be elicited in isolated and nonintegrated "bits" by brain stem stimulation, and integrated facial expressions can occur without affect. All of these statements apply to the vocal expression of emotion as well (cf. Jurgens, 1975).

The literature on the neural systems underlying expressive vocalization has recently been reviewed by Jurgens (1979), who suggests that these systems are arranged in a hierarchical manner. The first level involves the brain stem reticular formation at the level of the pons and medulla. These include the nuclei directly involved in facial movement and respiratory control. He suggests that the motor coordination of specific behaviors necessary for vocalization occurs at this level. However, the integrated neural patterns that characterize specific calls is not generated here, but requires the direction of higher structures.

The second level involves the midbrain region, specifically the caudal periaqueductal gray and laterally adjacent tegmentum between the inferior colliculus and the brachium conjunctivum (Jurgens, 1979, p. 38). Jurgens suggests that the "hardwired" neural patterns underlying specific vocal expressions occur at this level and that the motor integration of these patterns occurs at the pons-medulla level. Jurgens notes that the motivational/emotional systems in the hypothalamus and limbic system, in which stimulation causes vocalizations which presumably are secondary to those states, project directly into this midbrain area, and he suggests that the influences from the motivational/emotional systems normally trigger vocal patterns which are "hard-wired" in the midbrain region. Jurgens notes that this vocalization-eliciting system has great phylogenetic age: it has been related to call production in birds, reptiles, amphibians, and even fish, despite the very different call-producing systems in these different vertebrate classes.

The third and fourth hierarchical levels both involve the volitional control of vocalization. The third level is associated with the region of the cingulate gyrus, involving the anterior limbic cortex in the squirrel monkey and the supplemental motor area in humans. This area appears to control vocalizations independently of motivational/emotional states via facilitatory or inhibitory influences upon the midbrain mechanism. It is thus associated with *voluntary call initiation* in that it may initiate calls which are already "hard-wired" within the midbrain, but it cannot form new calls.

The fourth level is associated with *voluntary call formation* in that it involves the ability to form new calls which are not dependent upon those "hard-wired" in the midbrain. This function is particularly associated with the area of the precentral gyrus which represents the larynx. This area is dispensible in creatures with a wholly innate vocal repertoire, but it gains increasing importance as one moves from lower monkeys to humans, where damage causes severe disturbances. We have seen that emotional utterance—highly stereotyped verbal statements such as curses or salutations—often survive destruction in this area in humans, and Jurgens suggests that this is because the voluntary control of call formation is relatively unimportant for these utterances.

A Model of the Motor Systems of Emotional Expression

Based upon Jurgen's (1979) analysis, a provisional model of the motor systems underlying the facial and vocal expression of emotion may be suggested. This model

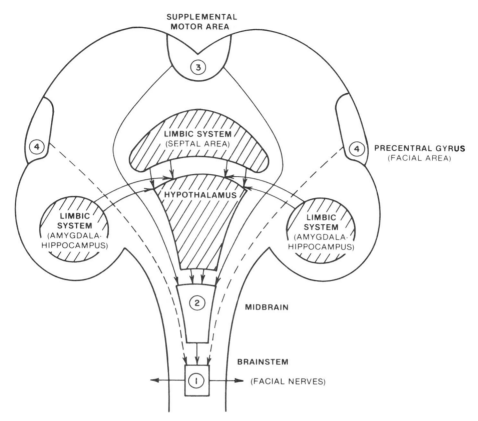

Figure 6-2. Neural bases of emotional expression. Reprinted with permission from Buck, *The Communication of Emotion*. New York: Guilford Press, 1984.

is presented in Figure 6-2. The model assumes that the mechanisms underlying facial expression are similar in general ways to those underlying vocal expression.

The model suggests that the motor coordination of facial as well as vocal expression occurs in the lower brain stem reticular formation (1), which may be controlled either by "hard-wired" systems of expression located in the midbrain region (2) or by voluntary influences from the precentral motor cortex (4) mediated via corticobulbar pyramidal fibers (dashed lines). The latter system involves *voluntary expression formation*, which is analogous to Jurgens' voluntary call formation system. The midbrain mechanism (2) may be activated by motivational/emotional systems in the limbic system and hypothalamus (cross-hatched in Figure 6-2), resulting in an externally accessible "readout" of the internal motivational/emotional state. This is the system involved in *spontaneous communication*. Alternatively, the midbrain mechanism may be activated by voluntary influences, which following Jurgens (1979) we shall tentatively locate in the supplemental motor area above the cingulate gyrus (3). This would constitute a system of *voluntary expression initiation* analogous to Jurgens' voluntary call initiation. It might be noted that the existence of an expression initiation mechanism would imply that posed emotional expression would differ significantly from the voluntary formation of facial expressions since the former would have the "assist" of the hard-wired midbrain mechanisms while the latter would not (cf. Buck, 1983, 1984).

Mechanisms of Excitation and Inhibition in Emotional Expression

This chapter has presented a general view of the nature of nonverbal communication, the role of the external expression of motivational/emotional states, and the neural systems involved in that expression. This section focuses on the determinants of individual differences in emotional expressiveness. In particular, it examines three points of view which, initially very different from one another, have recently converged, suggesting that they commonly reflect a basic dimension of behavior. These points of view are (a) the externalizing/internalizing distinction stemming from Jones's (1930, 1935) studies of the development of emotional expression, (b) Gray's theory, stemming from Pavlov's typology and Eysenck's theory of extraversion/introversion, and (c) the analysis of the role of cerebral lateralization in emotional expression. This author has pointed out the relationships between these points of view before (Buck, 1976, 1979a), but recent evidence has made this point of view even more compelling. I suggest that these points of view together have the potential to form a major integrative synthesis in psychology.

Externalizing/Internalizing Modes of Response

Jones's studies. The distinction between externalizing and internalizing modes of response was first suggested by Jones (1930, 1935), based upon the observations that the threshold for electrodermal responding in infants is higher than in older children, and that in nursery school-age children, some individuals show a consistent pattern of relationship between physiological responding and overt expressiveess. The *externalizing* pattern is associated with marked overt behavior but infrequent or reduced electrodermal responses, while the *internalizing* pattern is the reverse. Jones hypothesized that the increased electrodermal responding in older children is related to their increasing control over emotional expression: "in older children, the increased inhibition and apparent emotional control may not imply a diminished emotionality but merely a shift from outer to inner patterns of response" (Jones, 1960, p. 13).

In later studies of extreme high and low electrodermal reactors in adolescents, Jones found that high reactors were rated by others as exhibiting a high degree of emotional control; they were rated as being quiet, reserved, controlled, and deliberative. They were also seen as being poised, calm, good natured, cooperative, and responsible. In contrast, the low reactors were rated as being uninhibited in their emotional expression: impulsive, animated, active, and talkative. They were also judged in more negative terms; as assertive, attention-seeking, and bossy. Jones judged the low-electrodermally-reactive adolescents as showing an "infantile" and maladaptive mode of response. Interestingly, a later study by Block (1957) on medical school applicants found high and low electrodermal reactors to have generally similar characteristics as did Jones, but they were evaluated differently. The high reactors were seen as withdrawn, worrying, and generally maladjusted; the low reactors were seen as nonconforming, independent, and "aggressively direct." Perhaps the same behavior that seems pushy and assertive in an adolescent seems "aggressively direct" in a medical school applicant (Buck, 1979a).

Jones's distinction aroused new interest when it was found that measures of spontaneous facial expressiveness are negatively related (between subjects) with skin conductance measures (Buck, Savin, Miller, & Caul, 1969, 1972; Lanzetta & Kleck, 1970). In other words, facially expressive subjects tended to show smaller skin conductance responses than did those who remained "stone faced." These studies assessed facial expressiveness by techniques derived from Miller's studies of nonverbal communication in rhesus monkeys (cf. Miller, 1974): Lanzetta and Kleck used the facial expression associated with the threat of shock, and Buck et al. employed the slide-viewing technique described above.

The slide-viewing technique. A series of studies employing the slide-viewing technique to assess individual differences in spontaneous expressiveness has found the following major results: (a) in adults, females are markedly better senders than males; (b) there are substantial individual differences in expressiveness in nursery school-aged children, but the sex difference in expressiveness in these children is small or nonexistent; (c) age is negatively correlated with expressiveness in boys but not girls; (d) the change in the number of skin conductance responses to the slides is negatively correlated with expressiveness in both adults and children; and (e) the personality characteristics found by Jones and Block to distinguish high and low electrodermal reactors are related to low and high expressiveness, respectively, in children (cf. Buck, 1979a, 1979b). These results have been interpreted as suggesting that individual differences in facial/gestural expressiveness are based upon innate temperamental factors (which underly the large and consistent individual differences in expressiveness in children), but that these factors may be greatly altered by learning and experiential factors (which underly the sex difference in expressiveness in adults).

This author has suggested that these patterns may be based upon physiological mechanisms associated with the excitation and inhibition of emotional behavior, if it is assumed that these systems share the following characteristics: (a) that there are individual differences in the arousal and/or arousability of these systems early in life; (b) that learning experiences can result in situationally specific changes in these levels of arousal and/or arousability; and (c) that activity in the inhibitory system relative to the excitatory system is directly or indirectly associated with increased electrodermal responding (cf. Buck, 1979a, 1981).

This model is illustrated in Figure 6-3. It illustrates how one female and male (A and B) may have initial temperamental predispositions toward externalizing response patterns associated with high activity in the excitatory system relative to the inhibitory reponse system, while another female and male (C and D) initially show internalizing response patterns. In our culture, these four individuals would tend to experience sex-linked patterns of reward and punishment for overt emotional expression. These patterns alter the relative balance of activity in the excitatory and

| | EXTERNALIZING TEMPERAMENT | | INTERNALIZING TEMPERAMENT | |
	A (FEMALE)	B (MALE)	C (FEMALE)	D (MALE)
NEURAL SYSTEM:	REW. PUN.	REW. PUN.	REW. PUN.	REW. PUN.
INITIAL STATE (AMOUNT OF AROUSAL/ AROUSABILITY)	[10] [5]	[10] [5]	[5] [10]	[5] [10]
CHANGES IN GENERAL EMOTIONAL SITUATIONS	+5 −5	−5 +5	+5 −5	−5 +5
RESULTING ADULT PATTERN	[15] [0]	[5] [10]	[10] [5]	[0] [15]
CHANGES IN AGGRES- SIVE SITUATIONS	−5 +5	+5 −5	−5 +5	+5 −5
RESULTING ADULT PATTERN	[5] [10]	[15] [0]	[0] [15]	[10] [5]

Figure 6-3. Hypothesized changes in the degree of arousal in reward (BES) and punishment (BIS) systems caused by an interaction of innate temperament and social learning.

inhibitory systems in similar situations in the future. Being male, B and D tend to experience punishment for general emotional expression, but are rewarded for being aggressive, while A and C experience the opposite patterns of reinforcement. As a result, the females as adults tend to show externalizing patterns of response in emotional situations, while males show externalizing patterns of response in aggressive situations, regardless of their initial temperament. However, the initial temperament continues to affect adult behavior in that the social learning simply adds to or subtracts from the original amounts of activity in the systems.

Related findings. Several related series of findings are relevant to the externalizing/internalizing distinction and bring it into contact with the other points of view that we shall consider. First, a number of studies have linked low electrodermal responding to acting-out, sociopathic behavior. Beginning with Lykken (1957), it has been found that sociopaths are less electrodermally reactive that nonsociopaths (cf. Hare, 1965a, 1965b, 1965c, 1970, 1978; Schmauk, 1970). Studies by Waid and his colleagues have shown that, in college students, electrodermal responding is positively related to the degree of socialization (Waid, 1976), that less highly socialized subjects are more deceptive on polygraph examinations due to their lower electrodermal responding, and that in contrast the high electrodermal responding of highly socialized subjects may cause innocent subjects to be misclassified as deceptive (Waid, Orne, & Wilson, 1979a, 1979b). Also, Waid, Orne, Cook, and Orne (1980) have shown that a minimal dose (400 mg) of the antianxiety tranquilizer meprobamate reduces the phasic electrodermal response on a polygraph test, so that deception could not be detected. This result may be particularly significant, as we shall see.

A second series of findings which is of interest involves the relationships between spontaneous expressiveness and various measures of personality. Spontaneous facial expressiveness has been positively related to field dependence and performance IQ (which are related in turn to right hemisphere processing), repression on the Byrne Repression-Sensitization scale (related in turn to hysterical tendencies—Tucker, 1981), and extraversion (cf. Buck et al., 1972, 1974; Harper, Wiens, & Fugita, 1977; Harper, Wiens, & Matarazzo, 1979; Sabatelli, Dreyer, & Buck, 1979). It is noteworthy that Harper et al. (1977, 1979), who have made the most extensive investigation of personality correlates, found that measures of spontaneous expressiveness were more strongly and meaningfully related to personality measures than were measures of posed expressiveness.

A third relevant observation involves studies reported in Field and Walden (1981), which among other things investigated the facial expressiveness, cardiac responsiveness, and threshold to auditory stimuli in newborn infants. The authors found that facially expressive infants exhibited higher sensory thresholds and less cardiac responsivity compared with less expressive neonates. They point out that this finding is consistent both with Eysenck's theory of extraversion-introversion and the externalizing-internalizing literature (cf. Buck, 1976, 1979a).

A fourth relevant observation involves the meaning of the high electrodermal responding in the internalizing mode of response. Evidence relevant to this finding has been reviewed by Fowles (1980). Based upon an analysis of differences in heart rate and electrodermal responding, particularly in a study by Szpiler and Epstein (1976), Fowles suggested that electrodermal responses increase with activation of a behavioral inhibition system (BIS) associated with anxiety. Fowles's paper puts us directly into contact with the second point of view which we shall consider, Gray's theory.

Gray's Theory

The theory. Gray's theory is based upon Eysenck's theory of extraversion-introversion, which is based in turn upon notions of central nervous system excitation and inhibition such as Pavlov's theory of the strength of the nervous system (cf. Buck, 1976). Eysenck (1967) suggested that the ascending reticular activating system (ARAS) has a higher threshold for activation in extraverts than in introverts, which makes the extravert less subject to conditioning and, by extension, less susceptible to the process of socialization than the introvert. Some of Eysenck's predictions were not supported by subsequent conditioning studies, and in 1972 Gray proposed a reinterpretation of the theory in light of data on the effects of barbiturate drugs and lesions of the septal area in animals.

In essence, Gray (1972) proposes that the physiological site underlying the extraversion-introversion distinction involves the hippocampus and medial septal area, which appears to act as a pacemaker for 4.8 Hz theta rhythm in the hippocampus. Gray points out that this neural system is normally activated by punishment, frustration, or nonreward and is associated with the inhibition of overt behavior. He suggests that the more the activity in this system, the more effective punishment is in inhibiting behavior, and the more susceptible one is to punishment, the more introverted one would be. Gray suggests that this system is represented at a higher level in the orbito-frontal cortex, and the whole system is termed the "septal-hippocampus-frontal" (SHF) system (cf. Gray, 1972).

Gray's system is compatible with theories which emphasize the importance of reward/punishment mechanisms (cf. Olds & Milner, 1954; Olds & Fobes, 1981; Routtenberg, 1978), in that it posits that there are three kinds of systems involved in the motivation of behavior: the reticular formation, which mediates diffuse general arousal; a "behavioral activation system" (BAS) which initiates behavior in response to cues associated with reward or the active avoidance of punishment; and a "behavioral inhibition system" (BIS) associated with the SHF mechanisms. The latter is viewed as an "anxiety system" which inhibits behavior in response to cues associated with punishment (passive avoidance) and frustrative nonreward (extinction). We have seen that the activity of the BIS seems to be associated with increased electrodermal responding. Fowles (1980) also suggests that BIS activity is decreased by antianxiety drugs, such as alcohol, barbiturates, and the minor tranquilizers, which relates back to the Waid et al. (1980) results.

The septal syndrome. Among the most important implications of Gray's theory is that it identifies a wide variety of human personality patterns with neural systems which have known locations in the central nervous system and known pharmacological properties, and also with experimental procedures well known in animal research (cf. Fowles, 1980; Gorenstein & Newman, 1980). For example, animal studies have indicated that symptoms associated with lesions in the SHF system are remarkably similar to symptoms of "disinhibitory psychopathology" in humans. These symptoms include the disinclination to inhibit punished responses, a steep temporal gradient of fear arousal so that feared stimuli become effective in inhibiting behavior only when they are immediately at hand, an inability to delay gratification, poor impulse control in the face of rewards, and stimulation seeking. Gorenstein and Newman (1980) suggest that the septal syndrome constitutes a "basic manifestation of disinhibition uncontaminated by environmental influence" (p. 313) and that it may provide a functional animal research model for the analysis of disinhibitory psychopathology in humans. They suggest that such psychopathology involves a genetically determined diathesis which is normally modified by environmental influences, and that this diathesis is at the root of a wide variety of psychopathological disorders, including sociopathy, hysteria, hyperactivity, impulsivity, and alchoholism.

Cerebral Lateralization and Emotional Expression

There are intriguing suggestions that the BAS and BIS systems may be related to recent suggestions that the cerebral hemispheres have different functions in emotional expression (Buck & Duffy, 1980; Tucker, 1981). Although it is too soon to demonstrate conclusively and precisely how these systems are related, there are at least two major points of contact in the two literatures. One is the identification of both the BIS and the left cerebral hemisphere with anxiety and the inhibition of spontaneous expression, and the other is the apparent involvement of both in human disinhibitory psychopathology.

Anxiety and inhibition. We have seen that the BIS has been identified as an inhibitory system whose functioning is decreased by antianxiety drugs. Tucker (1981) has suggested in a comprehensive review of the literature in this area that the left cerebral hemisphere is likewise associated with anxiety and the inhibition of the emotionality associated with the right hemisphere. Tucker bases his analysis largely upon the known cognitive capacities of the left and right hemispheres. The left hemisphere is associated with an analytic and verbal form of cognitive strategy, the right hemisphere with a global and imaginal ideation. In recent studies, Tucker and his colleages have shown college students color slides with either sexual or aversive content. In one study, they asked subjects to facilitate or inhibit their emotional responses to the slides and analyzed the reports of the naturally occurring cognitive strategies used to accomplish this. They demonstrated that, as expected, subjects tended to use analytic and verbal ideation to inhibit emotion and that global and imaginal thinking was employed to facilitate arousal (Shearer & Tucker, 1981). In a second study, Tucker and Newman (1981) instructed subjects to inhibit their response using either an analytic or imaginal strategy and found that the former strategy was more effective using both self-reports and measures of autonomic arousal (finger temperature).

Tucker's thesis is quite compatible with the results of the study by Buck and Duffy (1980). The latter study found greater spontaneous facial expressiveness in left-hemisphere-damaged aphasic patients than in right-hemisphere-damaged patients and concluded that

> the left hemisphere may normally exert an inhibitory influence over spontaneous nonverbal expression. Damage to the left hemisphere, in this view, would decrease this inhibition and allow for greater nonverbal expression. The low expressiveness of the right hemisphere-damaged patients suggests that this expression may be mediated in part by the right cerebral hemisphere. (p. 357)

Disinhibitory psychopathology. Tucker (1981) has suggested that a variety of psychopathological processes may be related to differences in hemispheric processing, including the disinhibitory personality disorders: sociopathic personality, particularly in men, and hysterical personality patterns, particularly in women. Flor-Henry (1974), for example, has suggested that both hysteria and psychopathy involve disturbances of left hemisphere functioning, with a pattern of a higher performance than verbal IQ, and notes that psychopathy is particularly associated with males and hysteria with females. Related to this is the finding that the symptoms of conversion reactions tend to occur on the left side of the body, suggesting right hemisphere influence (Calin, Diamond, & Braff, 1977; Stern, 1977). Tucker contrasts the apparently low level of left hemisphere cognitive functioning in sociopathy and hysteria with obsessive-compulsive disorders in which there is evidence that left hemisphere cognitive functions are particularly strong.

Conclusions

There is converging evidence that externalizing-internalizing modes of emotional responding are related to a basic dimension of behavior involving central nervous system mechanisms of excitation and inhibition. It is too early to specify exactly what mechanisms are involved—there may in fact be a series of mechanisms at different levels in the nervous system. Nevertheless, the evidence suggests that nonverbal communication via spontaneous facial/gestural expressiveness is an important aspect of this dimension, doubly so because it involves such socially relevant behavior. This should probably not be considered to be a trait in the sense that traits involve consistent tendencies to respond that are carried across situations. In fact, it seems clear that externalizing-internalizing modes of response normally vary widely according to the situation. This is not as contradictory as it might first appear. As Figure 6-3 demonstrates, it is possible for a physiological substrate to be so organized as to actively encourage different responses in different situations; thus, a child may be inhibited from expressing his or her emotions in a given situation but not in others (cf. Buck, 1979a). It is possible that externalizing-internalizing modes of response affect behavior across most all situations only in the extreme cases of psychopathology, resulting in hysteria or sociopathy on one hand or obsessive-compulsive disorders on the other.

In this final section we have been discussing a puzzle, many pieces of which are not yet in place. However, an overall integrative picture is beginning to emerge, and the general boundaries and characteristics of the picture as a whole are becoming clearer. It encompasses that aspect of "nonverbal communication" that involves spontaneous emotional expression, ethological analyses of the evolution of emotional expression and communication, physiological theories of motivation and emotion, pharmacological studies of the effects of drugs on learning and performance, studies of the effects of brain manipulations in animals and brain pathology in humans, theories of human emotion and individual differences, etc. It is relevant to many levels of analysis, encompassing the levels of reflex and instinct, drive and emotion, and social learning and personality. In short we have the exciting prospect of a major synthesis, relating areas of investigation which have long been isolated from one another and which involve greatly different levels of analysis.

The Physiological Bases of Nonverbal Communication

The distinction between spontaneous and symbolic nonverbal communication has been defined as well as the respective relationship to right and left hemisphere functioning. The discussion outlined the nature of the primary motivational/emotional systems or primes underlying spontaneous communication, which are special-purpose processing systems associated with specific neural substrates. The nature of the motor systems underlying nonverbal behavior was outlined, using the work of Jurgens and Ploog to suggest that three such systems can be distinguished: a system concerned with spontaneous expression; a voluntary expression initiation system in which innate expressions are activated voluntarily, and an expression formation system involving the voluntary construction of expressions. We then considered the notion that general excitatory-inhibitory systems affect nonverbal expression, ending with the suggestion supported by Tucker's work and the Buck and Duffy results that the left hemisphere exerts an anxiety-like inhibitory control over spontaneous expressive tendencies mediated by the right hemisphere.

The foregoing suggest that the following factors must be considered in analyzing the physiological bases of nonverbal communication. Foremost is whether the non-verbal behavior involves spontaneous expression, voluntary expression initiation, or voluntary expression formation since widely different neural systems are involved in these types of expression. If the behavior involves spontaneous expression, one must consider the nature of the motivational/emotional system involved and its characteristics: i.e., the innate arousability of that system for that particular individual, the sorts of developmental experiences provided by the family and culture relevant to the expression of that system, the implications of the particular situation for the arousal and expression of that system, the presence of any physical factors (sleeplessness, drugs, disease) that might affect the physiological operation of the system, etc.

In addition to the specific motivational/emotional system, a broad variety of research suggests that general excitatory and inhibitory systems underlie nonverbal expressiveness. The particular nature of these systems is not yet understood nor are their interactions with specific motivational/emotional systems. However, it appears that the excitatory-inhibitory systems have several general features. Inhibition is associated with the internalizing pattern of increased electrodermal responding and decreased external expression, while excitation is associated with the opposite, externalizing, pattern of response. An extreme example of the externalizing pattern is acting-out sociopathic behavior (particularly in males) and hysterical behavior (particularly in females). An extreme example of the internalizing pattern may be found in obsessive-compulsive disorders and high anxiety. Antianxiety drugs such as meprobamate and alcohol appear to increase externalizing tendencies. The excitatory-inhibitory systems are related to personality measures, and their influence can be detected virtually from birth. Inhibition seems to be associated with the SHF system and the left hemisphere; excitation appears to be associated with the right hemisphere.

Summary

This discussion of the physiological bases of nonverbal communication has included: (a) a distinction between spontaneous and symbolic communication as different types of nonverbal communication based upon different physiological systems; (b) a definition of primary motivational/emotional systems that are the basis of spontaneous communication; (c) a discussion of the content of spontaneous communication as involving a "readout" of the state of the motivational/emotional systems; (d) a model of the motor systems underlying emotional expression; and (e) a discussion of the role of excitatory-inhibitory systems in emotional expressiveness, suggesting that a synthesis of major proportions is presently under way which will relate many diverse areas of study and levels of analysis.

Acknowledgment.   This chapter was written while the author was a visiting scholar at the Department of Psychology and Social Relations, Harvard University, and the Aphasia Research Center at the Boston Veterans Administration Hospital. Research reported here was supported by National Institute of Mental Health (NIMH) Grant No. 20268 and by funds from the University of Connecticut Research Foundation. The author is grateful for Drs. Joan Borod, Robert Duffy, Tiffany Field, and Harold Goodglass for their comments on this chapter.

References

Andrew, R. J. (1963). The origin and evolution of the calls and facial expressions of the primates. *Behavior, 20*, 1-109.

Andrew, R. J. (1965). The origins of facial expressions. *Scientific American, 213*, 88-94.

Bear, D. M. (1980, November). *Anatomy and pathology of emotion*. Presentation at the Boston Veterans' Administration Hospital, Boston.

Best, C., & Taylor, N. (1966). *The physiological basis of medical practice* (8th Ed.). Baltimore: Williams and Wilkins.

Block, J. (1957). A study of affective responsiveness in a lie detection situation. *Journal of Abnormal and Social Psychology, 55*, 11-15.

Borod, J., & Koff, E. (1982, February). *Facial asymmetry and lateral dominance in normal and brain-damaged adults*. Paper presented at the meeting of the International Neuropsychological Society, Pittsburgh, PA.

Buck, R. (1976). *Human motivation and emotion*. New York: Wiley.

Buck, R. (1978). The slide-viewing technique for measuring nonverbal sending accuracy: A guide for replication. *Catalog of Selected Documents in Psychology, 8*, 63 (Abstract).

Buck, R. (1979a). Individual differences in nonverbal sending accuracy and electrodermal responding: The externalizing-internalizing dimension. In R. Rosenthal (Ed.), *Skill in nonverbal communication: Individual differences*. Cambridge, MA: Oelgeschlager, Gunn & Hain.

Buck, R. (1979b). Measuring individual differences in the nonverbal communication of affect: The slide-viewing paradigm. *Human Communication Research, 6*, 47-57.

Buck, R. (1981). The evolution and development of emotion expression and communication. In S. Brehm, S. Kassin, & F. Gibbons (Eds.), *Developmental social psychology*. New York: Oxford.

Buck, R. (1982). Spontaneous and symbolic nonverbal behavior and the ontogeny of communication. In R. S. Feldman (Ed.), *The Development of Nonverbal Behavior in Children*. New York: Springer-Verlag.

Buck, R. (1983). Emotion development and emotion education. In R. Plutchik and H. Kellerman (Eds.), *Emotions in early development*. New York: Academic Press.

Buck, R. (1984). *The communication of emotion*. New York: Guilford Press. In press.

Buck, R., & Duffy, R. (1977). *Nonverbal communication of affect in brain-damaged patients*. Paper presented at the convention of the American Psychological Association, San Francisco.

Buck, R., & Duffy, R. (1980). Nonverbal communication of affect in brain-damaged patients. *Cortex, 16*, 351-362.

Buck, R. W., Miller, R. E., & Caul, W. F. (1974). Sex, personality and physiological variables in the communication of emotion via facial expression. *Journal of Personality & Social Psychology, 30*, 587-596.

Buck, R., Savin, V. J., Miller, R. E., & Caul, W. F. (1969). Nonverbal communication of affect in humans. *Proceedings of the 77th Annual Convention of the American Psychological Association*, 367-368.

Buck, R., Savin, V., Miller, R. E., & Caul, W. F. (1972). Nonverbal communication of affect in humans. *Journal of Personality and Social Psychology, 23*, 362-371.

Cofer, C. N., & Appley, M. H. (1964). *Motivation: Theory and research*. New York: Wiley.

Courville, J. (1966). Rubrobulbar fibers to the facial nucleus and the lateral reticular nucleus. *Brain Research, 1*, 317-337.

Critchley, M. (1975). *Silent language*. London: Butterworth.

Darwin, C. (1872). *Expressions of the emotions in man and animals*. London: John Murray.

Duffy, R. J., & Buck, R. (1979). A study of the relationship between propositional (pantomime) and subpropositional (facial expression) extraverbal behaviors in aphasics. *Folia Phoniatrica, 31*, 129-136.

Duffy, R. J., & Duffy, J. R. (1981). Three studies of deficits in pantomimic expression and pantomimic recognition in aphasia. *Journal of Speech and Hearing Research, 24*, 70-84.

Duffy, R. J., Duffy, J. R., and Pearson, K. (1975). Pantomime recognition in aphasics. *Journal of Speech and Hearing Research, 18*, 115-132.

Ekman, P., & Friesen, W. V. (1975). *Unmasking the face*. Englewood Cliffs: Prentice-Hall.

Ekman, P., Friesen, W. V., & Ellsworth, P. (1971). *Emotion in the human face*. New York: Pergamon Press.

Eysenck, H. J. (1967). *The biological basis of personality*. Springfield, IL: Charles C Thomas.

Field, T. M., & Walden, T. A. (1981). Perception and production of facial expressions in infancy and early childhood. In H. Reese & L. Lipsett (Eds.), *Advances in Child Development and Behavior* (Vol. 16). New York: Academic Press.

Flor-Henry, P. (1974). Psychosis, neurosis, and epilepsy. *British Journal of Psychiatry, 124*, 144-150.

Fowles, D. C. (1980). The Three Arousal Model: Implications of Gray's two-factor learning theory for heart rate, electrodermal activity, and psychopathy. *Psychophysiology, 17*, 87-104.

Galin, D., Diamond, R., & Braff, D. (1977). Lateralization of conversion symptoms: More frequent on the left. *American Journal of Psychiatry, 134*, 578-580.

Gainotti, G., & Lemmo, M. (1976). Comprehension of symbolic gestures in aphasia. *Brain and Language, 3*, 451-460.

Gibson, J. J. (1966). *The senses considered as perceptual systems*. Boston: Houghton-Mifflin.

Gibson, J. J. (1977). The theory of affordances. In R. E. Shaw & J. Bransford (Eds.), *Perceiving, acting and knowing: Toward an ecological psychology*. Hillsdale, NJ: Erlbaum.

Glickman, S. E., & Schiff, B. B. (1967). A biological theory of reinforcement. *Psychological Review, 74*, 81-109.

Goodglass, H., & Kaplan, E. (1963). Disturbance of gesture and pantomime in aphasia. *Brain, 86*, 703-720.

Gorenstein, E. E., & Newman, J. P. (1980). Disinhibitory psychopathology: A new perspective and a model for research. *Psychological Review, 87*, 301-315.

Gray, J. A. (1972). The psychophysiological nature of introversion-extraversion: A modification of Eysenck's theory. In V. D. Nebylitsyn and J. A. Gray (Eds.), *Biological basis of individual behavior*. New York: Academic Press.

Grossman, S. P. (1979). The biology of motivation. *Annual Review of Psychology, 30*, 209-242.

Hare, R. D. (1965a). Acquisition and generalization of a conditioned fear response in psychopathic and nonpsychopathic criminals. *Journal of Psychology, 59*, 367-370.

Hare, R. D. (1965b). Psychopathy, fear arousal and anticipated pain. *Psychological Reports, 16*, 499-502.

Hare, R. D. (1965c). Temporal gradient of fear arousal in psychopaths. *Journal of Abnormal Psychology, 70*, 442-445.

Hare, R. D. (1970). *Psychopathy: Theory and research*. New York: Wiley.

Hare, R. D. (1978). Electrodermal and cardiovascular correlates of psychopathy. In R. D. Hare & D. Schalling (Eds.), *Psychopathic behavior: Approaches to research*. New York: Wiley.

Harper, R. G., Wiens, A. N., & Fugita, B. (1977). *Individual differences in encoding-decoding of affect and emotional dissimulation*. Paper presented at the convention of the American Psychological Association, San Francisco.

Harper, R. G., Wiens, A. N., & Matarazzo, J. D. (1979). The relationship between endoding-decoding of visual nonverbal emotional cues. *Semiotica, 28*, 171-192.

Hebb, D. O. (1955). Drives and the C.N.S. (Conceptual nervous system). *Psychological Review, 62*, 243-354.

Hess, E. H. (1962). Ethology: An approach toward the complete analysis of behavior. In R. Brown, E. Galanten, E. H. Hess, & G. Mindler (Eds.), *New directions in psychology*, pp. 157-266. New York: Holt, Rinehart & Winston.

Izard, C. (1971). *The face of emotion*. New York: Appleton-Century-Crofts.

Izard, C. E. (1977). *Human emotions*. New York: Plenum Press.

Jenkins, J., Jimenez-Pabon, E., Shaw, R., & Sefer, J. (1975). *Schnell's aphasia in adults*. New York: Harper & Row.

Jones, H. E. (1930). The galvanic skin reflex in infancy. *Child Development, 1*, 106-110.

Jones, H. E. (1935). The galvanic skin response as related to overt emotional expression. *American Journal of Psychology, 47*, 241-251.

Jones, H. E . (1960). The longitudinal method in the study of personality. In I. Iscoe & H. W. Stevenson (Eds.), *Personality development in children*. Chicago: University of Chicago Press.

Jurgens, U. (1979). Neural control of vocalization in nonhuman primates. In H. D. Steklis & M. J. Raleigh (Eds.), *Neurobiology of social communication in primates*. New York: Academic Press.

Kimura, D. (1979). Neuromotor mechanisms in the evolution of human communications. In H. D. Steklis & M. J. Raleigh (Eds.), *Neurobiology of social communication in primates*, pp. 197-219. New York: Academic Press.

Lanzetta, J. T., & Kleck, R. E. (1970). Encoding and decoding of nonverbal affect in humans. *Journal of Personality and Social Psychology, 16*, 12-19.

Lindsley, D. B. (1951). Emotion. In S. S. Stevens (Ed.), *Handbook of experimental psychology*. New York: Wiley.

Lindsley, D. B. (1957). Psychophysiology and motivation. In M. R. Jones (Ed.), *Nebraska symposium on motivation*, pp. 44-105. Lincoln, NE: University of Nebraska Press.

Lykken, D. T. (1957). A study of anxiety in the sociopathic personality. *Journal of Abnormal and Social Psychology, 55*, 6-10.

MacLean, P. D. (1968). Contrasting functions of limbic and neocortical systems of the brain and their relevance to psychophysiological aspects of medicine. In E. Gellhorn (Ed.), *Biological foundations of emotion*. Glenview, IL: Scott, Foresman.

MacLean, P. D. (1969). The hypothalamus and emotional behavior. In W. Haymaker, E. Anderson, & W. J. H. Nanta (Eds.), *The hypothalamus*. Springfield, IL: Charles C Thomas.

MacLean, P. D. (1970). The limbic brain in relation to the psychoses. In P. H. Black (Ed.), *Physiological correlates of emotion*. New York: Academic Press.

MacLean, P. D. (1978). Effects of lesions of globus pallidus on species—typical display behavior of squirrel monkeys. *Brain Research, 149*, 175-196.

Miller, R. E. (1974). Social and parmacological influences on nonverbal communication in monkeys and man. In L. Krames, T. Alloway, & P. Pliner (Eds.), *Nonverbal communication*. New York: Plenum Press.

Olds, M. E., & Fobes, J. L. (1981). The central basis of motivation: Intracranial self-stimulation studies. *Annual Review of Psychology, 32*, 523-576.

Olds, J., & Milner, P. (1954). Positive reinforcement produced by electrical stimulation of septal area and other regions of rat brain. *Journal of Comparative and Physiological Psychology, 47*, 419-427.

Pickett, L. W. (1974). An assessment of gestural and pantomimic deficit in aphasic patients. *Acta Symbolica, 5*, 69-86.

Ploog, D. W. (1966). Biological basis for instinct and behavior: Studies on the development of social behavior in squirrel monkeys. In J. Wortis (Ed.), *Recent advances in biological psychiatry* (Vol. 8, 199-224). New York: Plenum Press.

Ploog, D. (1981). Neurobiology of primate audio-vocal behavior. *Brain Research Reviews, 3*, 35-61.

Routtenberg, A. (1978). The reward system of the brain *Scientific American, 239*(5), 154-164.

Russell, J. A. (1979). Affective space is biopolar. *Journal of Personality and Social Psychology, 37*, 345-356.

Russell, J. A., & Mehrabian, A. (1977). Evidence for a three-factor theory of emotions. *Journal of Research in Personality, 11*, 273-294.

Sabatelli, R., Dreyer, A., & Buck, R. (1979). Cognitive style and the sending and receiving of facial cues. *Perceptual and Motor Skills, 49*, 203-212.

Schlosberg, H. (1952). The description of facial expressions in terms of two dimensions. *Journal of Experimental Psychology, 44*, 229-237.

Schmauk, F. J. (1970). Punishment, arousal, and avoidance learning in sociopaths. *Journal of Abnormal Psychology, 76*, 325-335.

Schwartz, G. E., Ahern, G. L., & Brown, S. L. (1979). Lateralized facial muscle response to positive and negative emotional stimuli. *Psychophysiology, 16*, 561-571.

Shearer, S. L., & Tucker, D. M. (1981). Differential cognitive contributions of the cerebral hemispheres in the modulation of emotional arousal. *Cognitive Theory and Research, 5*, 85-93.

Steklis, H. D., & Raleigh, M. J. (1979). Behavioral and neurobiological aspects of primate vocalization and facial expressions. In H. D. Steklis & M. J. Raleigh (Eds.), *Neurobiology of social communication in primates*. New York: Academic Press.

Stellar, E. (1954). The physiology of motivation. *Psychological Review, 61*, 5-22.

Stern, D. B. (1977). Handedness and the lateral distribution of conversion reactions. *Journal of Nervous and Mental Disease, 164*, 122-128.

Szpiler, J. A., & Epstein, S. (1976). Availability of an avoidance response as related to autonomic arousal. *Journal of Abnormal Psychology, 87*, 73-82.

Thorpe, W. H. (1948). The modern concept of instinctive behavior. *Bulletin of Animal Behavior, 1*, 1-12.

Tomkins, S. (1962). *Affect, imagery, and consciousness: The positive affects (Vol. 1)*. New York: Springer

Tomkins, S. (1963). *Affect, imagery, and consciousness: The negative affects (Vol. 2)*. New York: Springer

Truex, R. C. (1959). *Human neuroanatomy*. Baltimore, MD: Williams & Wilkins.

Tucker, D. M. (1981). Lateral brain function, emotion, and conceptualization. *Psychological Bulletin, 89*, 19-46.

Tucker, D. M., & Newman, J. P. (1981). Lateral brain function and the cognitive inhibition of emotional arousal. *Cognitive Theory and Research, 5*, 197-202.

Varney, N. R. (1978). Linguistic correlates of pantomime recognition in aphasic patients. *Journal of Neurology, Neurosurgery and Psychiatry, 41*, 564-568.

Waid, W. M. (1976). Skin conductance response to both signaled and unsignaled noxious stimulation predicts level of socialization. *Journal of Personality and Social Psychology, 34*, 923-929.

Waid, W. M., Orne, E. C., Cook, M. R., & Orne, M. T. (1981). Meprobamate reduces accuracy of physiological detection of deception. *Science, 212*, 71-73.

Waid, W. M., Orne, M. T., & Wilson, S. K. (1979a). Effects of level of socialization on electrodermal detection of deception. *Psychophysiology, 16*, 15-22.

Waid, W. M., Orne, M. T., & Wilson, S. K. (1979b). Socialization, awareness, and the electrodermal response to deception and self-disclosure. *Journal of Abnormal Psychology, 88*, 663-666.

Weinstein, E. A., & Bender, M. B. (1943). Integrated facial patterns elicited by stimulation of the brain stem. *Archives of Neurology and Psychiatry, 50*, 34-42.

Wilson, W. P., & Nachold, B. S. (1972). The neurophysiology of affect. *Diseases of the Nervous System, 33*, 13-18.

Young, P. T. (1961). *Motivation and emotion*. New York: Wiley.

Chapter 7
Physiological Mediation of Attitude Maintenance, Formation, and Change

Mark P. Zanna, Richard A. Detweiler, and James M. Olson

The nature/nurture controversy is a recurring one in psychology, and the attitude formation and change literature has not been immune to it. Moore (1929) believed that there is a relation between biological factors (hereditary temperament) and attitude extremity. Klineberg (1940) noted that prejudicial racial attitudes are "sometimes stated in terms of direct, biologically determined hostility or aggressiveness between different racial groups" (pp. 346-347). Allport's (1935) view that attitudes are learned through experience or imitation has superceded this perspective, however, with a widely accepted contemporary definition of attitude being "a learned predisposition to respond in a consistently favorable or unfavorable manner with respect to a given object" (Fishbein & Ajzen, 1975, p. 6).

If this definition is valid, what role can biological factors play in attitude formation and change? While completely accepting the notion that attitudes are learned and not hereditary, it is possible that biological factors mediate attitude formation and change: between the occurrence of a stimulus and the learning of an attitude toward it, physiological factors (ranging from heart rate changes to drug effects) may be important. These factors might exert causal influence on the final attitude or merely be correlates of attitude processes. The primary issue that this chapter addresses is: Under what conditions do physiological factors mediate attitude processes? This issue will be addressed in three phases. First, the possible relations between existing attitudes and various physiological indices will be explored. Second, the role of physiological factors in attitude formation will be examined. Finally, the effects of physiological reactions on attitude change will be reviewed.

Attitudes and Psychophysiology

Attitude Definition

The definition of the term "attitude" has evolved and changed over the history of social psychology (see Allport, 1935; Oskamp, 1977). Perhaps reflecting the old notion that attitudes have cognitive, emotional, and behavioral components, there has been a tendency in the attitude psychophysiology literature to use the terms attitude and emotion interchangeably. Thus, theories and research on emotion have been used to substantiate particular approaches to attitude psychophysiology. Although attitudes and emotions are certainly related, it is misleading to equate them: An attitude is directed toward a referent or target, whereas an emotion is a label for an internal state. Research on the relation between these concepts is important, but theories and measures of emotion should be distinguished from theories and measures of attitudes. Because we deal in this chapter explicitly with attitudes, we will not discuss the emotion literature in detail. Consistent with most current theorizing about attitudes, we will use the term "attitude" to refer to the positive or negative evaluation of an object (person, thing, place, etc.). Attitudes are, therefore, distinct from beliefs and behaviors (see Fishbein & Ajzen, 1975), as well as from emotions. Thus, "I hate lima beans" or "I like soccer" represent attitudes because they reflect negative or positive evaluations of those objects, whereas "lima beans make me nauseated" or "soccer makes me feel excited" are emotions because they provide labels for internal states.

Assumptions about Attitudes and Physiological Response

Over the past 50 years, research on the relation between existing attitudes and physiological processes has taken one of three basic approaches. These approaches reflect different underlying assumptions about the nature of the attitude-physiology relation.

The first and earliest approach assumed that physiological response can be used as unbiased, objective measures of attitudes. Thus, physiological responses were equated with the attitude construct. For example, Chant and Salter (1937) examined the relations between attitudes toward war and GSR responses. They recorded GSR responses while generally pacifistic subjects were administered a scale made up of a series of militaristic and pacifistic items. They found an average correlation of $-.32$ between individual items and the associated GSR: Militaristic items resulted in greater GSR response. In a similar vein, Rankin and Campbell (1955) explored the use of GSR "as a potential measure of attitudes" (p. 30). In this study, two sets of GSR electrodes were connected to white, male subjects—one real set and one dummy set—and subjects responded to a word association task. On four occasions during this task, either a white or a black experimenter (or his assistant) adjusted the dummy electrodes, resulting in incidental physical contact. Significantly greater GSR responses ($p < .001$) occurred to the black than to the white personnel. This differential was greatest on the first contact. In addition, when scores on a previously administered attitudinal measure of prejudice were correlated with the differential in subjects' GSR responses to the black and white personnel, correlations of about .40 were obtained showing that greater prejudice was correlated with relatively larger physiological reactions to the black target. Finally, based upon previous work on emotion and prejudice (Cooper & Singer, 1956; Cooper & Siegel, 1956), Cooper and Pollock (1959) examined the relation between national/ethnic prejudice and GSR response. Subjects heard positive statements about nine national/ethnic groups (Austrian, Canadian, English, German, Irish, Japanese, Jewish, Mexican, Polish, and Swedish) while their GSR was recorded. Because previous data had demonstrated negative attitudes in this sample toward Japanese, Jews, and Mexicans, greater GSR reactivity to favorable statements about these groups was predicted. Analyses within subjects and across all subjects supported this hypothesis.

The assumption of these studies was that *attitudes result in physiological responses* which, because of "the general inability of the subject to inhibit the response voluntarily" (Rankin & Campbell, 1956, p. 30), can be used as indices of the attitudes. Despite the positive results reviewed above, research support for this perspective has been mixed, with null effects or inconsistent effects frequently obtained (e.g., Abel, 1930; Cattell et al., 1949; Gottlieb et al., 1967; Porier and Lott, 1967). More recently, however, Gormly's research has provided some support for this perspective in the context of interpersonal disagreement. Gormly (1974) found that larger GSR responses occurred when a confederate expressed a high proportion of counterattitudinal statements than when the confederate expressed a low proportion of counterattitudinal statements. Clore and Gormly (1974) replicated this basic finding and also found a significant correlation between GSR and attraction to the confederate. Although Baugher and Gormly (1975) did not replicate the attraction effect, they did replicate and extend the counterattitudinal effect: Greater GSR responses occurred to disagreement when the subject's self-rated competence on the topic under discussion was low or when the competence of the confederate was believed to be low.

The second approach to examining the relation between physiological responses and attitudes was stimulated by Schachter and Singer's (1962) theory of emotions and Bem's (1967, 1970, 1972) self-perception theory of attitudes. In Schachter and Singer's well-known study, subjects were injected either with epinephrine (a stimulant) or with a placebo and were then placed in a room with a happy or an angry confederate. Epinephrine subjects who were not informed of the true effects of the drug reported experiencing emotions similar to the confederate (euphoria or anger) more than did other subjects. The logic here is that an external stimulus (epinephrine) caused a generalized state of physiological arousal, which subjects then labeled on the basis of situational cues. Thus, the emotion a person experiences as a result of being aroused depends on contextual, situational factors. For the purposes of this chapter, the important point is that physiological states *precede* the emotion. Bem (1970) suggested that attitudes follow similar rules: Attitudes are inferences about internal states, which are guided by external cues. He cites Valins' (1966) research as support for this hypothesis. Valins found that male subjects' attractivenesss ratings of slides of nude females were affected by bogus physiological feedback: Subjects preferred slides to which they thought their heart rate changed. Although the feedback about heart rate changes was bogus, subjects apparently searched the slides to explain their perceived reactions. The assumption in this approach, then, is that *physiological responses (real or perceived) result in an attitude*. This hypothesis has generated a great deal of research, most of it within attributional context. The major question has been whether particular physiological responses are related to attitude valency. Is there one type of "gut reaction" that is reliably related to negative attitudes and another type to positive attitudes (a James–Lange perspective), or do physiological reactions involve only general activation, which is unrelated to attitude valence (a Cannon perspective)?

The third approach to investigating the relation between physiological responses and attitudes is best represented by a series of experiments by Cacioppo, Petty, and their colleagues. Rather than examining only the relation between physiological response and final attitude, these researchers have focused on the relation between physiological response and attitude processes. Their hypothesis is that "peripheral neurophysiological circuits and responses can reflect and/or influence cognitive processing, either because of the effects of the afferent activity from the peripheral response on brain functioning or because of the neural commands from a subcortical system influencing both information processing and peripheral response" (Cacioppo & Sandman, 1980, p. 93). The assumption here, then, is that *physiological measures can be used to assess the cognitive processing which is an inherent part of attitudes.*

Cacioppo and Petty (1979b) advocate the use of multiple physiological measurements, especially head and throat EMG, but also cardiac measures. The assumption is that heart rate gives a general measure of cognitive activity and that speech muscle EMG activity can reflect the depth of information processing in persuasion (Cacioppo & Petty, 1979b, p. 2183). In the first experiment reported by Cacioppo and Petty (1979b), subjects were forewarned that they would be hearing several different (counterattitudinal) advocacy messages and were asked to "collect their thoughts" about the message topic. As each topic was announced, subjects were instructed to sit quietly for 1 min and then to list all the thoughts they had been thinking and to indicate their agreement with the message. During this time, seven different physiological measures were taken: three oral EMG (lip, chin, and throat), one nonoral EMG (back), heart rate, respiration rate, and pulse amplitude. A comparison of the physiological measures from the 1-min intervals preceding and following topic announcement supported the researchers' hypotheses: There were significant changes in chin and lip EMG activity (both $p < .001$) and a marginal change in throat activity ($p < .10$), but no change in back EMG activity. In addition, there were significant changes in heart rate ($p < .02$) and breathing rate ($p < .01$), but no change in pulse amplitude. The canonical correlation between the oral EMG and heart rate measures and the cognitive measures, collapsed across all messages, was .42, indicating that greater physiological responsiveness is associated with more information processing. There was no relation between the attitude and physiological measures, however.

The second experiment replicated the first, with three modifications: Subjects were not asked to list their thoughts following the message announcement, which allowed an assessment of the natural occurrence of oral EMG activity; facial EMG electrode placement was used to test whether facial muscle responses associated with the expression of emotion would indicate the direction of subjects' attitudes; and proattitudinal and neutral topics were used in addition to counterattitudinal ones. The increased oral activity effect of the first experiment was replicated in the counterattitudinal condition (even though electrode placement was different), but not in the neutral or proattitudinal conditions. Attitudes were again unrelated to oral activity. The heart rate change effect was not replicated, although some differential effects occurred. The analysis of facial responses yielded the most interesting results: Different patterns of facial muscle activity were manifested in response to the counterattitudinal topic versus the neutral and proattitudinal topics. These patterns of facial muscle response were similar to those reported by Schwartz et al. (1976) as indicative of unpleasant states (the counterattitudinal pattern) and pleasant states (the neutral and proattitudinal pattern). Overall, then, the assumption of this research—that physiological activity is indicative of attitudinal information processing—was supported. Whether the physiological activity precedes or follows from the information processing is unclear. The notion that cardiac activity can facilitate information processing is supported by Cacioppo's (1979) study which will be discussed in detail in a later section.

Finally, Cacioppo and Petty's (1979b) finding that facial muscle activity showed distinct patterns for counterattitudinal versus neutral and proattitudinal topics suggests an intriguing new method for using physiological responses as direct measures of attitude. Previous research has typically attempted to relate specific physiological responses (e.g., heart rate, GSR, respiration rate, etc.) to attitudes. What Cacioppo and Petty (1979b; 1981a,b) suggest is that "measures of EMG activity over these (facial) muscle sites might yield a pattern of skeletomuscular response that would distinguish positive from negative reactions to a persuasive communication" (Cacioppo & Petty, 1981a, p. 453). Thus, by measuring facial EMG in addition to more traditional physiological measures *and* by looking for distinct patterns of responses, it may be possible to develop more sensitive physiological measures of attitude valence. The fact that no correlation is reported between facial EMG and rated attitude toward the topic, however, despite the relation of EMG to counterattitudinal versus neutral and proattitudinal topics, indicates that more work is needed to validate the technique.[1] Nevertheless, these possibilities constitute refreshing new developments in the exploration of the relation between physiological responses and attitude processes.

In summary, the three approaches to attitude psychophysiology reflect different assumptions about the role of arousal in attitude formation and changes: Attitudes cause physiological responses; physiological responses cause attitudes; or physiological responses are correlates of attitudinal information processes. That there is a linkage between biology and existing attitudes is certainly well documented: Both the early and more recent research support this notion. The unresolved issue is the nature of the linkage since each of these approaches posits a different causal sequence. One possibility is that arousal is associated with the maintenance of extant attitudes whenever those attitudes are threatened or made particularly salient. The thoughts associated with defending a cognitively threatened attitude might result in an information processing link to physiology; the evaluative characteristic of attitudes might result in a direct link of physiology with atti-

---

[1]Cacioppo (personal communication, August 31, 1981) reports that no correlation was computed because of the non-normality. He notes, however, that ". . . the experimental results would strongly suggest the existence of a between-groups correlation between attitude and facial muscle patterning."

whenever attitude salient stimuli are presented. This is, of course, speculative—future research utilizing systematic variations of attitude topic, salience, and threat as well as ranges of physiological manipulation and measures must be carried out before these issues can be clarified.

Attitude Formation and Psychophysiology

Physiological Response and Attitude Formation

The fundamental question concerning the psychophysiology of attitude formation is whether actual physiological responses can influence attitudes. The best strategy for answering this question is to directly manipulate physiological responses in an attitudinal context. Several techniques have been used to accomplish this goal. One method is to administer a drug that produces a change in physiological state. The study that first used this approach was Schachter and Singer's (1962) now-classic experiment. These authors manipulated general arousal by injecting epinephrine into some subjects. As noted earlier, they found that the induced arousal, when not otherwise explainable, resulted in an emotional state inferred from external cues (although this effect has been questioned by Marshall, 1976; Maslach, 1977; and Marshall and Zimbardo, 1979, among others). Research using a variety of similar stimulant drugs has been relatively common in research on emotion and has generally supported a basic Schachter–Singer perspective (e.g., Gerdes, 1979, used epinephrine; Erdman & Janke, 1978, used ephedrine; and O'Neal & Kaufman, 1972, used amphetamine). In an attitude formation context, O'Neal (1971) used caffeine to induce arousal in subjects. Specifically, he examined the strength of the halo effect (uniformity of trait evaluation) by having subjects rank photographs of possible team members on eight, evaluative, personality traits, while manipulating the importance of the decision (you will choose versus you probably will not choose your team members), arousal (caffeine arousal/misinformed versus caffeine arousal/informed versus no arousal), and the relevance of the photographs (photographs of men from whom the team could be chosen versus men from a previous study). His expectation was that the strongest attitudinal halo effect would occur when subjects were physiologically aroused (and misinformed) and were ranking the photos from whom they would actually choose team members. This prediction was confirmed, with the halo effect being significantly stronger ($p < .01$) in that condition than in the comparable aroused/informed and unaroused conditions. Thus, unexplained, actual physiological arousal, as induced by chemical means, has been found in the above cited studies to influence expressed attitudes.

Alternative approaches have also been used to manipulate physiological state in a context related to attitudes. For example, Zillman, Johnson, and Day (1974) used a stationary, exercise bicycle to produce general sympathetic arousal. Subjects who were high, moderate, or low in degree of prior physical conditioning were induced to ride an exercise bicycle for 1½ min, which resulted in a significant increase in blood pressure for all subjects. Half of the subjects were immediately given the opportunity to administer electrical shocks to a confederate who either had or had not previously provoked them. The remaining subjects waited 6 min before being given a similar opportunity. Based on previous research, the authors knew that subjects in good physical condition would show larger decreases in blood pressure after the 6-min delay than would subjects in poor condition; moreover, after the 6-min delay, the arousal cues would have disappeared even for those subjects in poor condition, whose blood pressure would still be elevated. The authors' prediction was that subjects with high residual arousal (i.e., the delayed, poorer conditioned subjects) would give more intense shocks to the provoker. That is, unperceived (and, therefore, not attributed to the exercise) but real arousal would facilitate negative expression toward a "disagreeable and obnoxious" (p. 509) person. Zillman et al. found, in fact, that "significant increments of aggressiveness were observed under conditions in which cues of prior arousal were no longer present but excitatory residues still prevailed" (p. 513).

Another creative method for inducing arousal was employed by Dutton and Aron (1974). These investigators measured male subjects' attraction to a female or a male interviewer. Subjects wre interviewed while crossing either a fear-provoking bridge (a tilting and swaying hand bridge over a 230-ft canyon) or a control bridge (heavy wood over a 10-ft ravine). As measured by the number of subjects accepting the experimenter's phone number and by the number of subsequent phone calls, subjects found the female interviewer in the arousing condition (fear-provoking bridge) more attractive than the interviewers in the other conditions. Although direct physiological measures were not obtained, arousal again seems to have influenced attitude formation processes.

Other techniques that have been used to manipulate physiological states include making self-revealing statements (Stein, 1971), noise (McArthur & Solomon, 1978), interpersonal disagreement (Gormly, 1974), staring (Strom & Buck, 1979), films (Geen, 1981; Green, 1975; Sapira et al., 1971), and frequency and duration of eye gaze (Coutts, Schneider, & Montgomery, 1980). The most direct and compelling manipulation of physiological reactions to date is probably that of Cacioppo (1979). In two experiments, he directly manipulated heart rate by placing a magnet over the pacemaker of subjects with implanted cardiac pacemakers. In half of the cases, the magnet was capped, resulting in no heart rate change, whereas in the other half, it was uncapped, resulting in an increase of 16 beats per minute. As mentioned earlier, Cacioppo found significant effects of heart rate change on information processing as measured by thoughts generated. Unfortunately, due to questionnaire design problems, it was not possible to ascertain whether there were attitudinal effects as well.

Taken together, these studies provide evidence that physiological states *can* influence attitudes—they are *sufficient*. This does not mean that such effects have been widely and repeatedly replicated. There appear to be three reasons for this lack of consistent results. First, very few researchers have directly manipulated and measured physiological states. Most investigators who have employed a direct physiological manipulation (e.g., a drug) have assumed that physiological changes occurred without taking running physiological measures. As O'Neal and Kaufman (1972) found, to their surprise, however, even a direct and obvious physiological manipulation (amphetamine) does not always result in *differences* between conditions in measured physiological state. For example, experimental procedures can produce as much arousal in control subjects as the physiological manipulation produces in experimental subjects.

Second, because of the influence of the extensive work in emotion and Schachter and Singer's landmark social-psychophysiological study, most researchers have used measures of emotion as their dependent variables, rather than measures of attitude. As previously noted, since attitudes and emotions are not necessarily equivalent, interpretive problems are the rule.

Third, few investigators have examined the relation between induced physiological responses and subjects' attitudes. Instead, the usual practice has been to examine the relation between the manipulation and subjects' physiological responses and then to examine the relation between the manipulation and subjects' attitudes. The analysis that has not been done or that has been done inadequately (a good technique would be Cohen's, 1968, regression approach to analysis of variance) concerns the relation between subjects' physiological responses and attitudes. Without this analysis, it is impossible to know whether physiological responses function as mediators of attitudes.

In sum, then, studies are needed that (a) manipulate and measure physiological states, (b) measure attitudes, and (c) appropriately analyze the relation between physiological states and attitudes. In addition, based on the previously reviewed work of Cacioppo and Petty, patterns of responses on a variety of physiological indices need to be examined: facial EMG, EEG, pupil dilation (Hess, 1965), voice modulation (Vanderkolk, 1976), blood pressure, respiration, and the traditional heart rate and GSR measures. Finally, Tognacci and Cook's (1975) proposal that conditioned autonomic responses might provide a directional measure of attitudes also deserves research attention.

Although additional research is needed, existing evidence indicates that actual physiological reactions are *sufficient* to influence attitudes. Four questions will now be addressed: Are actual physiological changes *necessary* for attitudinal effects? Are *perceived* physiological changes necessary for attitudinal effects? And are perceived physiological changes *sufficient* for attitudinal effects? These first three will be considered in the following section. The final question, a summary of the above, will constitute the concluding section: What role does physiology play in attitude formation?

The Necessity and Sufficiency of Physiological Responses for Attitude Formation

Although theories of emotion have typically included real physiological change as a mediator or correlate of emotional states, Valins (1966) stimulated extensive research by taking the position that perceived (cognitively believed) rather than actual physiological change is all that is necessary. As noted earlier, Valins gave subjects bogus information about their physiological reactions. In his study, he provided male subjects with bogus heart rate feedback indicating that their heart rate changed in response to the presentation of two out of seven photographs of nude females. Compared to no-change conditions and to conditions in which the feedback was labeled as irrelevant noise, these females were rated as significantly more attractive.

Whether, in fact, the perception of arousal (real or not) is a necessary and/or sufficient state for attitudinal effects has been and continues to be a controversial question.

There seems to be enough evidence to reject the notion that the perception of arousal is a *necessary* component of attitude processes. Studies (e.g., Zillman et al., 1974) have shown attitudinal effects due to nonperceived, actual physiological arousal and research has also documented the general insensitivity of people to their own internal states (e.g., see Chapter 4 of this volume). Katkin et al. (1981), in fact, report that females (though not males) are unable to learn to detect their own heartbeats. Similarly, Jones and Hollandsworth (1981) report that male runners are significantly more accurate discriminators of heart rate than female runners. Finally, Schandry (1981) reports that only emotionally labile and anxious persons are good heart rate discriminators. At the same time, however, extensive research utilizing bogus physiological feedback indicates that nonveridical information can influence affective responses. A problem with interpreting much of this research in terms of attitude processes is that, as Hirschman and Clark (1982) note, "The attitude and persuasion applications were attempts to induce or vary an emotion . . . ." As a result, dependent measures were frequently emotional rather than attitudinal in nature; for reasons discussed previously, our focus in this chapter is explicitly on attitudes, and we will limit ourselves to attitudinal bogus feedback studies.

Is there evidence that cognitively perceived physiological arousal is *sufficient* to cause attitudinal effects? This was Valins' original proposition, and, although it remains controversial, substantial support has accumulated for it (for reviews, see Hirschman & Clark, 1982; Liebhart, 1979). In the typical bogus feedback study, as in Valins' (1966) original experiment, subjects are presented with a stimulus while simultaneously receiving false feedback about their physiological state. Subsequently, subjects indicate their attitudes or emotions regarding the stimulus. In Goldstein, Fink, and Mettee's (1972) extension of Valins' experiment, male subjects were shown a series of eight female nudes. For the experimental subjects, bogus feedback was provided indicating an increase in heart rate to the fourth and seventh nudes. These subjects rated the two nudes associated with increases in heart rate significantly higher (by 12 points on the 100-point scale) than did the control subjects. In a later study, Hirschman (1975) used a similar paradigm to assess whether feedback effects could be obtained in a negative context. While watching 10 successive photographs of people who died violently, experimental subjects heard (bogus) feedback indicating a heart rate increase. Subjects rated their degree of discomfort while viewing each slide and the overall unpleasantness of all slides combined. Significant effects were obtained for both discomfort and unpleasantness, with the heart rate increase condition giving the most negative ratings.

Liebhart (1979) has developed a model that specifies the necessary preconditions for the bogus feedback effect to occur: First, the feedback (e.g., increasing heart rate) associated with the stimulus (e.g., a nude female) must seem incongruous to the subject, thereby initiating an information search to explain the reaction; second, the stimulus must be searched until a sufficient explanation for the feedback is found (e.g., beautiful breasts); and third, this attributed explanation must result in other types of responses (e.g., physiological responses, attitudes, etc.). Given these conditions, the perception of physiological changes does seem sufficient to have attitudinal effects.

This brings us to the last question: Are *actual* physiological changes *necessary* for attitude processes to be influenced? That is, does bogus information have an effect because it produces real physiological changes? This question has been raised repeatedly, beginning with Valins' original work and most recently with Hirschman and Clark's (1982) review. Stern, Botto, and Merrick (1972), for example, found different patterns of heart rate response to bogus feedback accompanying photos of nude females and speculated that real physiological changes may mediate the effects of bogus feedback. The most complete examination of bogus feedback, physiological changes, and attitudes was conducted by Detweiler and Zanna (1976). This study is unusual in that it did not use a single-response measure of attitude; as Fishbein and Ajzen (1975, p. 56) note, "single-response measures should not be taken as indicants of attitude, irrespective of the investigator's intuition regarding their affective (evaluative) nature." Detweiler and Zanna used the mean rating across 20 adjective descriptors to measure attitudes, thereby removing the effects of specific attributions and leaving only the evaluative component. Subjects received bogus feedback (increasing, decreasing, no change, no feedback) about their heart rate and GSR responses to the presentation of various nation names. Significant relations were found between bogus feedback/no feedback and actual heart rate and between actual heart rate and final attitude; no relation existed between bogus feedback and attitude. Thus, *real* physiological changes determined attitudes in this bogus feedback study.

This effect has not been obtained consistently in other studies, however. Several factors may account for the inconsistent findings. First, Detweiler and Zanna used methodologies not typically employed, which may have increased the effectiveness of the false feedback: Credibility trials using congruent heart rate feedback were employed; the order of feedback conditions was randomized; each subject's actual heart rate was used as the baseline for bogus heart rate feedback; and heart rate changes were not averaged over long (e.g., 10-sec) intervals, where phasic changes occur. Second, as previously noted, most studies have not included satisfactory measures of attitudes; the feedback effect, may, indeed, not occur for emotions. Finally, there may be individual differences in responses to bogus feedback (e.g., Hirschman & Hawk, 1978).

At this point, then, it seems most reasonable to conclude that physiology is a sufficient but not always necessary condition for attitudinal effects to occur. The necessity of real physiological changes can never be disproved, of course, but adequate tests of this issue await research with improved methodologies, improved designs (see the previous section), and multiple measures of various physiological responses (see the first section).

Thus, it seems that cognitively perceived physiological changes are sufficient but not necessary to cause attitudinal effects. More important to the present chapter, though, is the notion that actual physiological changes are also sufficient to produce attitudinal effects. We now turn to the general question of what role physiology might play in attitude formation.

The Role of Physiology in Attitude Formation

Based on the studies reviewed above, it seems clear that there is sufficient evidence supporting the role of physiology in attitude formation to reject the notion that physiological states never influence attitudes. What, then is the precise relation between internal states and attitudes? Three models can be posited, each of which specifies a somewhat different role of physiological responses in the formation of attitudes.

The first model assumes that physiological states have a direct and paramount effect on attitudes. That is, a stimulus is presented, a physiological response occurs, and from this response, an attitude is inferred. The second model is a modification of the first: Physiological responses are *one* of the factors that have a direct effect on attitudes. That is, other factors (e.g., amount of information, prior experience, personality factors, etc.) also have a direct impact. The third model assumes that the effects of physiology are indirect and have effects only through their influence on other processes (as in Cacioppo and Petty's idea that arousal influences information processing, which in turn influences attitudes). These three models have one assumption in common: Physiological factors are seen as *mediators* of attitudinal responses. That a mediating effect occurs seems obvious on the basis of existing evidence. But that it does not always occur also seems obvious, as exemplified by the bogus feedback research. A number of factors, such as the amount of prior knowledge (as in Detweiler & Zanna, 1976) and the amount of information processing (as in Cacioppo & Sandman, 1980), undoubtedly influence the nature and degree of mediation.

Detweiler and Zanna (1977), in response to Harris and Katkin's (1975) analysis of the role of autonomic feedback in emotion and attribution, suggest that physiological mediation of attitudes may occur only for relatively novel stimuli. They suggest that research in this area must distinguish between emotions and attitudes (as discussed in this chapter), examine all relations among stimuli, physiological responses, and attitudes using appropriate statistical techniques, and manipulate factors that may influence the degree to which physiology mediates attitudes (e.g., amount of knowledge, amount of information, etc.). Research following these suggestions seems necessary to evaluate adequately the alternative models of the role of physiology in attitude formation.

Attitude Change and Psychophysiology

To this point, we have discussed psychophysiological aspects of attitude maintenance and attitude formation. For the remainder of the chapter, we turn to the question of how attitude change and persuasion are affected by physiological reactions, especially physiological arousal. Few studies have included direct measures of subjects' physiological reactions as concomitants of persuasion, and even fewer have manipulated subjects' physiological states. Nevertheless, the existing data suggest that physiological processes can have certain consequences that impact on attitude change.

The relation between psychophysiological reactions and persuasion has interested many researchers; indeed, it has been a natural outgrowth of a variety of substantive concerns. It has been addressed, for example, by researchers interested in such diverse questions as the effectiveness of fear appeals, the effects of exogenous manipulations of heart rate on attitude change, the impact of drugs on persuasibility, the consequences of sensory deprivation, and the mechanisms underlying dissonance-motivated attitude change. Below, we review briefly each of these areas of research and identify their contributions to the understanding of the psychophysiology-persuasion relation.

Fear Appeals and Persuasion

Perhaps the earliest interest in the effects of physiological processes on persuasion was stimulated by research on fear appeals. This literature addressed the important question of whether or not "scare tactics" are effective: Will a persuasive message have more impact if it arouses fear in the listeners? The common sense or intuitive answer to this question, as indicated by the widespread use of fear appeals by parents, educators, politicians, and others, is affirmative. Like many intuitive analyses, however, this is at best an oversimplification.

An early experimental investigation of fear appeals was conducted by Janis and Feshbach (1953). These researchers presented high school students with one of three lectures about the importance of preventive, dental hygiene behaviors (e.g., brushing teeth). The "low fear" lecture simply informed subjects of the negative consequences of failing to care for one's teeth and made a number of recommendations about how to avoid such problems. The "moderate fear" lecture described the negative consequences in more detail. The "high fear" lecture made very fear-provoking statements (e.g., that dental infection can spread to other parts of the body and cause serious illness) and was accompanied by revolting slides of infected teeth and gums.

One week after hearing the lecture, subjects were asked to report their dental hygiene behaviors. Surprisingly, reported compliance with the recommendations was greatest in the low fear group and least in the high fear group. Janis and Feshbach therefore concluded that fear appeals reduce attitude and behavior change, possibly because listeners avoid highly threatening messages.

Subsequent investigators, however, generally failed to replicate the inverse relation between fear arousal and persuasion. Leventhal and Singer (1966), for example, found that a high fear communication on dental hygiene produced greater acceptance of recommendations by visitors to a state exposition than did a low fear communication. Similarly, Chu (1966) found that elementary school children expressed greater willingness to take a drug to counteract the danger of roundworms after hearing a high fear than a low fear message. Thus, although results have been somewhat variable, the most common finding has been a positive relation between the fearfulness of a message and persuasion (for reviews of the literature, see Beck & Frankel, 1981, Higbee, 1969; Leventhal, 1970; Rogers, 1982).

To reconcile and integrate these sometimes contradictory results, theorists have attempted to identify the psychological processes that mediate the effects of fear on attitude change. For example, Janis (1967) and McGuire (1969) have argued that fear has potentially competing effects: It may reduce listeners' attention (since it is aversive and motivates escape or avoidance), but it may simultaneously increase listeners' willingness to accept the recommendations (so as to avoid the negative consequences described in the message). These competing effects could produce inconsistent results and suggest that a curvilinear relation exists between fear arousal and persuasion: Moderate levels of fear may produce more attitude change than low levels, but extremely fear-provoking messages may be so aversive that people will avoid them and not change their attitudes.

The assumption underlying these models is that fear is an aversive state, which people are motivated to reduce. Thus, attitude change is seen as an avenue by which people can control their fear. Consistent with this position, Harris and Jellison (1971) found that subjects who were given false physiological feedback indicating that their arousal increased during a fear-provoking message and decreased during the presentation of recommendations showed greater acceptance of the recommendations than did subjects whose feedback indicated that their arousal increased during the message and did not change during the recommendations.

Unfortunately, other studies have not supported the drive-reduction model. For example, Leventhal and Singer (1966) found that the positioning of recommendations in a message affected fear reactions but not persuasion. Further, although specific instructions about how to comply with recommendations increase compliance (e.g., Leventhal, Singer, & Jones, 1965), this factor has equal impact for high and low fear messages—a finding that is inconsistent with the drive-reduction model (see Higbee, 1969; Leventhal, 1970).

As a result, theorists have moved toward cognitive explanations of the fear-persuasion relation, discounting the role of fear as a drive. For example, Higbee (1969) argued that threatening messages increase the perceived seriousness of failing to heed the recommendations, but also decrease the perceived likelihood of the consequences occurring (e.g., blindness may be seen as a serious but unlikely consequence of not brushing one's teeth). Thus, a curvilinear relation between message threat and persuasion should result: At some point, the threat becomes so unlikely that its improbability outweighs its seriousness. Note that the emotion of fear plays no direct role in this model—the cognitive appraisal of the danger is the critical factor determining attitude change.

In a similar vein, Leventhal (1970) has proposed a "parallel response" model, which distinguishes between emotional and acceptance responses to a threat. Essentially, Leventhal suggests that fear appeals contain elements that may influence emotional reactions (which, in turn, will initiate fear control processes, such as avoidance) or acceptance responses (which, in turn, will initiate danger control processes, such as attitude or behavior change) or both—but these responses do not necessarily affect one another. Further, the elements of fear appeals that influence acceptance responses are primarily cognitive, such as the perceived seriousness of the problem and knowledge about how to comply with the recommendations. Once again, then, the arousal of fear per se is relegated to the secondary role in the causal determination of attitude change.

The most comprehensive model of the effects of fear appeals has been developed by Rogers and his colleagues (Rogers, 1975, 1982; Rogers, Deckner, & Mewborn, 1978; Rogers & Mewborn, 1976). Using an approach similar to the "health belief model" in the preventive health literature (see Becker, 1974; Langlie, 1977; McKinlay, 1972; Rosenstock, 1966), Rogers's "protection motivation theory" assumes that threatening messages vary in the extent to which they convince listeners that (1) the depicted event is serious, (2) the depicted event is likely if coping responses are not adopted, and (3) the recommended coping responses will be effective in avoiding the depicted event. To the extent that listeners perceive the event to be serious and likely and the coping responses to be effective, protection motivation will be aroused, which will result in attitude and behavior change. Thus, the emotion of fear is not postulated to mediate the effects of message threat on persuasion; cognitive processes and resultant protection motivation are the critical mediators.

Research on these models, particularly Rogers's protection motivation theory, has generally been supportive, confirming the notion that cognitive appraisal determines the impact of a threatening message. For example, Rogers and Mewborn (1976) exposed subjects to a presentation on one of three topics (cigarette smoking, driving safety, or venereal disease). Noxiousness of the presentations was varied by using films that depicted the end result of the problems (e.g., surgery for lung cancer or venereal disease; victims of an automobile accident) or that were relatively innocuous. In addition, written messages following the film manipulated the alleged probability of the threatened event and the efficacy of the recommended coping responses. After viewing the film, subjects reported their level of fear. After reading the message, subjects reported their perceptions of the severity and probability of the event and the efficacy of the coping responses. At the end of the study, subjects' behavioral intentions to follow the recommendations were assessed.

The noxious films resulted in more reported fear than did the innocuous films. Fear did not necessarily translate into stronger intentions to follow the recommendations, however. Instead, the cognitive appraisal variables proved to be important in determining subjects' intentions. For example, on the venereal disease topic, the noxious film produced stronger intentions than the innocuous film to adopt the recommendations when the alleged efficacy of the coping response was high, but noxiousness did not affect intentions when efficacy was low. On the smoking topic, the message that depicted the threatening event as highly probable resulted in stronger intentions to follow the recommendations when efficacy was high, but weaker intentions when efficacy was low, than did the low probability message. Most important, a path analysis of the data indicated that the perceived efficacy of the coping responses was the strongest single determinant of behavioral intentions and that fear arousal affected intentions only indirectly, by increasing the perceived severity of the threatening event.

These and other findings (e.g., Hass, Bagley, & Rogers, 1975; Rogers et al., 1978; Rogers & Thistlethwaite, 1970) indicate that cognitive appraisal of the threatening event, rather than emotional arousal per se, determines listeners' attitudinal and behavioral reactions to fear appeals. But direct manipulations and/or measures of subjects' physiological states were not included in these studies. Fortunately, such data do exist.

Rogers and Deckner (1975) manipulated physiological arousal directly by injections of epinephrine, an autonomic arousal agent. Subjects were then exposed to one of several communications, some of which were fear-provoking. In Experiment 1, epinephrine increased reported fear, but did not affect attitude or behavior change. In Experiment 2, epinephrine had no effects on any measure of fear, attitudes, or behavior. In contrast to these weak effects for epinephrine, noxious messages resulted in more attitude change than innocuous messages in both studies and produced stronger intentions to follow the recommendations in Experiment 2. Also, a 3-month follow-up in Experiment 2 showed that messages that stressed the effectiveness of the recommendations produced more behavior change. Thus, message characteristics were shown to be important determinants of attitude and behavior change, but physiological arousal per se did not seem to play a critical role. Direct physiological measures were not obtained in these studies, however, and as discussed in a previous section, it is possible that the drug did not actually produce different physiological reactions (see O'Neal & Kaufman, 1972).

Mewborn and Rogers (1979) monitored subjects' physiological reactions during exposure to either a high or low noxiousness film on venereal disease (these films were used previously by Rogers & Mewborn, 1976). Parallel main effects for noxiousness emerged on self-report, heart rate, and skin conductance measures of arousal. Thus, convergent validity was provided for the manipulation of fear (noxiousness) and for the self-report measure of fear. On the other hand, fear was not associated with acceptance of the recommendations (whether fear was assessed by self-report or physiological measures). Instead, only a manipulation of "reassurance" (involving the perceived probability of contracting venereal disease and the alleged efficacy of medical treatment) affected behavioral intentions, with high reassurance producing stronger intentions to follow the recommendations.

Taken together, the research literature on fear appeals provides little evidence for the causal impact of physiological reactions per se on persuasion. Rather, attitude and behavior change following a threatening communication seem to be related primarily to individuals' cognitive appraisal of the severity of the problem, its probability of occurrence, and the efficacy of the recommended coping responses. Nevertheless, the extent to which physiological arousal is attributed to the message (and perhaps the extent to which reductions in arousal are attributed to the presentation of recommendations; see Harris & Jellison, 1971) may influence these cognitive processes. For example, individuals may consider their fear reaction to a message to be informative about the severity of the problem (Rogers & Mewborn, 1976). Also, arousal (or the perception of arousal) may be necessary to *initiate* cognitive appraisal. Beyond these general and indirect (via the appraisal process) effects, however, physiological reactions do not seem to play an important, causal role in the persuasive impact of fear appeals.

Exogenous Manipulations of Heart Rate

Cacioppo, Petty, and their colleagues have proposed an intriguing relation between cardiac activity and persuasion (for detailed discussions of their model and research, see Cacioppo & Petty, 1982; Cacioppo & Sandman, 1980). Their model is based on (and integrates) two related hypotheses. First, Lacey and Lacey (1958, 1974, 1978) have argued that heart rate acceleration is associated with *and facilitates* cognitive elaboration, whereas heart rate deceleration is associated with *and facilitates* sensory input and reception. Second, Petty and Cacioppo (1977, 1979a, 1979b) have argued that cognitive responses to a persuasive message affect attitude change, with the generation of favorable thoughts about the message increasing persuasion and the generation of counterarguments to the message inhibiting persuasion. Combining these hypotheses, Cacioppo and Petty have speculated that cardiac acceleration should reduce the persuasive impact of relatively unconvincing messages and increase the persuasive impact of cogent, compelling messages.

Regarding the impact of cardiac activity on cognitive elaboration versus sensory input, studies have shown that subjects' heart rates increase from baseline levels during the performance of complex intellectual tasks, but decrease during the performance of tasks that involve attention to external stimuli (e.g., Lacey, Kagan, Lacey, & Moss, 1963). More important, there is evidence that performance on a reading comprehension task is improved by exogenously accelerating heart rate (Cacioppo, 1979) and that sensory intake is facilitated during operantly conditioned decreases in heart rate (McCanne & Sandman, 1974). The precise neurophysiological mechanisms that mediate these effects of cardiac activity are unclear, although Lacey and Lacey (1978) have suggested that the baroreceptors (afferent receptors located along the arterial tree, which are sensitive to blood pressure) play a role.

The second link in the postulated sequence from cardiac activity to persuasion—the effects of cognitive responses on the persuasive impact of a message—has been explored in a systematic program of research by Petty, Cacioppo, and their colleagues. These researchers have demonstrated convincingly that subjects' cognitive responses to a message, especially the production of favorable thoughts and/or counterarguments, mediate attitude change. The assumption underlying this research is that individuals are not passive recipients of persuasive messages, but instead elaborate cognitively on the appeal. To the extent that the message leads the recipient to think of positive implications of the advocated position (favorable thoughts), attitude change should occur; to the extent that the message elicits counterarguments, however, attitude change should be inhibited.

In their research, Petty and Cacioppo have focused on how traditional, independent variables in persuasion affect the cognitive elaboration of a message and, subsequently, attitude change. Studies have shown that the cognitive response analysis can explain the effects on persuasion of forewarning (Cialdini, Levy, Herman, Kozlowski, & Petty, 1976; Petty & Cacioppo, 1977, 1979a), distraction (Petty, Wells, & Brock, 1976), message repetition (Cacioppo & Petty, 1979a), the personal relevance of the message (Petty & Cacioppo, 1979b), the use of rhetorical questions (Petty, Cacioppo, & Heesacker, 1981), and the number of sources presenting the message (Harkins & Petty, 1981). For example, Petty et al. (1981) presented subjects with a counterattitudinal message arguing in favor of senior comprehensive examinations, in which the major arguments were either convincing or weak and were summarized in either statement or rhetorical forms (e.g., "Whatever educational value the exams have for graduate students would also benefit undergraduates" versus "Wouldn't whatever educational value the exams have for graduate students also benefit undergraduates?"). When the issue was of low personal relevance to subjects, the use of rhetoricals enhanced cognitive elaboration (relative to the messages in statement form), producing more favorable thoughts about the convincing message and more counterarguments to the weak message. In contrast, when the issue was highly relevant to subjects, rhetoricals disrupted cognitive elaboration, producing fewer favorable thoughts about the convincing message and fewer counterarguments to the weak message. Moreover, the pattern of persuasion across conditions corresponded exactly to the cognitive elaboration findings (i.e., compared to the messages in statement form, rhetoricals increased the persuasive impact of the convincing message and reduced the impact of the weak message when relevance was low, but reduced the impact of the convincing message and increased the impact of the weak message when relevance was high), and subjects' final attitudes correlated significantly (within-cell) with both how many favorable thoughts they generated (.51) and how many counterarguments they generated (−.40). There is good evidence, then, that subjects' cognitive elaboration of a message is a causal determinant of the message's persuasive impact.

Taking together these findings that (a) cardiac activity affects cognitive elaboration and (b) cognitive elaboration affects attitude change, Cacioppo, Sandman, and Walker (1978) studied the effects of heart rate on persuasion. Subjects were trained for 5 days to accelerate and decelerate their heart rate by means of an operant shaping procedure. Specifically, subjects accumulated a monetary reward by surpassing criteria for cardiac acceleration or cardiac deceleration in response to different colored lights. At the end of the fifth training session, subjects were presented with counterattitudinal messages during periods of heart rate increase, heart rate decrease, and basal heart rate (i.e., the messages were presented while the different colored lights were illuminated, and subjects could still earn money by altering their heart rate). The plausibility of the supporting arguments in the messages was varied, although none of the arguments were especially compelling. Subjects indicated their agreement with each message after it was presented and provided retrospective reports of their thoughts about each message immediately following the final message.

The results of the study are displayed in Figure 7-1. Subjects' heart rates were significantly faster during acceleration trials than during either deceleration trials or base rate trials (which did not differ from one another). In addition, subjects generated more counterarguments to, and expressed greater disagreement with, the messages when they were presented during acceleration trials than when they were presented during deceleration trials. These effects occurred irrespective of the plausibility of the supporting arguments in the messages. Thus, cardiac activity was associated with cognitive elaboration and resistance to persuasion for these relatively unconvincing messages. It should also be noted that several other physiological measures, including chin muscle activity, respiration rate, and blood flow,

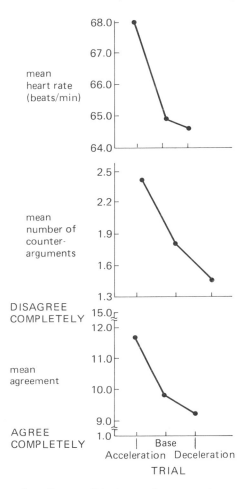

Figure 7-1. The effects of cardiac conditioning on heart rate (top panel), production of counterarguments (middle panel), and agreement with the message (bottom panel). (Copyright © 1978, The Society for Physiological Research. Reprinted with permission from Cacioppo, Sandman, & Walker, 1978).

did not show any differences between acceleration and deceleration trials, indicating that the conditioning procedure affected heart rate relatively independently of other physiological reactions.

Although the results of Cacioppo et al. (1978) are consistent with the postulated sequence involving cardiac activity, cognitive elaboration, and attitude change, they are not definitive. For one thing, subjects were aware of the changes in their heart rate because they received accurate feedback after each trial about whether or not they had surpassed the reward criterion (in postexperimental discussions, however, subjects could not articulate the hypothesis that heart rate would affect cognitive responding or attitude ratings). Also, the conditioning procedure might have elicited different affective experiences or been differentially distracting during acceleration versus deceleration trials. To overcome some of these problems, Cacioppo (1979) employed an exogenous manipulation of heart rate, which subjects could not detect, to study the proposed sequence.

Cacioppo (1979) recruited subjects who wore implanted, cardiac pacemakers, but who were otherwise in good health. Subjects were presented with counterattitudinal messages while their heart rate was either ostensibly or actually accelerated by 16 beats per minute. This manipulation was effected by placing a magnet, either capped or uncapped, over the reed of the pacemaker. Subjects could not accurately discriminate between trials on which their heart rate was accelerated and trials on which their heart rate remained unaffected. After each message, subjects listed all thoughts that occurred to them while reading the message and rated their agreement with the advocated position (plausibility of the messages was not manipulated; all messages were counterarguable).

Results showed that subjects generated more total thoughts and more counterarguments to the messages when heart rate was accelerated than when it was not accelerated; thus, elevated heart rate increased cognitive elaboration. The heart rate manipulation did not affect agreement with the messages, however. Inspection of the raw data revealed a positively skewed distribution of attitude responses: 50% of the subjects answered 1 ("disagree completely"). It seems, then, that subjects were able to counterargue and reject the messages even when their heart rate was not accelerated; the attitude measure may have been insensitive to possible treatment effects.

These experiments provide interesting, though not unequivocal, evidence in support of the postulated relation between cardiac activity and persuasion. The hypothesis that accelerated heart rate is associated with and facilitates cognitive elaboration seems well documented. The impact of heart rate on subsequent attitude change requires further investigation, however. In particular, research showing both facilitative and inhibitory effects of increased heart rate on attitude change (e.g., evidence that accelerated heart rate decreases the persuasive impact of unconvincing messages *and* increases the impact of cogent measures) would be compelling. Cacioppo and Petty's work constitutes a rare example of an a priori hypothesis about the effects of physiological reactions on attitude change, which is tested via direct manipulations of subjects' physiological states and which postulates mediating cognitive processes that are known to affect persuasion in other domains. Thus, their hypothesis provides a promising direction for future research.

Drugs and Persuasion

According to Bostrom (1980), theories of communication and persuasion have generally ignored altered physiological states because "to alter the reception of a message through the use of hunger or drugs is quite distasteful to most of us" (p. 174). But considering the amounts of caffeine, nicotine, alcohol, tranquilizers, and other drugs consumed in our society, one cannot assume that the typical recipient of a persuasive message is not in an altered physiological state. Therefore, it is important that researchers investigate the interaction between persuasive messages and the altered physiological states caused by various drugs. That is, researchers ought to determine which drugs enhance and which drugs inhibit the impact of a persuasive communication.

In his chapter, Bostrom (1980) addresses this issue. The first conclusion to be drawn from his review of the literature, however, is that there is little relevant research. In fact, Bostrom is forced largely to speculate on what moderating effects various drugs have on persuasion. Because past research (e.g., Kerber & Coles, 1978; Harris & Jellison, 1971; Mintz & Mills, 1971) has indicated that persuasion is enhanced when arousal is attributed to the persuasive message, Bostrom speculates that stimulants such as nicotine (from cigarettes), caffeine (from coffee and cola-type soft drinks), and amphetamine ought to enhance persuasive effects, especially if the arousal is misattributed, whereas depressants such as alcohol and tranquilizers ought to inhibit or diminish persuasion, possibly because such drugs reduce the discomfort caused by attitude-discrepant messages.

Only for alcohol and caffeine, however, is there direct evidence available. Smith (1974) used a version of the Asch situation to examine the effect of alcohol on the acceptance of social influence from one's dating partner. Smith reasoned that because alcohol apparently increases feelings of self-confidence, subjects ought to be less open to social influence when under the influence. In fact, alcohol, administered in two drinks (1.00 ml/kg for males; 0.84 ml/kg for females) reduced conformity on a perceptual task (deciding which of two rectangles contained the greater area of white) for rare drinkers (1 drink per month or less), but not for occasional drinkers (2-3 drinks per month). As might be expected, rare drinkers were also more impaired on a task that required subjects to walk a straight line, heel to toe. Thus, alcohol seemed to inhibit social influence, at least for some subjects. Because subjects' responses were public in nature, however, it is unclear whether alcohol inhibited public compliance or private acceptance (i.e., attitude change). Also, the factors that mediated the effect of alcohol are unclear since no attempt was made to assess potential physiological or cognitive mediators.

More recently, Bostrom and White (1979) directly tested whether individuals ingesting alcohol will be less affected by persuasive messages than individuals in a normal state. Subjects in this study read three (500-word) essays that attacked the validity of three cultural truisms (e.g., frequent toothbrushing is helpful). In the high alcohol condition, participants received a soft drink (Fresca) containing 0.77 ml of alcohol per kg of body weight; in the low alcohol condition, the drink contained 0.52 ml/kg. (According to Bostrom and White, these amounts translate into a 150-pound individual in the high alcohol group receiving the equivalent of 4.43 ounces of 80-proof whiskey.) Two control conditions, which are necessary to assess the impact of alcohol, were also run. In the no alcohol condition, the soft drink contained no alcohol; in the survey control condition, subjects' attitudes were assessed in the absence of drinks and essays. The results indicated that, contrary to the popular conception that "plying" people with alcohol will "lower their resistance," alcohol ingestion reduced the impact of the persuasive messages. Compared to the survey control condition, attitude change was apparent only in the no and low alcohol conditions. Subjects in the high alcohol condition did not differ from the survey controls and changed less than subjects in the no ($p < .05$) and low alcohol ($p < .10$) conditions.

Why did alcohol inhibit the impact of the persuasive messages? One possibility is that increased self-confidence leads to greater counterargumentation. After reading the essays and having their attitudes assessed, subjects were asked to identify counterarguments that had occurred to them while reading the essays. Although this procedure is different from the thought-listing technique advocated by Cacioppo and Petty (1981c), it is noteworthy that there were no differences between the conditions in the number of counterarguments reported. The authors suggest that "probably the best explanation (for alcohol's inhibitory effect) is that CNS depression reduced the discomfort which could have been created by the persuasive messages, so that the need for attitude change and counterarguments was reduced" (p. 79). Once again, however, no attempt was made to assess this mediating mechanism at either the physiological or cognitive level.

Finally, Mintz and Mills (1971) gave subjects caffeine, in the form of three crushed *No Doz* (Bristol-Myers) tablets, and either told them about the true effect of the drug or described an irrelevant side effect. These authors were interested in testing the hypothesis that an increase in physiological arousal will enhance attitude change to a convincing communication, but only if the arousal is misattributed, i.e., is interpreted as an emotion associated with the object of the attitude. The results indicated that subjects who were informed of caffeine's true effects were, in fact, less persuaded by a message arguing against chest X-rays than were subjects given misinformation (who would presumably misattribute their arousal). Although subjects given caffeine had higher pulse rates than subjects given a placebo, no within-cell correlations were reported between this measure of physiological arousal and attitude change.

Thus, caffeine seems to enhance the impact of a convincing persuasive message, but only when the arousal can be misattributed. This conclusion raises the interesting question of whether people in more natural settings are aware of the physiological effects of various stimulants such as caffeine. Although it seems reasonable to assume that people have some knowledge about the impact of certain drugs, there may be substances (e.g., tobacco, see Bostrom, 1980) for which a substantial number of persons are unaware of the effects and/or the time course of the effects. If so, many people may well qualify as "aroused-ignorant" recipients. Clearly, this issue is an important one for future research. Finally, these questions also raise the issue of whether individuals are normally sensitive to their internal, physiological states. As noted earlier in the chapter, some researchers (e.g., Jones & Hollandsworth, 1981; Katkin et al., 1981; Schandry, 1981) have found that many individuals cannot discriminate internal changes. Thus, whether the effects of drugs on persuasion are mediated by actual or perceived physiological changes is an open question.

In sum, although research on drugs and persuasion is important and promising, this is clearly an area that has been underinvestigated. The basic question of how various drugs impact on persuasion is only now beginning to receive research attention. The further question of how such effects, if they exist, are mediated physiologically and/or cognitively has yet to be addressed empirically. Finally, the question of whether (or, more precisely, under what conditions) the findings of laboratory investigations will generalize to real world settings has yet to be asked. With respect to this last issue, a recent study by Pennebaker and his colleagues (1979) is of interest. In this field study, a team of experimenters visited bars at various times in the evening and asked both male and female customers to rate the overall attractiveness of the opposite sex customers. Although there were undoubtedly alternative explanations, it is interesting to speculate that differential alcohol intake caused the results: Subjects rated members of the opposite sex as more physically attractive at closing time than earlier in the evening.

Sensory Deprivation and Persuasion

Over the last 15 years, Suedfeld and his colleagues have investigated the impact of sensory deprivation on subsequent resistance to persuasion. According to Suedfeld (1980), "there is no doubt by now that REST (Restricted Environmental Stimulation) increases the susceptibility of most subjects to influence from external sources" (p. 64). Suedfeld and Borrie (1978), for example, attacked subjects' attitudes toward the desirability of frequent toothbrushing after 24 hours (consisting of two, 12-hour sessions) of either sensory deprivation or nonconfinement. Sensory deprivation consisted of lying on a bed in a dark, silent room, with water and liquid diet food available at bedside and a chemical toilet in the chamber. Subjects were instructed not to move around nor to make any kind of noise. Nonconfinement, in this study, consisted of staying in or near the laboratory control room to serve as monitors. According to Suedfeld and Borrie, most of the nonconfinement subjects' time was spent in reading, conversation, eating, listening to the radio, doing schoolwork, and so on, with some walking around in and near the building.

At the end of the second session, the persuasive communication was presented over an intercom after appropriate warning but without any other disruption. The results of this experiment replicated the traditional finding: Subjects who heard the attack at the end of 24 hours of sensory deprivation were more persuaded than those who heard the persuasive communication after 24 hours of nonconfinement.

According to Suedfeld (1980), the traditional explanation for this effect (the so-called "stimulus hunger" explanation) is that sensory deprivation produces a need for stimulation, which causes the subject to attend carefully to messages that ordinarily would have little impact. Although there is minimal direct evidence to support this proposition, it has yet to be rejected (Suedfeld, 1980, p. 65). Another explanation, Suedfeld's disorganization hypothesis, follows from conceptualizing sensory deprivation as an arousal-inducing manipulation. Data on changes in skin resistance indicate that sensory deprivation produces increases in GSR, and, although heart rate data are less clear, heart rate seems to be positively related to feelings of boredom (Suedfeld, 1980). In addition, sensory deprivation produces cognitive effects typically associated with arousal-inducing manipulations; for example, performance on simple tasks tends to improve, whereas performance on complex tasks tends to be disrupted (e.g., Landon & Suedfeld, 1972). Since resisting a counterattitudinal message is a complex cognitive task (e.g., it involves generating or recalling counterarguments), the greater persuasibility of deprived subjects may result from the arousal-produced disruption of these complex, information-processing activities.

Of course, these explanations are not mutually exclusive, and Suedfeld's current position is that sensory deprivation produces stimulus hunger *and* disorganizes the complex cognitive functioning involved in the evaluation of persuasive messages (Suedfeld, 1980). With regard to disorganization effects, recent evidence suggests two elements: (1) deprived subjects are impaired at generating arguments against a persuasive communication (Suedfeld, Tetlock, & Borrie, in preparation), and (2) sensory deprivation, even without the introduction of any persuasive message, produces instability in the belief systems that underlie existing attitude structure (Tetlock & Suedfeld, 1976). Both disorganization effects would, of course, increase the persuasive impact of subsequent counterattitudinal communications.

Suedfeld and his colleagues have also used sensory deprivation to try to help people with health-related problems. For example, in a 2 by 2 design, Suedfeld and Ikard (1974) did or did not present antismoking communications to subjects who had or had not experienced 24 hours of sensory deprivation. The results indicated an impressive effect for sensory deprivation: Fully 2 years later, sensory deprivation subjects were smoking an average of 55% below baseline, compared to 18% for the nonconfined subjects. Unfortunately, there were no significant main or interactive effects for the persuasive communication. In retrospect, this may not be surprising because the subjects, though psychologically addicted or preaddicted according to the Tomkins-Ikard Smoking Scale (Ikard & Tomkins, 1973), were (1) already highly motivated to quit smoking and (2) technically capable of doing so.

Borrie (1977) also combined sensory deprivation and persuasive communications to treat patients, in this case overweight individuals. In contrast to the smoking study, the results revealed a significant interaction between sensory deprivation and the communications. After 6 months, weight loss, though not extensive, was greater for subjects receiving the combination of sensory deprivation and the persuasive messages (loss of approximately 6 kg) than for the other subjects (loss of approximately 1 kg). One explanation for the conflicting results of the smoking and weight loss studies is that people trying to lose weight need more technical help to achieve their goal than do people trying to quit smoking (Suedfeld, 1980, p. 278).

In sum, it seems clear that sensory deprivation enhances the impact of persuasion. This effect may reflect that sensory deprivation disrupts the processing of complex information through some mechanism such as arousal. It should be noted, however, that researchers have not taken measures of arousal and attitude change simultaneously.

Dissonance

To this point, we have examined attitude change that follows from being exposed to a persuasive communication. Over the past 25 years, however, social psychologists have determined that one of the best ways to change a person's attitude is not necessarily to present a persuasive communication, but instead to commit the person to some behavior relevant to the attitude. So, for example, if a campaign manager wanted someone to vote for his or her candidate, the manager would probably do better by getting the prospective voter to stuff envelopes for the candidate than by communicating the candidate's virtues.

Various theories exist that specify more precisely the conditions under which attitude change follows from behavior. Surprisingly, however, the two major theories—Festinger's (1957) cognitive dissonance theory and Bem's (1972) self-perception theory—tend to agree on the conditions. Their differences concern the underlying process that is proposed to mediate the effect. Dissonance theory posits the existence of a drive-like motivation to maintain consistency among relevant cognitions. When one's attitude is at variance with one's behavior, attitude change occurs as a means of reducing an unpleasant, tension state. Self-perception theory, in contrast, is best characterized as a "cool" information-processing model. According to Bem (1967), self-descriptive attitudes are based on the individual's observations of his or her own overt behavior and the external stimulus conditions under which it occurs. "In the self-perception explanation, there is no aversive motivational pressure postulated" (Bem, 1972, p. 17). Thus, to oversimplify, whereas dissonance theory holds that we rationalize, self-perception theory views us as rational.

Is dissonance an aversive, motivational state? Or, more precisely, do traditional dissonance-induction procedures produce an aversive, motivational state? Several early studies, reviewed by Kiesler and Pallak (1976), suggested that dissonance manipulations are indeed arousing. For example, Pallak and Pittman (1972) demonstrated that dissonance manipulations produce classic arousal effects on an irrelevant task, i.e., dissonance-aroused subjects performed better than control subjects on an easy (or low response competition) task and worse on a difficult (or high response competition) task.

More recently, Zanna and his colleagues have used a misattribution paradigm to investigate whether dissonance is arousing and, if so, precisely how it is experienced phenomenologically (Zanna & Cooper, 1976). In the initial study, Zanna and Cooper (1974) had subjects write counterattitudinal essays (defending the proposition that controversial speakers should be banned from college campuses) under conditions of either high or low perceived choice. Both dissonance theory and self-perception theory predict that attitude change will occur only when the person feels responsible for his or her behavior, i.e., only when the behavior is unconstrained. In addition, subjects (ostensibly in the context of a separate study) were given a placebo pill before they wrote the essay and were told either that it would make them feel tense, that it would make them feel relaxed, or were given no information about the pill's effects. If dissonance is arousing, then subjects who believe themselves to be under the influence of a tension-producing pill will have an adequate (although false) explanation for their arousal. Attributing their tension to the pill, these subjects should not feel any need to change their attitudes. In contrast, subjects whose inconsistent essay writing produces arousal despite their ingestion of an allegedly relaxing pill ought to feel a greater need to alter their attitudes.

The results are shown in Table 7-1. When the drug was supposed to have no side effect, the standard dissonance (or self-perception) effect was replicated: High-choice subjects agreed more with the position that they took in the counterattitudinal essay than did low-choice subjects. In the tense condition, this effect was virtually eliminated; in the relaxation condition, this effect was significantly enhanced. Clearly, these latter results are consistent with dissonance theory but cannot easily be explained by self-perception theory. It should be noted, however, that this study

Table 7-1 Agreement with Counterattitudinal Essay

Decision Freedom	Potential Side Effect of the Drug		
	Tenseness	None	Relaxation
High	3.4[a]	9.1	13.4
Low	3.5	4.5	4.7

Note: Adapted from Zanna and Cooper (1974). Copyright 1974 by the American Psychological Association. Adapted by permission.

[a] Higher scores indicate greater agreement (i.e., attitude change) on a 31-point scale.

did not directly test the hypothesis that dissonance is arousing. Rather, it tested one implication of the assumption that dissonance is arousing.

Subsequent research using the misattribution paradigm has suggested the following.

(1) Dissonance is phenomenologically aversive, i.e., it can only be misattributed to an external, arousing agent that is allegedly aversive in nature (Zanna, Higgins, & Taves, 1976).[2]
(2) Misattribution is preferred over attitude change as an avenue of dissonance reduction (Zanna, Higgins, & Taves, 1976).
(3) If dissonance is extreme, then subjects are motivated to place themselves in a potentially aversive situation, apparently to "mislabel" their arousal (Gonzalez, Cooper, & Zanna, 1975).
(4) Reinstating the counterattitudinal behavior after two weeks (by having subjects recall their counterattitudinal essays) produces attitude change in those conditions where it had been initially attenuated through misattribution (Higgins, Rhodewalt, & Zanna, 1979).
(5) Attitude change can be eliminated by misattribution when the behavior is inconsistent, i.e., when the person advocates a position in his or her latitude of rejection, but not when the behavior is generally consistent, i.e., when the person advocates a position in his or her latitude of acceptance (Fazio, Zanna, & Cooper, 1977).

Although these results demonstrate that attitude change will be eliminated if cues for misattribution of aversive arousal are available, they do not provide unequivocal evidence that attitude change must be accompanied by arousal or discomfort. A study by Cooper, Zanna, and Taves (1978) is relevant to this issue. These investigators addressed two questions: Is arousal necessary for attitude change following induced compliance?; and Will arousal from another source "add" (i.e., be misattributed) to the dissonance-produced arousal? Again, subjects were induced to write counterattitudinal essays (defending President Ford's pardoning of Richard Nixon) under either high- or low-choice conditions. Although all subjects were given a pill and told that it was a placebo, one-third actually received a tranquilizer (phenobar-

---

[2] In fact, in a follow-up study, Higgins, Rhodewalt, and Zanna (1979) found evidence suggesting that unpleasantness, rather than arousal per se, is the motivating factor in dissonance reduction (but see Fazio & Cooper, 1982).

bital), one-third received an amphetamine, and one-third received the expected placebo. If arousal or discomfort is necessary for dissonance-produced attitude change, then subjects should not change their attitudes in the tranquilizer condition; on the other hand, if amphetamine arousal is misattributed to the counterattitudinal behavior, then attitude change should be enhanced in the amphetamine condition, possibly even under low-choice instructions.

The results are shown in Table 7-2. When the drug was actually a placebo, the standard dissonance effect—more attitude change under high choice than low choice—was replicated. In the tranquilizer condition, this effect was eliminated, which suggests that arousal or discomfort is necessary to motivate attitude change following counterattitudinal advocacy. In the amphetamine condition, attitude change was increased under both high and low choice. Interestingly, only in this low-choice condition did subjects perceive that they had a choice to write the essay. Feeling aroused, subjects apparently deduced that they must have freely chosen to engage in the attitude-discrepant behavior. In this study, then, amphetamine-arousal seems to have been misattributed to the writing of the counterattitudinal essay.

In sum, research by Zanna and his colleagues suggests that (1) dissonance is an aversive state and (2) an aversive state is necessary to motivate cognitive changes following counterattitudinal advocacy. How do these data relate to the so-called controversy between dissonance theory and self-perception theory? Clearly, they suggest that dissonance theory provides a better account than self-perception theory of the process that mediates attitude change following attitude-discrepant behavior.

But do subjects actually experience arousal or discomfort when dissonance has theoretically been aroused? And does attitude change reduce this unpleasant state? There is some self-report evidence that suggests affirmative answers to both of these questions. Zanna and Cooper (1974) included a self-report measure of tension, which was taken after subjects wrote their essays but before their attitudes were assessed. Within the replication conditions (i.e., no side-effect conditions), subjects reported being significantly more tense in the high-choice than in the low-choice condition. Higgins, Rhodewalt, and Zanna (1979) also included self-report measures of mood state, taken both before and after subjects' postadvocacy attitudes were assessed. These authors found evidence that, in conditions where there was significant attitude change, subjects felt more comfortable than did subjects in con-

Table 7-2 Agreement with Counterattitudinal Essay

Decision Freedom	Drug Condition		
	Tranquilizer	Placebo	Amphetamine
High	8.6[a]	14.7	20.2
Low	8.0	8.3	13.9

Note: Adapted from Cooper, Zanna and Taves (1978). Copyright 1978 by the American Psychological Association. Adapted by permission.

[a] Higher scores indicate greater agreement (i.e., attitude change) on a 31-point scale.

ditions where there was no significant attitude change (i.e., where subjects apparently misattributed their dissonance-produced arousal), but these differences occurred only *after* (not before) subjects responded to the attitude measure.

Although this self-report evidence is interesting, an important question is whether there is any evidence that dissonance manipulations produce changes in subjects' physiological states. In their review, Kiesler and Pallak (1976) cite two studies that found evidence of dissonance manipulations (1) constricting finger pulse amplitude (Gerard, 1967) and (2) increasing the number of skin conductance responses (Quanty & Becker, 1974). More recently, Gleason and Katkin (1978) reported a study in which subjects were asked to give a speech in support of reducing average grades to solve the grade inflation problem (dissonant condition) or a speech in opposition to reducing average grades (consonant condition). Subjects in the dissonant condition showed significantly greater elevations in both heart rate and frequency of spontaneous fluctuations in skin conductance during the first minute of thinking about their upcoming speech than did subjects in the consonant condition.

Thus, evidence from a variety of studies indicates that dissonance is experienced as an unpleasant, emotional state (see also Fazio & Cooper, 1982). If direct changes in this state reduce the dissonance (see Cooper, Zanna, & Taves, 1978), then it seems reasonable to hypothesize that people experiencing dissonance may be motivated to engage in behavior that is designed to alter their physiological state (e.g., taking drugs or drinking alcohol). An innovative study by Steele, Southwick, and Crithlow (1981) explored this possibility for the case of alcohol consumption. The results indicated that although dissonance-aroused subjects did not consume more alcohol (in the context of rating different brands), the drinking that did take place was sufficient to eliminate dissonance-reducing attitude change.

The Role of Physiology in Attitude Change

The research that we have presented indicates that physiological reactions can impact on attitude change. Exogenous manipulations of heart rate, for example, have been shown to influence resistance to persuasion. Similarly, certain drugs appear to enhance (and others to inhibit) attitude change following exposure to a persuasive communication.

At the same time, however, it should be noted that these effects of physiological reactions on attitude change appear to be mediated by cognitive processes, such as cognitive elaboration and counterarguing. Whether physiological states affect subjects' *ability* or *motivation* to cognize is unclear. Nevertheless, the psychophysiology-persuasion relation does not seem to be a direct one; future research needs to address the possible mediators.

The literatures on sensory deprivation and dissonance provide less direct evidence that physiological reactions effect attitude change. Instead, researchers in these areas have accumulated various findings that implicate but do not prove the role of physiology. Individually, the findings are equivocal, but, taken together, they provide relatively convincing evidence that the effects of sensory deprivation and dissonance on attitude change are mediated by physiological reactions, especially physiological arousal. Perhaps the most important task facing researchers in these areas is to obtain measures of physiology and attitude change simultaneously and to examine directly the relation between these measures.

In closing, research on the physiological mediation of attitude change has begun the task of explicating this complex issue. Some important findings have been obtained, and some promising directions for future research have been identified. Until additional data are collected, however, the precise role of psychophysiology in persuasion will remain more speculation than fact.

Acknowledgments.   The preparation of this chapter was supported in part by a Social Sciences and Humanities Research Council of Canada Sabbatical Leave Fellowship to Mark P. Zanna. We wish to thank William M. Waid for his comments on an earlier version of the manuscript.

References

Abel, T. (1930). Attitudes and the GSR. *Journal of Experimental Psychology, 13*, 47-60.

Allport, G. (1935). Attitudes. In C. Murchison (Ed.), *A handbook of social psychology.* Worcester, MA: Clark University Press.

Baugher, D. M., & Gormly, J. B. (1975). Effects of personal competence on the significance of interpersonal agreement and disagreement: Physiological activation and social evaluations. *Journal of Research in Personality, 9*, 356-365.

Beck, K. H., & Frankel, A. (1981). A conceptualization of threat communications and preventive health behavior. *Social Psychology Quarterly, 44*, 204-217.

Becker, M. H. (Ed.). (1974). The health belief model and personal health behavior. *Health Education Monographs, 2*, (Whole No. 4).

Bem, D. J. (1967). Self-perception: An alternative interpretation of cognitive dissonance phenomena. *Psychological Review, 74*, 183-200.

Bem, D. J. (1970). *Beliefs, attitudes, and human affairs.* Belmont, CA: Brooks/Cole.

Bem, D. J. (1972). Self-perception theory. In L. Berkowitz (Ed.), *Advances in experimental social psychology* (Vol. 6). New York: Academic Press.

Borrie, R. A. (1977). *The use of sensory deprivation in a programme of weight control.* Unpublished Ph.D. dissertation, University of British Columbia.

Bostrom, R. N. (1980). Altered physiological states: The central nervous system and persuasive communications. In M. F. Roloff & G. R. Miller (Eds.), *Persuasion: New directions in theory and research.* Beverly Hills, CA: Sage.

Bostrom, R. N., & White, N. D. (1979). Does drinking weaken resistance? *Journal of Communication, 29*, 73-80.

Cacioppo, J. T. (1979). Effects of exogenous changes in heart rate on facilitation of thought and resistance to persuasion. *Journal of Personality and Social Psychology, 37*, 489-498.

Cacioppo, J. T., & Petty, R. E. (1979a). Effects of message repetition and position on cognitive response, recall, and persuasion. *Journal of Personality and Social Psychology, 37*, 97-109.

Cacioppo, J. T., & Petty, R. E. (1979b). Attitudes and cognitive response: An electrophysiological approach. *Journal of Personality and Social Psychology, 37*, 2181-2199.

Cacioppo, J. T., & Petty, R. E. (1981a). Electromyograms as measures of extent and affectivity of information processing. *American Psychologist, 36*, 441-456.

Cacioppo, J. T., & Petty, R. E. (1981b). Electromyographic specificity during covert information processing. *Psychophysiology, 18*, 518-523.

Cacioppo, J. T., & Petty, R. E. (1981c). Social psychological procedures for cognitive response assessment. The thought listing technique. In T. V. Merluzzi, C. R. Glass, & M. Genest (Eds.), *Cognitive assessment.* New York: Guilford Press.

Cacioppo, J. T., & Petty, R. E. (1982). A biosocial model of attitude change. In J. T. Cacioppo & R. E. Petty (Eds.), *Perspectives in cardiovascular psychophysiology*. New York: Guilford Press.

Cacioppo, J. T., & Sandman, C. A. (1980). Psychophysiological functioning, cognitive responding, and attitudes. In R. E. Petty, T. M. Ostrom, & T. C. Brock (Eds.), *Cognitive responses in persuasion*. Hillsdale, NJ: Erlbaum.

Cacioppo, J. T., Sandman, C. A., & Walker, B. R. (1978). The effects of operant heart rate conditioning on cognitive elaboration and attitude change. *Psychophysiology, 15*, 330-338.

Cattell, R., Maxwell, E., Light, B., & Unger, M. (1949). The objective measurement of attitudes. *British Journal of Psychology, 40*, 81-90.

Chant, S. H., & Salter, M. D. (1937). The measurement of attitude toward war and the galvanic skin response. *Journal of Educational Psychology, 28*, 281-289.

Chu, G. C. (1966). Fear arousal, efficacy, and imminency. *Journal of Personality and Social Psychology, 4*, 517-524.

Cialdini, R. B., Levy, A., Herman, C. P., Kozlowski, L., & Petty, R. E. (1976). Elastic shifts of opinion: Determinants of direction and durability. *Journal of Personality and Social Psychology, 34*, 663-672.

Clore, G. L., & Gormly, J. B. (1974). Knowing, feeling, and liking: A psychophysiological view. *Journal of Research in Personality, 8*, 218-230.

Cohen, J. (1968). Multiple regression as a data-analytic technique. *Psychological Bulletin, 70*, 426-443.

Cooper, J. B., & Pollock, D. (1959). The identification of prejudicial attitudes by the galvanic skin response. *Journal of Social Psychology, 50*, 241-245.

Cooper, J. B., & Siegel, H. E. (1956). The galvanic skin response as a measure of emotion in prejudice. *Journal of Psychology, 42*, 149-155.

Cooper, J. B., & Singer, D. (1956). The role of emotion in prejudice. *Journal of Social Psychology, 44*, 241-247.

Cooper, J., Zanna, M. P., & Taves, P. A. (1978). Arousal as a necessary condition for attitude change following induced compliance. *Journal of Personality and Social Psychology, 36*, 1101-1106.

Coutts, L. M., Schneider, F. W., & Montgomery, S. (1980). An investigation of the arousal model of interpersonal intimacy. *Journal of Experimental Social Psychology, 16*, 545-561.

Detweiler, R. A., & Zanna. M. P. (1976). Physiological mediation of attitudinal responses. *Journal of Personality and Social Psychology, 33*, 107-116.

Detweiler, R. A., & Zanna, M. P. (1977). *An alternative model of "primary and secondary emotional behavior: an analysis of the role of autonomic feedback affect, arousal, and attribution."* Unpublished manuscript, Drew University.

Dutton, D., & Aron, A. (1974). Some evidence for heightened sexual attraction under conditions of high anxiety. *Journal of Personality and Social Psychology, 30*, 510-517.

Erdman, G., & Janke, W. (1978). Interaction between physiological and cognitive determinants of emotions: Experimental studies of Schachter's theory of emotions. *Biological Psychology, 6*, 61-74.

Fazio, R. H., & Cooper, J. (1982). Arousal in the dissonance process. In J. T. Cacioppo & R. E. Petty (Eds.), *Social psychophysiology*. New York: Guilford Press.

Fazio, R. H., Zanna, M. P., & Cooper, J. (1977). Dissonance and self-perception. An integrative view of each theory's proper domain of application. *Journal of Experimental Social Psychology, 13*, 464-479.

Festinger, L. (1957). *A theory of cognitive dissonance*. Stanford, CA: Stanford University Press.

Fishbein, M., & Ajzen, T. (1975). *Belief, attitude, intention, and behavior: An introduction to theory and research*. Reading, MA: Addison-Wesley.

Geen, R. G. (1981). Behavioral and physiological reactions to observed violence: Effects of prior exposure to aggressive stimuli. *Journal of Personality and Social Psychology, 40*, 868-875.

Gerard, H. B. (1967). Choice difficulty, dissonance, and the decision sequence. *Journal of Personality, 35*, 91-108.

Gerdes, E. P. (1979). Autonomic arousal as a cognitive cue in stressful situations. *Journal of Personality, 47*, 677-711.

Gleason, J. M., & Katkin, E. S. (1978, September). *The effects of cognitive dissonance on heart rate and electrodermal response.* Paper presented at the meetings of the Society for Psychophysiological Research, Madison, WI.

Goldstein, D., Fink, D., & Mettee, D. (1972). Cognition of arousal and actual arousal as determinants of emotion. *Journal of Personality and Social Psychology, 21*, 41-51.

Gonzalez, A. F. J., Cooper, J., & Zanna, M. P. (1975). *Social affiliation and cognitive labeling under differential levels of dissonance-evoked arousal.* Unpublished manuscript, Princeton University.

Gormly, J. (1974). A comparison of predictions from consistency and affect theories for arousal during interpersonal disagreement. *Journal of Personality and Social Psychology, 30*, 658-663.

Gottlieb, A., Gleser, G., & Gottschalk, L. (1967). Verbal and physiological responses to hynotic suggestion of attitudes. *Psychosomatic Medicine, 29*, 172-183.

Green, R. (1975). The meaning of observed violence: Real vs. fictional violence and consequent effects on aggression and emotional arousal. *Journal of Research in Personality, 9*, 270-281.

Harkins, S. G., & Petty, R. E. (1981). Effects of source magnification of cognitive effort on attitudes: An information-processing view. *Journal of Personality and Social Psychology, 40*, 401-413.

Harris, V. A., & Jellison, J. M. (1971). Fear-arousing communications, false physiological feedback, and the acceptance of recommendations. *Journal of Experimental Social Psychology, 7*, 269-279.

Harris, V. A., & Katkin. E. S. (1975). Primary and secondary emotional feedback: An analysis of the role of autonomic feedback on affect, arousal, and attribution. *Psychological Bulletin, 82*, 904-916.

Hass, J., Bagley, G., & Rogers, R. W. (1975). Coping with the energy crisis: Effects of fear appeals upon attitudes toward energy consumption. *Journal of Applied Psychology, 60*, 754-756.

Hess, F. H. (1965). Attitude and pupil size. *Scientific American, 212*, 46-54.

Higbee, K. L. (1969). Fifteen years of fear arousal: Research on threat appeals, 1953-1968. *Psychological Bulletin, 72*, 426-444.

Higgins, E. T., Rhodewalt, E., & Zanna, M. P. (1979). Dissonance motivation: Its nature, persistence, and reinstatement. *Journal of Experimental Social Psychology, 15*, 16-34.

Hirschman, R. (1975). Cross-modal effects of anticipatory bogus heart rate feedback in a negative emotional context. *Journal of Personality and Social Psychology, 31*, 15-19.

Hirschman, R., & Clark, M. (1982). Bogus physiological feedback. In J. T. Cacioppo & R. E. Petty (Eds.), *Social psychophysiology.* New York: Guilford Press.

Hirschman, R., & Hawk, G. (1978). Emotional responsivity to nonveridical heart rate feedback as a function of anxiety. *Journal of Research in Personality, 12*, 235-242.

Ikard, F. E., & Tomkins, S. S. (1973). The experience of affect as a determinant of smoking behavior: A series of validity studies. *Journal of Abnormal Psychology, 81*, 172-181.

Janis, I. L. (1967). Effects of fear arousal on attitude change: Recent developments in theory and experimental research. In L. Berkowitz (Ed.), *Advances in experimental social psychology* (Vol. 3). New York: Academic Press.

Janis, I. L., & Feshbach, S. (1953). Effects of fear-arousing communications. *Journal of Abnormal and Social Psychology, 48*, 78-92.

Jones, G. E., & Hollandsworth, J. G. (1981). Heart rate discrimination before and after exercise-induced augmented cardiac activity. *Psychophysiology, 18*, 252-257.

Katkin, E. S., Blascovich, J., & Goldband, S. (1981). Empirical assessment of visceral self-perception: Individual and sex differences in the acquisition of heartbeat discrimination. *Journal of Personality and Social Psychology, 40*, 1095-1101.

Kerber, K. W., & Coles, M. G. H. (1978). The role of perceived physiological activity in affective judgments. *Journal of Experimental Social Psychology, 14*, 419-433.

Kiesler, C. A., & Pallak, M. S. (1976). Arousal properties of dissonance manipulations *Psychological Bulletin, 83*, 1014-1025.

Klineberg, O. (1940). *Social psychology*. New York: Henry Holt and Co.

Lacey, B. C., & Lacey, J. I. (1974). Studies of heart rate and other bodily processes in sensorimotor behavior. In P. A. Obrist, A. H. Black, J. Brener, & L. V. DiCara (Eds.), *Cardiovascular psychophysiology—Current issues in response mechanisms, biofeedback, and methodology*. Chicago: Aldine.

Lacey, B. C., & Lacey, J. I. (1978). Two-way communication between the heart and the brain: Significance of time within the cardiac cycle. *American Psychologist, 33*, 99-113.

Lacey, J. I., Kagan, J., Lacey, B. C., & Moss, H. A. (1963). The visceral level: Situational determinants and behavioral correlates of autonomic response patterns. In P. H. Knapp (Ed.), *Expression of the emotions in man*. New York: International Universities Press.

Lacey, J. I., & Lacey, B. C. (1958). Verification and extension of the principle of autonomic response stereotypy. *American Journal of Psychology, 71*, 50-73.

Landon, P. B., & Suedfeld, P. (1972). Complex cognitive performance and sensory deprivation: Completing the U-curve. *Perceptual and Motor Skills, 34*, 601-602.

Langlie, J. K. (1977). Social networks, health beliefs, and preventive health behavior. *Journal of Health and Social Behavior, 18*, 244-260.

Leventhal, H. (1970). Findings and theory in the study of fear communications. In L. Berkowitz (Ed.), *Advances in experimental social psychology* (Vol. 6). New York: Academic Press.

Leventhal, H., & Singer, R. P. (1966). Affect arousal and positioning of recommendations in persuasive communications. *Journal of Personality and Social Psychology, 4*, 137-146.

Leventhal, H., Singer, R. P., & Jones, S. (1965). The effects of fear and specificity of recommendations upon attitudes and behavior. *Journal of Personality and Social Psychology, 2*, 20-29.

Liebhart, E. H. (1979). Information search and attribution: Cognitive processes mediating the effect of false autonomic feedback. *European Journal of Social Psychology, 9*, 19-37.

Marshall, G. D. (1976). *The affective consequences of "inadequately explained" physiological arousal*. Unpublished doctoral dissertation, Stanford University.

Marshall, G. D., & Zimbardo, P. G. (1979). Affective consequences of inadequately explained physiological arousal. *Journal of Personality and Social Psychology, 37*, 970-988.

Maslach, C. (1977). Negative emotional biasing of unexplained arousal. In C. Izard (Ed.), *Emotions and emotion-cognition interactions in psychopathology*. New York: Plenum Press.

McArthur, L., & Solomon, L. (1978). Perceptions of an aggressive encounter as a function of the victim's salience and the perceiver's arousal. *Journal of Personality and Social Psychology, 36*, 1278-1280.

McCanne, T. R., & Sandman, C. A. (1974). Instrumental heart rate responses and visual perception: A preliminary study. *Psychophysiology, 11*, 283-287.

McGuire, W. J. (1969). The nature of attitudes and attitude change. In G. Lindzey & E. Aronson (Eds.), *The handbook of social psychology* (Vol 3, 2nd Ed.). Reading, MA: Addison-Wesley.

McKinlay, J. R. (1972). Some approaches and problems in the study of the use of services: An overview. *Journal of Health and Social Behavior, 13*, 115-152.

Mewborn, C. R., & Rogers, R. W. (1979). Effects of threatening and reassuring components of fear appeals on physiological and verbal measures of emotion and attitudes. *Journal of Experimental Social Psychology, 15*, 242-253.

Mintz, P. M., & Mills, J. (1971). Effects of arousal and information about its source upon attitude change. *Journal of Experimental Social Psychology, 7*, 561-570.

Moore, H. T. (1929). Innate factors in radicalism and conservatism. *Journal of Abnormal and Social Psychology, 35*, 220-238.

O'Neal, E. (1971). Influence of future choice importance and arousal upon the halo effect. *Journal of Personality and Social Psychology, 19*, 334-340.

O'Neal, E., & Kaufman, L. (1972). The influence of attack, arousal, and information about one's arousal upon interpersonal aggression. *Psychonomic Science, 26*, 211-213.

Oskamp, S. (1977). *Attitudes and opinions*. Englewood Cliffs, NJ: Prentice-Hall.

Pallak, M. S., & Pittman, T. S. (1972). General motivational effects of dissonance arousal. *Journal of Personality and Social Psychology, 21*, 349-358.

Pennebaker, J. W., Dyer, M. A., Caulkins, R. S., Litowitz, D. L., Ackreman, P. L., Anderson, D. B., & McGraw, K. M. (1979). Don't the girls get prettier at closing time: A country and western application to psychology. *Personality and Social Psychology Bulletin, 5*, 122-125.

Petty, R. E., & Cacioppo, J. T. (1977). Forewarning, cognitive responding, and resistance to persuasion. *Journal of Personality and Social Psychology, 35*, 645-655.

Petty, R. E., & Cacioppo, J. T. (1979a). Effects of forewarning of persuasive intent and involvement on cognitive responses and persuasion. *Personality and Social Psychology Bulletin, 5*, 173-176.

Petty, R. E., & Cacioppo, J. T. (1979b). Issue involvement can increase or decrease persuasion by enhancing message-relevant cognitive responses. *Journal of Personality and Social Psychology, 37*, 1915-1926.

Petty, R. E., Cacioppo, J. T., & Heesacker, M. (1981). Effects of rhetorical questions on persuasion: A cognitive response analysis. *Journal of Personality and Social Psychology, 40*, 432-440.

Petty, R. E., Wells, G. L., & Brock, T. C. (1976). Distraction can enhance or reduce yielding to propaganda: Thought disruption versus effort justification. *Journal of Personality and Social Psychology, 34*, 874-884.

Porier, G. W., & Lott, A. J. (1967). Galvanic skin responses and prejudice. *Journal of Personality and Social Psychology, 5*, 253-259.

Quanty, M. B., & Becker, L. A. (1974). *Physiological indices of dissonance arousal and reduction in a stressful situation*. Unpublished manuscript, University of Missouri-Columbia.

Rankin, R. F., & Campbell, D. T. (1955). Galvanic skin response to Negro and white experimenters. *Journal of Abnormal and Social Psychology, 51*, 30-33.

Rogers, R. W. (1975). A protection motivation theory of fear appeals and attitude change. *Journal of Psychology, 91*, 93-114.

Rogers, R. W. (1982). Cognitive and physiological processes in fear appeals and attitude change: A revised theory of protection motivation. In J. T. Cacioppo & R. E. Petty (Eds.), *Social psychophysiology*. New York: Guilford Press.

Rogers, R. W., & Deckner, W. C. (1975). Effects of fear appeals and physiological arousal upon emotion, attitudes, and cigarette smoking. *Journal of Personality and Social Psychology, 32*, 222-230.

Rogers, R. W., Deckner, C. W., & Mewborn, C. R. (1978). An expectancy-value theory approach to the long-term modification of smoking behavior. *Journal of Clinical Psychology, 34*, 562-566.

Rogers, R. W., & Mewborn, C. R. (1976). Fear appeals and attitude change: Effect of a threat's noxiousness, probability of occurrence, and the efficacy of coping responses. *Journal of Personality and Social Psychology, 34*, 54-61.

Rogers, R. W., Thistlethwaite, D. L. (1970). Effects of fear arousal and reassurance upon attitude change. *Journal of Personality and Social Psychology, 15*, 227-233.

Rosenstock, I. M. (1966). Why people use health services. *Millbank Memorial Fund Quarterly, 44*, 94-127.

Sapira, J., Scheib, F., Moriarty, R., & Shapiro, A. (1971). Differences in perception between hypertensive and normotensive populations. *Psychosomatic Medicine, 33*, 239-250.

Schachter, S., & Singer, J. (1962). Cognitive, social, and physiological determinants of emotional state. *Psychological Review, 69*, 379-399.

Schandry, R. (1981). Heart beat perception and emotional experience *Psychophysiology, 18*, 483-488.

Schwartz, G., Fair, P., Salt, P., Mandel, M., & Klerman, G. (1976). Facial muscle patterning to effective imagery in depressed and nondepressed subjects. *Science, 192*, 489-491.

Smith, R. C. (1974). Alcohol and the acceptance of social influence: An experimental study. *Psychopharmacologia, 36*, 357-366.

Steele, C. M., Southwick, L. L., & Crithlow, B. (1981). Dissonance and alcohol: Drinking your troubles away. *Journal of Personality and Social Psychology, 41*, 831-846.

Stein, S. H. (1971). Arousal level in repressors and sensitizers as a function of response context. *Journal of Consulting and Clinical Psychology, 36*, 386-394.

Stern, R. M., Botto, R. W., & Herrick, C. D. (1972). Behavioral and physiological effects of false heart rate feedback: A replication and extension. *Psychophysiology, 9*, 21-29.

Strom, J., & Buck, R. (1979). Staring and participant's sex: Physiological and subjective reactions. *Personality and Social Psychology Bulletin, 5*, 114-117.

Suedfeld, P. (1980). *Restricted environmental stimulation: Research and clinical applications*. New York: Wiley.

Suedfeld, P., & Borrie, R. A. (1978). Sensory deprivation, attitude change, and defense against persuasion. *Canadian Journal of Behavioural Science, 10*, 16-27.

Suedfeld, P., & Ikard, F. E. (1974). Use of sensory deprivation in facilitating the reduction of cigarette smokers. *Journal of Consulting and Clinical Psychology, 42*, 888-895.

Suedfeld, P., Tetlock, P. E., & Borrie, R. A. (in preparation). *The effects of restricted stimulation and a distracting task on counterarguing and attitude change*.

Tetlock, P. E., & Suedfeld, P. (1976). Inducing belief instability without a persuasive message: The roles of attitude centrality, individual cognitive differences, and sensory deprivation. *Canadian Journal of Behavioural Science, 8*, 324-333.

Tognacci, L., & Cook, S. (1975). Conditioned autonomic responses as bidirectional indicators of racial attitude. *Journal of Personality and Social Psychology, 31*, 137-144.

Valins, S. (1966). Cognitive effects of false heart rate feedback. *Journal of Personality and Social Psychology, 4*, 400-408.

VanderKolk, C. J. (1976). Physiological measures as a means of assessing reactions to the disabled. *New Outlook for the Blind, 70*, 101-103.

Zanna, M. P., & Cooper, J. (1974). Dissonance and the pill: An attribution approach to studying the arousal properties of dissonance. *Journal of Personality and Social Psychology, 29*, 703-709.

Zanna, M. P., & Cooper, J. (1976). Dissonance and the attribution process. In J. H. Harvey, W. J. Ickes, & R. F. Kidd (Eds.), *New directions in attribution research* (Vol. 1). Hillsdale, NJ: Erlbaum.

Zanna, M. P., Higgins, E. T., & Taves, P. A. (1976). Is dissonance phenomenologically aversive? *Journal of Experimental Social Psychology, 12*, 530-538.

Zillman, D., Johnson, R. C., & Day, K. D. (1974). Attribution of apparent arousal and proficiency of recovery from sympathetic activation affecting excitation transfer to aggressive behavior. *Journal of Experimental Social Psychology, 10*, 503-515.

Part III
Physiology and Social Behavior

Chapter 8
Social Interactions and Psychophysiology

John B. Gormly

Introduction

The most active period for research in the psychophysiology of face-to-face interactions was during the 1950s, when a large body of research was published on psychophysiological activation during various conditions of psychotherapy. Since that time, there has been a regular decline in the number of studies reporting physiological events during face-to-face interactions. Current interest in behavioral medicine is on the rise, and this area of psychology has recently been described in an excellent book by Surwit, Williams, and Shapiro (1982). We are witnessing a rebirth of research in social interactions and psychophysiology, particularly in the case of cardiovascular activity such as blood pressure and heart rate during socially stressful interactions (e.g., MacDougall, Dembroski, & Krantz, 1981), research which is relevant to an understanding of coronary-prone people.

It is hard to imagine a larger category of naturalistic human behavior than face-to-face interactions. Within this broad area, we find may prominent subareas of behavior such as teacher-student interactions and the educational process, labor-management negotiations, and socialization of children by their parents, just to illustrate a few interesting and socially relevant areas. Despite the interest in face-to-face interactions by many academic disciplines, particularly social psychology, only three subareas have produced a body of literature on physiological activity during social interactions. They are the areas of therapist-client interactions during psychotherapy, coronary-prone behavior patterns, and interpersonal disagreement. It is hoped that a consideration of research in those areas will lead to an appreciation of the significance of knowing about physiological activation during social interactions and will lead to an increased use of psychophysiological measures in research on face-to-face interactions.

Psychophysiological Activity and Psychotherapy

Research on psychophysiological activity and the conditions of therapy has been extensively reviewed by Lacey (1962). A more recent, although briefer, reviewer has been written by Lang (1971). Since Lang's review, very little has been reported in this area, although the early research was promising and most interesting. This is an excellent area for continuing psychophysiological study.

Much of the research in this area uses physiological change as a measure of the affective significance of events and topics to the client. Doust and Schneider (1955), for example, reported case studies on changes in the oxygen saturation of the blood as it was related to psychological conflicts. In one case, a man reported disabling anxiety while at home in the evening, although he felt well during the day while at work. The topics of "wife" and "sex" resulted in significant drops in oxygen saturation of his blood, thus revealing a source of conflict which made his symptoms more understandable.

The psychological conflict in this example involved social interactions, the client's social and, particularly, sexual relations with his wife. It is generally the case that studies on psychophysiological activations and psychological conflict are dealing with problems that involve social insecurities. Hence, this body of research is properly sociophysiological research. These very interesting studies on affective significance of experience, however, are not studies of face-to-face interactions and will not be discussed further in this chapter except to refer the reader to the reviews by Lacey and by Lang.

In addition to research in clinical settings on affective significance of topics to clients in therapy, there have been studies in three areas which do involve face-to-face interactions between client and therapist: the client's responses to conditions of the therapeutic interaction, the clients' responses to personal characteristics of the therapist, and the therapists' affective responses during therapy. In the review that follows, I will describe some studies which are representative of each area and discuss the kinds of studies which could continue the development of an understanding of the process of psychotherapy using psychophysiological measures in research on psychotherapy.

Client's Responses to the Conditions of Therapy

Research in which the therapist deliberately controls the nature of the therapist-client interaction during the psychotherapeutic interview has taken two general paths. In the first, the therapist directs the interaction so that it becomes an analogue to the patient's life-situation outside of therapy so that the patient's symptoms can occur and go into remission right in the therapy session. The second direction is for the therapist to direct the interaction in a general way, nondirective versus confrontative, for example, to investigate the "better" social climate for therapy.

An early study by Mittlemann, Wolff, and Scharf (1942) provides a good example of the first approach. They reported many case studies on patients who had severe gastroduodenal problems. When the therapist directed the discussion in a way that produced feelings of security, there was a measurable decrease in peristalic activity and stomach acidity. When the therapist induced feelings of resentment during the interview, peristalic activity and stomach activity increased.

The measures of physiological change in this study provided the definitive measure to test a general hypothesis about the quality of social interactions and psychosomatic symptoms. A natural development of this line of research is to provide for measuring of physiological activity in the naturally occurring conditions of the person's life outside the therapy situation. That kind of feedback very well could be the most direct way of achieving corrective action for the reduction or elimination of symptoms.

In a study of supportive versus confrontive styles of therapy, Malmo, Boag, and Smith (1957) recorded muscle tension in psychoneurotic patients while studying the effects of praising versus critical statements made to the patient by the psychologist. Critical comments results in high muscle tension which remained high throughout a rest interval, while praising comments by the psychologist were followed by reduced muscle tension. Dittes (1957), in a study that was conceptually similar to that of Malmo et al. (although not a direct manipulation of conditions), had raters judge the degree of permissiveness by the therapist and associated this with a measure of electrodermal activity during therapy sessions. Permissiveness was significantly related to reduced physiological activation during therapy.

More recently, Martin, Lundy, and Lewin (1960) added another piece of information to studies on conditions of therapy and their effects on the activities of the client. They varied the level of communicativeness of the therapist and measured the emotional content of the client's speech in addition to electrodermal activity. The study covered the first five sessions of therapy. In the condition where the therapist was most verbal, the clients increased their discussion of emotionally significant topics across the five sessions, while physiological activation decreased significantly in the final two sessions. In conditions of lower verbal communicativeness by the therapist, the clients' discussions of emotionally significant topics dropped to a low level.

We see an interesting beginning in the use of psychophysiological measures for studying the effects of various conditions of therapy. The results might be taken to indicate that supportive conditions with verbally active therapists are effective conditions for therapy. Of course, the missing pieces include a body of literature that relates physiological activity during therapy sessions to outcomes, such as whether the clients leave therapy prematurely or the number of sessions to the successful conclusion of therapy.

There is reason to believe that the pattern of physiological activation during therapy is an important measure. Mowrer, Light, Luria, and Seleny (1953), studying the change in electrodermal activity from session-to-session, reported that clients who left therapy prematurely were clients whose levels of skin conductance increased throughout the course of treatment; successful clients had decreasing activation. These results are supported by Fenz and Steffy (1968), who reported decreases in skin conductance to be associated with improvement in social behavior for psychiatric patients.

It is the effect on the outcome of therapy that primarily gives importance to studying conditions of the therapeutic interaction. It is important to know whether or not particular conditions in therapy are effective in reducing upsetting emotions and maladaptive behavior in the naturalistic setting where the problem occurs. Paul (1966) has reported the only study I know of that has used psychophysiological variables in such an investigation. Clients who reported excessive anxiety occurring while anticipating and speaking in public were treated with one of several alternative procedures of therapy. After the conclusion of treatment, measures of pulse rate and electrodermal activity were recorded along with behavioral ratings and self-report of anxiety just before the person was to make a public speech. The dependent measures converged in supporting the conclusion that systematic desentization was the most effective treatment in the study for reducing emotional and behavioral problems associated with public speaking.

Client's Responses to Personal Characteristics of Therapists

In the period that followed Eysenck's (1952) dramatic conclusion that no evidence supported the assumption that psychotherapy was better for the patient than no psychotherapeutic treatment, considerable research was directed toward demonstrating that some therapists were effective (see Truax & Mitchell, 1971). These studies were primarily directed at determining the interpersonal skills that made therapists effective. According to Truax and Mitchell, who did an extensive review of this research, two out of three therapists were ineffective or harmful. They argued that therapists needed feedback about their effects on the client. Levels of psychophysiological activation during therapy sessions and throughout the course of treatment could be a useful part of the feedback process, while at the same time adding to an understanding of the psychophysiological correlates of the process and successful outcome of therapy. Unfortunately, there was practically no interest in including psychophysiological variables in research on the personal characteristics of therapists. It is not too late!

There is some information on the effects of the *person* of the therapist on physiological activity of the client. DiMascio, Boyd, Greenblatt, and Solomon (1955) studied the effects of the therapist on the heart rates of patients during clinical interviews. All clients had their lowest heart rate with one particular therapist. A content analysis of the interaction, however, did not clarify why the therapist had this effect. Malmo et al. (1957) reported on the effect of the therapist's mood on the heart rate of a psychoneurotic patient. The psychologist kept notes on his moods during a 3-month period while the patient's heart rate was recorded throughout their meetings. The patient had a substantially elevated heart rate during the meetings with the therapist when he was in a "bad" mood. Dittes's (1957) study described earlier is also relevant to this topic. Content analysis of therapists' sessions where skin conductance was assessed from the client revealed that therapists' gentleness and attentiveness were related to lower physiological activation.

Thus, it is clear that the *person* of the therapist had an effect on the physiological states of the client as well as on the outcome of therapy. We do not have nearly enough information to make a definite statement about the interconnectedness of the three variables: personal qualities of therapist, physiological effects on client, and outcome of therapy. It is a promising area for research which could have an important impact on selection and training of therapists.

Therapist's Responses During Therapy

Malmo et al. (1957) recorded muscle tension from both the therapist and the client and found that therapist and patient had similar patterns of muscle tension in response to the therapist's presentation of supportive or critical comments. Critical therapists had increased muscle tension following their critical comments. While this research might have taken the direction of studying physiological hazards of different styles of therapy for the therapist, the interest in this area has generally been to study empathy as indicated by concordant physiological states between therapist and client. Other studies have described concordance for heart rate (Coleman, Greenblatt, & Solomon, 1956), heart rate and lability of heart rate (DiMascio, Boyd, & Greenblatt, 1957), and skin conductance (Robinson, Herman, & Kaplan, 1982).

The Robinson et al. study clearly indicates that the concordance in physiological activation was related to the construct of empathy rather than common reactions to the events occurring during therapy. They measured judgments about perceived empathy as well as continuous skin conductance. Concordance in phasic responding was greatest when clients and therapists judged that they were in empathic states.

The interest in this area is presumably related to an assumption that if the therapist is in an empathic relationship with the client, including psychophysiological empathy, then the process of therapy and the outcome of therapy will be advanced. At this time, this is an unsupported assumption, and it is one that would be extremely difficult to test. An easier task would be to investigate psychophysiological contagion: For example, does a person, either the client or therapist, who has an excessive cardiovascular reaction pattern produce that effect in the other?

Comments

The sample of studies described in this section illustrates the potential for psychophysiological variables in leading to an understanding of the process and outcome of the therapeutic interaction. Significant results are found using a wide variety of physiological indices, which most likely means that robust physical changes are occurring during therapy. Much could be said about the inadequacies of studies in this area and the need for a standard set of physiological measures. Lacey (1962) has already done this in an excellent fashion, and it would be useful to study his comments as part of any plan to do research in this area. The field of psychology would be advanced greatly by a renewed interest in investigating psychophysiology and psychotherapy. Perhaps the current interest in behavioral medicine will encourage this work. The most important studies will be those using psychophysiological variables as part of a converging set of measures to demonstrate the effectiveness of psychotherapy, measured in the naturalistic settings where emotional disturbances are occurring. When a convincing procedure is developed for establishing that effective therapy has occurred, then the problems can be worked backward. How do different therapists and different conditions of therapy affect outcome, and what are the covarying psychophysiological events for different therapists, qualities and different conditions of therapy? Such an area of knowledge would be helpful in training and evaluating therapists, and it would be valuable in the development of a general understanding of social interactions.

Psychophysiological Activity, Coronary-Prone Personality, and Social Interactions

It has long been held that personality factors have an influence on physical health; this is particularly the case for cardiovascular disorders (Wolff, 1953). The assessment of coronary-prone personalities advanced from assessment via clinical intuition by the work of Rosenman and Friedman (1974), who developed a structured interview procedure for the objective assessment of a coronary-prone personality (Type A) and the relative absence of coronary-prone behavior patterns (Type B). Longitudinal research on heart disease has demonstrated that descriptions of people according to their coronary-prone behavioral pattern account for a proportion of variance in heart disease which is independent of that associated with known physical risks, like blood pressure, smoking, obesity, etc. (Rosenman, Brand, Jenkins, Friedman, Straus, & Wurm, 1975). Thus, a challenging topic of research has been to discover the links between the coronary-prone personality and heart disease.

It is not surprising that investigators are "hitting pay dirt" by studying Type A and Type B persons during social interactions. Many years ago, Wolf, Cardon, Shepart, and Wolff (1955) demonstrated that blood pressure and other measures of cardiovascular performance are increased substantially by face-to-face interviews. Since then, this has been determined to be a general phenomenon involving social conversation (Williams, Kimball, & Willard, 1972; Lynch, Thomas, Long, Malinow, Chickadonz, & Katcher, 1980). Using various conditions of social interactions, researchers have reported that Type A people have a larger blood pressure increase than Type B people in performing tasks in which they are challenged (Dembroski, MacDougall, Shields, Petitto, & Lushene, 1978), in interactions with hostile opponents during competition but not to competition alone (Glass, Kraloff, Contrada, Hilton, Kehoe, Mannucci, Collins, Snow, & Elting, 1980), and during an interview but not during a quiz (Krantz, Schaeffer, Davia, Dembroski, MacDougall, & Shaffer, 1981). Thus, it appears that it is not simply that Type A people are physiologically responsive to difficult activities; the interpersonal qualities of the situation are most important in elevating cardiovascular responses. The interpersonal characteristics of the Type A person have been described by Jenkins (1979) as involving lack of interest in other people, that they have a self-centered quality. Is it not interesting, then, that Type A people project the image of being socially aloof while they are so reactive to social conditions at a physiological level? This pattern of contradiction in performance is likely to result from social fears, particularly fears of powerlessness, which are expressed as an attempt to be superior and competent. Such hypothesis can easily be tested using psychophysiological measures.

While Type A and Type B persons can be examined in laboratory studies where conditions of social insecurity are contrived, the manipulation of conditions are likely to create only weak threats compared to naturalistic events. This is not to discourage laboratory studies in this area; they should be done. The important and additional data that is needed would involve examining the frequency and extent of power struggles Type A and Type B people engage in while interacting with significant people in their lives (like parents, spouse, and supervisors) while recording cardiovascular responses. Relevant to the preceding section, we would also do well to investigate the cardiovascular activity of people as they interact with Type A and Type B people, a study of physiological contagion. It is quite likely that Type A and Type B people have different effects on those who interact with them.

Psychophysiological Activity and Interpersonal Disagreement

Interpersonal disagreement has been a leading topic is psychological research (Byrne, 1971; Findley & Cooper, 1981). It is a condition which can be created in the laboratory with direct relevance to behavior outside the laboratory. Casual friendships, satisfaction in marriage, and the harmony of international relations are all dependent on the way the participants create and respond to disagreement.

Research on psychophysiological activation during face-to-face disagreement can be divided into two areas. In the first case, the *conditions* under which disagreement occurs are varied. This is usually done to test predictions from competing theories that attempt to account for people's responses to disagreement. In the second case, disagreement is presented in order to assess individual differences in behavioral styles of coping with disagreement.

Varying the Conditions in which Disagreement Occurs

Burdick and Burnes (1958) appear to have reported the first study on physiological activation during disagreement. They studied the skin conductance of subjects who discussed two topics with an assistant to the experimenter. The higher level of activation during disagreement was taken to indicate a psychological strain in the subject that originated from a motivational state to be in balanced situations, that is, to be in agreement with a respected person. Gerard (1961) recorded electrodermal activity for subjects who were making judgments about lengths of lines along with three other students. The other students were accomplices of the experimenter and disagreed with his judgment according to plan. The experimenter varied the degree of disagreement and the subject's confidence in his abilities. Results were taken to support the ideas of balance theory, similar to the Burdick and Burnes study.

Murray (1963) studied the heart rate of students involved in a discussion and argument with a lawyer. Conditions were varied throughout their exchange to include times when the student criticized the lawyer and times when the lawyer insulted the student. While no particular social psychological theory was tested, empirical results demonstrated that heart rate was highest when the student was about to be active in the discussion, and that heart rate was higher when he was actively involved in discussion than when he was being insulted.

Three studies were conducted in which the subjects were in face-to-face presentations of their social attitudes with peers, who were also accomplices of the experimenter. These studies were designed to test competing predictions from social-psychological theories (Clore & Gormly, 1974; Gormly, 1974; Baugher & Gormly, 1975). All studies used levels of skin conductance to test predictions from the affect-reinforcement theory of Byrne and Clore (1967), balance theories (Heider, 1958; Newcomb, 1961), and dissonance theory (Festinger, 1957); each theory leads to different predictions about the social conditions of disagreement in which arousal would be greatest. In all three studies, the predictions from the affect-reinforcement theory best predicted the conditions in which skin conductance would be highest.

Aside from the value of these studies in testing predictions generated from competing theories, they also demonstrate the potency of using psychophysiological variables in social research. The psychological measures were the definitive dependent variables in these studies.

Individual Differences in Coping with Disagreement

The second area of study within the psychophysiology of interpersonal disagreement has been investigations of the levels of physical activation that accompany different personal styles of responding to disagreement. Steiner (1966) and Gormly (1971) demonstrated a replicated relation between the behavioral styles people use in "coping" with disagreement and levels of skin conductance during the interaction. Four styles were compared: people who were high in the amount of conformity (Conformers), people who were extreme in reporting less disagreement than actually occurred (Deniers), people who were extreme in rejecting the disagreeing other person (Rejecters), and people who were extreme in their devaluation of the significance of disagreement (Devaluaters).

Although conformity, denial, rejection, and devaluation have been described as coping styles, i.e., ways of attempting to reduce the arousal that is associated with the stress of being involved in a disagreement (Lazarus, 1966; Steiner, 1966; Hamilton, 1969; Gormly, 1971), the pattern of arousal for Conformers and Deniers does not fit the "coping-style" description or indicates maladaptive coping styles. People who respond to disagreement with conformity or denial have increasing levels of skin conductance during disagreement and immediately following it; these people have substantially more arousal than people who reject the disagreeing person or devalue the significance of disagreement. Psychophysiological variables can be used to further investigate conformity and denial as coping styles, and the following section will present research that does this.

Although this chapter has described many studies that have increased general knowledge about the process of human interactions and has pointed out natural areas for continued development, a reading of recent journals in social psychology, personality, and psychophysiology shows that there is no group of recent studies whose explicit purpose is to describe the psychophysiology of social interactions. The remainder of this chapter will describe two previously unpublished studies, one following the experimental approach to research and the other following the correlational approach. Cronbach (1957) has described these two approaches as competing traditions for how knowledge about psychology is gathered. Psychophysiological measures will be demonstrated as important variables in both approaches.

Most psychophysiological research on social interactions takes an experimental approach, seeking to answer questions about the effects of social conditions such as "Does a permissive therapist evoke fewer skin conductance responses than a confronting therapist?" It is equally important that we investigate questions that can really be answered only by correlational procedures such as "Are hypertensive people more likely to be avoided by significant people in their lives than people with normal blood pressure?" Thus, psychophysiological variables can be used to study the effects of environmental conditions, as well as individual differences in physiological traits. The data presented later in this chapter indicate that when care is taken to achieve stable physiological measures of the individual (usually through repeated measurement), certain physiological traits emerge that are substantially related to social-behavioral traits. It is hoped that these studies will serve to increase interest in conducting research on psychophysiology and social interactions.

The Experimental Approach: Conformity as a Deceptive Act

One way of viewing conformity is to see it as a way of coping with stress; this interpretation implies that if people whose general style of responding to disagreement was conformity were prevented from conforming, then their arousal would increase. This interpretation is similar to a Freudian explanation of defense mechanisms: when a person is not able to use a habitual defense mechanism, then the person experiences an excessive amount of arousal/anxiety.

Another way of viewing conformity, however, is to see it as an example of deception, such as a lie or misrepresentation of yourself to another person. When conformity is viewed as deception, then the high level of skin conductance for Conformers is consistent with other studies involving the detection of deception; lying is accompanied by increased arousal. This is the principle that has yielded the lie detector, although the detection of lying is not so simple according to recent writings (Lykken, 1974; Waid, Orne, & Wilson, 1979, for example). High levels of skin conductance during conformity are also consistent with Mowrer's theory of emotional disturbance, Integrity Therapy: When people are dishonest, they become upset or aroused because they fear being found out (Mowrer, 1961).

In the study which follows, people who typically respond to disagreement with conformity will be prevented from conforming by the experimental procedure being used. Following the ideas of Mowrer (1961) and the research on arousal and deception, it was hypothesized that this enforced honesty would result in lower levels of skin conductance than when people are allowed to conform their opinions to a disagreeing person's opinions.

It has already been demonstrated that a person's response to disagreement, whether it be conformity, denial, rejection, or devaluation, acts as a personality trait; that is, the style of responding is consistent from one situation to another (Gormly, Gormly, & Johnson, 1972). This was determined by exposing the same group of people to a succession of disagreement situations. Thus, a person who conforms his or her opinions in one situation is highly likely to conform in another.

Procedure of the Study

The present study had two parts. First, there was testing of a large group of male college students to identify those people who were extreme in their use of conformity in response to disagreement. People who were extreme in the use of underrecall were also identified and served as a control group. This aspect of the current study was modeled after the procedures of Gormly, Gormly, and Johnson (1972). The 1972 report has a detailed description of the method; the essential aspects of the method will be presented here. Next, 1 week after the initial testing, people high in conformity and people high in denial returned for a second testing. At this time, the procedure prevented the subjects from conforming. The procedure of this aspect of the study was modeled after Gormly (1971), which contains a detailed description of the procedure; only the essential aspects of the method will be presented here.

Identifying people who conform their opinions.[1] Eighty male students from General Psychology classes at Rutgers University participated in the first part. They completed a 30-item survey of social attitudes of high interest to college students. Each item had six alternatives, from strongly in favor of (pro) the topic to strongly against (con); the student was to check the alternative which best represented his position. The laboratory had several small rooms and when the person was finished with the 30 items, he was taken to another room where he met another student. The second student was an accomplice.

The subject was told that he and the other person would present their attitudes aloud, and based on that information, they were to make judgments about the other person's social and personality characteristics.

The accomplice had a sheet that indicated the other person's responses for the first 15 items from the survey of attitudes; the subject did not know this. The subject was handed an unmarked survey of attitudes and saw the accomplice being handed an unmarked booklet. The accomplice was told to state the option that best represented his opinion toward the first attitude-topic. Then the subject was to give his response to the same topic. This order of presentation was to continue for 15 topics. The opinions given by the accomplice were in disagreement with 12 of the subject's original attitudes. Disagreement was created by having the accomplice state the option that was three positions removed from the subject's original response; thus, if the subject had indicated that he was strongly pro some topic, then the accomplice was mildly con the topic, etc.

After the presentation of opinions, the two people were separated. The subject was asked to estimate the number of topics for which he and the other person were in disagreement and he was asked to go through a checklist of adjectives and to indicate which adjectives described the other person (filler activities for the study).

A record was kept of the position stated by the subject in the face-to-face meeting, and this was compared with the original responses. Conformity was measured by the number of positions the person moved in the direction of the position stated by the

---

[1] I wish to thank Steven Darby and Harold Busch for their assistance in this study.

accomplice minus the number of positions the person moved away from the accomplice's position for the 12 disagreement items. The 10 subjects with the highest conformity scores were selected for the main study.

A second group of people were also selected for further study. All subjects were asked to estimate the number of topics on which they and the other person were in disagreement. The 10 subjects with the lowest estimates were selected for further study; that is, the group that most underrecalled the extent of disagreement. In previous research (Steiner, 1966; Gormly, 1971), people who underrecalled the extent of disagreement were found to have high levels of skin conductance during and after disagreement, similar to people who used conformity, and the underrecall people served as a control group in the main study.

Prevention conformity. The 20 selected students returned to the laboratory in the following week. The procedure and explanations were similar to those of the first meeting. The subject was to meet another student (another accomplice of the experimenter), present his attitudes, listen to the other person's attitudes, and use that information for making judgments about the other person's social and personal characteristics. Two elements of the procedure were, however, modified. First, the subject had his completed attitude booklet with him, with the opinions he had given privately indicated on it. He was directed to state the position he had indicated as his. The accomplice was given the same directions as the subject was given. Second, skin conductance was recorded from the subject and accomplice while they stated the attitudes. The experimenter stated that he was interested in how skin conductance was influenced by "taking in information."

Skin conductance was recorded in the same manner as an earlier study (Gormly, 1971). The range of the subject's skin conductance was estimated by having the person rest for approximately 7 min while alone in the room (low point of skin conductance) and by having the experimenter suddenly end the rest period by entering the room and loudly clapping his hands three times in front of the person's face while saying loudly, "Wake up!" (high point of skin conductance). Knowing the range of responding for each person allows correcting skin conductance scores for individual differences in range of responding (Lykken, Rose, Luther, & Maley, 1966).

Prevent Conformity Reduces Arousal for Conformers

As in the earlier study, the person's skin conductance was scored from the highest level it reached in 5-sec intervals following the accomplice's statement of each of the 15 attitudes.

Skin conductance for Conformers and Deniers who had to state the positions they had indicated privately, thereby preventing conformity, was compared with the responses of the 10 people who had the highest conformity scores and the 10 people who had the highest denial scores from the earlier study, when conformity was a possibility. These data are illustrated in Figure 8-1. The apparent reduction in arousal for Conformers who were not allowed to conform is statistically significant; that is, the interaction between style of Responding (Conformers versus Deniers)

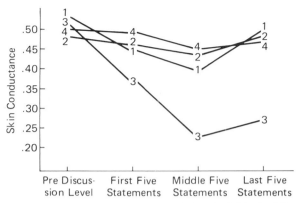

Figure 8-1. Level of skin conductance corrected for individual difference in range: 1 = Conformers in first study, 2 = Deniers in first study, 3 = Conformers when conformity was blocked, and 4 = Deniers when conformity was blocked.

and Treatment (Block Conformity versus Permit Conformity) is significant (F(1,35) = 7.76, p < .01). The means averaged for the 15 events are given in Table 8-1.

When people who typically respond to disagreement with conformity are prevented from conforming, they have less physiological arousal. As the graph illustrates, this is a substantial change for Conformers. The reduction in arousal was not a general effect of the second method. People who underrecalled the extent of disagreement had levels of skin conductance in the second condition that were quite similar to levels of skin conductance in the original condition.

Reconceptualizing the Act of Conformity.

The data support the position of Mowrer that deception or dishonesty is arousing and that honesty, even enforced honesty, results in lower arousal (Mowrer, 1961). It does not support the position that conformity is a way people respond in order to reduce arousal associated with disagreement. As such, this study illustrates the merit of using psychophysiological variables to improve our understanding of social interactions. It is hard to imagine how a study using traditional dependent measures of verbal report could have differentiated the two positions so clearly. Aside from the way in which this study supported one theoretical position (Mowrer's Integrity Therapy), I am taken by a broader issue. We seldom, and maybe never, read the words *conformity* and *lying* together in the professional psychological literature. Conformity seems to be an objective, scientific word; lying seems to be a subjective, moralistic word. I wonder, however, if we have not misled ourselves by relabeling old social phenomenon; the old word is lying, implying a violation of social trust; it is an old topic of law, religions, and socialization. When someone lies or when we lie, we expect there to be increased arousal. Conformity seems to be a neutral word, but it may be covering an old emotional social transaction. Taken from the viewpoint that conformity is another name for lying, the results of the present study seem expected: When you prevent a group of people from lying, they have less physiological activation.

Table 8-1 Levels of Skin Conductance Corrected for Individual Differences in Range Averaged across 15 Events

	Conformers	Deniers
Permit Conformity	.43	.46
Block Conformity	.29	.48

In any case, this study is offered as an example of the usefulness of psychophysiological variables in social research. Several research questions are stimulated by this study. What would happen to levels of arousal for Deniers, Rejecters, and Devaluators if they were prevented from responding to disagreeing others with their preferred behavioral response? What happens to the level of arousal of experimenters and accomplices as they engage in their deceptive roles?

Other issues include a rereading of the literature on conformity from the viewpoint that conformity is an action of deception. Findley and Cooper (1981) have reported that conformity is among the most frequently discussed topics in social-psychological textbooks. I believe that it would be highly stimulating for research and theory to attempt another conceptualization of conformity.

My final wondering here involves a re-examination of the general area of "presentation-of-self to others" as an arousing, deceptive act; that is, the deliberate presentation of a personal image for social consumption. Perhaps current-day emotional disturbances have in part a simple, basic origin, a consequence of deception. Certainly, the experimental conditions and related level of deception used by the subjects in the study reported in this chapter are miniscule compared to the activities of people outside the laboratory in their "real" lives; yet, the difference in arousal for Conformers in the two conditions of the study was substantial.

During the social interactions of people, there are psychophysiological responses. Recording the psychophysiological responses as well as the person's verbal activities and other actions provides a better data base from which to build theoretical accounts of social psychology.

The Correlational Approach: A Study on Psychophysiological Traits and Social Behavior Patterns

While the experimental approach centers around the manipulation of some conditions during the experiment, the correlational approach centers around investigation of natural variation among people. We easily recognize the wide variability among people in their approach-avoidance of social interactions (Gormly & Gormly, 1981) as well as their personal styles during face-to-face interactions. The coping styles, discussed in the previous section, are examples of variation in personal styles during interactions.

A good question for psychophysiological investigation is: "Are there psychophysiological traits, and are they related to styles of behaving during social interactions?" The remainder of this section will take up the correlational approach toward investigating this question, a question about the biological foundations of social behavior patterns.

The biological viewpoint in personality holds that differences among people at the biological level contribute to differences among people in their stable styles of behaving, personality traits (Williams, 1956). There is a large amount of indirect evidence in support of this viewpoint in the form of estimates of heritability for various temperaments, social traits, and ability measures. Vandenberg (1962) provided an extensive amount of information on the heritability of personality characteristics, and these kind of data continue to be reported with increasingly sophisticated methodologies (see Rose, Harris, Christian, & Nance, 1979; Lykken, 1982).

Heritability studies provide only indirect evidence for the contribution of biological factors in behavior because they do not identify specific biological variables that are related to specific personality traits (Wiggins, Renner, Clore, & Rose, 1976). Heritability estimates are a hint that such a relationship could be found if you assessed the right biological variables and the right social traits. The biological viewpoint is, of course, broader than heritability. Biological traits could result from environmental factors as well, including the prenatal environment.

Despite the heritability data, despite Eysenck's (1967) theorizing about cortical arousal and introversion/extraversion, and despite many research reports on the biological trait and personality trait relationships (see Grings & Dawson, 1978, for a recent review), there are no data which describe a substantial and replicated relationship between these two classes of variables.

In order to find a relationship between psychophysiological traits and social traits, it is necessary to demonstrate that (1) the biological variables have traitlike properties, that is, a person's score is reasonably stable across situations and time, and it is necessary to demonstrate that (2) the personality measures are reliable and valid indicators of behavioral traits. If either of the scores, biological or social, are unstable, then one would expect relationships to occur primarily by chance and to be equivocal, sometimes a positive relationship, sometimes a negative relationship, and mostly unrelated. Taking the research on extraversion/introversion and the cortical arousal hypothesis as an example, the data is often contradictory or inconclusive (Koriat, Averill, & Malmstrom, 1973; O'Gorman, 1974; Campbell, Baribeau-Braun, & Braun, 1981). These studies have not established that the psychophysiological measures they are using have traitlike properties; this methodological oversight encourages the use of unstable scores and encourages contradictory findings.

Traitlike Properties of Psychophysiological Variables[2]

One procedure for investigating the stability of physiological activity would be to expose a group of people to a set of experimental conditions while measuring the physiological variables of interest and to repeat the same experimental conditions at a later date. The research subjects would be a sample taken from the population to which the results are to be generalized. It is possible that the stability of psychophysiological responses will vary with age of the subject and possible with gender among other characteristics (Freixa i Baqué, 1982).

---

[2]I wish to thank Sari Preston for her assistance in this study.

In the study that follows, 65 members from two social fraternities from Rutgers University were examined for the test–retest stability of several physiological variables.

The psychophysiological variables. Five physiological systems were assessed: skin conductance, using a constant-voltage circuit; heart rate, using a cardiotachometer; blood pressure, using a manually inflated cuff; skin temperature; and respiration. Each system was extensively scored. Forty-one variables were scored from the skin-conductance record, for example, including frequency of skin conductance during various intervals, time of onset of skin conductance responses following stimulation, half-life times, and highest, lowest, and range of responses during various intervals. The procedures for recording and scoring the psychophysiological variables were generally similar to the procedures found in studies published in the journal *Psychophysiology*. A detailed description of the procedure is available from the author.

The events of the study. Five classes of events were included in the study: a rest period of 7 min, a startle period, a period of stimulation by onset and offset of a light, a period of stimulation by onset and offset of a series of tones, and a cold-pressor period, with the subject immersing his hand in water (4 °C) for 1 min. The study was repeated on the subject 1 week after the initial testing and at the same hour of day.

The stability of psychophysiological responses.
Blood pressure. The 12 test-retest correlations for blood pressure are presented in Table 8-2; in response to the question, "Is a person's blood pressure reading stable from one week to the next?" The answer has to be that it depends.

From the estimates of stability found in this study, it is clear that any single recording of blood pressure from one week to the next is not likely to be describing a stable value of blood pressure. That is, it could not be considered to be a reliable trait score. Things improve when blood pressure is taken during several events in one session and then the person is given an averaged blood pressure score. That score has higher stability from week to week. In that way, the test–retest value for systolic pressure is .74, and the correlation for diastolic pressure is .68. But how good is that

Table 8-2 The Test-Retest Correlation Coefficients for Blood Pressure during Six Events ($N=64$)

	Systolic	Diastolic
Rest	.59	.38
Startle	.30	.50
Lights	.71	.49
Tones	.53	.55
Cold Water Anticipation	.44	.37
Cold Water	.41	.50
Blood Pressure Averaged over the Six Events	.74	.68

for the purposes intended in the present study: to examine the relationships between biological traits and behavioral traits?

When the reliabilities of two measures (a biological variable and a social behavior pattern, in this case) are less than 1, and they always are, the maximum correlation that is possible is less than 1. The relationship between the reliabilities of measures and their maximum possible correlation can be seen in Eq. (1).

$$\max r_{12} = (\sqrt{r_{11}})(\sqrt{r_{22}}). \tag{1}$$

The maximum correlation between two variables, 1 and 2, is the product of the square roots of the reliability of variable 1 and the reliability of variable 2. This equation is a special case of the "correction for attenuation" presented later. For example, suppose we want to find the maximum correlation that could exist between some trait measure of aggressiveness and blood pressure at rest. Using the estimates of the reliability of blood pressure measurements from the study reported here and using .85 as a reasonable example of a self-report measure of aggressiveness, then we have $(\sqrt{.59})(\sqrt{.85}) = .71$; that would be for the systolic pressure. For the diastolic pressure it would be $(\sqrt{.38})(\sqrt{.85}) = .57$. These maximum relationships are for cases where there is a perfect relationship between the two variables, but the empirical relationship is limited by the reliabilities of the measurement procedures. The point here is that our chances of finding what we are looking for is reduced by unreliabilities of measurement. As Table 8-2 illustrates, and it is a general rule, reliability of measurement increases when the score is based on several relevant observations which are added together. When you have a better sample of relevant responses, your score is a better representation of the variable of interest.

We know from Table 8-2 that the most reliable scores come from blood pressure averaged over six events. That is not all, though. We can estimate the reliability of blood pressure when it is represented by the combined scores from both testing sessions; this is a blood pressure score that represents 12 samplings from the person, 6 events on each of 2 days separated by 1 week. The reliabilities of combined scores would be $r = .85$ systolic and $r = .81$ diastolic.

The estimations of reliabilities for systolic and diastolic pressures when the scores from both testing sessions are combined come from Eq. (2)

$$r_c = \frac{2r_{12}}{1 + r_{12}}. \tag{2}$$

The reliability of the combined score in a test–retest study is equal to two times the test–retest correlation divided by the test–retest correlation plus 1. The derivation of this formula, a standard correction in theory of measurement, can be read in Edwards (1970). The importance of increasing the number of observations of a person's physiological performance can be illustrated with a few simple calculations. In this example, suppose there is a real relationship between social aggressiveness and a person's blood pressure waiting for us to discover it. Suppose further that this relationship is .50, which we could find if we had perfectly reliable measures of each variable: blood pressure and social aggressiveness. Realistically, the reliability of the personality score might be $r = .85$. Let us examine what we could possibly hope to find with various (realistic) reliabilities of the physiological variable (Table 8-3).

Table 8-3 Hypothetical Relationships which Could be Found between a Personality Trait and a Physiological Trait when Measurment is Unreliable and the Real Relationship between the Two Variables is $r=.50$

Reliability of Diastolic Pressure	Reliability of Personality Measure	Maximum Correlation
$r=.38$ (from rest period)	$r=.85$	$r=.190$
$r=.68$ (from average, one session)	$r=.85$	$r=.340$
$r=.81$ (from average, two sessions)	$r=.85$	$r=.405$

The formula used to compute the maximum expected correlations depending on various reliabilities of the variables is

$$\max r_{12} = (r_{xy})(\sqrt{r_{11}})(\sqrt{r_{22}}) \ . \tag{3}$$

The maximum expected correlation between two variables, 1 and 2, is the product of the real relationship between the two variables (r_{xy}), the reliability of variable 1, and the reliability of variable 2. This formula is called correction for attenuation, a standard correction in theory of measurement and it can be read in McNemar (1966). Formula (1) is a variant of (3); in formula (1), r_{xy} was set at 1, so it was not included in the equation.

Table 8-3 illustrates a most important point. The possibility of finding a statistically significant relationship in a study when that relationship exists in reality is limited by the reliability of the measurement procedures. If you were to consider the situation in Table 8-3 when the size of the sample being tested was $N=25$, only the case in which diastolic pressure was the average from two sessions (reliability of the diastolic pressure equal to .81) would have a chance of being statistically significant at $p<.05$. With $N=25$, a correlation coefficient has to be .40 for $p<.05$.

One final point on the implications of correlational studies with unreliable scores: How does it come to be that some studies report correlations between unreliable scores that exceed the maximum expected? This can occur by chance or from a mistake. In either case, the excessively high correlations should not replicate. We should be more demanding about replicating results before they are published. No doubt there would be fewer published studies and less confusion in the literature.

Skin conductance. Most of the electrodermal measures were not suitable for studies on traits; the scores were too unreliable even when averaged over two testing sessions. The median test-retest reliability coefficient was $r=.34$. The number of skin conductance responses summed across all events had the best reliability, estimated $r=.84$. The second most reliable measure was the half-lives of the skin conductances averaged across all events, estimated $r=.73$. The reliability of the amplitude of the skin conductance responses, a frequently reported measure, was only $r=.43$. There is, of course, nothing fixed about the values of reliabilities reported here. With more events within the testing sessions and with multiple testing sessions, they are all likely to achieve higher values.

Heart rate. Heart rate as scored in the study and as stimulated by the procedures of this study is not stable from one testing sessions to another. The median reliability coefficient for the test–retest data was $r=.13$. The lowest heart rate averaged across the events of the study had an estimated reliability for two sessions of $r=.63$.

This same value, $r = .63$, was found for the number of acceleration-deceleration periods averaged across the events.

Skin temperature. It appears that skin temperature is a reliable characteristic of a person when measured from the face and averaged over six events. The lowest skin temperature had an estimated reliability of $r = .91$; the highest skin temperature had an estimated reliability of $r = .84$.

Respiration rate. While rate of respiration at specific times during the testing session did not have traitlike reliability values, the rate of respiration averaged across the events did. The estimated reliability for respiration for both sessions combined is $r = .90$.

Comments on stability scores. The data from this study of the reliability of psychophysiological data show that the individual measurements of physiological responses do not have traitlike properties; that is, they are too unreliable. When responses are averaged across the events of a single session, however, several responses have reliabilities that approach or exceed $r = .80$. The number of variables that have traitlike stability when averaged over two sessions increases over that from a single session. It is likely that more psychophysiological variables would have traitlike reliabilities if more events were included within a session and if there were multiple sessions. For the purposes in this chapter, to demonstrate the usefulness of including psychophysiological variables in studies of social interactions, only those measures having reliabilities greater than .80 for scores combined over two sessions will be carried forward into the next part of the research. These are systolic and diastolic blood pressure, the number of skin conductance responses, low and high skin temperature, and rate of respiration.

Social Judgments of Personality Traits

Personality traits refer to a person's styles of behaving which is consistent from one situation to another and from one time to another. The personality trait viewpoint has been challenged by Mischel (1968) who wrote that traits tell more about the cognitive activities of the observer than about the behavior of the person being described. That argument has merit to be sure, but nevertheless, there is good reason to believe that some traits measured by some procedures are descriptive of regularities in behavior.

One strategy of personality assessment seems to particularly result in valid indication of personality traits, peer ratings. Winder and Wiggins (1964) showed that peer ratings of aggressiveness and of dependency were related to observable behavior of aggression and dependence for school-aged children. Using college men who were members of social fraternities, Gormly and Edelberg (1974) demonstrated that ratings of interpersonal aggressiveness of the members by their fraternity brothers resulted in very high interrater agreement (raters agreed among themselves about the degree of assertiveness of the participants), even though the ratings were done independently. The second part of that study was even more supportive of the trait viewpoint. Fraternity members were brought into the laboratory and observed by a group of strangers for a brief time, and even from that brief exposure, the strangers had high agreement with the fraternity members in judging the aggressiveness of the participants. McGowan and Gormly (1976) compared peer ratings of energetic with objectively recorded behavior in naturalistic settings. The behavior sampled included speed of walking, rate of postural changes, rate of climbing stairs, and rate of head movements. The correlation between peer ratings and observed behavior was $r = .70$, obviously, a substantial relationship.

There are a large number of trait adjectives in the English language, many thousands. Fortunately, many of these have common meanings, and the list of personality traits can be reduced to a few. Wiggins (1968) has done this empirically for interpersonal traits, and the traits included in the following study are fairly representative of the dimensions of personality uncovered by Wiggins. Traits which have a low rate of occurrence in fraternity members' ratings of each other, e.g., sad, were excluded because they had insufficient variance to be useful for this study. A second consideration for keeping the number of traits in this study small was to reduce the chances of spurious correlations.

Procedure of the study. Thirty-two members of one fraternity and 30 members of a second fraternity rated the members in their own fraternity on a group of personality traits. This procedure was a yearly routine for members of these fraternities. A trait name appeared at the top of the page with the following instructions: "If the trait is a characteristic of any of the people listed below, print YES before that person's name. If the trait is not a characteristic of the person, then print NO before his name. Each person should have either a *yes* or *no* before his name." These instructions were followed by the names of the people participating in the study, listed in a single column. The following traits were used: Anxious, Energetic, Happy, Interpersonally Aggressive, Impulsive, Sociable.

The subjects from the psychophysiological assessment study reported here were the subjects who were rated on personality characteristics.

Results of the study. A person's score from the peer ratings was the proportion of raters who indicated that the trait was a characteristic of him. The raters within each fraternity were split into two groups and compared for degree of agreement in their ratings for each trait, two groups of raters for each person on all traits. This procedure, the split-half reliabilities of the raters, resulted in reliability coefficients for all traits equal to or greater than .90. This was true for each fraternity. Having two fraternities analyzed separately allows for a replication of each finding.

Correlations between Psychophysiological Traits and Social Behavior Patterns

The correlation between the two kinds of trait scores, psychophysiological traits and personality traits, resulted in three significant relationships that replicated. Trait scores for Happy correlated .56 with trait scores for Number of Skin Conductance Responses in Fraternity 1 and .51 for Fraternity 2; these values are significant at $p < .01$. Trait scores for Impulsive correlate negatively with trait scores for Number of Skin Conductance Responses, $-.47$ for Fraternity 1 and $-.55$ for Fraternity 2; again, both values are significant at $p < .01$. The third significant relationship was between trait scores for Blood Pressure and trait scores for Interpersonal Aggressiveness. Diastolic pressure was correlated with Interpersonal Aggressiveness, $r = .38$ for Fraternity 1 and $r = .44$ for Fraternity 2; both correlations were significant at $p < .05$.

The results averaged across the two samples of the trait study are presented in Table 8-4. Included in this table are the reliabilities of the variables and the estimate of the "true" correlation between the two trait scores, that is, corrected for the unreliability of the scores.

It is interesting to see that the same physiological trait, rate of skin conductance responses, is related to two personality traits. These personality traits are relatively independent of each other, at least the peer ratings of Happy and Impulsive are relatively independent, $r = .14$ for Fraternity 1 and $r = .29$ for Fraternity 2. Thus, the multiple correlation between the personality traits and the skin conductance variable would be quite high. There is not enough information in this report to resolve this triangle of Happy-Skin Conductance-Impulsive variables. One hypothesis that would interconnect these three variables is that there is a preference in people for a moderate amount of contrast in their sympathetic nervous systems, i.e., skin conductance responses. When a person has that frequency, the person is perceived as happy or content. When a person does not have that frequency, the person "impulsively" engages in activity, the purpose simply being the increase in sympathetic nervous system activity, which then produces a happier state for the impulsive person. The missing data for this hypothesis is the demonstration that when impulsive people behave impulsively they have an increase in skin conductance responses, and they have an increase in positive affect.

The relationship uncovered in this research between trait blood pressure and trait interpersonal aggressiveness would seem to be relevant to research on Type A behavior pattern and cardiovascular activity. Although the empirical relationship between Type A behavior people and elevated cardiovascular activity is clear and well-replicated (see Glass, 1977, and Surwit, Williams, Shapiro, 1982, for recent reviews), theoretical explanations for the relationship are still in the developmental stage. This development will be speeded by uncovering the relationship or lack of relationship between Type A behavior and cardiovascular activity in a broad range of conditions.

One line of theoretical speculation (Glass, 1977; Rhodewalt & Comer, 1982) implies that a disposition to control stressful events is central to the increased cardiovascular activity. While this may be true, the findings from the present study demonstrate that the relationship is broader than that. In this study, the physio-

Table 8-4 Correlations between Physiological Traits and Personality Traits

Physiological Trait	Personality Trait	Empirical Correlation	Corrected Correlation
(.84) SCRs	(.91) Happy	$r = .54$	$r = .62$
(.84) SCRs	(.92) Impulsive	$r = .51$	$r = -.58$
(.81) Dias. BP	(.95) Interpersonal Aggressiveness	$r = .41$	$r = .47$

Note: Numbers in ( ) are reliability scores; data are averaged for the two fraternities, $N = 65$.

logical response, increased blood pressure, is present as a trait, not as a differential response to stress. In fact, the subjects were familiar with the author's research procedures as a consequence of past experimentation on them; they were all informed volunteers, and there was nothing for them to control in the procedure.

It is all too easy for us to offer explanations about variables in terms of sequential functions, causes and effects. Does the behavioral style result in the cardiovascular trait or does the physical trait result in the behavioral trait? We may be chasing our tails with this logic, the consequence being a narrowing of the procedures of investigation. What we have is a correspondence between two ways of viewing a person, a biological viewpoint and a behavioral viewpoint. This might well be a simultaneous relationship and not a sequential one.

That which we call behavior is nothing more than the activities of the body, conceptualized in a particular way. It is not at all surprising that in measuring physiological traits and traits based on people's interactions with each other that we should find a correspondence. The correlation between skin conductance responses and impulsiveness is particularly stable. Gormly and Fagnant (1980) reported this association from another study.

Recognizing the unity of behavior and biology, what is the value of the present findings? The research on heritability of personality traits points to the connection between personality and the body, but it does not inform us of the specific biological systems involved. Findings such as those in the present study give us a toehold on beginning to understand human personality as an expression of physical traits. This is not to say that social experiences are not important; that is another source of individual differences in behavior, but not the only source. From the present findings we now have another set of researchable questions: what has the rate of bursts in the activity of the sympathetic nervous system (inferred from the rate of skin conductance responses) got to do with happiness as a trait or state?; what has it to do with impulsiveness?; how does it come to be that trait-diastolic pressure is related to interpersonal aggressiveness?; and is this important in the development of cardiovascular disease (Surwit, Williams, Shapiro, 1982)? Step by step we refine our understanding of man, particularly as a social-physiological being.

The research presented and the procedures reported in this chapter have not settled any issues about the assessment of psychophysiological traits. There may be several traits for rate of skin conductance responses, for example. It may well be that we would find a reliable, stable trait score for number of skin conductance responses during a set of social events that is independent of the trait scores for number of skin conductance responses from the procedures reported in this paper. When I do these studies again, I will attempt to make the events in the procedures better analogues of the events in the world outside the laboratory. This would include social conversations, studying academic matter, eating, physical activity, daydreaming, etc. The purpose underlying this chapter was not to close any research area with a pulling-together of a definitive set of studies. We do not have those studies. The purpose of this chapter was to illustrate a productive strategy for understanding people and their interactions. I hope the findings lead to wondering, like this. If happiness is related to more sympathetic nervous system activity, can we better understand why it is that people take stimulants like caffeine or cocaine? Can we better understand why taking a walk or jogging or having a massage makes some people feel better? Is it possible that the activity of participating in psychotherapy increases the rate of sympathetic nervous system change? Perhaps in attempting to understand people's efforts toward improving the conditions of emotional life, we labeled the problem incorrectly. Rather than say that people are pursuing happiness, and building our studies and theories from that construct, we might better say that people are pursuing some optimal rate of sympathetic nervous system activity, and build our studies and theories from the physiological construct. In the latter case, behavior is viewed as the activities of the body in the service of the body. Recording psychophysiological variables during social interactions allows us to bring the body back into our theories of behavior.

References

Baugher, D. M., & Gormly, J. (1975). Effects of personal competence on the significance of interpersonal disagreement: Physiological activation and social evaluations. *Journal of Research in Personality, 9*, 356-365.

Burdick, H. A., & Burnes, A. J. (1958). A test of "strain toward symmetry" theories. *Journal of Abnormal and Social Psychology, 57*, 367-370.

Byrne, D. (1971). *The attraction paradigm*. New York: Academic Press.

Byrne, D., & Clore, G. L. (1967). Effectance arousal and attraction. *Journal of Personality and Social Psychology Monograph, 6* (Whole No. 638).

Campbell, K. B., Baribeau-Braun, J., & Braun, C. (1981). Neuroanatomical and physiological foundations of extraversion. *Psychophysiology, 18*, 263-267.

Clore, G. L., & Gormly, J. B. (1974). Knowing, feeling, and liking: A psychophysiological study of attraction. *Journal of Research in Personality, 8*, 218-230.

Coleman, R., Greenblatt, M., & Solomon, H. C. (1956). Physiological evidence of rapport during psychotherapeutic interviews. *Diseases of the Nervous System, 17*, 2-8.

Cronbach, L. J. (1957). The two disciplines of scientific psychology. *American Psychologist, 12*, 671-684.

Dembroski, T. M., MacDougall, J. M., Shields, J. L., Petitto, J., & Lushene, R. (1978). Components of the Type A coronary-prone behavior pattern and cardiovascular responses to psychomotor performance challenge. *Journal of Behavioral Medicine, 1*, 159-176.

DiMascio, A., Boyd, R. W., & Greenblatt, M. (1957). Physiological correlates of tension and antagonism during psychotherapy: A study of 'interpersonal physiology.' *Psychosomatic Medicine, 19*, 99-104.

DiMascio, A., Boyd, R. W., Greenblatt, M., & Solomon, H. C. (1955). The psychiatric interview: A sociophysiologic study. *Diseases of the Nervous System, 16*, 2-7.

Dittes, J. E. (1957). Galvanic skin response as a measure of patient's reaction to therapist's permissiveness. *Journal of Abnormal and Social Psychology, 55*, 295-303.

Doust, J. W. L., & Schneider, R. A. (1955). Studies on the physiology of awareness: An oximetrically monitored controlled stress test. *Canadian Journal of Psychology, 9*, 67-78.

Edwards, A. L. (1970). *The measurement of personality traits*. New York: Holt, Rinehart, and Winston.

Eysenck, H. J. (1952). The effects of psychotherapy: An evaluation. *Journal of Consulting Psychology, 16*, 319-324.

Eysenck, H. J. (1967). *The biological basis of personality*. Springfield, IL: Charles C Thomas.

Fenz, W. D., & Steffy, R. A. (1968). Electrodermal arousal of chronically ill psychiatric patients undergoing intensive behavioral treatment. *Psychosomatic Medicine, 30*, 423-436.

Festinger, L. A. (1957). *A theory of cognitive dissonance*. Evanston, IL: Row, Peterson.

Findley, M., & Cooper, H. (1981). Introductory social psychology textbook citations: A comparison in five research areas. *Personality and Social Psychology Bulletin, 7*, 173-176.

Freixa i Baque, E. (1982). Reliability of electrodermal measures: A compilation. *Biological Psychology, 14*, 219-229.

Gerard, H. B. (1961). Disagreement with others, their credibility, and experienced stress. *Journal of Abnormal and Social Psychology, 62*, 559-564.

Glass, D. C. (1977). *Behavior patterns, stress, and coronary disease*. Hillsdale, NJ: Erlbaum.

Glass, D. C., Krakoff, L. R., Contrada, R., Hilton, W. F., Kehoe, K., Mannucci, E. G., Collins, C., Snow, B., & Elting, E. (1980). Effect of harassment and competition upon cardiovascular and plasma catecholamine responses in Type A and Type B individuals. *Psychophysiology, 17*, 453-463.

Gormly, J. (1971). Sociobehavioral and physiological responses to interpersonal disagreement. *Journal of Experimental Research in Personality, 5*, 216-222.

Gormly, J. (1974). A comparison of predictions from consistency and affect theories for arousal during interpersonal disagreement. *Journal of Personality and Social Psychology, 30*, 658-663.

Gormly, J., & Edelberg, W. (1974). Validity in personality trait attribution. *American Psychologist, 29*, 189-193.

Gormly, J. B., & Fagnant, D. (1980, April). *Impulsive people and the sympathetic nervous system*. Paper presented at the meeting of the Eastern Psychological Association, Hartford, CN.

Gormly, J., & Gormly, A. V. (1981). Approach-avoidance: Potency in physiological research *Bulletin of the Psychonomic Society, 17*, 221-223.

Gormly, J., Gormly, A., & Johnson, C. (1972). Interpersonal attraction, competence motivation, and reinforcement theory. *Journal of Personality and Social Psychology, 19*, 375-380.

Grings, W. W., & Dawson, M. E. (1978). *Emotions and bodily responses: A psychophysiological approach*. New York: Academic Press.

Hamilton, D. L. (1969). Responses to cognitive inconsistencies: Personality, discrepancy level, and response stability. *Journal of Personality and Social Psychology, 11*, 351-362.

Heider, F. (1958). *The psychology of interpersonal relations*. New York: Wiley.

Jenkins, C. D. (1979). The coronary-prone personality. In W. D. Gentry & R. B. Williams, Jr. (Eds.), *Psychological aspects of myocardial infarction and coronary care* (2nd Ed.). St. Louis: Mosby.

Koriat, A., Averill, J. R., & Malstrom, E. J. (1973). Individual differences in habituation: Some methodological and conceptual issues. *Journal of Research in Personality, 7*, 88-101.

Krantz, D. S., Schaeffer, M. A., Davia, J. E., Dembroski, T. M., MacDougall, J. M., & Shaffer, R. T. (1981). Extent of coronary atherosclerosis, Type A behavior, and cardiovascular response to social interaction. *Psychophysiology, 18*, 654-664.

Lacey, J. I. (1962). Psychophysiological approaches to the evaluation of psychotherapeutic processes and outcome. In E. A. Rubinstein & M. B. Parloff (Eds.), *Research in Psychotherapy* (Vol. 1). Washington, DC: American Psychological Association.

Lang, P. J. (1971). The application of psychophysiological methods to the study of psychotherapy and behavior modification. In A. E. Bergin & S. L. Garfield (Eds.), *Handbook of psychotherapy and behavior change*. New York: Wiley.

Lazarus, R. S. (1966). *Psychological stress and the coping process*. New York: McGraw-Hill.

Lykken, D. T. (1974). Psychology and the lie detector industry. *American Psychologist, 29*, 725-739.

Lykken, D. T. (1982). Research with twins: The concept of emergenesis. *Psychophysiology, 19*, 361-373.

Lykken, D. T., Rose, R., Luther, B., & Maley, M. (1966). Correcting psychophysiological measures for individual differences in range. *Psychological Bulletin, 66*, 481-484.

Lynch, J. J., Thomas, S. A., Long, J. M., Malinow, K. L., Chickadonz, G., & Katcher, A. H. (1980). Human speech and blood pressure. *The Journal of Nervous and Mental Disease, 168*, 526-534.

MacDougall, J. M., Dembroski, T. M., & Krantz, D. S. (1981). Effects of types of challenge on pressor and heart rate responses in Type A and B women. *Psychophysiology, 18*, 1-9.

Malmo, R. B., Boag, T. J., & Smith, A. A. (1957). Physiological study of personal interaction. *Psychosomatic Medicine, 19*, 105-119.

Martin, B., Lundy, R. M., & Lewin, M. H. (1960). Verbal and GSR responses in experimental interviews as a function of three degrees of "therapist" communication. *Journal of Abnormal and Social Psychology, 60*, 234-240.

McGowan, J., & Gormly, J. (1976). Validation of personality traits: A multicriteria approach. *Journal of Personality and Social Psychology, 34*, 791-795.

McNemar, Q. (1966). *Psychological Statistics*. New York: Wiley.

Mischel, W. (1968). *Personality and assessment*. New York: Wiley.

Mittelman, B., Wolff, H. G., & Scharf, J. (1942). Emotions and gastroduodenal function. *Psychosomatic Medicine, 4*, 5-61.

Mowrer, O. H. (1961). *The crisis in psychiatry and religion*. Princeton, NJ: Van Nostrand.

Mowrer, O. H., Light, D. H., Luria, Z., & Seleny, M. (1953). Tension changes during psychotherapy. In O. H. Mowrer (Ed.), *Psychotherapy: Theory and research*. New York: Ronald Press.

Murray, H. A. (1963). Studies of stressful interpersonal disputations. *American Psychologist, 18*, 28-36.

Newcomb, T. (1961). *The acquaintance process*. New York: Holt, Rinehart, & Winston.

O'Gorman, J. G. (1974). A comment on Korait, Averill, and Malstrom's "Individual differences in habituation." *Journal of Research in Personality, 8*, 198-202.

Paul, G. L. (1966). *Insight vs. desensitization in psychotherapy*. Stanford, CA: Stanford University Press.

Rhodewalt, F., & Comer, R. (1982). Coronary-prone behavior and reactance: The attractiveness of an eliminated choice. *Personality and Social Psychology Bulletin, 8*, 152-158.

Robinson, J. W., Herman, A., & Kaplan, B. J. (1982). Autonomic responses correlate with counselor-client empathy. *Journal of Counseling Psychology, 29*, 195-198.

Rose, R. J., Harris, E. L., Christian, J. C., & Nance, W. E. (1979). Genetic variance in nonverbal intelligence: Data from the kinships of identical twins. *Science, 205*, 1153-1155.

Rosenman, R. H., Brand, R. J., Jenkins, D., Friedman, M., Straus, R., & Wurm, M. (1975). Coronary heart disease in the Western Collaborative Group study: Final follow-up experience of 8½ years. *Journal of the American Medical Association, 233*, 872-877.

Rosenman, R. H., & Friedman, M. (1974). Neurogenic factors in pathogenesis of coronary heart disease. *Medical Clinics of North America, 58*, 269-279.

Steiner, I. D. (1966). The resolution of interpersonal disagreements. *Progress in Experimental Personality Research, 3*, 195-240.

Surwit, R. S., Williams, R. B., & Shapiro, D. (1982). *Behavioral approaches to cardiovascular disease*. New York: Academic Press.

Truax, C. B., & Mitchell, K. M. (1971). Research on certain therapist interpersonal skills in relation to process and outcome. In A. E. Bergin & S. L. Garfield (Eds.), *Handbook of psychotherapy and behavior change*. New York: Wiley.

Vandenberg, S. G. (1962). The hereditary abilities study: Hereditary components in a psychological test battery. *American Journal of Human Genetics, 14*, 220-237.

Waid, W. M., Orne, M. T., & Wilson, S. K. (1979). Effects of level of socialization on electrodermal detection of deception. *Psychophysiology, 16*, 15-22.

Wiggins, J. S. (1968). Personality structure. In P. R. Farnsworth (Ed.), *Annual review of psychology* (Vol. 19). Palo Alto, CA: Annual Reviews.

Wiggins, J. S., Renner, K. E., Clore, G. L., & Rose, R. J. (1976). *Principles of personality*. Reading, MA: Addison-Wesley.

Williams, R. J. (1956). *Biochemical individuality*. New York: Wiley.

Williams, R. B., Kimball, C. P., & Willard, H. N. (1972). The influence of interpersonal interaction on diastolic blood pressure. *Psychosomatic Medicine, 34*, 194-197.

Winder, C. L., & Wiggins, J. S. (1964). Social reputation and social behavior: A further validation of the Peer Nomination Inventory. *Journal of Abnormal and Social Psychology, 68*, 681-684.

Wolf, S., Cardon, P. V., Shepart, E. M., & Wolff, H. G. (1955). *Life stress and essential hypertension*. Baltimore: Williams & Wilkins.

Wolff, H. G. (1953). *Stress and disease*. Springfield, IL: Charles C Thomas.

Chapter 9
Cognition, Arousal, and Aggression

Brendan Gail Rule[1] and Andrew R. Nesdale

Although aggression and violence have always been an important human social problem, even cursory examination of the crime statistics for any western country leaves no doubt about the high incidence of homicides, muggings, rapes, bombings, and assassinations at the present time. Moreover, whether or not aggression and violence have increased in the past 10 or 20 years, the evidence indicates that people believe these to be violent times and are increasingly concerned for their safety (Scherer, Abeles, & Fischer, 1975).

Given the magnitude of the problem and the increasing concern felt by lay people, the possible causes of aggression have been addressed by neurologists, criminologists, sociologists, anthropologists, geneticists, and psychologists. Within psychology, a variety of accounts have been proposed ranging from broad-based instinctual theories of aggression to those focusing on acquired drives, conditioned reflexes, and, more recently, cognitive variables.

The frustration-aggression hypothesis (Dollard, Doob, Miller, Mowrer, & Sears, 1939) was a major focus of social psychological research on aggression from 1939 to 1960. Earlier notions from psychoanalytic theory (Freud, 1959) were framed into the testable proposition that frustration (defined as the blocking of ongoing goal-directed behavior) produces an instigation to aggression that is directed mainly toward injuring the person who is perceived as the cause of the goal blocking. The expression of aggression was considered to result in a carthartic reduction in the instigation to aggress.

Although Dollard et al. did not provide a label for the motivating force or "instigation to aggression," Berkowitz (1962) subsequently proposed that anger was the construct embodying instigation. This was considered to be a drive or force which energized aggression. At the same time, however, both Berkowitz (1962) and Bandura and Walters (1963) expressed their dissatisfaction with the frustration-

[1]This chapter was facilitated by a grant to B. G. Rule from the Social Sciences and Humanities Research Council of Canada and a grant to A. R. Nesdale from the Australian Research Grants Commission. The authors made an equal contribution to this chapter.

aggression formulation. These authors recognized anger as only a setting condition or a facilitator of aggression which required external stimulus events to prompt retaliation. Their shift from a tension reduction model of aggression to one emphasizing the role of external factors led to two different theoretical perspectives: one based on classical conditioning and the other on instrumental conditioning. In the Kuhnian sense, the transition represented a paradigm shift, which, with the development of the new perspectives, resulted in a paradigm clash (Kuhn, 1962). Berkowitz stressed the role of environmental stimuli that served to "pull" the aggressive response rather than "push" it from within, as entailed by a drive position. Bandura deviated further by rejecting frustration as a necessary condition for aggression, and by introducing environmental and cognitive factors as important influences on aggressive behavior.

The focus on external stimulus conditions and the rejection of tension or drive reduction models served as a background for an emerging general approach which has implicated arousal, emotional states (particularly anger), and cognition in the expression of aggression. Issues which have been addressed include how anger is experienced by individuals, the influence on anger and aggression of exposure to additional sources of arousal, and whether there is a reduction in anger and aggression (i.e., aggression cartharsis) following an aggressive response. The common approach that appears to underlie the treatment of each of these issues is that an individual's cognitions mediate the experience of an arousal state as the emotional state of anger and the subsequent level of aggression are displayed. The purpose of this chapter is to examine the research related to this general approach. Consistent with the issues noted above, the presentation is structured into several sections. First, we discuss the constructs of arousal, frustration, cognition, and aggression and their operationalizations in the literature. Second, we consider the view that the emotional state of anger depends upon the labeling of an arousal state in accordance with salient situational cues. Third, we examine the role of anger in the expression of aggression. Fourth, we examine how the state of anger and aggression may be enhanced or reduced by additional sources of arousal. Fifth, we review the literature relating to aggression catharsis.

Constructs of Arousal, Cognition, Frustration, and Aggression

Arousal

Arousal refers to an undifferentiated increase in sympathetic activity. Measurement of this activity is usually accomplished by finding and recording increases in heart rate, galvanic skin response, blood pressure, blood volume, respiration, and muscle potential. Despite the apparent reliability of these measures in response to experimental manipulations, exceptions often occur. Although insult usually increases autonomic reactivity as indexed by single or multiple measures (Zillmann, 1979), sometimes it does not. For example, insult may increase blood pressure, but not change palmar sweat (Geen, 1975). Observation of aggressive films that were unjustified compared to justified increased galvanic skin response but not heart rate (Geen & Rakosky, 1973). Given the opportunity to counteraggress reduced blood pressure, but not pulse rate and respiration (Baker & Schaie, 1969). The reasons for these inconsistencies rest on several interrelated methodological issues. These involve the relation of the measures to each other, the relation of the measures to the concept under investigation, and the confounding of operations that exert differential effects on specific measures.

The relation of physiological measures to each other has been a concern because the low intercorrelations which are frequently reported raise skepticism about a general arousal or activation syndrome (Ax, 1953; Lacey, 1967). This problem, called differential fractionation, is reflected in a rise in one measure and a fall in another (e.g., Dengerink, 1971). Two approaches to understanding the problem have been taken.

First, many authors have considered the low correlations to be an artifact due to inappropriate procedures or units of measurement (Schnore, 1959; Lazarus, Speisman, & Mordkoff, 1963). The assumption is that the relation between measures is positive and linear; failure to find positive correlations reflects error of measurement. Some authors have tried to pool over many measures that reflect total arousal and others have tried to improve measurement of individual measures (Malmstrom, Apton, & Lazarus, 1965). A recent model by Porges and colleagues (1980) offers a sophisticated and promising approach to measurement problems. They argue that examining the relation between physiological systems as well as between physiological and behavioral systems has been hampered by the use of descriptive statistics that are not sensitive to rhythmic relations. Instead, they propose a new cross-spectral analysis to examine rhythmic co-occurrence and covariation of two systems at specific frequencies.

Taylor and Epstein (1967) argued for a second position. They contended that it is more important to determine the properties of different physiological systems by studying how they vary as a function of stimulus input, including intensity, rate of stimulation, and time since onset. The subsystems of arousal must maintain homeostatic balance and may respond differentially to stimulus inputs. In accord with this view, Libby, Lacey, and Lacey (1973) observed that task demands for cognitive elaboration produced a different effect on heart rate than those requiring attention to the environment. Elliott (1969) reviewed data showing that heart rate was related to activation of responses, whereas galvanic skin response reflected general arousal. Several other authors have noted that the stimulus context may affect different systems . Ax (1953) and Schachter (1957) found that anger and fear produced arousal on different measures. Moreover, Geen and Quanty (1977) review conflicting evidence in the sensitivity of diastolic and systolic blood pressure after anger arousal, and they suggest that an overall index of blood pressure may be the better measure of anger (McGinn et al., 1974). Considering the results of these various authors, it is evident that parametric research must be undertaken extensively to document further the fragmented preliminary support for the second position.

Related to the notion that varying stimulus conditions may affect different physiological systems, it must be noted that procedures in both experimental and control conditions might obscure desired results. For example, both Feshbach (1964) and Zillmann (1979) have noted that procedures, such as giving angered participants the opportunity to aggress, may arouse guilt and anxiety. Consequently, although "aggressive" arousal may decrease, other kinds of arousal may increase tension. Different theoretical expectations derive from these considerations. In addition, control conditions may induce arousal independent of anger. When threat of shock is used as a control condition (e.g., Geen, 1975), physiological reactivity may not differ from that in an anger condition (see Rule & Nesdale, 1976). Until more parametric studies are done and better conceptualizations are offered, the contribution of physiological measures must be regarded with caution. Designs and experiments should include several physiological, experiential, and behavioral measures or employ two-stage designs (Cantor, Zillmann, & Bryant, 1975).

Frustration

Following the definition offered in the pioneering work by Dollard et al. (1939), frustration refers to an external stimulus condition (i.e., the blocking of ongoing goal-directed behavior) rather than an internal motivating state. Researchers have operationalized frustration by depriving a person of a desired goal, such as preventing a hungry person from eating, or inducing a person to fail on a task.[2]

Cognition

The term cognition is used broadly in this chapter and, indeed, generally by writers, to refer to both the process and products of inferences, evaluations, judgments, and decisions that may be made by individuals in relation to other people and events in social situations. Given that such cognitions are not directly observable or immediately accessible, measurement of particular cognitive activity is typically achieved via subjects' responses to standardized/controlled questions in a questionnaire following their exposure to a particular stimulus.

Aggression

"Aggression," "aggressive behavior," and "aggressive responding" are used interchangeably to refer to responses involving the delivery of noxious stimuli to a target. Aggression has been operationalized by providing experimental participants with the opportunity to deliver electric shock or aversive tones to a target (although the apparatus is, in both cases, not functional), to punch objects, to withhold rewards, and to insult a target verbally.

---

[2]Although many earlier studies purportedly examined the frustration-aggression relation, their operations did not satisfy the definitional requirements. In particular, frustration was usually varied by insult rather than by pure goal-blocking (see reviews by Berkowitz, 1962; Bandura, 1973). This procedure is acceptable only if the definition of frustration is stretched to include blocking self-esteem strivings; this would make the concept too protean for scientific usefulness (Kaufmann, 1970). In addition, aggression was frequently measured by expressions of hostility, which were not made known to the frustrator. Thus, no injurious consequences occured for the frustrator.

Arousal, Cognition, and Anger

The theoretical underpinnings of the current cognitive approaches are embodied in Schachter and Singer's theory (1962) linking arousal and emotion. Schachter and Singer's attempt to account for the link between arousal and emotion is encompassed by three propositions:

(1) when an individual has no immediate explanation for a state of physiological arousal, he will label the state and describe his feelings according to the cognitions available to him
(2) when the individual has a completely appropriate explanation for his physiological arousal, no evaluative needs will arise and the individual will label his feelings according to the alternative cognitions available
(3) the individual will react emotionally and will report emotions only to the extent that he experiences the state of physiological arousal.

The initial propositions were partially supported by Schachter and Singer's findings that physiologically aroused persons who were uninformed or who were misinformed about the various physiological effects of epinephrine injections were more verbally hostile in the presence of an angry confederate, or, were more euphoric in the presence of a happy confederate than were persons who were informed of the physiological effects of the drug. These apparent labeling effects were consistent with the experimental context.

Drawing upon the work of Schachter and Singer, aggression researchers have suggested that the extent to which an individual experiences the emotional state of anger depends upon the level of sympathetic activity resulting from threats to the individual's physical or psychological well-being (Zillmann, 1978) and the individual's interpretation of the situation in which the threat occurs (Rule, Ferguson, & Nesdale, 1979).[3] Consistent with this view, research has shown that frustration that is interpreted as arbitrary or intentional induces anger more readily than that which is nonarbitrary (e.g., Burnstein & Worchel, 1962; Rule, Dyck, & Nesdale, 1978; Kulik & Brown, 1979). In addition, Dyck and Rule (1978) found that intended attack facilitates anger and aggression more than does unintended attack, and that justification for intended attack mitigates anger and retaliation.

While it is plausible that an insulted person would label his arousal as anger rather than happiness given the situation, the more controversial implication of Schachter and Singer's approach relates to the plasticity of emotion labeling. As suggested by the Schachter and Singer study outlined previously, the labeling position incorporates the possibility that an individual may label his arousal state erroneously. Thus, given the presence in the situation of two or more possible sources of the individual's arousal state, only one of which contributed to that state, the individual may

---

[3]It is assumed that emotional labeling is not necessarily a conscious process. Cognitive processes may occur without conscious awareness or unaided by intentional strategies (see Posner & Snyder, 1975). Emotional information activated in memory may or may not affect conscious cognitions. Moreover, "labeling" can occur within a very short time period. While these assumptions are viable theoretically (Nisbett & Wilson, 1977) they pose problems for using questionnaire responses as indicative of cognitive activities.

label his arousal state erroneously such that it is consistent with a nonveridical source rather than the veridical source. For example, an individual might receive an insult from one person and praise from another, experience an increase in arousal from the insult, yet label his emotional state as happiness in accordance with the praise received.

In addition to Schachter and Singer's initial results, several other studies have reported findings consistent with this position (e.g., Nisbett & Schachter, 1966; Ross, Rodin, & Zimbardo, 1969). It has been reasoned that if labeling of arousal occurs as a result of search for external cues, then one should be able to induce people to relabel their arousal in terms of certain specific external cues. For example, Nisbett and Schachter (1966) examined the idea that naturally occurring states of arousal induced by threat of shock could erroneously be attributed to a nonemotional source such as a placebo pill if people were led to expect arousal symptoms from the latter source. In their study, people who were led to believe that they were in an artificial state of arousal actually tolerated more intense shock.

Despite these supportive studies, however, several challenges to the cognitive labeling perspective have been advanced. First, two studies have unsuccessfully attempted to replicate Schachter and Singer's two-factor model of emotion. Maslach (1979) employed a new paradigm using amnesia for hypnotically induced arousal. Subjects either did or did not experience unexplained arousal in the presence of a confederate who exhibited either happy or angry emotions. Her results illustrated that subjects with unexplained arousal reported negative emotions regardless of the confederate's mood. Similarly, in a more direct attempt to replicate former results, Marshall and Zimbardo (1979) examined the emotional states of placebo-injected and epinephrine-injected subjects who were misinformed about possible bodily effects from these injections. These subjects were exposed to a euphoric confederate, but their reports of affect did not differ according to the information provided about their injections. Thus, their inadequately explained psychological arousal did not make them more susceptible to changes in affect. Like Maslach (1979), these authors also found that the physiological arousal was interpreted in terms of negative emotions despite the happy behavior of the confederate. While neither of these experiments represented direct methodological replications of the original Schachter and Singer results, their conceptual replication attempts failed to support the original theoretical expectations.

Second, Vuchinich and Tucker (1980) have criticized the cognitive labeling explanation of the effects of alcohol on emotions. They observed that if individuals believe that they have consumed a potent drug, such as alcohol, it is likely that the lack of ambiguity about the probable source of arousal would preclude misattribution via a cognitive labeling process. Consequently, Vuchinich and Tucker (1980) argue that the interpretations offered by several researchers (e.g., Pliner & Cappell, 1974; Wilson, 1977, 1978) may be questioned because they have not adequately differentiated expectations about the effects of alcohol from the cognitive labels applied to alcohol-induced arousal through misattribution of arousal to other situational cues. It should be noted that while these objections to the applications of Schachter and Singer's original model are apt, they are based on strict interpretations of that model rather than some extrapolations from it (e.g., Zillmann's excitation transfer paradigm).

Third, several studies have assessed whether an available additional explanation for arousal reduces perceived anger and aggression. These studies have yielded equivocal results. Geen, Rakosky, and Pigg (1972) found reduced aggression when shock-provoked participants were given feedback that their arousal was due either to reading a sexually arousing prose passage or to taking a mildly arousing drug rather than electric shock. In their provision of information about whether participants were aroused by other sources or by receiving shock, however, they inadvertently manipulated the degree of anger instigation. They did so by relating shock arousal feedback to strong feelings of anger and aggressiveness, and by relating the additional source feedback to feelings not associated with anger or aggressiveness. Similarly, although Younger and Doob (1978) reported that angered participants who supposedly took a relaxing pill aggressed more than those who supposedly took an arousing pill, they did not find anger or behavioral differences between unprovoked participants and provoked participants who had ingested the relaxing pill.

In summary, there is evidence consistent with the view that the amount of arousal instigated and the particular label given to that arousal state is governed by the interpretation based on the external cues in the situation. However, the evidence is ambiguous regarding the possibility that an individual who is aroused by one source can label his arousal state erroneously in accordance with another stimulus which might be a potential source of his arousal. While this issue will only be resolved by additional research, it might be noted that a variant of the mislabeling notion is also discussed later, under "Effects of Additional Arousal Sources." In that case, the issue concerns the labeling of arousal when an individual is subjected to two sources of arousal, one of which typically produces anger.

Anger and Aggression

In addition to substantiating Berkowitz' (1962) claim that anger mediates the frustration-aggression relationship, research findings have indicated that anger is an apparently important determinant of aggression in people whose well-being has been physically or psychologically threatened (e.g., Rule & Hewitt, 1971; Rule & Leger, 1976; Rule & Nesdale, 1974; Rule & Percival, 1971). For example, Rule and Percival (1971) found that goal blocking and unjustified insult compared with controlled conditions increased aggression. Moreover, both the frustration and insult manipulations produced feelings of annoyance and negative evaluations of the partner's performance.

In attempts to operationalize more directly the mediating variable of anger, several researchers have monitored physiological changes during the experiments. Some researchers have found that in instigating an aggressive response, goal blocking produces an increase in autonomic activity, as measured by blood pressure (Doob & Kirshenbaum 1973; Fishman, 1965). However, in other studies, frustration (manipulated by failure on a learning task) did not increase autonomic activity and aggression to the same extent as did insult (Gentry, 1970; Rule & Hewitt, 1971). In these studies, neither heart rate nor blood pressure increased in failure conditions, while both increased when participants were insulted during their failure experience.

Although it may be argued that the subjects in the failure condition were not frustrated and consequently an increase in autonomic activities did not occur (see Rule & Hewitt, 1971), it is generally recognized that insult and attack are more powerful and more reliable instigators of aggression than is frustration. Several studies have documented that insult or attack increases emotional reactivity as reflected by increases in heart rate (e.g., Ferguson, Rule, & Lindsay, 1982), basal skin conductance (e.g., Taylor, 1967; Shortell, Epstein, & Taylor, 1970), and blood pressure (e.g., Ax, 1953; Funkenstein et al., 1954). It can be concluded that frustration and, to a greater extent, insult promote an increase in anger and that this is revealed in enhanced emotional reactivity and in accompanying verbal reports of anger.

Given that anger is an important mediator of aggression, under what conditions is this state most conducive to aggression? First, as stated previously (Rule, 1974; Rule & Nesdale, 1976), anger is primarily likely to influence aggressive behavior primarily when the response is uniquely directed toward injuring the target (i.e., hostile aggression). While anger may mediate hostile aggression, it would not be expected to underlie an aggressive response that had some social purpose (i.e., prosocial aggression) or which served to obtain a goal for purely extrinsic reasons unrelated to the victim's behavior (i.e., personal-instrumental aggression).[4] This view is supported by research demonstrating that conditions assumed to induce anger increase only hostile responses and not responses serving prosocial goals (Rule & Hewitt, 1971; Rule & Leger, 1976; Rule & Nesdale, 1974). In these studies, participants are asked to play the role of a teacher, using shock as punishment for errors in a learning task. Participants are frustrated or angered by their partner, after which they are given the opportunity to retaliate by administering shocks.

Rule and Hewitt (1971) found more aggression following nonfrustration and high frustration compared with moderate frustration conditions. The aggression displayed under high frustration (manipulated by learning failure plus insult) conditions was interpreted as reflecting anger because higher shock levels administered were accompanied by elevated cardiac activity and high annoyance ratings. The nonfrustrated (i.e., learning success) subjects delivered a similar high number of shocks, apparently assuming that the shock could aid their partner's performance. On the other hand, the moderately frustrated (i.e., learning failure) subjects, using their own previous failure as a comparison, apparently assumed that punishment would contribute little to the other's goal achievement and hence delivered fewer shocks. In both the low and moderate thwarting conditions, there was no evidence from either physiological or self-report measures to indicate that subjects were angered. The subjects seemed to give shock either to hurt physically an insulting

---

[4]Although aggression can be defined as harm or injury at the descriptive level, some typing of aggression is needed at the construct level (Feshbach, 1964; Rule, 1974). Aside from accidental aggression, the types of intentional aggression receiving most attention in the literature are hostile and instrumental. Hostile aggressive behavior is directed primarily at injuring another person. Instrumental aggressive behavior is directed primarily toward attaining a nonagressive goal. Instrumental aggression may be perpetrated for personal reasons (e.g., to obtain money or prestige) or for prosocial reasons (e.g. to save the country, or teach someone a lesson).

partner who had angered them or to promote learning if the learning seemed feasible on the basis of their past experience.

In another experiment (Rule & Nesdale, 1974), subjects participating as teachers were either told specifically that increasing shock inflicted pain which helped (prosocial function of aggression) or hindered (hostile function) a learner's performance. The learner either succeeded or failed on his task, thereby winning or losing a reward for himself and either insulting or not insulting the teacher. As expected, subjects administered shock levels according to both the value of aggression and their partner's insult. When shock presumably could hinder their partner's performance, insulted subjects expressed more aggression; but when shock presumably could help their partner, noninsulted participants expressed more aggression. The insulted teachers reported that they were more upset when the shock helped rather than hindered their provoker's performance, whereas the noninsulted subjects reported that they were more upset when shock hindered rather than helped their partner's performance. Moreover, the insulted subjects indicated that they were more angry and disliked the target more than did the noninsulted subjects. Other results showed that the increasingly successful performance of the partner activated prosocial but diminished hostile aggression. These findings have been confirmed in a subsequent study by Rule and Leger (1976).

Considered together, the results of this series of experiments show that insult that generates anger leads to the expression of hostile aggression. Insult facilitates hostile responses and decreases helpful responses. In contrast, more prosocial aggression occurred when it presumably might improve the performance of the other person on the learning task.

Second, although anger apparently mediates hostile aggression, it may be a necessary but not a sufficient condition for this response. Indeed, in an early statement of this view, Berkowitz (1962) contended that although anger mediated the effect of frustration on aggression, the drive of anger would "not lead to drive specific behavior (aggression in this case) unless there are appropriate cues or releasors" (pp. 32-33). While such aggressive cues could be internally represented, Berkowitz focused on external cues, such as violent films, weapons, or people's names.

Berkowitz has reviewed numerous studies that provide data consistent with this position (Berkowitz, 1965, 1969, 1970, 1974). An early study provides an example of his paradigm. A confederate of the experimenter angered subjects who then observed an aggressive film or an exciting nonaggressive film. The participants were subsequently permitted to deliver electric shocks to the accomplice whose name was the same or different from the loser in the fight film. Aggression was expressed toward the accomplice when his name was the same as that of the losing boxer in the fight film condition. Apparently, the high association of the confederate with the aggressive film enhanced his aggressive cue value. However, although aggressive cues may exert a directing influence on aggression by angered persons, Berkowitz (1969) has acknowledged and other research has shown (e.g., Rule & Hewitt, 1971) that anger increases the likelihood of aggression even in the absence of strong external aggressive cues.

Furthermore, the presence of aggressive cues may also serve as a source of general arousal that increases aggression by exacerbating the experience of anger. Zillmann

(1979) has provided an extensive review of literature that supports the proposition that exposure to materials involving aggressive behavior maintains a state of elevated excitation and correspondingly high levels of aggressive retaliation. In contrast to the conclusion of other authors (Berkowitz, 1965; Geen, 1976; Goranson, 1970) that exposure to such aggressive stimuli directly facilitates aggression. Zillmann argues that this exposure has its effect through the maintenance of, rather than increases in, anger. Both Zillmann and Johnson (1973) and Donnerstein, Donnerstein, and Barrett (1976) have shown that exposure to nonaggressive stimuli in a control condition actually reduces aggression. For example, Zillmann and Johnson (1973) found that a minor provocation had no effect on excitation and, although observing a violent film increased arousal to some extent, not very much change occurred. In contrast, when subjects were provoked severely, an increase in excitation as measured by blood pressure and vasoconstriction was maintained during exposure to a violent film, but reduced by exposure to a nonhostile film. Aggressive responses measured by delivering electric shock to a provocateur was a function of the difference in level of excitation after exposure to the films. Because the arousal coming from the violent stimuli may add to arousal from the provocation (Doob & Kirshenbaum, 1973), the relatively high arousal in the violent film condition may have been misattributed to the provocation and, hence, labeled as anger. Thus, although aggressive cues may exert a directing selective effect on aggression, as suggested by Berkowitz (1962), these cues may increase anger and subsequent aggression by contributing an additional component of arousal.

While external aggressive cues do not appear to be necessary prerequisites for an aggressive response, however, other features of the situation may influence the response of even a highly angered person. For example, if an aroused person is unable to aggress for some reason, or engages in a neutral activity, or is exposed to other, nonhostile communications, anger and aggression may be reduced. While anger arousal might be expected to diminish over time. (Konecni, 1975a), engaging in other tasks and exposure to nonhostile communications might produce a similar effect by distracting the angered person's attention (Bandura, 1965; Rule, Haley, & McCormack, 1971) or by providing incompatible emotional response states (Baron, 1974c; Baron & Bell, 1977; Zillmann & Sapolsky, 1977). Konecni (1975a) has provided results consistent with this view. In this study, subjects were either annoyed or treated neutrally. Subjects were assigned either to give shocks to the annoyer, to wait, or to work on mathematical problems with an interpolated period lasting 7 or 13 min. After this, the number of shocks delivered to the annoyer was measured. Waiting subjects delivered more shocks than did the subjects who were in the annoyed-math and annoyed-shock conditions, suggesting a distracting task reduces anger and aggression, although, within the 7-min conditions, shock decreased aggression more than in engaging in a cognitive task. In addition, the fewer shocks administered by subjects waiting 13 min compared to 7 min showed that arousal dissipates with time.

Third, while these results show that other factors in the situation can influence an individual's level of anger and hence aggression, other features of the situation may simply serve to *inhibit* the expression of aggression. In particular, aggression is likely to be inhibited by situational factors which arouse fear of punishment or disapproval, internal standards of conduct prohibiting aggression, or other conflicting goals involved in the interaction situation.

As others have noted (e.g., Berkowitz, 1962), any features of the situation that enhance the perception of likely disapproval for an action may inhibit the expression of aggression. Rule, Dyck, and Nesdale (1978) found that aggressive inclinations were significantly increased by the knowledge that frustration was intended rather than unintended. In addition, subjects were more instigated and expressed more aggression according to that instigation when they were able to reject their provoker under private, anonymous conditions rather than publicly. More directly, research has shown that aggression is reduced when it is assumed that an audience is likely to disapprove of aggression (Borden & Taylor, 1973; Borden, 1975) although this depends upon the attractiveness of the peers or the audience (Baron, 1972).

Furthermore, if an angered person is made aware that retaliation is considered inappropriate, he may express less aggression than if that standard were not so salient. Results of several experiments (Berkowitz, Lepinski, & Angulo, 1969; Berkowitz & Turner, 1974; Turner & Simons, 1974) have been interpreted as indicating that angered subjects inhibit their aggression because of anxiety about the appropriateness of retaliation. In fact, several recent studies have demonstrated that if subjects are simply made more aware of their own behavior by observing themselves in a mirror or on a videotape, they express less aggression when the salient standard in the situation prohibits aggression and more aggression when the salient standard encourages aggression (Carver, 1974; Scheier, Fenigstein, & Buss, 1974; Rule, Nesdale, & Dyck, 1975).

Finally, whether or not a person aggresses might depend upon other goals in the situation. For example, if the person expects or needs further interaction with the target person, aggression may be reduced to ensure that the additional goals can be realized. Hokanson et al. (1968) reported that when a friendly response was instrumental in reducing further aggression, its use increased. Alternatively, Berscheid, Boye, and Walster (1968) found that retaliation was expressed in order to reduce further harm from an antagonist. These results may provide a partial interpretation for Baron's findings (1973, 1974c) that threat of retaliation reduced aggression only in nonangry persons. Nonangered persons may have wanted to avoid provoking a potential retaliator, whereas angered persons may have wanted to convey their anger not only to even the score but to warn the provoker to calm down. Even when received abuse is considered to reflect the attacker's aggressive nature, whether or not the victim retaliates might depend upon whether he or she expects that retaliation would reduce further aggression or would enhance the nastiness of the provoker. In sum, although anger appears to mediate aggression when the function of that response is to injure another person, a number of factors may inhibit aggression, regardless of the person's level of anger.

Effects of Additional Arousal Sources on Anger and Aggression

Aside from the research that has established the anger-aggression link by examining the effect of one arousal source (i.e., frustration, provocation) on aggression, other research has considered the combined effects of provocation and another source of arousal on anger and aggression. In this research, subjects are typically provoked by a confederate, exposed to another arousing stimulus, and then given the opportunity to respond aggressively to the provoker. The results have revealed that arousal by a secondary source sometimes does and at other times does not enhance the expression of aggression.

Enhancement of aggression by insulted participants has been reported when they have been exposed to strenuous physical exercise (Zillmann & Bryant, 1974; Zillmann, Katcher, & Milavsky, 1972), white noise (Donnerstein & Wilson, 1976; Konecni, 1975b), moderate heat (Baron, 1977a), and erotica (Donnerstein et al., 1975; Meyer, 1972; Zillmann, 1971; Zillman, Hoyt, & Day, 1974). On the other hand, nonenhancement effects on aggression have been reported when provoked persons were exposed to erotica (Baron, 1974a,b; Baron & Bell, 1977; Donnerstein, Donnerstein, & Barrett, 1976; Donnerstein, Donnerstein, & Evans, 1975), high heat (Baron, 1977a), and when attention was diverted from the insulter to erotica (Geen, Rakosky, & Pigg, 1972), to an arousing drug (Younger & Doob, 1978), or to noise (Harris & Huang, 1974).

As was discussed earlier in the section on "Arousal, Cognition, and Anger," one approach to understanding the effects of two arousal sources on anger and aggression is via some variant of the Schachter and Singer labeling position. Two such approaches will be considered: excitation transfer and cue salience.

Excitation Transfer

Tannenbaum and Zillmann (1975) and Zillmann (1978) have proposed an "excitation transfer" model according to which residues from an earlier arousal state intensify a subsequent arousal state. A residue of sympathetic arousal engendered by first viewing an erotic film may be transferred and thereby enhance an emotional state such as anger. Or if an insulted person is subsequently aroused by a second, different stimulus and is reconfronted by the original anger-provoking stimulus, anger will be reinstated and enhanced by the arousal residue from the second arousal-producing stimulus. In the original formulation of the model (Tannenbaum & Zillmann, 1975), arousal transference occurred when the person was aroused but did not link cues from one source of arousal to the other source. The cues for linkage were presumably derived from exteroceptive sources such as trembling. Hence, when such cues were unavailable, the person presumably misattributes this residual excitation to another source with a decline in the awareness of being aroused by the residual source. With lessened awareness of earlier arousal, a person presumably does not discriminate the contribution of the separate sources of arousal that occurred immediately prior to the time of the response.

According to Zillmann (1978), two experiments uniquely support this attributional position. In one study by Zillmann, Johnson, and Day (1974), the presence or absence of cues linking arousal to physical exercise was varied by delay and no-delay conditions, respectively, between the physical exertion and the aggression phase of the experiment. These authors demonstrated that when provoked subjects could attribute their arousal to immediately preceding excessive physical exertion, they administered less shock to their provokers than when they had a time delay that presumably reduced the cues linking their arousal to exertion.

The second study (Cantor, Zillmann, & Bryant, 1975) assessed the diminution of the subjects' awareness of arousal due to one source (physical exercise) and its effects on subsequent attribution of arousal to a succeeding arousal stimulus (erotica). In the first stage of a two-part experiment, participants exercised physically and then later reported at different time intervals the extent to which they were still aroused by the exercise. On the basis of measures of the perceived and actual physiological excitation, three recovery phases were constructed. In phase 1, measured excitation was elevated and subjects reported that they were aroused from the prior exercise; in phase 2, measured excitation was significantly elevated but subjects reported that they had recovered from their prior excitation and; in phase 3, both actual physiological arousal and perceived arousal showed recovery. In the second stage of the experiment, different subjects in the first, second, or third exercise recovery phase were exposed to erotic stimuli after which perceived sexual arousal was measured. Consistent with expectations, participants in the second recovery phase perceived themselves as being more sexually aroused than did participants in the other two recovery phases.

The excitation transfer model has been challenged, however, by recent lines of investigation. The first comes from a study by Donnerstein et al. (1975) in which subjects were exposed to neutral, mildly erotic, or highly erotic stimulation immediately *prior* to provocation. Donnerstein et al. found that aggression increased linearly as the degree of eroticism of the stimuli increased despite the lack of any time delay between exposure to erotic and insult stimuli. Second, there is an accumulating literature (e.g., Baron, 1974a,b; Donnerstein et al., 1975) indicating that the supplementary arousal produced by mild erotica and humor does not enhance aggression when viewed *subsequent* to provocation and, as acknowledged by Zillmann and Sapolsky (1977), these data cannot be explained by the excitation transfer model. Despite attempts to resolve the issue (Baron & Bell, 1977; Malamuth, Feshbach, & Jaffe, 1977; Zillmann, Bryant, Comisky, and Medoff, 1981), differences in the type of erotic stimuli used and their variation on numerous dimensions, including the occasional confounding of aggression, preclude satisfactory resolution of the problem.

Cue Salience

Aside from the "excitation transfer" notion, a further variant of the cognitive labeling position assumes that the likelihood and intensity of aggression is a function of the extent to which the label of anger is attached to the overall state of arousal arising from the two or more sources. However, rather than the arousal, hence emotional state, being incremented by a *residue* of unlabeled arousal from another source, this position suggests that the emotional state labeled depends upon the relative salience of the cues associated with each arousal source in the immediate environment (see

Rule, Ferguson, & Nesdale, 1979, for a fuller account of this). Here, "cues" refer to dimensions or attributes that are descriptive of, or associated uniquely with, different stimuli. Provocation, for example, is describable in terms of dimensions such as its intensity and the presence or absence of intent.

It is assumed that certain cues associated with a particular source or a variety of sources are more vivid to an individual than others; that is, they receive more attention than other cues in the situation (Pryor & Kriss, 1977). Different people may react differently to the same source or sources depending upon which feature of the source(s) is the focus of attention. It is assumed that cues may be differentially salient to an individual because of, for example, the intensity of arousal that each cue produces, the ego-involving capacity (or importance) of the cues, the meaning of the cues to the individual because of his partial experience with situations like the target situation, the sequential presentation of the arousing stimuli, etc.

In addition to the research literature employing two sources of arousal, the cues associated with one source of arousal may be more salient than those associated with another source. For example, if a person has had a previously traumatic experience with aversive noise or has coronary problems and is asked to engage in strenuous exercise, the cues associated with the noise or exercise may be more salient than those associated with something like insult, and the level of arousal experienced may be greater. On the other hand, if the person has not had this kind of traumatic experience and is exposed to personal insult and white noise or exercise, personal insult may be more ego-involving or important than either noise or exercise. Therefore, personal insult is likely to be more salient to the individual and would receive more attention with the result that anger is experienced and the likelihood of aggression is enhanced. In brief, arousal from an additional source will increment anger and aggression if the cues to the anger source are salient, whereas anger and aggression will diminish if the cues to the additional arousal are salient.

Although the cue salience notion has not been systematically examined in research studies, the procedures employed in several experiments might be considered to be relevant. It will be recognized, however, that most of these studies utilized a similar paradigm to the studies reviewed earlier under "Anger and Aggression." In this paradigm, the salience of a particular arousal source is manipulated by instructions. While the intent of these studies has been to assess whether an available additional explanation for arousal reduces anger and aggression, equivocal findings have been obtained. For example, in a study by O'Neal and Kaufmann (1972), participants were given a stimulant, Dexedrine, that was described as either a vitamin or a stimulant. Aggression was highest in the stimulant attack condition relative to the remaining conditions regardless of information about the arousing properties of the pill. Nevertheless, neither self-report nor pulse rate data indicated that Dexedrine increased arousal, thereby precluding an unambiguous interpretation of their results.

In a subsequent study, Ferguson, Rule, and Lindsay (1982) conducted an experiment based on the assumption that the perception of anger and its behavioral manifestation will be reduced when an additional source of arousal is perceived as a plausible explanation for arousal that may otherwise be associated with anger only.

To examine the implications of this analysis, they provided a change in the plausibility of an additional source of arousal. They reasoned that if a plausible additional source of arousal reduces the attribution of arousal solely to the provoker who has insulted the person, then reducing the explanatory plausibility of the additional source should subsequently increase attributions of arousal to the provoker. Further, it was considered that the plasticity in the labeling of arousal should produce corresponding changes in anger (Liebhart, 1979). If physiologically aroused people can attribute their arousal only to a provoker's behavior, their anger and aggression should be greater than if they can attribute their state to both the provocation and an additional source, such as an arousing pill. Finally, compared with the latter condition, perceived anger and aggression should increase when a joint attribution to the provoker and an arousing pill is undermined by information that the pill is actually a placebo and therefore not arousing.

Men received 200 mg of caffeine and were led to believe that they had ingested either an arousing drug or a harmless placebo. They were then either provoked or not provoked by their partner during a bogus reaction time task. After receiving four bogus opportunities to deliver aversive tones to their partners, they were told that they had been misinformed of their pill assignments. Those who had been initially told they had been given a drug were told that they had received a placebo, and those who had been initially told they had received a placebo were told that they had received the drug. After reversing the assignments, the subjects received four more opportunities to express aggression. When rating their reactions at the end of the session, provoked relative to unprovoked participants attributed their annoyance and feelings of anger to both the drug and their partner's behavior. These results showed that we had manipulated multiple sources of arousal. Contrary to expectations, however, angered compared with nonangered participants delivered more aversive tones when they thought they had taken the drug, but reduced their aggression when subsequently told that they had been injected by a placebo rather than an arousing drug. Thus, even under conditions where an alternative source is plausible, anger is not reduced. Instead, the results seem to reflect these participants' tendency to use the drug as an excuse to release hostility. Such results accord with other findings in which stimulating drugs such as caffeine or alcohol show an increase in emotional behavior (Lange, Goeckner, Adesso, & Marlett, 1975; Cotton, Baron, & Borkovec, 1980; Vuchinich, Tucker, & Sobell, 1979).

Based on the findings reviewed in this section, there does not appear to be clear support for either the excitation transfer or cue salience explanations of the effects of additional arousal on the anger and aggression of angered persons. However, while it is evident at this stage that at least the range of application of the excitation transfer model is restricted, research on the cue salience notion is scant.

To provide a more adequate assessment of the cue salience notion, research is needed which, as a first step, determines the differential cue salience of a number of different sources of arousal (Rule, Ferguson, & Nesdale, 1979). Cue salience could be determined independently using tasks which, for example, assess the relative number of cues recalled that are related to each source of arousal, the order in which each kind of cue is recalled, recognition latency of cues, and so on. Using the results of these studies, research could be conducted which examined predictions regarding the magnitude of anger and aggression as a function of arousal from two or more sources.

Aggression Catharsis

The final issue to be discussed concerns the notion of aggression cartharsis, i.e., that attacking a provoker results in the attacker's purging himself of hostility and anger toward his victim (Dollard et al., 1939). A considerable amount of research has examined the effect of an angry person's retaliation upon his or her subsequent degree of anger arousal and his or her level of aggression. In accord with a recent analysis of catharsis (Konecni, 1975a), we consider as relevant those instances involving the actual expression of aggression by an angered person; this excludes the observation of aggression as it affects aggression. Research on this issue has shown that the expression of aggression reduces physiological arousal (Baker & Schaie, 1969; Gambaro & Rabin, 1969; Hokanson, 1970) but not always (Holmes, 1966). Moreover, it sometimes increases behavioral aggression (e.g., Geen, Stonner, & Shope, 1975), and sometimes decreases it (e.g., Konecni & Doob, 1972).

Differing interpretations of the literature have been offered. Konecni (1975) has argued that aggression may lower arousal, the degree of experienced anger, and subsequent aggression under highly specific conditions. According to these writers, the acts must be preceded by anger, aim at the source of anger, appear to harm the target, and not be anticipated to produce other aversive events. In research illustrating these points, Doob and his colleagues (Doob & Wood, 1972; Konecni & Doob, 1972) and Konecni (1975a) observed that participants angered by a verbally abusive partner decreased subsequent aggression when the annoyed individuals had been given an opportunity to deliver shock to their tormentor or an innocent bystander.

Moreover, it was suggested that aggressive behavior can be enhanced by "repetition of a mode of release" (Dollard et al., 1939). According to Konecni (1975a), administering a large number of shocks that no longer decrease arousal (anger) may result in the person's adopting a standard of giving many shocks. Using a design with a number of control conditions, Konecni showed that using the same mode of activity (shock) resulted in increases of subsequent aggression, whereas using a different but equally punishing mode of activity (noise) decreased subsequent aggression.

Some authors (Geen & Quanty, 1977; Quanty, 1976) have suggested that the participants in the Doob studies may have felt guilty about responding to verbal insult by shocking their partner. Under these conditions, restraints against aggression may have been increased. The implication of this view is that minimizing restraints may increase hostility. Other studies that have measured both physiological responses and behavior suggest that expressing aggression may make the person feel better but lead to more hostility, especially when the restraints against aggressing are lowered (Kahn, 1966; Geen, Stonner, & Shope, 1975). For example, subjects in the Geen et al. study were angered by excessive shock or mild insult. Subjects were assigned to one of three conditions: (1) deliver a fixed amount of shock for learning errors, (2) the experimenter shocks the partner, or (3) no shock was mentioned. Subjects were then permitted to administer shocks for errors on a learning task. Angered subjects' blood pressure increased and those who gave shock on the first task dropped in blood pressure. Angered subjects who had delivered shock on the first task were more aggressive and more hostile toward their partner.

Fishman (1965) reported suggestive but not significant data for the notion that when aggression against an instigator is appropriate, aggression is followed by tension reduction; when it is not appropriate, it increases tension; and, when appropriateness is ambiguous, there is no consistent relation between aggression and tension. The perceived appropriateness of aggression apparently decreases restraints against aggressing as well as subsequent tension. This pattern of results is consistent with findings that low guilt persons experience greater blood pressure decreases than do high guilt persons who express aggression (Schill, 1972). Although the latter results deal with a trait characteristic and have not always been replicated (Gambaro & Rabin, 1969), they suggest that the perceived appropriateness of aggression may indeed be an important determinant of tension reduction.

Zillmann (1979) interprets the reduction of arousal in a series of studies by Hokanson (Hokanson & Burgess, 1962; Hokanson & Shetler, 1961) to the fact that retaliation reduces arousal if annoyance is attributable to malice. Zillmann recognizes that if the annoyance is ambiguously attributed to malice, some of the specific conditions suggested by Geen and Quanty might effect arousal reduction as they propose. Zillmann also notes that anxiety may prevent the decay of excitation and this apprehensiveness about the appropriateness of behavioral retaliation may maintain or produce arousal. The introduction of anxiety greatly compromises the interpretation of arousal as an aggression-motivating force. His summary statement is that in coping with intense annoyances through aggressive action, the individual will experience a reduction in arousal if the actions reduce the threat or punish the annoyer and if the actions do not produce the apprehension of further danger by the annoyer or the expectation of social reproach. Even if retaliation neither has utility nor is free of expectation of further annoyance, the maintenance of arousal, however, cannot last for extended periods of time simply due to fatigue alone. However, other conditions in the environment may promote continued appraisal of the danger; especially when annoyed, the individual may rehearse his or her grievance and maintain the state of elevated excitation. Any stimulation that promotes this rehearsal prevents recovery and any disruption of this process should accelerate the decay of excitation.

In summary, the evidence suggests that the expression of aggression by an angered person does not exert a simple cathartic effect on the aggressor's subsequent arousal and hostility. Whether one or both of the aggressor's arousal and hostility are reduced or are maintained at a high level appears to depend upon the potential aggressor's cognitions in the situation. Relevant considerations include the characteristics of the target, the amount of aggression expressed, differences between the amount of aggression received and the amount expressed, and the mode of aggressing. Together, these influence a person's judgment of the appropriateness of his retaliation and hence affect his subsequent level of anger arousal and aggression.

Conclusions

Contrary to earlier approaches to aggression, the research reviewed in this chapter indicates that an aggressive response is the product of a complex interaction between arousal, cognition, and emotional states, especially anger. While previous views (e.g., Berkowitz, 1962) delineated an important role for anger in the expression of aggression, more recent approaches have stressed the important influence exerted by an individual's cognitions on his arousal state and its influence on aggression. Whether or not a person experiences an elevated state of arousal, what specific state he or she experiences, and the extent to which this state instigates an aggressive response appears to depend upon the person's cognitions. Again, this is not to say that our understanding of the interrelationship between cognition and arousal is clear: at best, the relationship is certainly complex and multifaceted, reflecting the nature of both concepts. While we have noted previously some of the conceptual and measurement problems in dealing with arousal, much along similar lines can be said of cognition. As was mentioned at the outset, the term "cognition" was, and has been, used broadly to refer to a range of operations in the context of aggression research. Such operations may include, for example, the individual's *perception* or awareness of an event (e.g., that a verbal comment has been directed at him), his *interpretation* of the meaning of that event (e.g., that the verbal comment comprises an insult), the *labeling* of his subsequent arousal stae (e.g., as "anger"), his *decision* to retaliate, a *judgment* of the type and level of retaliation which is desired and/or appropriate, and so on. As might be anticipated, these lists of operations probably vary on several dimensions (e.g., duration, consciousness, complexity, implications) which contribute to the difficulty of unraveling the cognition-arousal relationship empirically.

Given this level of complexity, many issues remain to be resolved. For example, although research has shown that people are more angered by arbitrary versus nonarbitrary thwarting (e.g., Kulik and Brown, 1979) and, inferentially, that some type of cognitive appraisal has been implicated, little is known concerning the mechanics of this process. For example, on what basis do people respond to particular cues? How is a state of anger "labeled" or experienced? To what extent are arousal states plastic such that they can be experienced as one of several emotional states? Similarly, although the research indicates that additional arousal from nonprovocative sources sometimes does and sometimes does not increment the individual's level of anger, the available evidence is unclear concerning the possibility that arousal from one source to another is "transferred" or "misattributed" to another source. While this state of affairs may owe much to problems of measurement, it is at least equally likely that the cognitions involved are particularly complex, varying with the particular situation under scrutiny. Thus, as suggested by Rule et al. (1979), certain cues may be more salient in particular contexts, and these may influence the arousal state as well as the level of retaliation. In addition, while individuals may partition the sources of their arousal, cues may have meaning as a justification and thereby strengthen the tendency for angered people to express aggression. While such issues must be resolved before our understanding of the cognition-arousal relationship is complete, it is also clear that future research must be undertaken with more attention being paid to the measurement of excitatory changes with explicit care taken for the methodological refinements suggested in the contemporary literature.

References

Ax, A. F. (1953). The physiological differentiation between fear and anger in humans. *Psychosomatic Medicine, 15*, 433-442.

Baker, J. W., II, & Schaie, K. W. (1969). Effects of aggressing "alone" or "with another" on physiological and psychological arousal. *Journal of Personality and Social Psychology, 12*, 80-86.

Bandura, A. (1965). Vicarious processes: A case of no-trial learning. In L. Berkowitz (Ed.), *Advances in experimental social psychology* (Vol. 2). New York: Academic Press.

Bandura, A. (1973). *Aggression: A social learning analysis.* Englewood Cliffs, NJ: Prentice-Hall.

Bandura, A., & Walters, R. H. (1963). *Social learning and personality development.* New York: Holt, Rinehart & Winston.

Baron, R. A. (1972). Reducing the influence of an aggressive model: The restraining effects of peer censure. *Journal of Experimental Social Psychology, 8*, 266-275.

Baron, R. A. (1973). Threatened retaliation from the victim as an inhibitor of physical aggression. *Journal of Research in Personality, 7*, 103-115.

Baron, R. A. (1974a). Sexual arousal and physical aggression: The inhibiting influence of "cheesecake" and nudes. *Bulletin of the Psychonomic Society, 3*, 337-339.

Baron, R. A. (1974b). The aggression-inhibiting influence of heightened sexual arousal. *Journal of Personality and Social Psychology, 30*, 318-322.

Baron, R. A. (1974c). Threatened retaliation as an inhibitor of human aggression: Mediating effects of the instrumental value of aggression. *Bulletin of the Psychonomic Society, 3*, 217-219.

Baron, R. A. (1977a). Aggression and heat: The "long hot summer" revisited. In A. Barum & S. Valins (Eds.), *Advances in environmental research* (Vol. 1). Hillsdale, NJ: Erlbaum.

Baron, R. A., & Bell, P. A. (1977). Sexual arousal and aggression by males: Effects of type of erotic stimuli and prior provocation. *Journal of Personality and Social Psychology, 35*, 79-87.

Berkowitz, L. (1962). *Aggression: A social psychological analysis.* New York: McGraw-Hill.

Berkowitz, L. (1965). The concept of aggressive drive: Some additional considerations. In L. Berkowitz (Ed.), *Advances in experimental social psychology* (Vol. 2). New York: Academic Press.

Berkowitz, L. (1969). The frustration-aggression hypothesis revisited. In L. Berkowitz (Ed.), *Roots of aggression.* New York: Atherton Press.

Berkowitz, L. (1970). The contagion of violence: An S-R mediational analysis of some effects of observed aggression. In J. K. Cole (Ed.), *Nebraska symposium on motivation* (Vol. 19). Lincoln, NE: University of Nebraska.

Berkowitz, L. (1974). Some determinants of impulsive aggression. The role of mediated associations with reinforcements for aggression. *Psychological Review, 81*, 165-176.

Berkowitz, L., Lepinski, J. P., & Angulo, E. J. (1969). Awareness of own anger level and subsequent aggression. *Journal of Personality and Social Psychology, 11*, 293-300.

Berkowitz, L., & Turner, C. W. (1974). Perceived anger level, instigating agent, and aggression. In H. London & R. E. Nisbett (Eds.), *Cognitive alteration of feeling states.* Chicago: Aldine.

Berscheid, E., Boye, D., & Walster, E. (1968). Retaliation as a means of restoring equity. *Journal of Personality and Social Psychology, 10*, 370-376.

Borden, R. J., (1975). Witnessed aggression: Influence of an observer's sex and values on aggressive responding. *Journal of Personality and Social Psychology, 31*, 567-573.

Borden, R. J., & Taylor, S. P. (1973). The social instigation and control of physical aggression. *Journal of Applied Social Psychology, 3*, 354-361.

Burnstein, E., & Worchel, P. (1962). Arbitrariness of frustration and its consequences for aggression in a social situation. *Journal of Personality, 30*, 528-541.

Cantor, J. R., Zillmann, D., & Bryant, J. (1975). Enhancement of experienced sexual arousal in response to erotic stimuli through misattribution of unrelated residual excitation. *Journal of Personality and Social Psychology, 32*, 69-75.

Carver, C. S. (1974). Facilitation of physical aggression through objective self-awareness. *Journal of Experimental Social Psychology, 10*, 365-370.

Cotton, J. L., Baron, R. S., & Borkovec, T. D. (1980). Caffeine ingestion, misattribution therapy and speech anxiety. *Journal of Research and Personality, 14*, 196-206.

Dengerink, H. A. (1971). Anxiety, aggression and physiological arousal. *Journal of Research in Personality, 5*, 223-232.

Dollard, J., Doob, L. W., Miller, N. E., Mowrer, O. H., & Sears, R. R. (1939). *Frustration and aggression.* New Haven, CN: Yale University Press.

Donnerstein, E., Donnerstein, M., & Barrett, G. (1976). Where is the facilitation of media violence? The effects of nonexposure and placement of anger arousal. *Journal of Research in Personality, 10*, 386-398.

Donnerstein, E., Donnerstein, M., & Evans, R. (1975). Erotic stimuli and aggression: Facilitation or inhibition. *Journal of Personality and Social Psychology, 32*, 237-244.

Donnerstein, E., & Wilson, D. W. (1976). Effects of noise and perceived control on ongoing and subsequent aggressive behavior. *Journal of Personality and Social Psychology, 34*, 774-781.

Doob, A. N., & Kirshenbaum, H. M. (1973). The effects on arousal of frustration and aggressive films. *Journal of Experimental Social Psychology, 9*, 57-64.

Doob, A. N., & Wood, L. E. (1972). Catharsis and aggression: The effects of annoyance and retaliation on aggressive behavior. *Journal of Personality and Social Psychology, 22*, 156-162.

Dyck, R. J., & Rule, B. G. (1978). Effects on retaliation of causal attributions concerning attack. *Journal of Personality and Social Psychology, 36*, 521-529.

Elliott, R. (1969). Tonic heart rate: Experiments on the effects of collative variables lead to a hypothesis about its motivational significance. *Journal of Personality and Social Psychology, 12*, 211-228.

Ferguson, T. J., Rule, B. G., & Lindsay, R. (1982). The effects of caffeine and provocation on aggression. *Journal of Research in Personality, 16*, 60-71.

Feshbach, S. (1964). The function of aggression and the regulation of aggressive drive. *Psychological Review, 71*, 257-272.

Fishman, C. G. (1965). Need for approval and the expression of aggression under varying conditions of frustration. *Journal of Personality and Social Psychology, 2*, 809-816.

Freud, S. (1959). *Beyond the pleasure principle.* New York: Bantam.

Funkenstein, D. H., King, S. H., & Drolette, M. (1954). The direction of anger during a laboratory stress-inducing situation. *Psychosomatic Medicine, 16*, 404-413.

Gambaro, S., & Rabin, A. I. (1969). Diastolic blood pressure responses following direct and displaced aggression after anger arousal in high- and low-guilt subjects. *Journal of Personality and Social Psychology, 12*, 87-94.

Geen, R. G. (1975). The meaning of observed violence: Real vs. fictional violence and consequent effects on aggression and emotional arousal. *Journal of Research in Personality, 9*, 270-281.

Geen, R. G. (1976). Observing violence in the mass media: Implications of basic research. In R. G. Geen & E. C. O'Neal (Eds.), *Perspectives on aggression.* New York: Academic Press.

Geen, R. G., & Quanty, M. B. (1977). The catharsis of aggression: An evaluation of a hypothesis. In L. Berkowitz (Ed.), *Advances in Experimental Social Psychology* (Vol. 10). New York: Academic Press.

Geen, R. G., & Rakosky, J. J. (1973). Interpretations of observed aggression and their effect on GSR. *Journal of Experimental Research in Personality, 6*, 289-292.

Geen, R. G., Rakosky, J. J., & Pigg, R. (1972). Awareness of arousal and its relation to aggression. *British Journal of Social and Clinical Psychology, 11*, 115-121.

Geen, R. G., Stoner, D., & Shope, G. L. (1975). The facilitation of aggression by aggression: Evidence against the catharsis hypothesis. *Journal of Personality and Social Psychology, 31*, 721-726.

Gentry, W. D. (1970). Effects of frustration, attack, and prior aggressive training on overt aggression and vascular processes. *Journal of Personality and Social Psychology, 16*, 718-725.

Goranson, R. E. (1970). Media violence and aggressive behavior: A review of experimental research. In L. Berkowitz (Ed.), *Advances in experimental social psychology* (Vol. 5). New York: Academic Press.

Harris, M. B., & Huang, L. C. (1974). Aggression and the attribution process. *Journal of Social Psychology, 92*, 209-216.

Hokanson, J. E. (1970). Psychophysiological evaluation of the catharsis hypothesis. In E. I. Megargee & J. E. Hokanson (Eds.), *The dynamics of aggression: Individual, group, and international analyses*. New York: Harper & Row.

Hokanson, J. E., & Burgess, M. (1962). The effects of three types of aggression on vascular processes. *Journal of Abnormal and Social Psychology, 64*, 446-449.

Hokanson, J. E., & Shetler, S. (1961). The effect of overt aggression on physiological arousal level. *Journal of Abnormal and Social Psychology, 63*, 446-448.

Hokanson, J. E., Willers, K. R., & Koropsak, E. (1968). The modification of autonomic responses during aggressive interchange. *Journal of Personality, 30*, 386-404.

Holmes, D. S. (1966). Effects of overt aggression on level of physiological arousal. *Journal of Personality and Social Psychology, 4*, 189-194.

Kahn, M. (1966). The physiology of catharsis. *Journal of Personality and Social Psychology, 3*, 278-286.

Kaufmann, H. (1970). *Aggression and altruism: A psychological analysis*. New York: Holt, Rinehart & Winston.

Konecni, V. J. (1975a). Annoyance, type and duration of postannoyance activity and aggression: The "cathartic" effect. *Journal of Experimental Psychology, General, 104*, 76-102.

Konecni, V. J. (1975b). The mediation of aggressive behavior: Arousal level versus anger and cognitive labeling. *Journal of Personality and Social Psychology, 32*, 706-712.

Konecni, V. J., & Doob, A. N. (1972). Catharsis through displacement of aggression. *Journal of Personality and Social Psychology, 23*, 379-387.

Kuhn, T. S. (1962). *The structure of scientific revolutions*. Chicago: University of Chicago Press.

Kulik, J. A., & Brown, R. (1979). Frustration, attribution of blame and aggression. *Journal of Experimental Social Psychology, 15*, 183-194.

Lacey, J. I. (1967). Somatic response patterning and stress: Some revisions of activation theory. In M. H. Appley & R. Trumbull (Eds.), *Psychological stress: Issues in research*. New York: Appleton-Century-Crofts.

Lange, A. R., Goeckner, D. J., Adesso, V. J., & Marlett, G. A. (1975). Effects of alcohol on aggression in male drinkers. *Journal of Abnormal Psychology, 84*, 508-518.

Lazarus, R. S., Speisman, J. C., & Mordkoff, A. M. (1963). The relation between autonomic indicators of psychological stress: Heart rate and skin conductance. *Psychosomatic Medicine, 25*, 19-30.

Libby, W. L., Lacey, B. C., & Lacey, J. I. (1973). Pupillary and cardiac activity during visual attention. *Psychophysiology, 10*, 270-294.

Liebhart, E. H. (1979). Information search and attribution: Cognitive processes mediating the effect of false autonomic feedback. *European Journal of Social Psychology, 9*, 19-37.

Malamuth, N. M., Feshbach, S., & Jaffe, Y. (1977). Sexual arousal and aggression: Recent experiments and theoretical issues. *Journal of Social Issues, 33*, 110-133.

Malmstrom, E. J., Apton, E., Jr., & Lazarus, R. S. (1965). Heart rate measurement and the correlation of indices of arousal. *Psychosomatic Medicine, 27*, 546-556.

Marshall, G. D., & Zimbardo, P. G. (1979). Affective consequences of inadequately explained physiological arousal. *Journal of Personality and Social Psychology, 37*, 970-988.

Maslach, C. (1979). Negative emotional biasing of unexplained arousal. *Journal of Personality and Social Psychology, 37*, 953-969.

McGinn, N. F., Harburg, E., Julius, S., & McLeod, J. M. (1974). Psychological correlates of blood pressure. *Psychological Bulletin, 61*, 209-219.

Meyer, T. P. (1972). The effects of sexually arousing and violent films on aggressive behavior. *Journal of Sex Research, 8*, 324-331.

Nisbett, R. E., & Schachter, S. (1966). Cognitive manipulation of pain. *Journal of Experimental Social Psychology, 2*, 227-236.

Nisbett, R. E., & Wilson, T. D. (1977). Telling more than we can know: Verbal reports on mental processes. *Psychological Review, 84*, 231-259.

O'Neal, E., & Kaufmann, L. (1972). The influence of attack, arousal, and information about one's arousal upon interpersonal aggression. *Psychonomic Science, 26*, 211-214.

Pliner, P., & Cappell, H. (1974). Modification of the affective consequences of alcohol: A comparison of social and solitary drinking. *Journal of Abnormal Psychology, 83*, 418-425

Porges, S. W., Bobrer, R. E., Cheung, M. N., Drasgow, F., McCabe, P. M., & Keren, G. (1980). New time series statistic for detecting rhythmic co-occurrence in the frequency domain: The weighted coherence and its application to psychophysiological research. *Psychological Bulletin, 88*, 580-587.

Posner, M. I., & Snyder, C. R. (1975). Attention and cognitive control. In R. L. Solso (Ed.), *Information processing and cognition*. New York: Wiley.

Pryor, J. B., & Kriss, M. (1977). The cognitive dynamics of salience in the attribution process. *Journal of Personality and Social Psychology, 35*, 49-55.

Quanty, M. B. (1976). Aggression catharsis: Experimental investigations and implications. In R. G. Geen & E. C. O'Neal (Eds.), *Perspectives on aggression*. New York: Academic Press.

Ross, L., Rodin, J., & Zimbardo, P. G. (1969). Toward an attribution therapy: The reduction of fear through induced cognitive-emotional misattribution. *Journal of Personality and Social Psychology, 12*, 279-288.

Rule, B. G. (1974). The hostile and instrumental functions of human aggression. In J. de Wit & W. W. Hartup (Eds.), *Determinants and origins of aggressive behavior*. The Hague: Mouton.

Rule, B. G., Dyck, R., & Nesdale, A. R. (1978). Arbitrariness of frustration: Inhibition or instigation effects on aggression. *European Journal of Social Psychology, 8*, 237-244.

Rule, B. G., Ferguson, T. J., & Nesdale, A. R. (1979). Emotional arousal, anger and aggression: The misattribution issue. In P. Pliner, K. Blankstein, & T. Spigel (Eds.), *Advances in the study of communication and affect*, pp. 119-137. New York: Plenum Press.

Rule, B. G., Haley, H., & McCormack, J. (1971). Anti-Semitism distraction and physical aggression. *Canadian Journal of Behavioral Science, 3*, 174-182.

Rule, B. G., & Hewitt, G. L. (1971). Effects of thwarting on cardiac response and physical aggression. *Journal of Personality and Social Psychology, 19*, 181-187.

Rule, B. G., & Leger, G. (1976). Pain cues and differing functions of aggression. *Canadian Journal of Behavioral Science, 8*, 213-222.

Rule, B. G., & Nesdale, A. R. (1974). Differing functions of aggression. *Journal of Personality, 42*, 467-481.

Rule, B. G., & Nesdale, A. R. (1976). Emotional arousal and aggressive behavior. *Psychological Bulletin, 83*, 851-863.

Rule, B. G., Nesdale, A. R., & Dyck, R. (1975). Objective self-awareness and differing standards of aggression. *Representative Research in Social Psychology, 6*, 82-88.

Rule, B. G., & Percival, E. (1971). The effects of frustration and attack on physical aggression. *Journal of Experimental Research in Personality, 5*, 111-118.

Schachter, J. (1957). Pain, fear, and anger in hypertensives and normotensives. *Psychosomatic Medicine, 19*, 17-29.

Schachter, S., & Singer, J. E. (1962). Cognitive, social and physiological determinants of emotional state. *Psychological Review, 69*, 379-399.

Scheier, M. F., Fenigstein, A., & Buss, A. H. (1974). Self-awareness and physical aggression. *Journal of Experimental Social Psychology, 10*, 264-273.

Scherer, K. R., Abeles, R. P., & Fischer, C. S. (1975). *Human aggression and conflict.* Englewood Cliffs, NJ: Prentice-Hall.

Schill, T. R. (1972). Aggression and blood pressure responses of high- and low-guilt subjects following frustration. *Journal of Consulting and Clinical Psychology, 38*, 461.

Schnore, M. M. (1959). Individual patterns of physiological activity as a function of task differences and degree of arousal. *Journal of Experimental Psychology, 58*, 117-128.

Shortell, J., Epstein, S., & Taylor, S. P. (1970). Instigation to aggression as a function of degree of defeat and the capacity for massive retaliation. *Journal of Personality, 38*, 313-338.

Tannenbaum, P. H., & Zillmann, D. (1975). Emotional arousal in the facilitation of aggression through communcation. In L. Berkowitz (Ed.), *Advances in experimental social psychology* (Vol. 8). New York: Academic Press.

Taylor, S., & Epstein, S. (1967). The measurement of autonomic arousal. *Psychosomatic Medicine, 29*, 514-525.

Taylor, S. P. (1967). Aggressive behavior and physiological arousal as a function of provocation and the tendency to inhibit aggression. *Journal of Personality, 35*, 297-310.

Turner, C. W., & Simons, L. S. (1974). Effects of subject sophistication and evaluation apprehension on aggressive responses to weapons. *Journal of Personality and Social Psychology, 30*, 341-348.

Vuchinich, R. E., & Tucker, J. A. (1980). A critique of cognitive labeling explanations of the emotional and behavioral effects of alcohol. *Addictive Behaviors, 5*, 179-188.

Vuchinich, R. E., Tucker, J. A., & Sobell, M. B. (1979). Alcohol, expectancy, cognitive labeling and mirth. *Journal of Abnormal Psychology, 88*, 641-651.

Wilson, G. T. (1977). Alcohol and human sexual behavior. *Behaviour Research and Therapy, 15*, 239-252.

Wilson, G. T. (1978). Booze, beliefs, and behavior: Cognitive processes in alcohol use and abuse. In P. E. Nathan, G. A. Marlatt, & T. Loberg (Eds.), *Alcoholism: New directions in behavioral research and treatment.* New York: Plenum Press.

Younger, J. C., & Doob, A. N. (1978). Attribution and aggression: The misattribution of anger. *Journal of Research in Personality, 12*, 164-197.

Zillmann, D. (1971). Excitation transfer in communication-mediated aggressive behavior. *Journal of Experimental Social Psychology, 7*, 419-434.

Zillmann, D. (1978). Attribution and misattribution of excitatory reactions. In J. H. Harvey, W. J. Ickes, & R. F. Kidd (Eds.), *New directions in attribution research* (Vol. 2). Hillsdale, NJ: Erlbaum.

Zillmann, D. (1979). *Hostility and aggression.* Hillsdale, NJ: Erlbaum.

Zillmann, D., & Bryant, J. (1974). Effect of residual excitation on the emotional response to provocation and delayed aggressive behavior. *Journal of Personality and Social Psychology, 30*, 782-791.

Zillmann, D., Bryant, J., Comisky, P. W., & Medoff, N. J. (1981). Excitation and hedonic valence in the effect of erotica on motivated intermale aggression. *European Journal of Social Psychology, 11*, 233-252.

Zillmann, D., Hoyt, J. L., & Day, K. D. (1974). Strength and duration of the effect of aggressive, violent, and erotic communication on subsequent aggressive behavior. *Communication Research, 1*, 286-306.

Zillmann, D., & Johnson, R. C. (1973). Motivated aggressiveness perpetuated by exposure to aggressive films and reduced by exposure to nonaggressive films. *Journal of Research in Personality, 7,* 261-276.

Zillmann, D., Johnson, R. C., & Day, K. D. (1974). Attribution of apparent arousal and proficiency of recovery from sympathetic activation affecting excitation transfer to aggressive behavior. *Journal of Experimental Social Psychology, 10,* 503-515.

Zillmann, D., Katcher, A. H., & Milavsky, B. (1972). Excitation transfer from physical exercise to subsequent aggressive behavior. *Journal of Experimental Social Psychology, 8,* 247-259.

Zillmann, D., & Sapolsky, B. S. (1977). What mediates the effect of mild erotica on annoyance and hostile behavior in males? *Journal of Personality and Social Psychology, 35,* 587-596.

Chapter 10
Social Processes, Biology, and Disease

Lawrence F. Van Egeren

Introduction

Sociophysiology is a field concerned with relating what happens socially *between* people to what happens physiologically *inside* them. Its roots lie in physiology, social science, human ethology, and medicine. Interactions in progress between social and biological systems are often monitored by means of noninvasive techniques. The goal is to study "traffic" on bridges connecting social and biological levels of organization without disturbing the flow.

The motive force behind clinical sociophysiology is the assumption that the human body is adapted to a limited range of social environments. When some limit of tolerance is exceeded socially, physiological changes may be set in motion that damage the body. What are these "tolerances" and "physiological changes?"

We can approach this question at many levels of analysis. We might begin with the fact that human society has experienced dazzling changes over the last 10,000 years while the human body has changed little if at all (Leakey, 1981). Can we safely ignore this fact? Is the human body equally well adapted to the social life of hunter-gatherers in the steamy jungles of Brazil and the social life of urbanites in the concrete canyons of New York City? We might ask the more specific question about whether biological costs and benefits are unequally distributed across the status rungs of a particular society. Still more specifically, we might ask about the response of person X to social stimulus Y in physiological parameter Z. Historically, the trend is to ask more and more detailed questions that are falsifiable in the laboratory. The danger here is that of losing sight of the "big picture." The difficulty is knowing how to *put together* the sociology, psychology, and physiology of a specific disease. Literature reviews (Barchas & Barchas, 1975; Henry & Stephens, 1977; Weiner, 1977; Weiner, Hofer, & Stunkard, 1981; Weisfeld, 1982; Wolf, 1981) make it plain that we are just now beginning to learn which questions to ask and how to ask them.

Suppose that we symbolize a clinically important social-biological linkage as $S-R_m-R_d$, where S = social situation, R_m = momentary physiological response (observed in the laboratory), and R_d = permanently dysfunctional or diseased response of the tissue or organ under study. Then we can ask three basic questions. Which social variables are relevant to the disease of interest, i.e., how do we choose "S"? What chain of causes links the social situation to the physiological parameter(s) monitored in the laboratory; how do we explain $S-R_m$? What processes transform reversible physiological changes observed in the laboratory into the irreversible pathology seen in real life; how do we account for R_m-R_d?

Each of the classes of variables listed above, as well as the functional pathways between them, are layered like an onion or like geologic strata of the Grand Canyon, so that a given social stimulus may trigger responses of very diverse origin. Some of the responses may be counterproductive and may possess no clear relationship to the "social nature" of the stimulus.

Illustrative Example

Imagine a smartly dressed executive in New York who is told by his superior that he cannot have a dataphone installed in his office. Sitting alone and staring at the telephone, which reminds him of the missing dataphone, gastric acid is stimulated in the executive's stomach which aggravates an old ulcer. How are we to understand this $S-R_m$ linkage (telephone-acid hypersecretion, let us say)? Will this help us explain the gastric erosion (ulceration, R_d)?

Suppose that you are asked to answer these questions and told that you may consult any "expert," living or dead, to help you. Whom would you consult, and on what grounds? To continue the fantasy, you begin by noting that copious secretion of gastric acid toward a telephone is "biologically absurd." Gastric secretions are physiologically adapted to food, not to telephones. Remembering that it also seems silly to salivate to bells, you summon Pavlov for advice. Pavlov reminds you that in conditioning experiments what makes the salivation response adaptive and allows us to rationally understand it as part of the animal's design is that the ringing of the bell forecasts the giving of food powder. The bell "warms up" the digestive system for the soon-to-arrive food powder, the natural object to which salivation is adapted. Look at the executive's conditioning history, Pavlov advises. There must be some telephone-food-acid secretion pathways ($S-S'-R_m$) there, however indirect and tortuous they may be. Find the "food powder," the missing link that will make everything fall into place.

Tortuous pathways remind you of Freud, to whom you turn next. Freud explains that the telephone is merely incidental, a minor prop on a broader stage. It is acting here simply as a tag for a large class of psychologically important objects, namely, "rejecting people." The executive is unconsciously trying to recover a lost, unsupportive milk-giving mother by secreting gastric acid "as if" the milk and the mother are still actually present. The body is trying to deny the rejection by the mother and her surrogate, the boss. Look for the missing links in a telephone–boss–mother–food–acid secretion chain ($S-S'''-S''-S'-R_m$) in the executive's life, he advises.

You consult Franz Alexander (1950), the intellectual father of modern psychosomatic medicine. He agrees with Freud's explanation, as far as it goes, but adds that it does not go far enough. It especially does not bridge the gap between gastric secretion and ulceration, R_m and R_d. Not all hypersecreters develop ulcers and not all people with ulcers are hypersecreters (Weiner, 1977). Perhaps there is some missing genetic factor "X" operating here, he notes.

The telephone-boss $(S-S''')$ link puzzles you. What is so important about possessing a dataphone, of which the telephone is merely a reminder? You decide to consult a social psychologist who is familiar with the corporate organization. She explains that the dataphone is a key status marker in this particular company. Middle-level executives on the way "up" have a dataphone, even when access to corporate information files is unnecessary, and executives who are stagnant or on the way "down" do not have one. What rather casually has been labeled "S" in the formula, the telephone, is a door that opens onto an important world outside the body, the corporation. The corporation, in turn, opens onto something larger still, society itself. "S" is really part of a complex social system which has its own structure, dynamics, and biological significance. Specifically, the telephone-dataphone S is linked to a status system S'''', of which the executive and his boss are parts.

We now have the cumbersome formula $S-S''''-S'''-S''-S'-R_m-X-R_d$ (telephone- status-boss-mother-food-hypersecretion-genotype-ulcer), a tangled jungle of unknown but potentially important relationships. Which ones will stand up to laboratory experimentation? In what forms will they be amenable to falsifiable tests? Where is the "pay dirt" likely to be?

Our problem has grown more complicated, seemingly calling for truly heroic advice, say from a Nobel Laureate. So you consult with Konrad Lorenz next, specifically on the possible biological significance of S'''', social status. Lorenz (1966) explains that, at least in animal communities, status or "peck order" is a very important biosocial organizer. It is a ranking of animals' access to biological goods (food, mates, nesting sites; Morse, 1980). Status is a fundamental property of the animal's lifeline to an ecological niche, a survival station which makes life itself possible. The higher the status the better the niche quality and, often, the greater the buffering from natural selection pressures (physical and biological "stresses"). Loss of status is biologically threatening for the same basic reason that loss of limb is threatening; it reduces biological fitness. Animals do not suffer loss of status quietly, but are aroused to action, either bluffing or fighting to stay on top (Wilson, 1975). Lorenz argues that a significant part of the linkage between status loss and physiological response $(S''''-R_m)$ is guided by code located in the animals' genes and innate brain "wiring." Wilson (1975, 1978) advises you that the response of humans to status loss, like the response of lower animals, has important genetic, phylogenetically archaic, origins. Gould (1977a) disagrees, a point to which we will return.

Perhaps some genetic factor Y is wedged between S and R_m, as Lorenz and Wilson suggest, so that our formula becomes telephone-status-boss-mother-food-genotype-hypersecretion-genotype-ulcer $(S-S''''-S'''-S''-S'-Y-R_m-X-R_d)$. It may turn out that factor Y, if it exists, does not influence gastric secretions, but does influence some other response R_m' involved in gastric ulceration. Whether ulcers develop depends in part on the barrier or "defense" that gastrointestinal tissues erect between themselves and the highly acidic contents of the gut. The barrier includes alkaline mucous secretions and frequent replacement of cells that are in contact with the acidic contents (Vander, Sherman, & Luciano, 1980). Physiological defenses (cell turnover, alkaline secretions, etc.) as well as challenges (hypersecretion of acid, etc.), the so-called "soil" as well as the "seed" of disease, must be considered in ulcer formation. Two additional facts encourage us to follow this line of reasoning for hypothetical factor Y. First, as will be reviewed later, subordinate animals who are defeated by dominant animals show prolonged elevation of adrenocortical hormones (Bronson & Desjardins, 1971; Eleftheriou & Scott, 1971), as do emotionally depressed or "defeated" human beings (Carroll, 1976). Second adrenocortical hormones inhibit cell division, and therefore the rate of cell replacement, in many tissues (Bullough, 1965).

The Expanding Circle

Someone trying to unravel a social-biological relationship is often confronted with a situation that looks very much like salivating to a bell. He or she may possess observations on S, R_m, and R_d and is searching for the many possible "food powders," the missing links (S ', S '', etc.) that will make everything fall into place and finally make sociobiological "sense." What are the key social, psychological, and physiological parameters of $S-R_m-R_d$? What important unconditional adaptations to social events were formed during the phylogeny of *Homo sapiens*? How did responses to social conditions radiate outward from these unconditional response epicenters during the ontogeny of the individual? That is, what is the individual's social-biological conditioning history?

Findings in clinical sociophysiology do not exist in a vacuum. They are integral pieces in the larger puzzle of human adaptation. Social stress used to be a "default" explanation for illnesses that could not yet be explained by faulty genes, poor nutrition, or known microorganisms and toxins. It is now becoming more widely appreciated that these broad classes of causes interact deeply (McKeown, 1979). In the illustrative example above we barely scratched the surface of the landscape, or more accurately the modern "cityscape," upon which problems in clinical sociophysiology are strewn. Even so, it was necessary to constantly expand the circle enclosing psychosocial and physiological factors that are potentially relevant to understanding the etiology of the disease.

Tracking leads in the sociophysiological literature nowadays is like picking up the beginning of a thread whose end is never in sight. The thread winds through environmental, neural, hormonal, cellular, and chemical layers and compartments of an integrated whole. The twistings and turnings have little respect for the boundaries of professional disciplines and dichotomies like biological-social, body-environment, and intracellular-extracellular.

Closing the Circle

We need a vantage point, a way to limit the expanding circle of potential causal influences. We begin with the fact that sociophysiology is not concerned with society or the body per se. Its object of study is their interaction, the no-man's land *between* them. In the most general sense, its interests point toward the interlevel dynamics of hierarchic living systems (Miller, 1978; Pattee, 1973).

The neurologist Jackson (1884/1958) postulated that new structures or levels of organization are integrated into organic systems by suppressing or damping down already existing structures. The theme of "competitive exclusion," or organic growth by "addition and suppression," dominated the thinking of Marx, Freud, and Darwin (see discussions by Heilbroner, 1980, on Marx; Sulloway, 1979, on Freud; and Mayr, 1982, on Darwin). Some inescapable mechanism seemed to fatefully pitch upper class against lower class, higher functions of the body (reason) against lower functions (instincts), and the "fittest" animals against the less fit, and in so doing set the fundamental trajectories of social, psychological, and biological change, respectively. In the pitched battle for limited resources, which Darwin and Marx clearly saw was the crux of the problem, the "exploited" lower classes, "repressed" feelings, and "dominated" animals had to struggle to escape annihilation. This very process of struggle was the means of perfecting society, mental life, and organisms. It was the motor behind their evolution to higher states. Of course, there were casualties along the way.

This perspective on interlevel dynamics (interactions between upper and lower strata of society, the body, and animal communities) casts the problem into an economic or resource budget form. The stage upon which the drama unfolds in the "struggle for life" is the competition for and distribution of limited resources. In modern parlance, the basic formative influence in life is seen as "ecological" in nature.

There are many modern variations of this theme. The outlook in many branches of biology has expanded from interests in what might be called, in the words of Cannon (1929), "biological wisdom" (how the body works as an information handling machine; how information is stored in genes, transferred to proteins, steers chemical reactions, etc.; Monod, 1971) to what might be called "biological politics" (the struggle for the *control* of information and energy). Studies of biological politics concern power and which interests will be served when there are conflicts of interest. They include explorations of what controls the balance between (a) "selfish" interests of individual cells and the larger interests of the body as a whole (Bullough, 1965; Yabrov, 1980), (b) normal cells and tumorigenic cells for control of cell cycles (Potter, 1980; Trosko & Chang, 1980), (c) the community of microorganisms present in the body and the host body itself (Axelrod & Hamilton, 1981), and (d) new (neocortical) and old (limbic) structures of the human brain, imbalances of which may cause psychopathology (MacLean, 1970) and sociopathology (Koestler, 1978).

Budget "Comptrollers"

A kernel idea of modern ecology is that life is a complicated "balancing act." Like a house of cards, everything alive leans into everything else alive, and health and life itself depends on the maintenance of a delicate balance (Dubos, 1965; Ehrlich, Ehrlich, & Holdren, 1977). Elements within and between various levels of organization must remain harmonious and well-balanced.

When a social event enters the body it releases activity in the hypothalamic-pituitary-adrenal, or neuroendocrine, system (Ader, 1981; Mason, 1975). The hypothalamus and the adrenal glands are extraordinarily complex organs. They appear to function as the body's main energy budget "comptrollers" or "bookkeepers." They are crossroads of homeostatic regulation primarily responsible for maintaining balance in the face of competing claims for investment of limited energy in essential biological functions or "accounts," such as feeding (Teitelbaum, 1967), reproduction (Goldman, 1974), growth (Bullough, 1965), heat production (Satinoff, 1974), maintenance of status position (Eleftheriou & Scott, 1971), and defense against microorganisms (Ader, 1981; Riley, 1981). By intercellular control of cell division and cell function the hypothalamic-pituitary-adrenal axis can fine tune bodily structure and function to the body's epigenetic life-cycle program and to the resource environment, including the social environment, to which the body's internal program must be adapted. By the operation of this system the surrounding world may deposit the "seed" and prepare the "soil" for health and disease. The biological budget perspective will guide our discussion.

Levels of Organization

When examining the complex literature on clinical aspects of social-biological interactions, certain patterns of biological organization are helpful to hold in mind as mental moorings. These perspectives on intracellular, extracellular, and social functioning aid in clarifying some stress effects that possess no obvious adaptive value.

Intracellular Organization

It now appears that cells have a small number of integrated, gene-controlled basic programs of protein synthesis. Bullough (1965) reviews extensive evidence identifying three such programs: one for cell maintenance (e.g., for making enzymes controlling the Krebs cycle), a second for cell division (for proteins controlling mitosis), and a third for specialized proteins that are specific to cell type but not essential to either maintenance or division of the cell (e.g., genetic programs for synthesis of myosin and other proteins involved in muscle contraction). Programs "2" and "3" are controllable from outside the cell by hormones, neurotransmitters, and mitotic stimulating and inhibiting agents.

Bullough (1965) reviews data showing that cells may either "function" or "divide" but cannot do both at once, i.e., gene programs "2" and "3" are competitively exclusive. Epinephrine appears to play a key role in causing cells to switch from one program to the other by combining with tissue-specific chemicals called "chalones." When the local concentration of the epinephrine-chalone complex is high, cells in the area do not divide. It appears that when the body is under stress and in a state of emergency alert, adrenal hormones signal many cells to perform their tissue-specific functions instead of entering a mitotic cycle. The immediate danger calls for action by already existing cells, not the addition of new cells to the body. In "budget" terminology, the body shifts calories from growth and repair accounts to work accounts of the energy budget. When the period of stress has passed and is followed by rest or sleep, the normal process of cell renewal continues (Bullough, 1965).

Cell-to-Cell Organization

A cell's biggest *internal* jobs are maintaining self and dividing whenever the opportunity permits (programs "1" and "2"). Its biggest *external* jobs are responding to the demands of other cells and telling other cells what to do (program "3"). Yabrov (1980) argues that inadequate functioning and disease often arise from some failure to carry out this *dual* (internal-external) commitment of cells, and health rests on a proper balance between the needs of individual cells and the needs of the organism as a whole. The nervous, endocrine, and immune systems are the three major systems commanding, coordinating, and integrating program "3" of cells throughout the body; they also may inhibit program "2" (Bullough, 1965; Iacobelli, King, Lindner, & Lippman, 1980).

Cell-to-cell communication by means of hormones, including stress-released hormones, appears to be deeply implicated in immune responses (Riley, 1981) and tissue growth control (Yotti, Chang, & Trosko, 1979). Such communication is thought to provide crucial regulatory functions in the two-stage theory of tumorigenesis, proposed originally by Berenblum (1941) and confirmed by extensive subsequent research (Potter, 1980; Trosko & Chang, 1978). Tumor development appears often to involve "initiation" of a mutant cell, followed by the clonal expansion of the initiated cell by a variety of agents which inhibit intercellular communication (Potter, 1980; Trosko & Chang, 1980; Yotti, Chang, & Trosko, 1979). Hypotheses and evidence presented by Trosko and Chang (1980) suggest that the two-stage theory of tumorigenesis may help explain a wide variety of degenerative diseases in which stress is also thought to be implicated. They speculate that atherosclerosis, cancer, and diabetes develop by means of similar cellular dynamics involving initiation and promotion of mutant cells in coronary arteries (yielding atherosclerosis), the pancreas (yielding diabetes), and other bodily tissues (yielding cancer).

Social disturbances of intercellular communication may account for some aspects of "failure to thrive" syndromes in humans and animals characterized by severely retarded growth. Emotional disturbances and abnormal home environments appear to be a central feature of "deprivation dwarfism" in children. When the children are removed from the home and placed in a socially enriched hospital environment, a condition of hypopituitarism with subnormal production of adrenocorticotropic and growth hormones is reversed and the children often show dramatic catch-up growth spurts without the aid of chemical intervention (Gardner, 1972; Powell, Hopwood, & Barratt, 1973). Social variables also affect the growth rates of nonhuman animals (Butler, Suskind, & Schanberg, 1978). Crowding in several animal species results in stunted growth (Christian, 1971).

Organism-to-Microorganism Organization

The human body abounds with microbes living inside it or on its surface. Like landlord and tenant, the relationship between symbiont and body host is often open to negotiation, which sometimes fails. The nature of the process of negotiation between normal body cells and foreign (microbial, tumorigenic) cells appears to hold many keys to understanding infectious and neoplastic diseases (Potter, 1980). Insofar as social condition and emotions tip the bodily balance toward infection or cancer, they must do so by somehow affecting the biological systems that regulate transactions between normal and foreign cells that together form what in effect is a complex "social colony."

Thomas (1974) and Selye (1976) draw attention to two unsolved puzzles. Why does any microorganism ever become pathogenic? Why do stress responses impair the body's immunological control, thus making the stress-compromised body less able to defend itself against cancer cells and infectious agents (Riley, 1981; Selye, 1976)? Microbial pathogenesis and stress-induced immunosuppression are paradoxical because they seem to be "suicidal." What evolutionary conditions would favor selection of microbes which kill their host and in so doing destroy their living quarters, their food supply, and themselves? What conditions favor selection of a mammalian body which, when it is under the siege of environmental stresses (say, food shortages, attack by enemies), *lowers* its resistance to microbes and tumorigenic cells via adrenocortical activation and lysis of lymphocytes and thymocytes (Riley, 1981)? These look like evolutionary paths to extinction instead of survival. Thomas and Selye explain these two cases of apparent self-destruction by saying simply that they are not adaptations, but rather mistakes, blunders, and limitations in ordinarily marvelous but delicate negotiations between microbes and man over biological turf.

Extensions of evolutionary theory by Hamilton (1964) and Trivers (1971) and more recently by Axelrod and Hamilton (1981) may shed light on the puzzles presented above. They are especially interesting because they suggest how (a) self-destructive survival strategies may evolve, (b) interlevel linkages (e.g., social-cellular) may evolve, and (c) many diseases function as something "social" in nature and result from a defection from a previously cooperative exchange of benefits between cell-cell, symbiont-host, and organism-organism interactants.

These theoretical developments were needed to deal with a crisis in evolutionary theory caused by the existence of altruistic behavior in many social animals. Altruism is defined in biology as behavior benefiting others at some cost in reproductive fitness to oneself. Altruism poses problems for Darwinian evolutionary theory because it seems to contradict the fundamental premise that organisms function so as to maximize their *own* reproductive fitness, not someone else's.

Evolutionary theory was rescued from the embarrassment of social cooperation based on self-sacrifice from two directions, Hamilton's (1964) genetical kinship theory and Triver's (1971) reciprocal altruism theory. Kinship theory states that under certain conditions it pays off, biologically, to sacrifice self for kin ("blood relatives"). What is maximally reproduced by the biologically fittest is not bodies but copies of their genes. Since copies of some of one's genes exist in one's own generation in the bodies of kin, behaving so as to benefit kin at a cost to one's self (i.e., behaving altruistically) may make evolutionary "sense," i.e., maximize reproductive fitness. On the grounds of this theory, animals, including man, should have a natural (gene-coded) leaning toward behaving altruistically as far into the social community as their genes are spread, but no farther. The advice here is, "Be good to family."

The reciprocation theory of Trivers extends the biological basis of social cooperation to nonrelatives, on the basis of exchange of benefits, i.e., "reciprocated" altruism. Animals, it is assumed, can form and keep social contracts. They have woven into their genes social exchange strategies, especially the variant of the Golden Rule known as the tit-for-tat strategy: Do unto others as they have done unto you. The advice here is, "Be good to others who are good to you." It is germane to the problem of disease, and its possible social causation, that Trivers' model and supporting examples suggest that reciprocal altruism (exchange of benefits by, say, host and microorganism) is favored by a high probability of continued association, which is dependent upon the stability of their relationship and the amount of time they have left to live.

A surprising implication of the kinship and reciprocation theories is that animals may be designed, as an evolved strategy, to *self-destruct*, on the important condition that the death will sufficiently benefit kin. By mathematical modeling and computer simulation Axelrod and Hamilton (1981) have explored this implication and its possible significance for understanding disease processes. The probability of future beneficial interactions is a central parameter of the Axelrod–Hamilton model. Whatever disrupts a biological association or compromises survivorship of one of the partners may cause the other partner to switch from cooperation to exploitation, with possibly lethal consequences. Axelrod and Hamilton (1981) give examples of symbionts becoming parasitic following a change in host-symbiont relationship, and tumors (e.g., Burkitt's lymphoma) becoming malignant when the body contracts infection (malaria). Examples can be given from other sources (see reviews by Ader, 1981; Finch, 1976; Riley, 1981) which support the authors' contention that when the body becomes enfeebled or distressed, whether the cause is social or nonsocial, bacterial and viral infections and tumorigenesis are often accelerated.

The Axelrod–Hamilton model predicts that as survivorship indicators in the body drop, foreign cells living in the body will increasingly attack normal cells because the likelihood of future benefits to the symbionts of living cooperatively is decreasing. By actively eliminating a nonviable resource-using body, the body's and the microbes' more viable kin may benefit.

The biology of aging is of interest here because many intracellular and extracellular chemicals change systematically with age (see Eisdorfer & Raskind, 1975; Finch, 1976; Strehler, 1972) and therefore may act as indices of survivorship. Adrenal cortisol and hypothalamic gonadotropin releasing factors drop, pituitary gonadotropins approach castrate levels in senescence, and brain monoamine (norepinephrine, dopamine, serotonin) concentrations are reduced (Finch, 1976). Finch holds that the brain catecholamines may function as a pacemaker of cellular aging. Many of the changes in chemical (neurotransmitter, hormonal) traffic between cells associated with aging are also associated with stress. Years ago Selye (1956) noted that stress effects are similar to premature aging. By "reading" chemical concentrations linked to aging and stress, along with signs of current systemic disease, host and symbionts may estimate the survivorship of the body. Single-chromosome bacteria reading chemical concentrations to make survival estimates may seem far-fetched. Bacteria read chemical concentrations to make other conditional decisions on protein synthesis (Jacob, 1966) and there is no inherent reason why some of these chemicals should not be related to survival of the body.

What is important to us is that whether negotiations going on inside the body become problematic, and the body as a social colony of cells (foreign and domestic) begins to "self-destruct," depends in part on conditions *outside* the body. Some of these conditions may be social. The Axelrod–Hamilton model of biological negotiations may help us conceptualize linkages between events on social and cellular levels in the following way. What is characteristic of a human way of life (i.e., species-specific survival strategies of *Homo sapiens*) is an intensely social cooperative economy (Leakey, 1981; Lovejoy, 1981) which (a) depends on a stable social structure that is maintained by pair-bonding (parent-offspring and adult-adult), dominance-submission (status, authority) and obligation (kinship, contractual) behavioral systems which (b) if destabilized, reduces survivorship (this is true of impairment of mutualistic behavioral strategies of any social species; Morse, 1980; Wilson, 1975) which (c) shifts chemical-cellular indices of survivorship (neurotransmitters and hormones correlated with stress and aging) downward which (d) changes cell-cell and host-symbiont negotiations in the direction of less cooperation and greater microbial infectivity and tumorigenicity which (e) tips the body away from health and toward disease either by directly causing disease or by preparing the cellular environment for disease later in life. There are clearly many "ifs" and "buts" here, but they may be preferable to the glaring holes in our current understanding.

Organism-to-Environment Organization

One of the puzzling outcomes of recent neurobiological research is the evidence of deep involvement of the brain in bodily processes that are usually assumed to be "autonomous," e.g., microbial defense and control of body weight and size at maturity (see extensive reviews in Ader, 1981, and Weiner, Hofer, & Stunkard, 1981). As noted earlier, the hypothalamus is a key structure. Hypothalamic lesions may alter the body's immune response to bacteria, viruses, tissue grafts, and implanted tumors (Fox, 1981; Plaut & Friedman, 1981; Stein, Keller, & Schleifer, (1981). They may either strengthen or weaken these responses, depending on the site of the lesion, and modify the body's susceptibility to a variety of illnesses (infections, neoplasia, allergic hypersensitivities, and autoimmune diseases).

Why does the brain meddle so deeply in basic bodily functions like immunity and growth control? Why not handle these problems exclusively through gene-coded information? The field biology of "life-history tactics" (Stearns, (1976) and behavioral ecology (Morse, 1980) may provide some answers. These studies remind us that the energy needed by the body exists outside it in the environment and that there is often intense competition for it. The brain needs to be sensitive to fluctuating resource conditions and to help somatic tissues make decisions about growth, etc., that are appropriate for those conditions. What are the optimal strategies of growth (fast or slow?), reproduction (many or few offspring?), micro-defense (combative or cooperative relations with microbes?), behavior (increased foraging or energy conservation when food is scarce?), and social organization (food-sharing or no food-sharing, tight or loose social ranking?) to best exploit resources in the environment? How should the tactics change at different stages of the life cycle or as population density increases?

A growing literature indicates that the brain helps tailor the body to its resource environment by downstsream influences on cell division and cell function. Hypothalamic-pituitary-adrenal regulation of the production of sex cells, immune cells, and somatic cells may alter the rate and intensity at which the body reproduces (Christian, 1950, 1975), grows (Bullough, 1965; Leibowitz, 1974), repairs damaged tissue (Bullough, 1961; King, 1962), ages (Finch, 1976), and defends against microorganisms (Riley, 1981; Stein, Keller, & Schleifer, 1981). The superimposi-tion of neuroendocrine controls onto the complex regulation of cell mitosis and meiosis allows the addition of new cells to the body, and new bodies to the popula-tion, to be finely adapted to external resource conditions. Adjusting energy con-sumption (tissue volume and function) to energy supply (food volume) is a fun-damental energy budget problem and an essential condition of life (Calow, 1978).

Past neuroendocrine stress research has focused on cell function (e.g., Mason, 1975) rather than on cell birth and cell death. The latter may be critical for understanding how the environment, flowing into body cells on the neurohumoral courier system, prepares the cellular "soil" of health and disease.

Stress in natural populations, such as human ancestral populations, is often linked to food shortages and predator pressures (Dobzhansky, 1962; Dubos, 1965; Morse, 1980) and therefore tends to be population density dependent. For years Christian (1950, 1975) has gathered evidence on how animals control their own population numbers. The hypothalamus and the adrenal gland are deeply implicated. As the population density of many mammals rises, so does the level of fighting and the secretion of adrenal corticoid and androgen hormones. Gonadotropin, leutinizing, and follicle stimulating hormone levels drop, as well as the weight of seminal vesicles, especially in subordinate animals (Bronson & Marsden, 1973). Crowding may cause complete cessation of reproduction, interrupted pregnancies, lower fetal weights, and slower postnatal growth (see Christian, 1975, for details).

Internal mechanisms of the body that respond to density-dependent stress (crowding) by lowering birthrates and raising deathrates should be self-limiting and should improve the biological fitness of the population. The sequence is expected to be (a) population grows, (b) density-dependent stress increases, (c) hypothalamic-pituitary-adrenal and sympathetic-adrenal axes become more active, (d) production of sex cells, immune cells, and replacement cells for damaged tissues is adrenal-inhibited, (e) mortality rises and natality falls, (f) population shrinks, (g) stress and stress-induced adrenal hormone levels drop, and (h) normal reproduction, immun-ity, and healing are restored. The population has a double gain in fitness because it is better tailored to available resources and it has lost animals that were most suscep-tible to damage and infection. The evolutionary advantages of such cycles would favor genetic retention of the hypothalamic-adrenal controls involved.

Organism-to-Organism Organization

We have now arrived at the level of adaptive organization toward which we were pointed from the start, the social level. Most animals live in groups because it pays off biologically to do so (Allee, 1943; Kropotkin, 1903). The struggle for life is a group matter, involving mutual support for food-getting, rearing of the young, and defense against enemies. The basic behavioral strategies and life-history tactics of survival in social species are themselves deeply social (Morse, 1980; Wilson, 1975).

Social behavior is an "adaptive zone," in Simpson's (1944) terminology. It is the topmost layer in the hierarchic tree of characteristic relationships between the environment and social organisms. It draws its "biological wisdom" primarily from two of the three depositories of information (genetical, neural, extrasomal) which guide our way of life, the neural (information stored in the unusually large brain of *Homo sapiens*) and the extrasomal (information deposited outside the body in books, blueprints, computer files, etc.). It is what makes our form of adaptation human instead of rodentlike or apelike.

The social zone of adaptation interacts with other adaptive zones (cellular, morphological, etc.) and is often wedged between lower zones and the resource environment. We have multilayered adaptations or solutions to basic biological problems. For example, our way of maintaining body calories is the supermarket, a *social* (and technological) adaptation or solution. Failing that, we can forage for natural flora and fauna, which is a *behavioral* solution used by other animals. Failing that, we can metabolize body fat and structural proteins for energy, a *physiological* solution. Failing that, we will die. To control body temperature, we have hierarchically ordered social (e.g., houses, clothing), behavioral (seek sunlight, natural cover), and physiological (conserve heat by constricting blood vessels in skin, produce heat by increasing metabolic rate) adaptations. So too, multilayered adaptations have developed for defending ourselves against microorganisms (socially building sewage systems and antibiotic drugs, behaviorally washing hands and avoiding infected people, and physiologically mobilizing immunological responses of the body) and against crowding (socially designing "defensive" housing and landscaping, behaviorally withdrawing or acting nasty to repel other people, and perhaps physiologically producing adrenocortical hormones which elevate deathrates and thin out a crowded population; Christian, 1975; Finch, 1976).

Faced with difficult problems of living, we play from strength. The strength of *Homo sapiens* is to think, to cooperate, and to use tools (Leakey, 1981; Washburn & Moore, 1974). Given a choice, we solve problems by mental, social, and technological means. Other animals do not possess these means to the degree we do. Consequently, generalizing from them to us needs to be guided by understanding of how mental-social-technological adaptations work *biologically*. Because we have tools in our survival kit other animals do not have, what are problems for them may not be problems for us, and vice versa. This will be illustrated for the problem of crowding later. On the other hand, once our humanity, our species' diagnostic adaptations, have been breached or stripped away, we revert to solutions to biological problems which we share with other animals and our distant ancestors. These "default" adaptations may seem strange and maladaptive because they are solutions to ancient problems (too little food, too many predators, harsh weather) rather than to modern problems (unemployment notices, uncontrollable inflation, etc.). Socially stimulated gastric changes may tell us simply that food shortages were a major stress in *past* evolutionary environments. The ghosts that haunt us today may be very different from those that haunted our forefathers and foremothers and molded our lower level stress response equipment. But the "biological remembrance" of things past, as Dubos (1968) puts it, which is woven into our lower level "biological wisdom," may bring them back to life when higher level defenses fail. When push meets shove, and shove crumbles, we may behave like simpler animals after all.

On the social level the problems of adaptation group together to form broad classes of behavior. Among them we shall distinguish social bonding, social ranking, and social obligation behavioral systems. They represent social subsystems of increasing size and complexity. Many important biological effects, and psychosomatic phenomena, tend to cluster at these three major strata of social organization. These behavioral systems are defined as follows.

Social Bonds: Social behaviors promoting physical proximity; attachment behaviors (smiling, caressing, etc.); attractive social signals (cries of alarm, affectional gestures, etc.) signaling interest in contact.

Social Ranks: Social behaviors showing asymmetry in exchanges and access to biological goods (dominance and submission); repulsive social signals (threats, bluffs, rejections, aggression, etc.) signaling interest in separation.

Social Obligations: Symbols and behaviors creating or signaling indebtedness and claims on future behavior; reciprocation behaviors (Trivers); kinship systems; formal contracts; duties and restrictions imposed by attachments to powerful priests (religion), rulers (citizenship), and merchants (economic commitments).

Social bonds. Severe disruption or distortion of social bonds has serious physiological consequences. In view of the biological benefits of social living it would be surprising if this were not the case. In general, higher disease rates and mortality follow the rupture of social bonds, and lower disease rates and mortality accompany intact bonds (major reviews are those of Cobb, 1976; Lynch, 1977; Wolf, 1981, for human literature, and Ader, 1975; Henry & Stephens, 1977; Hofer, 1981; Levine, 1974, for animal literature).

Just as much may be learned about a gland of secretion by removing it from the body or injecting its products into the body, much may be learned about bond attachments by interrupting or removing them (social isolation studies) or adding stimuli by handling, etc., to the animal's normal sensory "diet" (extra stimulation studies). Hofer (1981) summarizes the effects of separating newborn rodents from the mother on the newborn's behavior (initial agitation and attempts to reestablish contact, followed by later apathy, loss of appetite, and sleep disturbances), emotional responses (initial separation distress followed by later depression-like responses), autonomic activity (initial increase and later decrease in cardiac and respiratory rates), hormone levels (drop in growth hormone), and brain chemistry (reduced brain ornithine decarboxylase, a critical enzyme in protein synthesis, and temperature-dependent changes in brain catecholamines). The broad pattern of response is similar in rodents, kittens, dogs, primates, and humans (Bowlby, 1973; Hofer, 1981).

A classic finding in this area is that manipulation of the mother-infant bond affects the infant's adrenal cortical response to stress at an adult age. Social isolation of the neonate is associated with larger responses later in life and extra stimulation (handling) with smaller responses (Ader, 1975; Levine, 1974). The emotionality of the animal's response to stress tends to be proportional to its adrenocortical response. Elevated adrenocortical activity has been associated with higher infectious and neoplastic disease rates (Riley, 1981), emotional depression in humans (Carroll, 1976) and animals (Henry & Meehan, 1981), and subordination in social status systems (Chamove & Bowman, 1978; Henry & Meehan, 1981; Lloyd, 1975). Thus, subnormal parenting and lack of social stimulation at early stages of growth may predispose the offspring to adrenal-mediated disease, emotional depression, and retreat from dominance challenges later in life.

Some illnesses that follow the rupture of social bonds in humans may not be adrenal-mediated. Bartrup, Lazarus, Luckhurst, Kiloh, and Penny (1977) compared recently bereaved adults with controls and found a subnormal T cell lymphocyte response to injection of a mitogen (an antigen that normally induces lymphocytes to multiply) in the patients but no difference between patients and controls in adrenal cortisol level. The implication is that the bodies of the grief-stricken patients failed to respond normally to antigen challenges, thus increasing their susceptibility to infection, but this failure was not caused by elevated cortisol production.

Montagu (1981) describes an interesting way in which intact relationships may be protective during periods of distress. The mucous membrane of the nose normally protects the body from airborne bacterial assaults because it is rich in lysozymes which kill bacteria. During distress the nasal membrane tends to dry out, weakening its bacteriocidal action. Human weeping, which is often contagious and a sympathy response to tragedy, may restore its effectiveness. Human tears which are rich in lysozymes bathe and humidify the nasal mucosa during weeping, allowing fewer bacteria to enter the body at a time when its immunological defenses may be adrenal-suppressed. Benefits such as this may have favored the evolution of socially released crying reflexes.

The mammalian mother provides her newborn with a physical environment (body heat), a biological environment (milk, transferred immunity), and a social environment (caretaking behavior) which profoundly influence the newborn's energy budget. This is especially so in (altricial) species in which offspring are born relatively underdeveloped and helpless, possess unstable homeostatic controls during early stages of growth, and develop slowly, thus exposing the young to parental influence during a prolonged period of biological vulnerability. Thus, the mother may affect the infant's growth and development through physical, biological, and/or behavioral channels embedded in the total environment she provides. Hofer (1981) finds that maternal influences on the neonate often act through the body heat (physical input) and nutrition (biological input) the mother supplies. Duke University biochemists have shown that maternal handling of rodent pups stimulates a critical enzyme involved in protein synthesis, ornithine decarboxylase (ODC) (Butler, Suskind, & Schanberg, 1978; Kuhn, Butler, & Schanberg, 1978). The activity of this enzyme was depressed by 50% in heart and brain tissues during rapid periods of growth in unhandled neonates. Nicely executed controls demonstrated that the critical independent variable was the lack of maternal behavior (licking, retrieval to the nest, etc.) and not the lack of nourishment and warmth the mother's body provides. This impressive work shows how the early social environment may simultaneously modify the maturation of the body, perhaps preparing the "soil" for future disease, and the neonates' social development (which is likely to be affected by subnormal mothering), thus forging early links for later correlations between social behavior and disease.

Much about the environment confronting the newborn is uncertain. What *is* certain is that the newborn will have a mother. The mother is a "buffer zone" between the neonate and the external world. Her parenting behavior expresses one of the accounts of her energy budget, which in turn shadows resource conditions (Calow, 1978; Morse, 1980). Under most circumstances, we can assume that the mother's own survival has a higher priority than survival of her offspring, at least in nonhuman species (see Trivers, 1974, for discussion of parental investment strategies). Then, parenting behavior may give the newborn body information about energy supply and demand in its surroundings. Most importantly, it may indicate how close to the edge of survival the mother is living, on the basis of the "surplus" energy she has available for investment in offspring. It is conceivable that there has been some genetic retention of the ability of the neonatal body to use mother-supplied behavioral information about the world to form its life-history tactics, i.e., to make decisions about how big and how fast to grow, how early to reproduce, etc. The neonatal redirection of body calories from growth to microdefense or the provision of body heat, etc., when parenting is inadequate may reflect the operation of these decisions. Hormonal changes induced in the infant's body by the mother's behavior may in part replace during the postnatal period the developmental direction that was imposed on the fetus by the mother's own blood-borne hormones during pregnancy.

Social rank. While all members of a group benefit from group living, they do not benefit equally, a fact that agonized Karl Marx. The fact is expressed in animal colonies as a ranking of animals into a "peck order." Low ranking animals have less access to biological goods (food, mates, superior habitats) (Allee, 1943; Wilson, 1975). Animal dominance systems have some resemblance to social power stratification in human societies.

Social ranking may affect health through rank-dependence of nutrition (McKeown, 1979). Lower ranking group members may also experience more stress and be less able biologically to adapt to it. In animal societies at least, the dominance system performs important stabilizing and regulating biological functions (Hinde, 1974; Wilson, 1975). Its own stability, and peace and tranquility in the social community, depends on the willingness of the "poor" (low ranking members) to stay in their place. Because the poor are not always willing to accept their lot, there are challenges to the established "peck order." Turmoil caused by social inequality and social mobility may be a major source of stress in animal and human communities (Henry & Stephens, 1977). Evidence from animal studies indicates that the stress-induced damage caused by status challenges disproportionately harms low ranking members.

Dominance-submission tests affect dominant and subordinate animals differently for two reasons. First, they are different physiologically prior to the test, as subordinate animals tend to have greater output of adrenal corticosterone than dominant animals (Chamove & Bowman, 1978; Lloyd, 1975). Second, subordinates are usually defeated by dominants, and the physiological consequences of triumph and defeat are quite different (Eleftheriou & Scott, 1971). Repeated defeats or chronic subordination may significantly affect hormone levels, protein synthesis, and maturation of the brain. For example, defeated mice show prolonged elevations of adrenal corticosterone and depressed brain RNA (Bronson & Desjardins, 1971). The mere threat of defeat (visual presence of a trained fighter mouse) may produce the effects in previously defeated mice.

For years Henry and co-workers have systematically studied the effects of social breakdown on communities of rodents (Henry & Stephens, 1977). They have created ingenious rodent "urban parks" by connecting home cages with plastic tubing feeding into a central shared space for feeding and watering. By sewing magnets into the animals and stationing magnetic field transducers on the tubing passageways they are able to monitor the movements of animals into and out of all compartments, as well as the outcomes of all dominance struggles, with the aid of a computer. By manipulating early social experience (isolation), the frequency of dominance tests, and other social parameters, and measuring their effects on behavior, blood pressure, hormone levels, adrenal medullary enzyme activity, and histological evidence of damage to the heart and the kidney, they have been able to demonstrate the relationship of well-controlled social variables to the development of atherosclerosis, hypertension, myocardial fibrosis and necrosis, interstitial nephritis, and what appears to be some instances of cardiac sudden death. Animals at different social ranks tend to show different neuroendocrine responses to stress, pituitary-adrenocortical responses predominating in subordinate animals and sympathetic-adrenomedullary responses predominating in dominant animals (Henry & Ely, 1976).

Social ranking in effect creates microenvironments inside an animal colony differing in life-support quality. Dominant animals live in higher quality environments (more or better quality food, superior nesting sites) and subordinate animals in lower quality environments. When there is some social mobility (movement of animals up and down the status system), this socially created environmental diversity may confer important evolutionary advantages. Dominants produce more offspring than subordinates (Wilson, 1975) and subordinates have higher adrenal-mediated deathrates than dominants (Christian, 1975). The systematic cycling of bodies generated at high ranks through inferior, more demanding environments existing at low ranks should speed the rate of evolution of successful adaptations to low quality environments (intense selection pressures) and thus benefit the phylogeny of the species. There is no evidence that such benefits accrue to humans (Dobzhansky, 1962; Mayr, 1970).

Social obligations. Social organization achieved through formal and informal agreements is highly developed in humans. Integrating and regulating society through a system of exchanges, grounded in implicit or explicit understandings, may not be unique to human beings. Trivers (1971) argues that the tit-for-tat exchange strategy, which is the strategy most often employed by humans playing mixed-motive games (Rapaport & Chammah, 1965), has ancient evolutionary sources and may have a deep genetic representation in humans. Aside from this issue, three points seem indisputable: (a) no other species depends on the symbolic form of this social adaptation to the degree we do, (b) the adaptation is significantly shaped by experience and history (cultural evolution), and (c) "moralistic aggression," as Trivers calls it, caused by failures in this mode of adaptation (cheating, unfairness, injustice, deception, broken agreements, betrayal) is an important source of stress in human cultures, even in the !Kung hunter-gatherers of Botswana (Lee & DeVore, 1976).

Feelings of anger and resentment accompanying moralistic aggression were important in the writings of a number of psychosomatic theorists. One can interpret the frustrated dependency and emotional rage and compensatory striving, thought by Alexander (1950) to play a major etiologic role in some psychosomatic illnesses, as the result of a broken "implicit agreement" by which the infant understands that he or she will be nursed and succored forever. The child (and the child remaining inside the adult) may feel deeply betrayed by the parents during independence training. Trivers (1974) holds that some misunderstandings between parent and child, and conflicts of interest between them, are deeply rooted in human phylogeny and inescapable. Many "psychosomatic equations" linking specific illnesses to specific emotional attitudes (Graham, 1972) include the implication of being shortchanged or betrayed in a relationship (duodenal ulcer = "felt deprived of what was due him," acne = "felt he was being picked on," ulcerative colitis = "felt he was being injured and degraded").

Research on combat troops in Viet Nam by Bourne (1971) illustrates the importance of social agreements and relationships as a moderator of stress (see also Cobb, 1976; Lynch, 1977). Helicopter ambulance medics and members of a Special Forces (Green Beret) team were studied during dangerous combat. The excretion of 17-hydroxycorticosteroids was much lower than expected from the objective threat to life. High morale, team unity and mutual support, the gratitude of wounded soldiers expressed to the medics, and the action of psychological defenses were thought to significantly reduce the stress of the combat situation. High levels of psychological and social organization may greatly modify stress responses and distinguish adrenocortical responses of humans and nonhuman animals to aggression and threat to life (Eleftheriou & Scott, 1971).

Given its importance to human social organization, we would like to know a great deal about the effects on the body of social obligation behavioral systems. Because of the dependence of these behaviors on symbolic processes, animal models will be of little help. We have used mixed-motive games to study dominance-submission and social agreement (exchange) behaviors of subjects at risk for heart disease (see below).

Crowding. Social closeness is biologically beneficial. But is it possible to have too much of a good thing? Is there an optimum "concentration" of people? What regulatory devices prevent crowding from becoming overcrowding? What happens socially and physiologically when they fail? Given the explosive growth of the human population, these are nontrivial questions.

Crowding in the physical or geographical sense is not a social variable. Language and technology can warp space and time, so that it is possible to be geographically far away but socially close together, or vice versa. The social bonding, ranking, and obligating behavioral systems described above have the important effects of creating social distances and organizing group members into a common social space which may have no simple one-to-one relationship to physical space. They create social "valences" or the probability of pairwise social interactions among equally spaced people, just as chemical valences are indices of chemical reactivity among equally spaced or concentrated chemicals.

One can make the case that human beings and even apes have a fundamental need for privacy as well as for contact (Chance & Jolly, 1970; Midgley, 1978). People and apes seem to possess an optimum level of attention-getting and social interaction. They do not want to be either excessively looked over (stared at) or overlooked (ignored). These two excesses may contribute to paranoia and depression, respectively, and be central problems of our times when life is often not only densely packed but anonymous. Upper echelon defenses against crowding, which were cited earlier, may modify the relationship between physical and psychosocial distances. They may help the individual achieve the amount of private space he or she needs. Evidence suggests that subjectively perceived or psychosocial distance is what likely matters physiologically (Aiello, DeRisi, Epstein, & Karlin, 1977).

It should be clear from the aforementioned that the linkage of population density to adrenal hyperfunction (Christian, 1975) and of adrenal hyperfunction to elevated susceptibility to infection (Riley, 1981), which has been established on rodents, does not permit us to write a neat $S-R_m-R_d$ (crowding–adrenal hyperfunction–infection) formula for humans. First, the "S" here is not a social stimulus. Second, humans possess means for dealing with physical crowding which rodents do not possess. Animal experimentation may nonetheless be useful because it may indicate what is likely to happen to a crowded human population when and if its defenses against crowding fail.

Crowding which is not successfully defended against increases the *intensity* of social stimulation, i.e., the touches, odors, sights, and sounds of other animals. Crowding experiments manipulate this basic social variable. The effects of crowding on the physiology of animals has an impressive literature (major reviews are those of Calhoun, 1962; Christian, 1975; Wilson, 1975). In the words of Wilson 1975,

> In general, raising the population density increases the rate of individual interactions, and this effect triggers a complex sequence of physiological changes: increased adrenocortical activity, depression of reproductive function, inhibition of growth, inhibition of sexual maturation, decreased resistance to disease, and inhibition of growth of nursing young apparently caused by deficient lactation. (p. 84)

Just as the body grows up to a preset size and then stops growing, apparently a mammalian population also controls its size by mechanisms built into the body. According to the homeostatic theory of the biologists Christian (1975) and Wynne-

Edwards (1965), the mammalian body intrinsically controls the concentration of bodies, just as it controls the concentration of molecules and cells.

A crowded colony of rodents eventually becomes socially pathological. There is too little room for building nests. Marauding males enter and trample the nests and attack the females. Males which ordinarily protect the nests do not or are unable to do so. Fighting escalates and is often vicious. Some males withdraw and become recluses, others roam about the cage restlessly without homes (nests). Fewer young are born and infant mortality rises sharply. Those that are born are handled aggressively, pushed out of the nest prematurely, and robbed of normal socialization experiences. A growing number of undersocialized animals do not respect territory or respond to social signals which normally keep life in a rodent colony relatively orderly and peaceful. The general picture is one of spiraling social chaos, eventually culminating in total social collapse (see Calhoun, 1962; Freedman, 1975; Henry & Stephens, 1977).

It is often assumed that there is little parallel between crowding in animals and humans. Crowding may tear apart the social fabric of a mouse community and sharply increase stress-induced, adrenal-mediated deathrates. In contrast, human beings live in Hong Kong under very crowded conditions and yet do not seem to suffer mentally or physically (Mitchell, 1971). Freedman (1975) sums up the contrast this way, "Under some conditions crowding may have disastrous effects on rats, mice, rabbits, and other animals, but crowding does not have generally negative effects on humans" (p. 1). Studies relating crime rates to population densities in neighborhoods of New York City and in different cities supported this conclusion. Statistical removal of variance in income, education, and ethnicity caused density–crime correlations to shrink to insignificant values. Freedman concludes that density per se does not matter for humans, though it obviously does for animals.

There are two good reasons for not accepting this conclusion in a sweeping form. First, the damage due to crowding may surface in ways that are different from those thus far studied. Second, in order to see its *potential* effects on the body (those effects which we may see in the New Yorks and Hong Kongs of the future, rather than today), current protective defenses against crowding must be stripped away. Analogously, in order to see the potential effects on the body of a poisonous gas, we need to examine all the tissues that take up the gas and must not allow subjects to wear gas masks.

Learning how to live together well in ever more densely packed quarters is one of the great achievements of civilized peoples, not unlike single cells learning how to live together in compact multicellular bodies (Miller, 1978). It is extraordinarily difficult. Consequently, we have developed an enormous cadre of defenses against the socially and physiologically disabling effects of crowding. We can escape from crowds and social overload *physically* by jet travel to uncongested parts of the world, or drive to secluded mountains, etc. for people of means; *psychologically* by taking journeys of imagination sitting in front of a television screen, for people who are less well-off financially; *socially* by focusing on a small circle of friends and ignoring strangers, even when they need help, being cranky with intruders, getting an unlisted telephone number, and leaving the receiver off the hook in the evenings; and *architecturally* by barricading ourselves in soundproof, odorproof, and burglarproof "defensive" housing, for which Hong Kong is justly well known. None of these stimulus and response conditions which mediate between a crowded world and our bodies may show up in crime statistics, though they may affect the quality of life. They may not have a measurable impact on health either, unless for some reason the protective devices crumble and the full impact of a crowded world is allowed to reach and penetrate the body. Then, perhaps, physiologically we will begin to resemble more closely crowded mice than crowded men.

Because of physical and behavioral adaptations wedged between the crowded environment and our bodies, some complex formula, $S-S'''-S''-S'-R_m'-R_m$, rather than a simple relationship between crowding and adrenal hyperfunction, $S-R_m$, better describes our sociophysiological response system. We are fortunate to have these adaptive capacities. It is well to remember from time to time that upon which our good fortune rests. Under crowded conditions people show elevations of sympathetic-mediated skin conductance (Aiello, DeRisi, Epstein, & Karlin, 1977; Aiello, Epstein, & Karlin, 1975; Aiello, Nicosia, & Thompson, 1979) and sometimes, but not always, more aggression, competitiveness, and discomfort (reviewed in Aiello, Nicosia, & Thompson, 1979). In view of the physiological changes which may accompany anger and aggression (Frankenhaeuser, 1975; Hamburg, Hamburg, & Barchas, 1975; Weiner, 1977) and competitiveness (see below), more sociophysiological studies of crowding in both humans and animals is needed. Crowding in human experiments is mild compared to animal experiments, and can only weakly foreshadow what may be in store for us as the world becomes dramatically more crowded. There are currently no facts upon which to base the hope that if the crowding becomes severe, or our species' specific defenses against it are blocked, we will be able to escape the physiological fate of crowded rodents and primates, namely, adrenal hyperfunction and a host of stress-mediated diseases (Henry & Stephens, 1977).

Competition. For several years we have studied the physiological effects of social competition in people who differ in behavioral risk for coronary heart disease. It had been established that someone possessing the so-called "Type A" behavior pattern had roughly twice the likelihood of having a heart attack as someone who possesses few Type A traits and is labeled "Type B" (Brand, 1978; Rosenman, 1974). The coronary-prone or Type A person is described as being unusually aggressive, competitive, hard driving, ambitious, restless, and impatient, while the coronary-resistant or Type B person is more unhurried and relaxed in behavioral style.

In this problem area the R_d states of our $S-R_m-R_d$ formula are fairly well established. They are heart attacks associated with myocardial ischemia and their clinical precursors, especially advanced atherosclerosis and coronary obstruction (Eliot, 1979). The challenge was to find S and R_m, social stimuli and consistent physiological responses to them, which are related to R_d and could also be studied in humans in the laboratory by noninvasive methods. We chose competitive social situations defined by mixed-motive games (Rapaport & Chammah, 1965) as the primary S and sympathetic-mediated responses of the heart and peripheral blood vessels as the primary R_m states. The latter included the heart rate, parameters of the electrocardiogram that reflect changes in oxygen supply–demand (ST–T waves) and blood volume (R wave) in the left ventricle of the heart, and blood volume changes in digital skin.

The depression of the ST segment of the electrocardiogram is the most reliable predictor of future heart attacks when assessed on an exercise treadmill (Ellestad, 1975). This and the other electrocardiographic responses examined are influenced by the level of traffic in sympathetic nerves that supply the heart. Extensive work by Verrier and Lown (Verrier & Lown, 1981; Verrier, Thompson, & Lown, 1974) shows that elevated cardiac sympathetic tone is associated with malignant cardiac arrhythmias, myocardial infarctions, and reinfarctions in dogs. It also increases the amount of physical work the heart performs with each beat. We felt that, in view of the fact that the heart beats around 2.5 billion times during a 70-year life span, repetitive socially induced increases in cardiac sympathetic tone (R_m) could very well predispose a human being to the catastrophic myocardial events that Verrier and co-workers had demonstrated so effectively in dogs.

The interpersonal games we employ are computer-controlled. Two people (e.g., two Type As or two Type Bs) interact cooperatively or competitively for points later convertible to money. In two experiments, paired subjects were able to cooperate, compete, punish, reward, or withdraw on each play of the game (Van Egeren, 1979a; Van Egeren, Sniderman, & Roggelin, 1982). Between plays they could send messages via a television screen expressing feelings, making requests, and offering behavioral deals. The laboratory computer monitored the social exchanges, paced the interaction, delivered feedback on the television screen, and automatically sampled and scored both interactants' cardiovascular responses. In other experiments, the target subject appeared to interact with another bona fide subject (our confederate) while in fact interacting with the computer which was programmed to play the game according to a predetermined strategy (Van Egeren, Abelson, & Thornton, 1978; Van Egeren, 1979b; Van Egeren, Abelson, & Sniderman, 1983; Van Egeren, Fabrega, & Thornton, 1983). By controlling one-half of the interaction, we were able to quantitatively vary social parameters and observe their effects on the cardiovascular systems of Type A and Type B people. The results of these experiments are summarized in Table 10-1.

The research focused on two questions. Are Type As more competitive than Type Bs in the laboratory? Do they exhibit larger sympathetically controlled cardiovascular reponses to social competition? The answer to the first question was "yes," and to the second question was a qualified "yes."

Type A subjects were generally more aggressive, competitive, and dominating in two-person interactions than Type B subjects (Table 10-1). They also broke more agreements and behaved more deceptively. For example, they were much more likely to send the message, "If you cooperate, I will cooperate," and then compete on the following play and outgain a cooperating partner three points to one (Van Egeren, 1979a). They were also more likely to block the transmission of messages which the partner attempted to send, which was a disinterest response and a potential snub or insult.

In some but not all experiments Type As exhibited greater sympathetic-dominated responses in heart rate (Van Egeren, 1979b), digital vasoconstriction (Van Egeren, 1979a), cardiac arrhythmias (Van Egeren, Abelson, & Sniderman, 1983), and ven-

Table 10-1 Summary of Research

Study	Subjects	Game[a]	Results Behavioral	Results Physiological
Van Egeren, Abelson & Thornton (1978)	20 males	2 × 2	Aggression inversely related to aggression guilt	Unpredictable partner stimulated greater speed of transmission of blood volume pulses from heart to finger, smaller drop in blood pressure
Van Egeren (1979a)	30 Type As 30 Type Bs	5 × 5	Type As more dominating, aggressive, deceptive	Greater digital vasoconstriction in Type As
Van Egeren (1979b)	32 unselected subjects given Type A test	2 × 2	Test scores unrelated to behavior	Larger acceleration of heart rate in subjects who scored high on Type A test
Van Egeren, Sniderman & Roggelin (1982)	20 Type As 20 Type Bs	5 × 5	Type As more aggressive, competitive	Type As and Bs indistinguishable in heart rate and digital vasomotor response
Van Egeren, Abelson, & Sniderman (1983)	24 Type As 24 Type Bs	2 × 2 3 × 3	Type As more aggressive	More arrhythmias in Type As; ST depression proportional to aggression
Van Egeren, Fabrega, & Thornton (1983)	36 Type As 36 Type Bs	2 × 2 4 × 4	Type As more often act to remove delays	Greater shifts in ST segment, T wave, and R wave of ECG in Type As when delays present

[a] 2 × 2 games = partners cooperated or competed on each play without communicating
   5 × 5 games = partners cooperated, competed, punished, rewarded or withdrew and could send
           messages

tricular electrocardiographic parameters (greater ST segment depression, and greater reductions in T wave and R wave; Van Egeren, Fabrega, & Thornton, 1983) during social interactions. The same cardiovascular response did not distinguish Type As and Type Bs in all experiments. However, when they were distinguishable, the direction of the difference was always the same: the Type As' cardiovascular reactions suggested more powerful innervation by the sympathetic branch of the autonomic nervous system. The differences in cardiovascular response of healthy college-age Type A and Type B subjects were dependent upon social stimulation. They did not appear during rest preceding social interactions but only while the interactions were actually in progress.

The last two experiments cited above are especially interesting because they involved detailed computer analysis of the electrocardiogram. The computer played the mixed-motive game identically against Type A and Type B subjects, so that we could examine whether the same social stimulus had a different impact on the two groups of subjects. In one experiment (Van Egeren, Abelson, & Sniderman, 1983) Type As and Type Bs differed in the rhythmicity of the heart in response to social stimulation, the Type As showing more frequent computer-detected arrhythmias. The two groups did not differ in ST segment depression. The more often the subject "punished" the confederate the greater the electrocardiographic ST segment depression he or she exhibited ($r = -.48, p < .01$), regardless of whether the subject was classified Type A or Type B prior to the experiment. Actual "Type A" behavior was more important than preexperiment classification. In another series of three experiments (Van Egeren, Fabrega, & Thornton, 1983), the computer delayed its responses during the social exchanges in order to stimulate the subject's impatience. This maneuver seemed to stimulate greater force of contraction of the heart, and therefore greater myocardial work, in the Type As than in the Type Bs. We inferred that there was greater myocardial oxygen demand (from ST–T wave findings) and reduced ventricular blood volume (from R wave findings) in the Type A subjects in response to the computer-controlled social stimulation.

These early observations suggest that people at the extremes of Type A behavior differ in neurally or chemically mediated connections between the social environment and the heart. From such observations we would like to make inferences about the pathophysiology of heart disease. For example, due to unusual susceptibility to competitive social conditions (S) Type As may experience chronically elevated cardiac sympathetic tone (R_m'') which produces stronger ventricular contractions (R_m') and greater demands for myocardial oxygen (the supply of which may be compromised by atherosclerotic coronary obstruction), along with a greater likelihood of cardiac arrhythmias (R_m), which leads someday to irreversible ventricular damage (R_d) associated with lethal arrhythmic events, myocardial fibrosis, etc. So far we have only bits and pieces of this imaginary $S-R_m''-R_m'-R_m-R_d$ formula. We have some evidence bearing on $S-R_m'$ and $S-R_m$ relationships, the reliability and generalizability of which are yet unknown. Under some but not all competitive conditions Type As displayed more frequent computer-scored arrhythmias than Type Bs, as well as ST–T and R wave shifts of the electrocardiogram suggestive of stronger ventricular contractions. Whether these functional relationships are associated with elevated sympathetic traffic to the heart (R_m'') and future damage to the heart (R_d) can only be decided by animal research where the necessary controls are ethically and operationally possible. When sociophysiological research is aimed at unraveling some problem of disease etiology, linking up human research and animal research is not only desirable but essential.

The findings cited here are consistent with observations by others that, in general, Type As respond to environmental challenges with greater sympathetic-dominated cardiovascular responses than do Type Bs (Dembroski, MacDougall, & Shields, 1977; Williams, Friedman, Glass, Herd, & Schneiderman, 1978), even in children (Lawler, Allen, Critcher, & Standard, 1981). Our work extends these findings to computer-assisted interpersonal situations and detailed computer analysis of the electrocardiogram. The fact that direct stimulation of cardiac sympathetic nerves can cause fatal cardiac arrhythmias and infarctions in dogs (reviewed in Verrier & Lown, 1981) and that chronic social competition and intense dominance challenges can cause endorgan damage in rodents resembling cardiac myopathies in humans (Henry & Ely, 1976; Henry & Meehan, 1981; Henry & Stephens, 1977) makes the human research all the more interesting and potentially relevant clinically. The fact that the human research is dependent upon animal experimentation to fill in some of the obvious gaps in knowledge of the pathophysiology of the disease is frustrating at times but need not discourage us. Given the worldwide trends toward explosive population growth and shrinking natural resources (Forrester, 1973; Barney, 1981), there are few forecasts of the future which do not include intense social competition. We had better learn what we can about the effects of social strife on the body, however diverse and imperfect the source of knowledge.

There is currently no well-formed theory of Type A behavior. Glass 1977 emphasizes the Type A's exaggerated need to control the surrounding world and we have cast this control into the broader ecological framework of resource-gathering strategies. Specifically, we view the Type A pattern as the behavioral expression of an ecological strategy for exploiting resources in the environment.

> The strategy is to maximize production by scrambling vigorously for resources, i.e., by being aggressive and competitive, overcoming environmental resistance (being impatient and controlling of the environment), gaining privileged access to resources via high social status (being ambitious), and hoarding resources as a hedge against future shortages (being acquisitive). This strategy should be effective in environments with plentiful goods and less adaptive and more stress-inducing as competition for goods increases and time pressures mount. (Van Egeren, Abelson, & Sniderman, 1983, p. 53)

Years ago, Chess, Thomas, and Birch (1967) identified an early pattern of development which predisposed children to later behavior problems, characterized by "irregularity in biological functions . . . nonadaptability or slow adaptability to change . . . and predominantly intense reactions" (pp. 338-339). Perhaps these children exhibit, or are predisposed toward, Type A behavior. They may be unusually biologically unstable and nonadaptable to change and therefore poorly prepared to handle the accelerating spiral of change, our mad race against ourselves, which is the hallmark of the modern world. Excessive need to impose control on surroundings may represent a protective effort to slow down change, to make the unpredictable a little more predictable, by those of us who are least able to manage the chaotic swirl of change in an age of uncertainty. Technological society may have the disease for which premature cardiovascular deaths, occurring predominantly in people classified as "Type A," are early symptomatic warnings to us all.

Explanation of Social-Biological Relations

The Problem

Some specific social stimuli dependably elicit some specific physiological responses. It is doubtful that social stress can cause disease of a cumulative and degenerative nature unless this is so. The difficulty in explaining manifest social-biological pairings is that they are so often biologically meaningless. Why does uncertainty, helplessness, and the "executive stress" of making decisions under pressure cause gastric erosion and ulceration (Weiss, 1972)? Constriction of the pupil is an adaptation to light. To what are gastric changes preceding ulceration an adaptation? If they are not an adaptation, but rather an incidental or fortuitous response (Williams, 1966), why are they reliably caused by certain classes of environmental conditions? If they are an adaptive response, albeit one gone awry, what is the biological problem for which they are the solution "by design?"

The two groups of scientists who more than anyone else assume the responsibility of explaining social-biological causation work from very different perspectives and methods of study. Psychosomatic theorists focus on the individual's ontogenetic (especially, conditioning) history and sociobiologists focus on human phylogeny. There is some need to put the two together, as field biologists attempt to do in behavioral ecology (Morse, 1980) and the analysis of life-history tactics (Stearns, 1976). The goal is to generate from an understanding of human phylogeny and ontogeny falsifiable hypotheses about disease that are testable in the laboratory or under naturalistic conditions.

Traditional Psychosomatic Models

To the question, "To what is the stress response (psychosomatic symptom) adapted?," writers in the psychosomatic tradition of medicine have given a variety of answers: repressed emotions (Deutsch, 1949), personality characteristics (Dunbar, 1943), emotional conflicts (Alexander, 1950), and emotional attitudes (Graham, 1972). These are the intermediary conditions filling the gap between the social environment and disturbed tissue functions. They are the hidden "food powders" which, it is thought, will make the individual's maladaptive bodily responses more intelligible to reason.

To cause cumulative-degenerative disease the causative agent(s) must persist in time. Enduring tensions in the form of unresolved emotional conflicts, etc., satisfy this condition. The psychoanalytic theory of repetition compulsion of symptoms, implying the notion that the underlying unconscious forces are timeless and unchanging, invited the idea that unresolved conflicts could work their damage continuously and unabated, regardless of the individual's shifting conscious thoughts and actions.

Thermodynamic-hydraulic physical models were important in traditional psychosomatic thinking (Grinker, 1973). It was believed by Dunbar and Alexander, for example, that inexpressible emotions (rage, resentment, etc.) could redirect energy away from voluntary nervous pathways mediating thoughts and actions toward involuntary-autonomic pathways innervating visceral tissues. The result was chronic hyperresponse (hyperemia, hypersecretion, hypermotility) of target tissues, eventually causing them to break down. It is possible to recast these "surplus energy" theories into the language we have been employing. As a result of conflicts of interest between the individual and surrounding social agents, energy may be redirected from external work accounts (calories spent on work in the external environment) to internal work accounts (calories spent on work in the internal environment) of the body's energy budget. The surplus or excessive energy invested in tissue-specific functions of circulating blood, moving air in and out of the lungs, breaking down foodstuffs in the gut, etc., eventually overstrains and damages the tissues.

Traditional psychosomatic models stimulated a great deal of research and altered the way illness is perceived by introducing the brain (and therefore psychological processes) into the processes of bodily regulation in a comprehensive way. The major failings of these models are that (a) the *specific* connections between emotions, etc., and patterns of response were never proven (Grinker, 1973), (b) adaptive responses were viewed too narrowly (dominated by Cannon's emergency response theory and Freud's psychoanalytic theory); adaptation to stress by means involving other types of energy expenditure, energy conservation, and regulation of cell cycles (adjustments in growth, immunity, and so on) were virtually unknown when Dunbar and Alexander were writing, and (c) it is difficult, although by no means impossible, to develop reliable tests of falsifiable hypotheses from these models.

Evolutionary-Ethological Models

Sociobiologists tend to seek answers to the question, "To what are social responses adapted?," in the animal's phylogenetic history. Developmental history, or ontogeny, is not ignored. Sociobiologists simply look beyond personal experience (nurture) to phylogenetic experience (nature) for the origins of social behavior. To the psychosomatic researcher the sense organs, and the conditional or modifiable neurons which lie beyond them, are the door of the body that opens onto social behavior and physiological responses to social stimuli. Sociobiologists recognize and emphasize a second door, the genes which prepare the body carrying them for social living, as a survival strategy, in ways peculiar to the species.

Sociobiologists contend that human genes channel social responses (physiological and behavioral) of human beings in specific ways. They argue that gene-coded biases of perceptual, intellectual, and emotional response systems impart leanings toward behavioral asymmetries in the direction of bonding deeply to people nearby, being aggressive, conforming to authority, fearing strangers, and dominating women (if a man) and being submissive to men (if a woman) (Eibl-Eibesfeldt, 1971; Hinde, 1974; Lorenz, 1966; Lumsden & Wilson, 1981; Tiger & Fox, 1971; Wilson, 1975). Experience in a particular culture may modify or amplify these biases, but they give human societies an indelible imprint which distinguishes us as a species.

The claim that some specific human social behaviors, such as altruism, are determined by possession of specific genes has stimulated vigorous debate (Sahlins, 1976; see Caplan, 1978, for collected papers). Gould (1977a) argues that human beings are genetically endowed for behavioral plasticity. We are the biologically unspecialized and adaptively versatile animal. Human beings are not genetically biased toward either aggression, dominance, greed, and sexism, on the one hand, or peacefulness, equality, altruism, and androgeny, on the other hand. We possess the biological potentiality to be any or all of these things. *Homo sapiens* is the genetically open and unfinished animal whose behaviors are fashioned and specified by culture and experience.

The philosopher Midgley (1978) occupies a middle ground in the sociobiology debate. She agrees with Gould that human beings are enormously flexible and also with Wilson that we possess evolved behavioral specificities and limits. We are not a passive wax impression of society. Human beings *create* culture, along certain species-distinctive lines, and then must adapt to their own creation. We are statue and sculptor simultaneously, as someone once put it. We prefer acceptance over rejection, kindness over cruelty, and honesty over deception. Such behavioral biases are not matters of choice which we are free to dispense with or to ignore. Cultures which systematically reject children, honor nastiness, and reward dishonesty and injustice are probably on the road to extinction rather than biological success.

The study of evolution tells us something about the biology of social organization and the origin of asymmetries in behavioral repertoires. It may provide clues about the kinds of social conditions to which we are phylogenetically adapted and which exerted major selection pressures during periods of rapid hominization. Studies of human origins (Leakey, 1981; Lovejoy, 1981; Mayr, 1970; Washburn & Moore, 1974; Young, 1971) suggest that the following kinds of forces were decisive in fashioning our unique biology: (a) a major climate change (warming-drying trend of the Miocene-Pliocene period) in Africa and Asia inhabited by hominoids, causing a shift from a forest to a risky plains habitat, which (b) favored bipedal locomotion (freeing the hands for new behavioral tasks of tool making, tool use, and carrying of food and infants) and hunting of large animals, (c) spectacular brain expansion between 1.3 and 0.3 million years ago, (d) limitation on expansion of pelvic girdle imposed by bipedal locomotion, (e) "premature" birth of human fetus to allow large fetal brain to pass through a small, approximately 4-inch birth canal (compared to other animals, our gestation period "should be" roughly 18 months rather than 9 months; Gould, 1977b; Montagu, 1981), (f) prolonged period of vulnerability and dependency of human neonate who is born underdeveloped and matures very slowly, which (g) favors selection of intense mother–infant and male–female pair bonding and of powerful sexual and parenting interests, (h) gradual expansion outward from sexual bond attachments (emphasized by Freud) and parental bond attachments (emphasized by Eibl-Eibesfeldt, among others) in ever-widening and deepening zones of social cooperation, which first includes genetical kin ("blood relatives"; Hamilton, 1964) and later embraces genetically unrelated individuals united by social contracts (Trivers, 1971), until (i) the current worldwide network of social and technological interdependence, or "global village," which supports our current sociobiological way of life is reached. Viewed synoptically, the deep interdependence of social and biological changes and the central place of neotony (slow development of young and "youthfulness" of adults) in the making of humankind stand out vividly.

The twin dangers in the sociobiology program are the tendency to substitute plausibility for proof and to make unwarranted interspecies generalizations. Ontogeny must be joined to phylogeny in detailed, demonstrable ways. Animal studies may tell us what is possible or plausible for humans, but not what is probable or proven. Nonetheless, we must rely on animal research to some degree because we cannot, for ethical reasons, deliberately cause disease in humans, even though that is clearly the best way to demonstrate that we understand its etiology.

Sociobiological "Fitness"

In "Civilization and Its Discontents," Freud (1930) expressed a dim view of society. Civilization, he contended, is built upon a renunciation of biological instincts. The instincts which are blocked are asocial (selfish, aggressive, and indiscreetly sexual). Our animal past, which is transparently evident in the infant and in products of unconscious processes, is excessively tamed and straightjacketed by society in ways which are unnatural and biologically damaging. The asocial body is poured into a poorly fitting social mold.

Psychosomatic theorists like Dunbar and Alexander pointed out that the "fit" between body and society is neither inherently good or bad. There is negotiation between biological givens and socializing agents during early development. The outcome of this period of conditioning and learning is a set of derived "tissue tensions" (socially conditioned emotional needs, personality traits, etc.) which may or may not be excessive and harmful.

Sociobiologists add to this picture the notion that the human body is inherently *social*, not asocial. Some of its biological givens are social in nature. Social survival strategies are represented in the body, especially in the brain, as perceptual–emotional–learning biases which structure adaptive transactions with the environment and result in species-specific behavioral asymmetries (bond attachments, altruism, dominance patterns, etc.). Massive data from the hominid fossil record, the behavior of primates, and the evidence of evolutionary continuity between humans and primates suggest that the human body itself is *socio*biological in nature. The extensive human brain tissue that is devoted to the social tasks of speech, recognition of faces, etc., gives dramatic evidence of this fact. Frustration of human needs to share and exchange goods fairly (Hamilton), to control cheating and deception (Trivers), and to bond affectionately to others and creatively to the world (Montagu) may harm the body no less than frustration of sexuality (Freud) and dependency needs (Alexander).

Multilevel Causation

The multilayered organization of the body offers little reason to hope that causal connections between social variables and physiological variables will turn out to be simple. For example, dialing a telephone is a biologically arbitrary act. We have no gene-coded instructions for it. Wanting to *connect* to others (by telephone) is less biologically neutral and is likely shaped by phylogeny and ontogeny. Should we be told by telephone of the death of a loved one, the social message may trigger a cascade of biological responses of very diverse origin. The message will enter the body's information processing (neural–immunological) system at the ear and descend into the body. It will be coded and recoded into informational molecules (neurotransmitters, hormones, cyclic AMP, genes) and will have been retranslated extensively by the time it reaches the adrenal glands. Adrenal tissues are phylogenetically ancient, having appeared in evolutionary time as early as jawless fishes like the lamprey (Young, 1962). The adrenals did not evolve to solve social problems. It is doubtful whether the original social message will still possess social meaning as it passes through this gland.

How "we" (that is, the body on the level of organization mediating conscious experience) and adrenal cells understand the telephone message is bound to be vastly different. The two levels will have different views of what the problem is and what must be done to correct it. On the psychosocial level we may attempt to adapt to the personal loss by examining its significance for our future and by seeking out friends, while the adrenal glands are preparing the body for a major shift in food resource conditions through carefully orchestrated changes in the production of chemicals and cells. When the social level is ruptured, ancient evolutionary designs for survival may be exposed. Efforts of the body to maintain social homeostasis, tissue homeostasis, and population homeostasis may function on various levels of adaptive organization simultaneously to create a complex and confusing array of physiochemical changes. These possibilities need to be considered when designing clinical sociophysiological experiments and interpreting the results.

Conclusions

1. Stability is a precondition of life, as Claude Bernard maintained.

2. By evolving culture human beings mitigated physical and biological variations (changes in weather, food supply, etc.) which constitute the major selection pressures (during phylogeny) and stresses (during ontogeny) dominating the lives of wild animals.

3. The stability of society itself must be maintained. Its stability depends significantly on the integrity of social bonding, ranking, and obligating behavioral systems. With the exception of certain third world countries, social instability has largely replaced physical and biological stresses threatening human biology.

4. Human beings escape the clutches of their biological past only to the degree that social solutions to life's problems remain intact. We live in multiple worlds, on multiple levels of body organization, simultaneously. When upper level adaptations fail, lower level mechanisms are exposed.

5. Conflicts of interest between members of pair-bond dyads, of different social strata, and of social contracts may destabilize social systems.

6. Efforts by the body to restore social stability (social homeostasis) may be channeled through various energy budget categories (for work, reproduction, maintenance and repair, immunity, growth, etc.), guided by behavioral tactics (e.g., skills in interpersonal negotiation on the social level), developmental tactics (e.g., adjustments in growth rate and age at sexual maturity), and ecological tactics (e.g., evolved mechanisms to adjust mortality and natality to external resource conditions). The conscious person will be aware of only a small part of the body's total effort to adapt, of the tip of the iceberg. Both recently evolved and phylogenetically ancient means of adaptation may be activated simultaneously on different levels of organization.

7. Psychosomatic researchers and sociobiologists concentrate on ontogenetic and phylogenetic adaptations to social stress, respectively. The two viewpoints need to be joined to form hypotheses about disease which are testable in the laboratory or under naturalistic conditions.

Acknowledgments. Research by the author reported here was supported by National Heart, Lung, and Blood Institute Grant 1 R01 HL21319-1. I wish to thank Drs. Ronald Simons, James Trosko, Thomas Stachnik, Bertram Stoffelmayr, and Hiram Fitzgerald for their helpful reviews of an earlier draft of this chapter.

References

Ader, R. (1975). Early experience and hormones: Emotional behavior and adrenocortical function. In B. Eleftheriou & R. Sprott (Eds.), *Hormonal correlates of behavior*. New York: Plenum Press.

Ader, R. (1981). *Psychoneuroimmunology*. New York: Academic Press.

Aiello, J., DeRisi, D., Epstein, Y., & Karlin, R. (1977). Crowding and the role of interpersonal distance preference. *Sociometry, 40*(3), 271-282.

Aiello, J., Epstein, Y., & Karlin, R. (1975). Effects of crowding on electrodermal activity. *Sociological Symposium, Human Crowding, 14*, 43-57.

Aiello, J., Nicosia, G., & Thompson, D. (1979). Physiological, social, and behavioral consequences of crowding on children and adolescents. *Child Development, 50*, 195-202.

Alexander, F. (1950). *Psychosomatic medicine*. New York: Norton.

Allee, W. (1943). Where angels fear to tread: A contribution from general sociology to human ethics. *Science, 97*, 517-525.

Axelrod, R., & Hamilton, W. (1981). The evolution of cooperation. *Science, 211*, 1390-1396.

Barchas, P., & Barchas, J. (1975). Physiological sociology: Endocrine correlates of status behaviors. In D. Hamburg & H. Brodie (Eds.), *American handbook of psychiatry* (Vol. 6). New York: Basic Books.

Barney, G. (1981). *The global 2000 report to the president*. Charlottesville, VA: Blue Angel.

Bartrup, R., Lazarus, L., Luckhurst, E., Kiloh, L., & Penny, R. (1977). Depressed lymphocyte function after bereavement. *Lancet, 1*, 834-836.

Berenblum, I. (1941). The cocarcinogenic action of croton resin. *Cancer Research, 1*, 44-48.

Bourne, P. (1971). Altered adrenal function in two combat situations in Viet Nam. In B. Eleftheriou & P. Scott (Eds.), *The physiology of aggression and defeat*. New York: Plenum Press.

Bowlby, J. (1973). *Separation*. New York: Basic Books.

Brand, R. (1978). Coronary-prone behavior as an independent risk factor for coronary heart disease. In T. Dembroski, S. Weiss, J. Shields, S. Haynes, & M. Feinleib (Eds.), *Coronary-prone behavior*. New York: Springer-Verlag.

Bronson, F., & Desjardins, C. (1971). Steroid hormones and aggressive behavior in mammals. In B. Eleftheriou & P. Scott (Eds.), *The physiology of aggression and defeat*. New York: Plenum Press.

Bronson, F., & Marsden, H. (1973). The preputial gland as an indicator of social dominance in male mice. *Behavioral Biology, 9*, 625.

Bullough, W. (1961). *Vertebrate reproductive cycles*. London: Methuen.

Bullough, W. (1965). Mitotic and functional homeostasis: A speculative review. *Cancer Research, 25*, 1683-1727.

Butler, S., Suskind, M., & Schanberg, S. (1978). Maternal behavior as a regulator of polyamine biosynthesis in brain and heart of the developing rat pup. *Science, 199*, 445-447.

Calhoun, J. (1962). Population density and social pathology. *Scientific American, 206*, 139-148.

Calow, P. (1978). *Life cycles*. London: Wiley.

Cannon, W. (1929). *Bodily changes in pain, hunger, fear, and rage*. New York: Harper & Row.

Caplan, A. (1978). *The sociobiology debate*. New York: Harper & Row.

Carroll, B. (1976). Limbic system-adrenal cortex regulation in depression and schizophrenia. *Psychosomatic Medicine, 38*, 106-121.

Chamove, A., & Bowman, R. (1978). Rhesus plasma cortisol response at four dominance positions. *Aggressive Behavior, 4*, 43-55.

Chance, M., & Jolly, C. (1970). *Social groups of monkeys, apes and men.* London: Cape.

Chess, S., Thomas, A., & Birch, H. (1967). Behavior problems revisited. *The Journal of the American Academy of Child Psychiatry, 6*(2), 321-331.

Christian, J. (1950). The adreno-pituitary system and population cycles in mammals. *Journal of Mammalogy, 31*, 247.

Christian, J. (1971). Population density and reproductive efficiency. *Biology of Reproduction, 4*, 248.

Christian, J. (1975). Hormonal control of population growth. In B. Eleftheriou & R. Sprott (Eds.), *Hormonal correlates of behavior.* New York: Plenum Press.

Cobb, S. (1976). Social support as a moderator of life stress. *Psychosomatic Medicine, 38*, 300-314.

Dembroski, T., MacDougall, J., & Shields, J. (1977). Physiologic reactions to socia challenge in persons evidencing the Type A coronary-prone behavior pattern. *Journal of Human Stress, 3*, 2-10.

Deutsch, F. (1949). "Thus speaks the body." *Transactions of the New York Academy of Medicine, 12*, 2.

Dobzhansky, T. (1962). *Mankind evolving.* New Haven, CN: Yale University Press.

Dubos, R. (1965). *Man adapting.* New Haven, CN: Yale University Press.

Dubos, R. (1968). *So human an animal.* New York: Scribner's.

Dunbar, H. (1943). *Psychosomatic diagnosis.* New York: Hoeber.

Ehrlich, P., Ehrlich, A., & Holdren, J. (1977). *Ecoscience.* San Francisco: Freeman.

Eibl-Eibesfeldt, I. (1971). *Love and hate.* New York: Schocken.

Eisdorfer, C., & Raskind, M. (1975). Aging, hormones and human behavior. In B. Eleftheriou & R. Sprott (Eds.), *Hormonal correlates of behavior.* New York: Plenum Press.

Eleftheriou, B., & Scott, J. (1971). *The physiology of aggression and defeat.* New York: Plenum Press.

Eliot, R. (1979). *Stress and the major cardiovascular disorders.* Mount Kisco, NY: Futura.

Ellestad, M. (1975). *Stress testing.* Philadelphia: Davis.

Finch, C. (1976). The regulation of physiological changes during mammalian aging. *The Quarterly Review of Biology, 51*, 49-82

Forrester, J. (1973). *World dynamics.* Cambridge, MA: Wright-Allen Press.

Fox, B. (1981). Psychosocial factors and the immune response in human cancer. In R. Ader (Ed.), *Psychoneuroimmunology.* New York: Academic Press.

Frankenhaeuser, M. (1975). Experimental approaches to the study of catecholamines and emotion. In L. Levi (Ed.), *Emotions.* New York: Raven.

Freedman, J. (1975). *Crowding and behavior.* San Francisco: Freeman.

Freud, S. (1930). *Civilization and its discontents.* New York: Norton.

Gardner, L. (1972). Deprivation dwarfism. *Scientific American, 227*, 76-82.

Glass, D. (1977). *Behavior patterns, stress, and coronary disease.* New York: Wiley.

Goldman, B. (1974). The hypothalamic-pituitary-gonadal axis and the regulation of cyclicity and sexual behavior. In F. Schmitt & F. Worden (Eds.), *The neurosciences: Third study program.* Cambridge, MA: MIT Press.

Gould, J. (1977a). *Ever since Darwin.* New York: Norton.

Gould, J. (1977b). *Ontogeny and phylogeny.* Cambridge, MA: Harvard University Press.

Graham, D. (1972). Psychosomatic medicine. In N. Greenfield & R. Sternbach (Eds.), *Handbook of psychophysiology.* New York: Holt, Rinehart & Winston.

Grinker, R. (1973). *Psychosomatic concepts.* New York: Jason Aronson.

Hamburg, D., Hamburg, B., & Barchas, J. (1975). Anger and depression in perspective of behavioral biology. In L. Levi (Ed.), *Emotions.* New York: Raven.

Hamilton, W. (1964). The genetical theory of social behaviour, I, II. *Journal of Theoretical Biology, 7*, 1-52.

Heilbroner, R. (1980). *Marxism: For and against.* New York: Norton.

Henry, J., & Ely, D. (1976). Biological correlates of psychosomatic illness. In R. Grenell & S. Galay (Eds.), *Biological foundations of psychiatry*. New York: Raven.

Henry, J., & Meehan, J. (1981). Psychosocial stimuli, physiological specificity, and cardiovascular disease. In A. Weiner, M. Hofer, & A. Stunkard (Eds.), *Brain, behavior, and bodily disease*. New York: Raven.

Henry, J., & Stephens, P. (1977). *Stress, health, and the social environment*. New York: Springer-Verlag.

Hinde, R. (1974). *Biological bases of human social behavior*. New York: McGraw-Hill.

Hofer, M. (1981). Toward a developmental basis for disease predisposition: The effects of early maternal separation on brain, behavior, and cardiovascular system. In H. Weiner, M. Hofer, & A. Stunkard (Eds.), *Brain, behavior, and bodily disease*. New York: Raven.

Iacobelli, S., King, R., Lindner, H., & Lippman, M. (1980). *Hormones and cancer*. New York: Raven.

Jackson, J. H. (1958). Evolution and dissolution of the nervous system (1884). Selected papers (Vol. 2). New York: Basic Books.

Jacob, F. (1966). Genetics of the bacterial cell. *Science, 152*, 1470.

King, D. (1962). Effect of injury on the cell. *Federation Proceedings, 21*, 1143-1146.

Koestler, A. (1978). *Janus*. New York: Vintage.

Kropotkin, P. (1903). *Mutual aid: A factor of evolution*. New York: McClure Phillips.

Kuhn, C., Butler, S., & Schanberg, S. (1978). Selective depression of serum growth hormone during material deprivation in rat pups. *Science, 201*, 1034-1036.

Lawler, K., Allen, M., Critcher, E., & Standard, B. (1981). The relationship of physiological responses to the coronary-prone behavior pattern in children. *Journal of Behavioral Medicine, 4*(2), 203-217.

Leakey, R. (1981). *The making of mankind*. New York: Dutton.

Lee, R., & DeVore, I. (1976). *Kalahari hunter-gatherers*. Cambridge, MA: Harvard University Press.

Leibowitz, S. (1974). Adrenergic receptor mechanisms in eating and drinking. In F. Schmitt & F. Worden (Eds.), *The neurosciences: Third study program*. Cambridge, MA: MIT.

Levine, S. (1974). Developmental psychobiology. In D. Hamburg & H. Brodie (Eds.), *American handbook of psychiatry*, Vol. 6, *New psychiatric frontiers*. New York: Basic Books.

Lloyd, J. (1975). Social behavior and hormones. In B. Eleftheriou & R. Sprott (Eds.), *Hormonal correlates of behavior*. New York: Plenum Press.

Lorenz, K. (1966). *On aggression*. New York: Harcourt, Brace, Jovanovich.

Lovejoy, C. (1981). The origin of man. *Science, 211*, 341-350.

Lumsden, C., & Wilson, E. O. (1981). *Genes, mind, and culture*. Cambridge, MA: Harvard University Press.

Lynch, J. (1977). *The broken heart*. New York: Basic Books.

MacLean, P. (1970). The triune brain, emotion, and scientific bias. In F. Schmitt (Ed.), *The neurosciences: Second study program*. New York: Rockefeller.

Mason, J. (1975). Emotion as reflected in patterns of endocrine integration. In L. Levi (Ed.), *Emotions*. New York: Raven.

Mayr, E. (1970). *Populations, species, and evolution*. Cambridge, MA: Harvard University Press.

Mayr, E. (1982). *The growth of biological thought*. Cambridge, MA: Harvard University Press.

McKeown, T. (1979). *The role of medicine*. Princeton, NJ: Princeton University Press.

Midgley, M. (1978). *Beast and man*. Ithaca, NY: Cornell University Press.

Miller, J. (1978). *Living systems*. New York: McGraw-Hill.

Mitchell, R. (1971). Some social implications of high-density housing. *American Sociological Review, 36*, 18-29.

Monod, J. (1971). *Chance and necessity*. New York: Vintage.

Montagu, A. (1981). *Growing young*. New York: McGraw-Hill.

Morse, D. (1980). *Behavioral mechanisms in ecology*. Cambridge, MA: Harvard University Press.

Pattee, H. (1973). *Hierarchy theory*. New York: G. Braziller.

Plaut, S., & Friedman, S. (1981). Psychosocial factors in infectious disease. In R. Ader (Ed.), *Psychoneuroimmunology*. New York: Academic Press.

Potter, V. (1980). Initiation and promotion in cancer formation: The importance of studies on intercellular communication. *The Yale Journal of Biology and Medicine, 53*, 367-384.

Powell, G., Hopwood, N., & Barratt, E. (1973). Growth hormone studies before and during catch-up growth in a child with emotional deprivation and short stature. *Journal of Endocrinology and Metabolism, 37*, 674-679.

Rapaport, A., & Chammah, A. (1965). *Prisoner's dilemma*. Ann Arbor, MI: University of Michigan Press.

Riley, V. (1981). Psychoneuroendocrine influences on immunocompetence and neoplasia. *Science, 212*, 1100-1109.

Rosenman, R. (1974). The role of behavior patterns and neurogenic factors in the pathogenesis of coronary heart disease. In R. Eliot (Ed.), *Stress and the heart*. Mount Kisco, NY: Futura.

Sahlins, M. (1976). *The use and abuse of biology*. Ann Arbor, MI: University of Michigan Press.

Satinoff, E. (1974). Neural control of thermoregulatory responses. In L. DiCara (Ed.), *Limbic and autonomic nervous systems research*. New York: Plenum Press.

Selye, H. (1956). *The stress of life*. New York: McGraw-Hill.

Selye, H. (1976). *Stress*. Boston: Butterworth.

Simpson, G. (1944). *The major features of evolution*. New York: Simon & Schuster.

Stearns, S. (1976). Life-history tactics: A review of the ideas. *The Quarterly Review of Biology, 51*, 3-47.

Stein, M., Keller, S., & Schleifer, S. (1981). The hypothalamus and the immune response. In H. Weiner, M. Hofer, & A. Stunkard (Eds.), *Brain, behavior, and bodily disease*. New York: Raven.

Strehler, B. (1972). The understanding and control of the aging process. In J. Behnke (Ed.), *Challenging biological problems*. New York: Oxford University Press.

Sulloway, F. (1979). *Freud, biologist of the mind*. New York: Basic Books.

Teitelbaum, P. (1967). The biology of drive. In G. Quarton, T. Melnechuk, & F. Schmitt (Eds.), *The neurosciences: A study program*. New York: Rockefeller.

Thomas, L. (1974). *The lives of a cell*. New York: Bantam.

Tiger, L., & Fox, R. (1971). *The imperial animal*. New York: Delta.

Trivers, R. (1971). The evolution of reciprocal altruism. *Quarterly Review of Biology, 46*, 35-57.

Trivers, R. (1974). Parent-offspring conflict. *American Zoologist, 14*, 249-264.

Trosko, J., & Chang, C. (1978). Genes, pollutants and human disease. *Quarterly Review of Biophysics II, 4*, 603-627.

Trosko, J., & Chang, C. (1980). An integrative hypothesis linking cancer, diabetes and atherosclerosis: The role of mutations and epigenetic changes. *Medical Hypotheses, 6*, 455-468.

Vander, A., Sherman, J., & Luciano, D. (1980). *Human physiology*. New York: McGraw-Hill.

Van Egeren, L. (1979a). Social interactions, communications, and the coronary-prone behavior pattern: A psychophysiological study. *Psychosomatic Medicine, 41*(1), 2-18.

Van Egeren, L. (1979b). Cardiovascular changes during social competition in a mixed-motive game. *Journal of Personality and Social Psychology, 37*, 858-864.

Van Egeren, L., Abelson, J., & Sniderman, L. (1983). Interpersonal and electrocardiographic responses of Type A's and Type B's in competitive socioeconomic games. *Journal of Psychosomatic Research, 27*, 53-59.

Van Egeren, L. F., Abelson, J., & Thornton, D. W. (1978). Cardiovascular consequences of expressing anger in a mutually dependent relationship. *Journal of Psychosomatic Research, 22*, 537-548.

Van Egeren, L., Fabrega, H., & Thornton, D. (1983). Electrocardiographic effects of social stress on coronary-prone (Type A) individuals. *Psychosomatic Medicine, 45*, 195-203.

Van Egeren, L., Sniderman, L., & Roggelin, M. (1982). Competitive two-person interactions of Type A and Type B individuals. *Journal of Behavioral Medicine, 5*(1), 55-66.

Verrier, R., & Lown, B. (1981). Autonomic nervous system and malignant cardiac arrhythmias. In A. Weiner, M. Hofer, & A. Stunkard (Eds.), *Brain, behavior, and bodily disease*. New York: Raven.

Verrier, R., Thompson, P., & Lown, B. (1974). Ventricular vulnerability during sympathetic stimulation: Role of heart rate and blood pressure. *Cardiovascular Research, 8*, 602-610.

Washburn, S., & Moore, R. (1974). *Ape into man*. Boston: Little, Brown.

Weiner, H. (1977). *Psychobiology and human disease*. New York: Elsevier.

Weiner, H., Hofer, M., & Stunkard, A. (1981). *Brain, behavior, and bodily disease*. New York: Raven.

Weisfeld, G. (1982). An extension of the stress-homeostasis model based on ethological research. *Perspectives in Biology and Medicine, 26*(1), 79-97.

Weiss, J. (1972). Psychological factors in stress and disease. *Scientific American, 226*, 104-113.

Williams, G. (1966). *Adaptation and natural selection*. Princeton, NJ: Princeton University Press.

Williams, R., Friedman, M., Glass, D., Herd, A., & Schneiderman, N. (1978). Mechanisms linking behavioral and pathophysiological processes. In T. Dembroski, S. Weiss, J. Shields, S. Haynes, & M. Feinleib (Eds.), *Coronary-prone behavior*. New York: Springer-Verlag.

Wilson, E. O. (1975). *Sociobiology*. Cambridge, MA: Harvard University Press.

Wilson, E. O. (1978). *On human nature*. Cambridge, MA: Harvard University Press.

Wolf, S. (1981). *Social environment and health*. Seattle, WA: University of Washington Press.

Wynne-Edwards, V. (1965). Self-regulating systems in populations of animals. *Science, 147*, 1543-1548.

Yabrov, A. (1980). Adequate function of the cell: Interactions between the needs of the cell and the needs of the organism. *Medical Hypotheses, 6*, 337-374.

Yotti, L., Chang, C., & Trosko, J. (1979). Elimination of metabolic cooperation in Chinese hamster cells by a tumor promoter. *Science, 206*, 1089-1091.

Young, J. Z. (1962). *The life of vertebrates*. New York: Oxford University Press.

Young, J. Z. (1971). *An introduction to the study of man*. New York: Oxford University Press.

Author Index

Abel, T., 165, 190
Abeles, R. P., 225, 247
Abelson, J., 269, 271, 272, 281
Adamson, L., 87, 98, 109
Ader, R., 253, 254, 257, 258, 260, 262, 278
Adesso, V. J., 239, 245
Ahern, G. L., 73, 85, 146, 161
Aiello, J., 266, 268, 278
Ainsworth, M. D. S., 66, 81, 87, 106, 109
Ajzen, T., 163, 164, 172, 191
Alexander, F., 250, 265, 273, 274, 276, 278
Alexander, R. D., 55, 56, 80, 81
Alfert, E., 12, 18
Allee, W., 260, 263, 278
Allen, M., 271, 280
Allport, G., 163, 190
Als, H., 87, 98, 109
Andrew, R. J., 68, 81
Andrews, R. J., 139, 158
Angulo, E. J., 235, 243
Anschel, C., 30, 44
Appley, M. H., 143, 158
Arditti, M., 25, 42
Argyle, M., 29, 42
Aron, A., 169, 191
Ashton, R., 127, 136
Augenbraun, C. B., 129, 136
Averill, J. R., 13, 16, 212, 221
Ax, A. F., 7, 16, 38, 42, 81, 227, 232, 243
Axelrod, R., 253, 256, 257, 278
Ayala, F. J., 50, 52, 66, 81, 82

Bagley, G., 176, 192
Baisel, E. J., 93, 112
Bakan, P., 29, 42
Baker, J. W. II, 227, 240, 243
Bandura, A., 68, 81, 225, 226, 228, 234, 243
Barash, D. P., 48, 49, 52, 55, 64, 76, 80, 81
Barchas, J., 249, 268, 278, 279
Barchas, P., 249, 278
Baribeau-Braun, J., 212, 220
Barlow, J. D., 29, 42
Barney, G., 272, 278
Baron, R. A., 119, 136, 234, 235, 236, 237, 243
Baron, R. M., 78, 79, 82
Baron, R. S., 239, 243
Barrett, E., 255, 281
Barrett, G., 119, 136, 234, 236, 244
Bartrup, R., 262, 278
Bates, J. E., 103, 109
Baugher, D. M., 165, 190, 205, 220
Bear, D. M., 147, 158
Beck, K. H., 174, 190
Becker, L. A., 189, 194
Becker, M. H., 176, 190
Bell, P. A., 119, 136, 234, 236, 237, 243
Bell, S. M., 106, 109
Bem, D. J., 165, 186, 190
Bender, M. B., 147, 161
Benjamin, L. S., 38, 42
Berg, K. M., 91, 109
Berg, W. K., 91, 109
Bergman, J. S., 126, 136
Berkowitz, L., 225, 226, 228, 231, 233, 234, 235, 242, 243

Berlyne, D. E., 8, 9, 12, 16
Bernstein, G. L., 127, 137
Bernstein, I. S., 72, 82
Berscheid, E., 120, 138, 235, 244
Best, C., 146, 158
Birch, H., 272, 279
Bjorkvall, C., 7, 17
Blackwell, B., 126, 138
Blanchard, E. B., 125, 138, 126, 136
Blankstein, K. R., 126, 136
Blascovich, J., 121, 127, 137
Blehar, M. C., 87, 109
Block, J., 150, 151, 158
Bloom, G., 13, 16
Bloom, S. W., 22, 43
Boag, T. J., 201, 222
Boffa, J., 13, 14, 16
Borden, R. J., 235, 244
Borkovec, T. D., 36, 42, 239, 244
Borod, J., 142, 158
Borrie, R. A., 184, 185, 190, 195
Bostrom, R. N., 181, 182, 183, 190
Botto, R. W., 36, 41, 44, 122, 138, 172, 195
Boukydis, C. F. Z., 103, 104, 109
Bourne, P., 265, 278
Bowlby, J., 65, 66, 67, 82, 100, 101, 109, 262, 278
Bowman, R., 262, 264, 279
Boyd, R. W., 3, 4, 16, 202, 203, 220
Boye, E., 235, 244
Brackbill, Y., 15, 17, 90, 109
Bradford, S., 16, 19
Braff, D., 155, 159
Brand, R., 268, 278
Brand, R. J., 204, 222
Braun, C., 212, 220
Brazelton, T. B., 87, 98, 109
Brehm, J. W., 119, 136
Brener, J., 125, 126, 136
Bretherton, I., 94, 109
Brickett, P., 28, 42
Brobeck, J. R., 32, 42
Brock, T. C., 178, 194
Bronson, F., 252, 259, 278
Bronson, G. W., 93, 109
Brookes, S., 27, 43
Brooks, J., 96, 111
Brown, C. C., 25, 42
Brown, R., 229, 242, 245
Brown, S. L., 73, 85, 146, 161
Brunswik, E., 80, 81, 82
Bryant, J., 123, 138, 228, 237, 243, 236, 237, 247

Buck, R., 4, 140, 141, 142, 144, 145, 146, 149, 150, 151, 153, 154, 155, 156, 158, 161, 169, 195
Buck, R. W., Jr., 119, 136
Bullough, W., 252, 253, 254, 255, 259, 278
Burch, N. R., 5, 6, 7, 10, 16
Burdick, H. A., 205, 220
Burgess, M., 241, 245
Burnes, A. J., 205, 220
Burnstein, E., 229, 244
Buss, A. H., 235, 247
Butler, S., 255, 263, 278
Byrne, D., 205, 206, 220

Cacioppo, J. T., 28, 40, 42, 166, 167, 169, 170, 173, 178, 179, 180, 181, 183, 190, 191, 194
Calhoun, J., 266, 267, 278
Calow, P., 259, 263, 278
Campbell, C. B. G., 60, 83
Campbell, D. T., 53, 55, 58, 80, 82, 164, 165, 194
Campbell, H., 91, 111
Campbell, K. B., 212, 220
Campos, J. J., 90, 93, 94, 95, 96, 97, 98, 109, 110, 112
Cannon, W., 253, 274, 278
Cannon, W. B., 35, 37, 42, 117, 118, 119, 123, 136
Cantor, J. R., 123, 136, 228, 237, 243
Caplan, A., 274, 278
Cappell, H., 230, 246
Cardon, P. V., 204, 223
Carducci, B. J., 120, 136
Carpenter, J. A., 7, 17
Carroll, B., 252, 262, 278
Carroll, D., 125, 136
Carver, C. S., 235, 243
Cattell, R., 165, 191
Caul, W. F., 151, 158
Caulfield, C., 101, 107
Cavanaugh, P. M., 8, 18
Chammah, A., 265, 268, 281
Chamove, A., 262, 264, 279
Chance, M., 266, 279
Chang, C., 253, 255, 281, 282
Chant, S. H., 164, 191
Chapman, A. J., 27, 43
Chess, S., 272, 279
Chevalier-Skolnikoff, S., 68, 82
Chickadonz, G., 204, 222
Chomsky, N., 63, 82

Christian, J., 255, 259, 260, 264, 266, 279
Christian, J. C., 212, 222
Christie, M. J., 33, 34, 45
Chu, G. C., 174, 191
Cialdini, R. B., 178, 191
Clark, M., 171, 172, 192
Clark, R. D., 40, 44
Clemens, T. L., 7, 10, 16
Clore, G. L., 165, 191, 206, 220, 212, 222
Cobb, S., 261, 265, 279
Cofer, C. N., 143, 158
Cohen, A. R., 119, 136
Cohen, J., 169, 191
Cohen, S. I., 5, 6, 16
Coleman, R., 40, 42, 203, 220
Coles, M. G. H., 182, 193
Collins, C., 204, 221
Collmer, C., 106, 111
Comer, R., 218, 222
Comfort, A., 8, 16
Comroe, J. H., 30, 42
Comsky, P. W., 237, 247
Contrada, R., 204, 221
Cook, M., 29, 42
Cook, M. R., 33, 42, 152, 161
Cook, S., 170, 195
Cooper, H., 205, 211, 221
Cooper, J., 119, 136, 186, 187, 188, 189, 191, 195
Cooper, J. B., 164, 191
Corah, N. L., 13, 14, 16
Cortell, L., 38, 43
Cotton, J. L., 239, 243
Cottrell, N. B., 120, 136
Courville, J., 146, 158
Coutts, L. M., 169, 191
Cozby, P. C., 120, 136
Crider, A., 3, 19, 21, 22, 44
Criderm A., 129, 136
Critcher, E., 271, 280
Critchley, M., 140, 141, 158
Crithlow, B., 189, 195
Cromwell, L., 24, 25, 42
Cronbach, L. J., 206, 220
Crowell, D. H., 16

Darrow, C. W., 8, 16, 38, 42
Darwin, C., 29, 35, 42, 47, 48, 68, 82, 139, 142, 159
Davia, J. E., 204, 221
Davidson, M. A., 7, 16

Davidson, L. A., 12, 19
Davidson, R. J., 132, 138
Davis, C. M., 22, 23, 25, 28, 42, 45
Davis, R. C., 38, 42
Dawson, M. E., 15, 17, 212, 221
Day, H. I., 10, 18
Day, K. D., 168, 195, 236, 248
Day, K. D., 236, 247
Décarie, T. G., 95, 111
Deckner, W. C., 176, 177, 194
DeFries, J. C., 52, 84
DeLoach, L. L., 102, 112
Dembroski, T., 271, 279
Dembroski, T. M., 199, 222, 204, 220, 204, 221
Dengerink, H. A., 227, 244
DeRisi, D., 266, 268, 278
Desjardins, C., 252, 264, 278
Detweiler, R. A., 4, 172, 173, 191
Deutsch, F. J., 273, 279
DeVore, I., 265, 280
Dimascio, A., 202, 203, 220
DiMascio, A., 3, 4, 16
Dimberg, U., 3, 71, 72, 73, 75, 82, 84
Disbrow, M. A., 101, 107, 109
Dittes, J. E., 4, 5, 6, 17, 201, 202, 220
Dobzhansky, T., 50, 51, 52, 55, 58, 59, 65, 82, 259, 264, 279
Doerr, H. O., 101, 107, 109
Dollard, J., 225, 228, 240, 244
Donchin, E., 27, 42
Donnerstein, E., 119, 136, 234, 236, 237, 244
Donnerstein, M., 234, 236, 244
Donovan, W. J., 101, 105, 110
Doob, A. N., 231, 234, 236, 240, 244, 245, 247
Doob, L. W., 225, 244
Doust, J. W. L., 200, 220
Dovidio, J. F., 40, 44
Drescher, V. M., 126, 138
Dreyer, A., 153, 161
Dubos, R., 253, 259, 260, 279
Duffy, E., 8, 16, 35, 40, 42, 88, 110
Duffy, J. R., 140, 159
Duffy, R. J., 140, 141, 142, 154, 155, 156, 158, 159
Dunbar, H., 273, 274, 276, 279
Dutton, D., 169, 191
Dyck, R., 229, 235, 244, 246

Easterbrook, J. A., 14, 17, 106, 111
Eckerman, C. O., 94, 112

Edelberg, R., 6, 8, 14, 17, 33, 42
Edelberg, W., 216, 221
Edwards, A. L., 214, 220
Ehrlich, P., 253, 279
Ehrlichman, H., 29, 43
Eibl-Eibesfeldt, I., 49, 59, 63, 67, 68, 69, 82, 274, 275, 279
Eisdorfer, C., 257, 279
Ekman, P., 68, 69, 82, 84, 144, 159
Eleftheriou, B., 252, 254, 264, 265, 279
Eliot, R., 268, 279
Ellestad, M., 269, 279
Elliot, R., 89, 90, 110, 227, 244
Ellsworth, P., 68, 82, 144, 159
Elting, E., 204, 221
Elul, M. R., 27, 43
Ely, D., 264, 272, 280
Emde, R. N., 94, 96, 102, 109, 110
Eppinger, H., 37, 43
Epstein, S., 6, 12, 13, 17, 22, 43, 153, 161, 227, 232, 247
Epstein, Y., 266, 268, 278
Erdman, G., 9, 10, 17, 168, 191
Euler, U. S. von, 13, 16
Evans, R., 236, 244
Eysenck, H. J., 150, 153, 159, 202, 212, 220

Fabrega, H., 269, 270, 271, 281
Fagnant, D., 219, 221
Fair, P. L., 73, 85
Fazio, R. H., 119, 136, 187, 189, 191
Feather, B. W., 15, 19
Feldman, J., 38, 43
Fenigstein, A., 235, 247
Fenz, W. D., 12, 13, 17, 201, 220
Ferguson, T. J., 229, 232, 238, 239, 244, 246
Feshbach, S., 174, 192, 227, 232, 237, 244, 246
Festinger, L., 119, 137, 186, 191
Field, T. M., 87, 97, 98, 99, 110, 153, 159
Finch, C., 257, 259, 260, 279
Findley, M., 205, 211, 221
Fink, D., 122, 137, 171, 192
Fischer, C. S., 225, 247
Fishbein, M., 163, 164, 172, 191
Fishman, C. G., 231, 241, 244
Fitzgerald, H. E., 15, 17
Flor-Henry, P., 155, 159
Fobes, J. L., 145, 146, 154, 160
Forrester, J., 272, 279

Fowles, D. C., 153, 154, 159
Fox, B., 32, 43, 258, 279
Fox, C. A., 32, 43
Frank, J. D., 5, 18
Frankel, A., 174, 190
Frankenhaeuser, M., 7, 13, 17, 81, 82, 268, 279
Fredrikson, M., 63, 83, 84
Freedman, J., 267, 279
Freeland, C. A. B., 103, 109
Freixa i Baque, E., 212, 221
Freud, S., 225, 244, 250, 253, 274, 275, 276, 279
Friedman, M., 204, 222, 271, 282
Friedman, S., 258, 281
Friesen, W. V., 68, 82, 144, 159
Froberg, J., 7, 17
Frodi, A. M., 3, 87, 100, 101, 102, 103, 104, 106, 107, 110
Frykolm, G., 78, 79, 80, 84
Fugita, B., 153, 159
Funkenstein, D. H., 232, 244

Gaeblein, C. J., 90, 111
Gaensbauer, T. J., 94, 109
Gaertner, S. L., 40, 44
Gainotti, G., 140, 159
Gale, A., 27, 43
Galin, D., 155, 159
Galosy, R. A., 90, 111
Gambaro, S., 240, 241, 244
Garcia, J., 60, 61, 82
Gardner, L., 255, 279
Gatchel, R. J., 15, 17
Geddes, L. A., 25, 43
Geen, R. G., 226, 227, 228, 231, 234, 236, 240, 241, 244, 245
Geiselman, J. H., 119, 137
Gellhorn, E., 8, 9, 12, 17, 38, 43
Gentry, W. D., 231, 245
Gerard, H. B., 119, 137, 189, 192, 205, 221
Gerdes, E. P., 168, 192
Ghiselin, M. T., 48, 62
Gibson, E. J., 92, 110
Gibson, J. J., 69, 78, 82, 140, 159
Gillman, A., 7, 17
Glass, D., 271, 272, 279, 282
Glass, D. C., 204, 218, 221
Gleason, J. M., 119, 137, 189, 192
Glickman, S. E., 142, 159
Godkevitch, M., 10, 17

Goeckner, D. J., 239, 245
Goldband, 121, 127, 137
Goldman, B., 254, 279
Goldstein, D., 122, 137, 171, 192
Gonzalez, A. F. J., 187, 192
Goodall, J., 68, 71, 82
Goodglass, H., 140, 159
Goodman, L. S., 7, 17
Goranson, R. E., 234, 245
Gorenstein, E. E., 154, 159
Gormly, A. V., 207, 208, 211, 221
Gormly, J., 165, 169, 190, 191, 192, 206,
    207, 208, 209, 211, 216, 217, 219,
    220, 221
Gottlieb, A., 165, 192
Gottlieb, G., 54, 83
Gould, J., 251, 274, 275, 279
Gowen, A. H., 124, 137
Graham, D., 265, 273, 279
Graham, F. K., 31, 36, 43, 90, 91, 110
Gray, J. A., 150, 153, 154, 159
Green, K. F., 60, 82
Green, R., 169, 192
Green, R. G., 169, 191
Greenberg, L. A., 7, 17
Greenblatt, M., 3, 16, 40, 42, 202, 203,
    220
Greiner, T. H., 7, 10, 16
Grings, W. W., 15, 17, 212, 221
Grinker, R., 273, 274, 279
Grossman, S. P., 145, 159
Gur, R. C., 131, 137, 132, 138
Gur, R. E., 131, 137
Gurland, B. J., 5, 18
Guyton, A. C., 7, 17

Hagdahl, R., 7, 17
Hager, J. C., 69, 83
Hager, J. E., 49, 59, 60, 85
Hahn, W. W., 89, 90, 109
Hailman, J. P., 54, 83
Haley, H., 234, 246
Hamburg, B., 268, 279
Hamburg, D., 268, 279
Hamilton, D. L., 206, 221
Hamilton, W., 253, 256, 257, 275, 276,
    278, 279
Hamilton, W. D., 55, 83
Hantas, M., 130, 131, 132, 135, 137
Hare, R. D., 7, 10, 17, 152, 159
Harkins, S. G., 178, 192
Harlow, J. F., 66, 83
Harlow, M. K., 66, 83

Harper, R. G., 67, 83, 153, 159
Harris, E. L., 212, 222
Harris, M. B., 236, 245
Harris, V. A., 3, 11, 13, 17, 118, 119,
    121, 123, 124, 137, 173, 175, 177,
    182, 192
Hass, J., 176, 192
Hassett, J., 4, 17
Hastrup, J. L., 129, 137
Haviland, J., 96, 111
Hawk, G., 172, 192
Hebb, D. O., 146, 160
Heesacker, M., 178, 194
Heider, F., 206, 221
Heilbroner, R., 253, 279
Heiman, P., 126, 138
Hein, P. L., 15, 18
Henderson, C., 93, 94, 109
Henry, J., 249, 261, 262, 264, 267, 268,
    272, 280
Herd, A., 271, 282
Herman, A., 203, 222
Herman, C. P., 178, 191
Herrick, C. D., 122, 138
Hess, E. H., 29, 43, 143, 160
Hess, F. H., 170, 192
Hess, L., 37, 43
Hewitt, G. L., 231, 232, 233, 246
Hiatt, S., 93, 109
Higbee, K. L., 174, 175, 192
Higgins, E. T., 187, 188, 192, 195
Hilton, W. F., 204, 221
Hinde, R., 263, 274, 280
Hinde, R. A., 59, 61, 65, 68, 72, 83
Hirschman, R., 11, 18, 171, 172, 192
Hirschman, R. D., 122, 137
Hjortsjö, C. H., 73, 74, 83
Hodgson, G., 127, 136
Hodos, W., 60, 83
Hoehn-Saric, R., 5, 18
Hofer, M., 249, 258, 261, 262, 280, 282
Hoffman, M. L., 55, 80, 83
Hokanson, J. E., 235, 240, 241, 245
Holland, P. C., 62, 84
Hollandsworth, J. G., 135, 137, 171, 183,
    192
Holmes, D. S., 240, 245
Hopwood, N., 255, 281
Horowitz, F. D., 69, 86
Hovland, C. K., 6, 18
Howard, J. L., 90, 111
Hoyt, J. L., 236, 247
Huang, L. C., 236, 245
Hugdahl, K., 63, 83, 84

Hull, C. L., 48, 83
Hume, W. I., 7, 18
Hygge, S., 79, 83

Iacobelli, S., 255, 280
Ikard, F. E., 185, 192, 195
Izard, C., 144, 160
Izard, C. E., 69, 83

Jackson, J. H., 253, 280
Jacob, F., 258, 280
Jacobson, E., 27, 43
Jaffe, Y., 237, 246
James, W., 38, 43, 117, 137
Janis, I. L., 174, 175, 192
Janisse, M. P., 29, 43
Janke, W., 9, 10, 17, 168, 191
Jellison, J. M., 175, 177, 182, 192
Jenkins, C. D., 204, 221
Jenkins, D., 204, 222
Jenkins, J., 140, 160
Jimenez-Pabon, E., 140, 160
Johansson, G., 80, 83
Johnson, C., 207, 208, 221
Johnson, H. J., 90, 109, 126, 136
Johnson, R. C., 168, 195, 234, 236, 248
Johnston, T. D., 49, 60, 62, 76, 80, 81, 83
Jolly, C., 266, 279
Jones, G. B., 12, 13, 17
Jones, G. E., 135, 137, 171, 183, 192
Jones, H. E., 150, 151, 160
Jones, J. M., 126, 136
Jung, C. G., 33, 43
Jurgens, U., 148, 149, 156, 160

Kagan, J., 89, 91, 110, 111, 178, 193
Kahn, M., 240, 245
Kalafat, J., 91, 111
Kalat, J. W., 60, 61, 62, 84
Kaplan, B. J., 203, 222
Kaplan, E., 140, 159
Kaplan, H. B., 22, 43
Kärker, A. C., 63, 83
Karlin, R., 266, 268, 278
Katcher, A. H., 204, 222, 236, 248
Katkin, E. S., 3, 11, 13, 17, 118, 119, 121, 123, 124, 127, 128, 129, 130, 131, 133, 137, 171, 173, 183, 189, 192,
Kaufman, L., 168, 169, 177, 194

Kaufmann, H., 228, 245
Kaufmann, L., 238, 246
Kehoe, K., 204, 221
Keller, S., 258, 259, 281
Kerber, K. W., 182, 193
Kerr, J., 31, 43
Khatchaturian, Z. S., 31, 43
Kiesler, C. A., 15, 19, 186, 189, 193
Kiloh, L., 262, 278
Kimball, C. P., 204, 223
Kimball, W. H., 27, 28, 42, 44
Kimura, D., 140, 160
King, D., 259, 280
King, R., 255, 280
Kingsley, E., 27, 43
Kirshenbaum, H. M., 231, 234, 244
Kleck, R. E., 151, 160
Klein, K., 14, 17
Klerman, G. L., 73, 85
Klineberg, O., 163, 193
Klorman, R., 101, 102, 112
Koella, G. B., 7, 18
Koenigsberg, M. R., 4, 133, 137
Koestler, A., 253, 280
Koff, E., 142, 158
Konecni, V. J., 234, 236, 240, 245
Koriat, A., 212, 221
Koss, M. C., 7, 16
Kozlowski, L., 178, 191
Krakoff, L. R., 204, 221
Krantz, D. S., 199, 222, 204, 221
Kriss, M., 238, 246
Kropotkin, P., 260, 280
Kruger, R., 31, 43
Kuhn, C., 263, 280
Kuhn, T. S., 76, 83, 226, 245
Kulik, J. A., 229, 242, 245
Kutas, M., 27, 42

LaBarbera, J. D., 69, 83
LaBok, J., 25, 42
Lacey, B. C., 39, 43, 88, 89, 90, 100, 110, 111, 178, 193, 227, 245
Lacey, J. I., 36, 38, 39, 40, 43, 88, 89, 90, 100, 108, 110, 111, 178, 193, 199, 200, 203, 220, 227, 245
LaCroix, J. M., 124, 137
Lader, M., 7, 18
Lader, M. H., 7, 18
Lamb, M. E., 65, 84, 87, 100, 101, 103, 104, 106, 107, 110, 111, 112
Landon, P. B., 184, 193
Lang, P. J., 199, 200, 221

Lange, A. R., 239, 245
Langevin, R., 10, 18
Langlie, J. K., 176, 193
Lanzetta, J. T., 71, 73, 74, 75, 83, 85,
    151, 160
Lasswell, H. D., 4, 18
Lawler, J. E., 90, 111
Lawler, K., 271, 280
Lazarus, L., 262, 278
Lazarus, P. S., 89, 111
Lazarus, R. S., 9, 12, 13, 15, 18, 206,
    221, 227, 245, 246
Leakey, R., 249, 258, 260, 275, 280
Lee, R., 265, 280
Leger, G., 231, 232, 233, 246
Leibowitz, S., 259, 280
Lemmo, M., 140, 159
Lenneberg, E., 51, 83
Lepinski, J. P., 235, 243
Lester, B. M., 103, 113
Leventhal, H., 35, 43, 174, 175, 193
Levine, J. M., 8, 18
Levine, S., 261, 262, 280
Levy, A., 178, 191
Levy, H., 16, 19
Levy, J., 131, 137
Lewin, M. H., 201, 222
Lewis, M., 90, 91, 96, 110, 111
Lewis, N. L., 34, 44
Lewontin, R. C., 52, 63, 77, 78, 80, 83
Libby, W. L., 227, 245
Liebhart, E. H., 171, 193, 239, 245
Lienert, G. A., 7, 18
Light, D. H., 201, 222
Lindner, H., 255, 280
Lindsay, R., 232, 238, 244
Lindsley, D. B., 35, 43, 88, 111, 145,
    146, 160
Lippman, M., 255, 280
Lippold, O. C. L., 28, 44
Lloyd, J., 262, 264, 280
Lockhard, R. B., 60, 83
Logue, A. W., 62, 83
Long, J. M., 204, 222
Lorenz, K., 251, 274, 280
Lounsbury, M. L., 103, 109
Lovejoy, C., 258, 275, 280
Lown, B., 269, 271, 282
Luciano, D., 251, 281
Luckhurst, E., 262, 278
Lumsden, C., 274, 280
Lundy, R. M., 201, 222
Luria, Z., 201, 222
Lushene, R., 204, 220

Luther, B., 209, 221
Lykken, D. T., 13, 18, 24, 44, 152, 160,
    207, 209, 212, 221
Lynch, J., 261, 265, 280
Lynch, J. J., 204, 222
Lynn, R., 36, 44

MacDougall, J., 271, 279
MacDougall, J. M., 199, 222, 204, 220
Mace, W. M., 81, 85
MacLean, P., 253, 280
MacLean, P. D., 145, 146, 147, 160
Maer, F., 132, 138
Magoun, H. W., 7, 19
Malamuth, N. M., 237, 246
Malatesta, C. Z., 102, 104, 106, 107, 112
Maley, M., 209, 221
Malinow, K. L., 204, 222
Malmo, R. B., 13, 18, 35, 39, 44, 88,
    110, 201, 202, 203, 222
Malmstrome, E. J., 227, 246
Malstrom, E. J., 212, 221
Mandel, M. R., 73, 85
Mandler, G., 11, 12, 18, 118, 125, 137
Mandler, J. M., 125, 137
Mannucci, E. G., 204, 221
Marlett, G. A., 239, 245
Marsden, H., 259, 278
Marshall, G. D., 10, 18, 118, 119, 137,
    168, 193, 230, 246
Martin, B., 5, 18, 201, 222
Martin, I., 22, 25, 44
Maslach, C., 36, 44, 118, 120, 137, 168,
    193, 230, 246
Mason, J., 253, 259, 280
Matarazzo, J. D., 67, 83, 153, 159
Matas, L., 94, 95, 112
Mathews, A. M., 5, 6, 18
Maynard-Smith, J., 55, 83
Mayr, E., 47, 50, 52, 54, 61, 63, 65, 66,
    67, 84, 253, 264, 275, 280
McArthur, L., 169, 193
McBurney, D. H., 8, 18
McCall, R. B., 91, 111
McCanne, T. R., 178, 193
McCarthy, G., 27, 42
McClearn, G. E., 52, 84
McCormack, J., 234, 246
McCurdy, H. G., 8, 19
McFarland, R. A., 126, 137
McGinn, N. F., 227, 246
McGowan, B. K., 60, 82
McGowan, J., 216, 222

McGuire, W. J., 175, 193
McKeever, W. F., 132, 138
McKeown, T., 252, 263, 280
McKinlay, J. R., 176, 193
McLeod, P., 126, 136
McMillan, D. L., 119, 137
McNemar, Q., 215, 222
McNichol, D., 27, 128, 137
Medoff, N. J., 237, 247
Meehan, J., 262, 272, 280
Mehrabian, A., 144, 161
Merrick, C. D., 172, 195
Mettee, D., 171, 192
Mettee, D. R., 122, 137
Mewborn, C. R., 176, 177, 194
Meyer, T. P., 236, 246
Meyers, K. A., 90, 111
Midgley, M., 266, 275, 280
Mieske, M., 73, 85
Milavsky, B., 236, 248
Miller, J., 252, 267, 280
Miller, N. E., 125, 137, 225, 244
Miller, R. E., 141, 151, 160, 151, 158
Mills, J., 182, 183, 193
Milner, P., 154, 160
Mineka, S., 65, 66, 84
Mintz, P. M., 182, 183, 193
Mischel, W., 216, 222
Mitchell, K. M., 202, 222
Mitchell, R., 267, 280
Mittelmann, B., 33, 44
Mittleman, B., 200, 222
Monod, J., 253, 280
Montagna, W., 9, 19
Montagu, A., 262, 275, 276, 280
Montgomery, S., 169, 191
Moore, H. T., 163, 193
Moore, R., 260, 275, 282
Mordkoff, A. M., 12, 19, 89, 111, 227, 245
Morell, M. A., 127, 137
Morgan, G. A., 94, 111
Morris, D. L., 90, 112
Morse, D., 251, 258, 259, 260, 263, 273, 280
Moruzzi, G., 7, 19
Moss, H. A., 178, 193
Mowrer, O. H., 201, 207, 210, 222, 225, 244
Mueller, C., 119, 137
Murdock, G. P., 63, 84
Murray, A. D., 100, 111
Murray, H. A., 205, 222

Nachold, B. S., 147, 161
Nance, W. E., 212, 222
Nesdale, A. R., 228, 229, 231, 232, 233, 235, 238, 239, 246
Newcomb, T., 206, 222
Newman, J. P., 154, 155, 159, 161
Nicosia, G., 268, 278
Nisbett, R. E., 229, 230, 246
Nomikos, M. S., 12, 18

O'Gorman, J. G., 212, 222
O'Neal, E., 168, 169, 177, 194, 238, 246
Obmascher, P., 65, 84
Obrist, P. A., 90, 93, 111
Odling-Smee, F. J., 47, 52, 56, 57, 59, 63, 64, 76, 84
Öhman, A., 3, 62, 63, 71, 72, 73, 84
Olds, M. E., 145, 146, 154, 160
Olson, J. W., 4
Opton, E. M., Jr., 12, 18
Orne, E. C., 152, 161
Orne, M., 15, 18
Orne, M. T., 4, 5, 19, 34, 45, 152, 161, 207, 222
Oskamp, S., 163, 194
Oster, H., 68, 84
Oster, P. J., 29, 44

Page, M., 15, 19
Pallak, M. S., 186, 189, 193
Parisi, S. A., 69, 83
Parke, R. D., 106, 111
Pattee, H., 252, 281
Paul, G. L., 15, 19, 201, 222
Pavlov, I. P., 36, 44
Pearson, K., 140, 159
Pennebaker, J. W., 121, 138, 184, 194
Penny, R., 262, 278
Percival, E., 231, 247
Pervin, L. A., 13, 14, 19
Petitto, J., 204, 220
Petrinovich, L., 80, 81, 84
Petty, R. E., 28, 40, 42, 166, 167, 170, 173, 178, 181, 183, 190, 191, 192, 194
Pfeiffer, E. A., 24, 25, 42
Pick, A. D., 69, 84
Pickett, L. W., 140, 160
Pigg, R., 231, 236, 245
Piliavin, I., 120, 138
Piliavin, J. A., 40, 44, 120, 138
Pilkonis, P. A., 15

Pittman, T. S., 186, 194
Plaut, S., 258, 281
Pliner, P., 230, 246
Plomin, R., 52, 84
Ploog, D., 147, 156, 160
Pollock, D., 164, 191
Porges, S. W., 227, 246
Porier, G. W., 165, 194
Posner, M. I., 229, 246
Potter, V., 253, 255, 256, 281
Powell, G., 255, 281
Procktor, J. D., 15, 17
Provost, M., 95, 111
Pryor, J. B., 238, 246

Quanty, M. B., 189, 194, 227, 240, 241,
    245
Quintanar, L. R., 40, 42

Rabin, A. I., 240, 241, 244
Raczynski, J. M., 27, 44
Rajecki, D. W., 61, 65, 84
Rakosky, J. J., 226, 231, 236, 245
Raleigh, M. J., 146, 161
Ramsay, D., 93, 109
Rankin, N. O., 12, 18
Rankin, R. F., 164, 165, 194
Rapaport, A., 265, 268, 281
Raskind, M., 257, 279
Ray, W. J., 3, 6, 22, 23, 25, 27, 45
Reed, E. S., 81, 85
Reed, S. R., 130, 137
Renner, K. E., 212, 222
Rescorla, R. A., 62, 84
Revusky, S., 61, 62, 84
Rheingold, H. L., 94, 112
Rhodewalt, E., 187, 188, 192
Rhodewalt, F., 218, 222
Ricciuti, H. N., 94, 111
Riddle, E. M., 30, 44
Riesen, A. H., 6, 18
Riley, V., 254, 255, 256, 257, 259, 262,
    266, 281
Rissler, A., 7, 17
Roberts, R., 81, 86
Robinson, J. W., 203, 222
Rodin, J., 120, 138, 230, 246
Roessler, R., 5, 19
Rogers, R. W., 174, 176, 177, 194
Rogers, T., 27, 44
Roggelin, M., 269, 282
Rose, R., 209, 221

Rose, R. J., 212, 222
Rosenfeld, H. M., 69, 86
Rosenman, R., 268, 281
Rosenman, R. H., 204, 222
Rosenstock, I. M., 176, 194
Ross, L., 230, 246
Rothbart, M. K., 97, 112
Routtenberg, A., 154, 160
Rozin, P., 60, 61, 62, 84
Rubin, Z., 29, 44
Rule, B. G., 228, 229, 231, 232, 233,
    234, 235, 238, 239, 242, 244, 246,
    247
Runeson, S., 78, 79, 80, 84
Rushmer, R. F., 47, 84
Russell, J. A., 144, 161
Russell, M. J., 8, 19

Sabatelli, R., 153, 161
Sackeim, H. E., 132, 138
Sackett, G. P., 69, 84
Sagan, C., 63, 85
Sahlins, M., 274, 281
Sandman, C. A., 166, 173, 178, 179, 180,
    191, 193
Sapira, J., 169, 194
Sapolsky, B. S., 234, 237, 248
Satinoff, E., 254, 281
Saucy, M. C., 132, 138
Saunders, G. S., 120, 138
Savin, V. J., 151, 158
Schachter, J., 31, 43, 227, 229, 230, 236,
    246, 247
Schachter, S., 3, 9, 11, 12, 14, 19, 35,
    36, 40, 41, 44, 118, 119, 120, 121,
    122, 138, 165, 168, 179, 194
Schaeffer, M. A., 204, 221
Schaffer, H. R., 93, 112
Schaie, K. W., 227, 240, 243
Schanberg, S., 255, 263, 278
Schandry, R., 171, 183, 195
Scharf, J., 200, 222
Scheier, M. F., 235, 247
Scherer, K. R., 225, 247
Schiff, B. B., 142, 159
Schill, T. R., 241, 247
Schleifer, S., 258, 259, 281
Schlosberg, H., 144, 161
Schmauk, F. J., 152, 161
Schneider, F. W., 169, 191
Schneider, R. A., 200, 220
Schneiderman, N., 271, 282
Schnore, M. N., 227, 247

Schwartz, A. N., 93, 112
Schwartz, B., 60, 62, 73, 85
Schwartz, G., 167, 195
Schwartz, G. E., 3, 19, 22, 44, 132, 138, 146, 161
Schwartz, H. G., 6, 19
Scott, J., 252, 254, 264, 265, 279
Scott, J. P., 69, 85
Sears, R. R., 225, 244
Sefer, J., 140, 160
Seleny, M., 201, 222
Seligman, M. E. P., 49, 59, 60, 62, 71, 85, 105, 112
Selye, H., 256, 257, 281
Shaffer, R. T., 204, 221
Shagass, C., 39, 44
Shapiro, A. H., 32, 44
Shapiro, D., 3, 19, 22, 44, 199, 218, 219, 222
Shaw, R., 140, 160
Shaw, R. E., 81, 85
Shearer, S. L., 155, 161
Shepart, E. M., 204, 223
Sherman, J., 251, 281
Shetler, S., 241, 245
Shields, J. L., 204, 220
Shope, G. L., 240, 245
Shortell, J., 232, 247
Shotland, R. L., 40, 44
Siegel, H. E., 164, 191
Silverman, A. J., 5, 6, 16
Simons, L. S., 235, 247
Simpson, G., 260, 281
Singer, D., 164, 191
Singer, J., 165, 168, 179, 194
Singer, J. E., 3, 9, 11, 12, 14, 19, 35, 36, 40, 41, 44, 118, 119, 120, 121, 122, 138, 229, 230, 236, 247
Singer, R. P., 174, 175, 193
Skarin, K., 94, 97, 112
Skinner, B. F., 48, 50, 56, 61, 62, 64, 85
Smallbone, A., 27, 43
Smith, A. A., 201, 222
Smith, D., 27, 43
Smith, R. C., 182, 195
Sniderman, L., 269, 271, 272, 281, 282
Snow, B., 204, 221
Snyder, C. R., 229, 246
Sobell, M. B., 239, 247
Sokolov, E. N., 6, 14, 19, 40, 44, 90, 112
Solley, C. M., 8, 19
Solomon, H. C., 40, 42, 202, 203, 220
Solomon, L., 169, 193
Sostek, A. J., 129, 138

Soumi, S. J., 65, 66, 84
Southwick, L. L., 189, 195
Speisman, J. C., 12, 19, 89, 111, 227, 245
Spitz, R. A., 93, 112
Spratt, G., 27, 43
Sroufe, L. A., 68, 85, 90, 94, 95, 97, 98, 99, 112
Staats, A., 15, 19
Staats, C., 15, 19
Staddon, J. E. R., 56, 85
Standard, B., 271, 280
Stayton, D. J., 106, 109
Stearns, S., 258, 273, 281
Stebbins, C., 40, 44
Stebbins, G. L., 50, 82
Stechler, G., 16, 19
Steele, B., 25, 42
Steele, C. M., 189, 195
Steffy, R. A., 201, 220
Stein, M., 258, 259, 281
Stein, S. H., 169, 195
Steiner, I. D., 206, 209, 222
Steklis, H. D., 146, 161
Stellar, E., 146, 161
Stephan, W., 120, 138
Stephens, P., 249, 261, 264, 268, 272, 280
Stern, D. B., 155, 161
Stern, D. N., 87, 98, 112
Stern, J. A., 29, 44
Stern, R. M., 3, 6, 22, 23, 25, 28, 30, 36, 41, 42, 44, 45, 122, 138, 172, 195
Sternberg, R. J., 61, 85
Stevenson-Hinde, J., 59, 83
Stoner, D., 240, 245
Strauss, R., 204, 222
Strehler, B., 257, 281
Strom, J., 169, 195
Stunkard, A., 249, 258, 282
Suberi, M., 132, 138
Suedfeld, P., 184, 185, 193, 195
Sulloway, F., 253, 281
Surwit, R. S., 199, 218, 219, 222
Suskind, M., 255, 263, 278
Sutterer, J. R., 90, 111
Svejda, M., 93, 109
Szpiler, J. A., 153, 161

Tannenbaum, P. H., 119, 138, 236, 247
Taves, P. A., 187, 188, 189, 195
Taylor, N., 146, 158
Taylor, S., 227, 247

Taylor, S. P., 232, 235, 244, 247
Teitelbaum, P., 254, 281
Tellegen, A., 13, 18
Tetlock, P. E., 185, 195
Thetford, P. E., 8, 19
Thistlethwaite, D. L., 176, 194
Thomas, A., 272, 279
Thomas, L., 256, 281
Thomas, S. A., 204, 222
Thompson, D., 268, 278
Thompson, J. N., Jr., 48, 49, 86
Thompson, P., 269, 282
Thompson, R. A., 3, 87, 100, 112
Thornton, D. W., 269, 270, 271, 281
Thorpe, W. H., 143, 161
Tiger, L., 274, 281
Tognacci, L., 170, 195
Tomkins, S., 144, 161
Tomkins, S. S., 185, 192
Traxler, W., 7, 18
Trivers, R., 256, 257, 263, 265, 275, 276, 281
Trivers, R. L., 80, 85
Tronick, E., 87, 98, 109
Trosko, J., 253, 255, 281, 282
Truax, C. B., 202, 222
Truex, R. C., 147, 161
Tryon, W. W., 29, 45
Tucker, D. M., 153, 154, 155, 156, 161
Tucker, J. A., 230, 239, 247
Turkey, M. T., 60, 62, 76, 80, 81, 83, 85
Turner, C. W., 235, 243, 247
Tursky, B., 32, 45

Usselmann, L. B., 24, 42
Uviller, E. T., 125, 137

Valentine, J. W., 50, 82
Valins, S., 3, 9, 11, 12, 19, 41, 45, 121, 122, 138, 165, 170, 171, 172, 195
van der Berghe, P. L., 63, 64, 85
Van Egeren, L. F., 4, 15, 19, 269, 270, 271, 272, 281, 282
van Hooff, J.A.R.A.M.A., 69, 85
Vandenberg, S. G., 212, 222
Vander, A., 251, 281
Vanderkolk, C. J., 170, 195
Varney, N. R., 140, 161
Vaughan, K. B., 74, 75, 85
Vaughn, B., 97, 98, 112
Venbles, P. H., 22, 25, 33, 34, 44, 45
Verrier, R., 269, 271, 282

Vietze, P., 69, 83
Vine, I., 68, 85
Vuchinich, R. E., 230, 239, 247

Waid, W. M., 4, 5, 13, 19, 34, 45, 152, 154, 161, 207, 222
Walden, T. A., 153, 159
Walker, B. R., 179, 180, 191
Wall, S., 87, 109
Walster, E., 120, 138, 235, 244
Walters, R. H., 225, 243
Ward, C. D., 120, 136
Washburn, S., 260, 275, 282
Washburn, S. L., 50, 51, 76, 77, 81, 86
Waters, E., 68, 85, 87, 90, 94, 95, 98, 99, 109, 112
Watson, J. B., 48, 86
Webb, R. A., 90, 111
Weerts, T. C., 81, 86
Weibell, F. J., 24, 25, 42
Weil-Malherbe, H., 7, 19
Weinberger, A., 29, 43
Weiner, H., 249, 251, 258, 268, 282
Weinstein, E. A., 147, 161
Weisfeld, G., 249, 282
Weiss, J., 273, 282
Weiss, J. M., 13, 19
Wells, G. L., 178, 194
Wenger, M. A., 38, 45
Wheeler, L., 10, 19
White, K. D., 127, 136
White, N. D., 182, 190
Whitehead, W. E., 124, 126, 127, 135, 138
Whitman, P. B., 106, 107, 113
Wiens, A. N., 67, 83, 153, 159
Wiesenfeld, A. R., 101, 102, 104, 106, 107, 112, 113
Wiggins, J. S., 212, 216, 217, 222, 223
Wilcott, R. C., 8, 18
Wilder, J., 38, 45
Willard, H. N., 204, 223
Williams, G., 273, 282
Williams, G. C., 58, 86
Williams, R., 271, 282
Williams, R. B., 199, 218, 219, 222, 204, 223
Williams, R. J., 212, 222
Williamson, D. A., 125, 138
Wilson, D. W., 236, 244
Wilson, E. O., 7, 19, 49, 50, 51, 59, 62, 63, 86, 251, 258, 260, 263, 264, 266, 274, 275, 280, 282

Wilson, G. T., 239, 247
Wilson, S. K., 152, 161, 207, 222
Wilson, T. D., 229, 246
Wilson, W. P., 147, 161
Winder, C. L., 216, 223
Wing, L., 7, 18
Wise, J. A., 127, 137
Wise, S., 87, 98, 109
Wispe, L. G., 48, 59, 86
Wolf, S., 204, 223, 249, 261, 282
Wolff, B., 7, 17
Wolff, H. G., 200, 204, 222, 223
Wood, L. E., 240, 244
Worchel, P., 229, 244
Wurm, M., 204, 222
Wynne-Edwards, V., 266, 267, 282

Yarbrov, A., 253, 255, 282

Yotti, L., 255, 282
Young, J. Z., 275, 276, 282
Young, L. D., 126, 136
Young, P. T., 143, 161
Young-Browne, G., 69, 86
Younger, J. C., 231, 236, 247

Zahn, T. P., 7, 19
Zajonc, R., 120, 138
Zanna, M. P., 4, 15, 19, 172, 173, 186,
    187, 188, 189, 191, 195
Zeskind, P. S., 103, 113
Zillman, D., 119, 121, 122, 123, 138,
    168, 169, 171, 195, 226, 227, 228,
    229, 230, 233, 234, 236, 237, 241,
    244, 247, 248
Zimbardo, P. G., 10, 18, 118, 119, 137,
    168, 193, 230, 246

Subject Index

Ability, physiological state and, 189
Activation syndrome, 227
Adaptation, social zone of, 260
Adult characteristics, 104–107
Adult responsiveness, to infant signals, 100–101
Aggression, 225–243
 anger and, 231–235
 arousal sources and, 235–240
 constructs of, 228
 environmental stimuli for, 226
 inhibition of, 234–235
 instigation to, 225
Aggression catharsis, 240–242
Aging, biology of, 257–258
Alcohol, and diminished persuasion, 182–183
Alpha activity, of brain, 27
Altruism, 80
 definition, 256
Amplifiers, 25–26
Anger, 229–231
 and aggression, 231–235
 and appropriateness of retaliation, 235
 and arousal sources, 235–240
Animal communities, status in, 251
Antisocial behavior, 119–120
Appraisal, 12
 of social stimuli, 15
Architectural defense, against crowding, 267–268
Arousal, 12–13, 225–243
 and aggressive behavior, 119–120
 concepts of, 35–36
 constructs of, 226–228
 electrodermal

and behavior, 8–9
 ontogeny of, 16
 and emotion, link between, 229
 heartbeat as index of, 124–125
 misattribution of, 11
 origins of, 6–7
 perceived, and emotion, 11–12
 physiological, 9
 from provocation, 234
 reduced, 209–210
 self-perception of, 121
 social stimuli for, 15
 source of, 238
 from violent stimuli, 234
"Attachment behavior," 100
Attack, and emotional reactivity, 232
Attitude change
 and psychophysiology, 173–190
 role of physiology in, 189–190
Attitude formation
 physiological response and, 168–170
 necessity and sufficiency of, 170–172
 and psychophysiology, 168–173
Attitude maintenance, physiological mediation of, 163–190
Attitudes
 concepts of, 119
 definition, 163–164
 false feedback of, 41–42
 and physiological response, 164–168
 and psychophysiology, 163–168
Autonomic balance, 37–38
Autonomic liability score, LIV and, 38
Autonomic nervous system (ANS), action of, 23

Autonomic perception questionnaire (APQ), 125–126
Autonomic self-perception, 117–136
Axelrod-Hamilton model, 257
    of biological negotiations, 258

Behavior
    antisocial and prosocial, 119–120
    electrodermal arousal and, 8–9
    heritability and, 212
    social and interpersonal, 119–120
Behavior therapy, 5–6
Behavioral adaptation, to biological problems, 260
Behavioral systems, definitions, 261
Beta activity, of brain, 27
Biological constraints, on learning, 59–63
Biological systems, vs. social systems, 249–277
Biology, of social organization, 275
Birth status, temperament and, 103
Blood, changes in oxygen saturation of, 200
Blood pressure
    and interpersonal aggressiveness, 217–218
    measurement of, 32
    stability of, 213–215
Bodily responses, recording, 22–35
    equipment for, 24–26
Brain
    and bodily processes, 258–259
    response recording of, 27
Brain-damaged patients, nonverbal communication in, 140–142

Caffeine
    and emotional behavior, 239
    and enhanced persuasion, 183
Cardiac activity
    mother-infant interaction and, 98–99
    and temporal patterning of emotional response, 97–98
Cardiac activity discrimination test, 126–127
Cardiac response
    to infant smiles and cries, 99–108
    interpretation of, 95–97
    meaning of, 88–91
    and socioemotional responsiveness, in infants, 91–99

Cardiovascular system, measurement of, 31–33
Cardiovascular-CNS mechanisms, functioning of, 89
Caregiving experiences, prior, 104–106
Catharsis, aggression, 240–242
Cells, internal-external commitment of, 255
Cell-to-cell organization, 255
Central nervous system (CNS)
    electrical stimulation of, 6
    physiological measures mediated by, 22
    significance of EDA, 7
Cerebral lateralization, and heartbeat discrimination, 130–133
Child-abusing parent, 106–107
Cholinomimetic agents, EDA and, 7
Cognition, 225–243
    constructs of, 228
Cognitive attribution theory, 121–122
Cognitive dissonance theory, 186
Cognitive labeling, challenges to, 230–231
Cognitive-physiological theory
    three-factor, 122
    two-factor, 121
Communication, 57
    nonverbal, physiological bases of, 139–157
    spontaneous, 139
    spontaneous vs. symbolic, 139–142
    symbolic, 139
Computers, in sociophysiological recordings, 26
Conditioned stimulus (CS), facial response to, 71–73
Conformers
    arousal levels for, 211
    and deniers, 209
Conformity, 210
    as deceptive act, 207–211
    measurement of, 208
    opinions and, 208–209
    prevention of, 209
    and reduced arousal, 209–210
    reconceptualizing, 210–211
Convariance, LIV and, 38
Coronary-prone personality, 204–205
Coronary-prone Type A traits, 268–272
Coronary-resistant Type B traits, 268–272
Couplers, 25–26
Courtship behavior, 66
Criticism, electrodermal arousal and, 6
Crowding, 265–268
    body mechanisms reponse to, 259

defenses against, 267–268
effects of, 266–267
in physical or geographical sense, 266
Cue salience, 237–240
ego-involving capacity of, 238
Cultural evolution, 58–59
Cultural pool, 57–58
Culture, priority of, 63–64
Cumulative-degenerative disease, 273

Deceptive act, conformity as, 207–211
Defensive response, 37
Deniers
arousal levels for, 211
conformers and, 209
Depressants, and diminished persuasion, 182
Depth perception, 92
Devaluators, arousal levels for, 211
Directional selection, 55
Disagreement
individual differences in, 206–207
interpersonal, 205–207
varying conditions of, 205–206
Disruptive (diversifying) selection, 55
Dissonance, 119, 185–189
Dominance-submission tests, 264
Drive-reduction model, fear appeals effect and, 175
Drugs, and persuasion, 181–184

Eccrine sweat glands, 34
Electric shocks, ANS responses to, 21–22
Electrodermal activity (EDA)
cholinomimetic agents and, 7
measurement of, 33–35
neurological account of, 6–7
studies of, 4
Electrodermal arousal
and behavior, 8–9
ontogeny of, 16
Electrodermal functioning, genetic effects on, 7
Electrodermal lability, heartbeat discrimination and, 129
Electrodermal responses (EDR)
in infancy, 16
situations affecting, 5
Electrodes, for bioelectrical recordings, 24–25
Electroencephalogram (EEG), 27

Electromyogram (EMG), muscle activity and, 27–28
Emergency response theory, 274
Emotion, 14
arousal and, 229
arousal-based theories of, 117–119
autonomic self-perception and, 117–136
cognitive-physiological approach to, 118
determinants of, 3
epinephrine and, 9
perceived arousal and, 11–12
physiological arousal and, 9
placebo effect on, 9–10
primary and secondary, 23–124, 118–119
"sham," 117, 119
visceral perception and, 120–124
Emotional behavior, stimulating drugs and, 239
Emotional responses, cardiac activity and temporal patterning of, 97–98
Epinephrine
effects on emotions, 9
and skin conductance level, 7
Epinephrine-chalone complex, 254
Evolution
cultural, 58–59
human, 49–52
Evolutionary biology, 47–49
basic, 49–66
framework from, 52–59
Evolutionary perspective, problems with, 76–78
Evolutionary theory, 76–77
extensions of, 256–257
Evolutionary-ethological models, 274–275
Evolutionary-ethological theory, of infantile attachment, 65–66
Excitation transfer, 122–123, 236–237
challenges to, 237
Eyes
measurement of, 28–30
movement of, 29–30

Facial expressions
emotional, 68–75
production of, 68–69
recognition of, 69
Facial stimuli
conditioning to, 69–73
facial responses to, 73–75
"Failure to thrive syndrome," 255
Fear appeals, and persuasion, 174–177

Females, electric shocks in, ANS responses to, 21–22
Frustration, constructs of, 228
Frustration-aggression hypothesis, 225
Frustration-aggression relationship, anger and, 231

Gender, responsiveness due to, 104
Gene pool, 53–54
Genetic and neural programs, 54–55
Genetic diversity, 49–52
  in populations, 52
Genetic programs
  closed, 67–68
  open and closed, 64–66
Goal blocking, 231

Habituation, concepts of, 36
Hamilton's kinship theory, 256–257
Happy-skin conductance-impulsive variables, 217–218
Heart disease, social environment and, 271
Heart rate
  exogenous manipulations of, 178–181
  as index of arousal, 11, 124–125
  measurement of, 31–32
  reliability of, 215–216
Heartbeat discrimination
  cerebral lateralization and, 130–133
  and electrodermal lability, 129
  sex differences in, 129–130
    instructions and, 133–134
Homeostasis, 37
  body efforts to maintain, 277
Homo sapiens, strength of, 260
Hostile aggression, anger and, 233
Human, open genetic programs in, 65
Human evolution, 49–52
Human social behavior
  evolutionary interpretation of, 77–78
  evolutionary perspective on, 47–81
  implications of, 66–75
Human sweating, olfactory discrimination in, 8–9
Humor, psychophysiological studies of, 10

Individual response stereotypy, 38–39, 89
Infant familiarity, 101–103
  responsiveness due to, 101–102
Infant signals, adult responsiveness to, 100–101

Infantile attachment, evolutionary-ethological theories of, 65–66
Infants
  cardiac and socioemotional response in, 91–99
  cardiac-behavioral convergence in, 96–97
  and caregivers, 87–109
  EDR in, 16
  smiles and cries of, 99–108
  stranger reactions in, 93–95
Information referents, 52–53
Insult, and emotional reactivity, 232
Interpersonal aggressiveness, 217–218
Interpersonal behavior, 120
Interpersonal disagreement, 205–207
Interpersonal interactions, 40
Intracellular organization, 254

Law of initial values (LIV), 38
Learning, 56–57
  biological constraints on, 59–63
Lying, 210

Males, electric shocks in, ANS responses to, 21–22
Maternal influences, on neonate, 262–263
Microbial pathogenesis, 256
Microenvironments, in social ranking, 264
Mother-infant bond, 262
Mother-infant interaction, cardiac activity and, 98–99
Motivation, physiological state and, 189
Muscles, response recording of, 27–28

Natural selection, 55–56
Neonate, maternal influences on, 262–263
Nervous system, organization of, 22–24
Neural activity, in skin, 8
Nonverbal communication
  in brain-damaged patients, 140–142
  physiological bases of, 139–157

Opinions, and conformity, 208–209
Organism-to-environment organization, 258–259
Organism-to-microorganism organization, 255–258
Organism-to-organism organization, 260–272

Orienting response, 36–37

Pantomime recognition, 140
"Parallel response," 175
Parent, abusing vs. nonabusing, 106–107
Parent-offspring relationship, 65, 65–66
Parenting behavior, 263
Pavlovian paradigm, 71
Pen-writers, 26
Perceived arousal, and emotion, 11–12
Peristaltic activity, therapy conditions and, 200
Personality
  biological viewpoint in, 212
  dimensions of, 106
Personality traits
  social judgements of, 216–217
  study procedure of, 217
Persuasion, fear appeals and, 174–177
Pharmacological studies, CNS significance of EDA, 7
Photoelectric plethysmograph, 33
Physical defense, against crowding, 267
Physiological adaptation, to biological problems, 260
Physiological arousal
  and sociocognitive processes, 9
  temporal patterns in, 12–13
Physiological communication, 41
Physiological information, false feedback of, 41–42
Physiological response
  and attitude formation, 168–170
    necessity and sufficiency of, 170–172
  origins of, to social stimuli, 14–16
Placebo, effects on emotions, 9–10
Polygraphs, 25, 32
Populations, genetic diversity in, 52
Prosocial behavior, 119–120
Protein synthesis, gene-controlled programs of, 254
Provocation, arousal from, 234
Psychological defense, against crowding, 267
Psychophysiological activity
  coronary-prone personality, 204–205
  and interpersonal disagreement, 205–207
  and psychotherapy, 199–204
Psychophysiological responses, stability of, 213–216
Psychophysiological traits, and social behavior patterns, 217–220
  study of, 211–220

Psychophysiological variables, 213
  traitlike properties of, 212–216
Psychophysiology
  attitude change and, 173–190
  attitude formation and, 168–173
  attitudes and, 163–168
  social interactions and, 199–220
  and sociophysiology, 21–22
"Psychosomatic equations," 265
Psychosomatic illnesses, 265
Psychotherapy
  context of, 3
  psychophysiological activity and, 199–204
  as social and physiological interaction, 4–14
Pupillography, 29

Race, sociophysiological investigations, 21
Rejecters, arousal levels for, 211
Respiration rate, reliability of, 216
Respiratory system, 30–31
Respiratory transducer, 30
Response systems, specific, recording, 27–35
Restricted environmental stimulation (REST), 184
Rodent communities, social breakdown in, 264

Scala Naturae, 60
Schachter and Singer paradigm, 9–11
Selection processes, relationships between, 59–66
Self-perception
  autonomic, 117–136
  theory of, 186
Sensory deprivation, and persuasion, 184–185
Sex, in sociophysiological investigations, 21–22
Sex differences
  in heartbeat discrimination, 129–130
  instructions and, 133–134
  in visceral perception, 132
Sham emotion, 117
Signal detection paradigm, 129
Skin, neural activity in, 8
Skin conductance
  EDA measure and, 34
  reliability of, 215

Skin conductance level (SCL), epinephrine and, 7
Skin conductance responses, social events and, 219–220
Skin preparation, for bioelectrical recordings, 25
Skin temperature, reliability of, 216
Social adaptation, to biological problems, 260
Social agreements, as moderator of stress, 265
Social and biological process, interaction of, 4
Social and physiological interaction, psychotherapy as, 4–14
Social behavior
   arousal-based theories of, 119–120
   biological constraints on, 66–68
   human
      evolutionary interpretation of, 77–78
      evolutionary perspective on, 47–81
      implications of, 66–75
   major aspects of, 4
Social behavior patterns, psychophysiological traits and, 217–220
   study of, 211–220
Social bonds, 261–263
   definition, 261
   rupture of, 261–262
      illnesses following, 262
Social competition, 268–272
   physiological effects of, 268
Social defense, against crowding, 267
Social environment, and heart disease, 271
Social events, skin conductance responses and, 219–220
Social interactions, and psychophysiology, 199–220
Social knowing, evolutionary implications of, 78–80
Social obligations, 265
   definition, 261
Social organization, biology of, 275
Social perception, ecological approach to, 79–80
Social processes, biology, disease and, 249–277
Social rank, 263–264
   definition, 261
   equality in, 263–264
   microenvironments in, 264
Social stimuli
   appraisal of, 15
   for arousal, 15

ectodermal response to, 14
   physiological response to, 14–16
Social stress, illness and, 252
Social survival strategy, 276
Social-biological interactions
   budget "comptrollers" in, 253–254
   closing circle in, 252–253
   expanding circle in, 252
   organization levels in, 254–272
Social-biological linkage, illustrative example, 250–252
Social-biological relations
   evolutionary-ethological models, 274–275
   explanation of, 272–277
   multilevel causation, 276–277
   problem of, 272–273
   psychosomatic models, 273–274
Sociobiological "fitness," 276
Sociobiology, 274
Sociocognitive processes, physiological arousal and, 9
Sociophysiological research
   concepts related to interpretation of, 35–36
   interpretation of, 35–39
   new vistas in, 39–42
Sociophysiology
   current research in, 3–4
   implications for, 80–81
   of infants and caregivers, 87–109
   methods in, 21–42
   origins of, 3–16
   psychophysiology as, 21–22
Spontaneous communication, 139, 141–142
   definition, 139–140
   vs. symbolic communication, 139–142
Stability scores, of psychophysiological data, 216
Stabilizing (normalizing) selection, 55
Status, in sociophysiological investigations, 22
Stimulants, and enhanced persuasion, 182
Stimulus-response specificity, 38–39
Strangers
   infants reactions to, 93–95
   reactions to, 93–95
Stress
   manipulations affecting, 12
   in natural populations, 259
   social agreements and, 265
   social inequality causing, 264
Stress reactions, processes modulating, 12

Stress-induced immunosuppression, 256
Stressful events, control of, 13
Sweating, human, olfactory discrimination
   in, 8–9
Symbiotic relationships, changes in, 257
Symbolic communication, 139
   definition, 140
Sympathetic activity
   increase in, 226
   level of, 229
Sympathicotonics, definition of, 38

Tape recorders, 26
Temperament, and birth status, 103
Theory of signal detection (TSD), 127
Therapists, client's responses to, 202
Therapy
   conditions of, client's responses to, 200–
      202
   supportive vs. confrontive, 201
   therapist's responses during, 203

Transducers, for bioelectrical recordings,
   24–25
Triver's reciprocation theory, 257
Tumorigenesis, 255

Ulcer formation
   challenges in, 251–252
   physiological defenses in, 251
Unconditioned stimulus (US), facial response to, 71

Vagotonics, definition, 37–38
Vasomotor activity, 33
Visceral perception
   background history of, 124–128
   and emotion, 120–124
   empirical results, 129–134
   methods and procedures, 124–135
   sex differences in, 132
Visual cliff, fear on, 92–93

Date Due

DEC 3 1 1990

UML 735